MW01026405

SUBURB

SUBURB

Planning Politics and the
Public Interest

Royce Hanson

CORNELL UNIVERSITY PRESS   **ITHACA AND LONDON**

Copyright © 2017 by Cornell University

All rights reserved. Except for brief quotations in a review, this book, or parts
thereof, must not be reproduced in any form without permission in writing from
the publisher. For information, address Cornell University Press, Sage House,
512 East State Street, Ithaca, New York 14850.

First published 2017 by Cornell University Press
Printed in the United States of America

Library of Congress Cataloging-in-Publication Data

Names: Hanson, Royce, author.
Title: Suburb : planning politics and the public interest / Royce Hanson.
Description: Ithaca ; London : Cornell University Press, 2017. | Includes
    bibliographical references and index.
Identifiers: LCCN 2016037980 (print) | LCCN 2016038977 (ebook) | ISBN
    9781501705250 (cloth : alk. paper) | ISBN 9781501708077 (epub/mobi) |
    ISBN 9781501708084 (pdf)
Subjects: LCSH: City planning—Political aspects—Maryland—Silver Spring. |
    Silver Spring (Md.)—Politics and government.
Classification: LCC HT168.S55 H36 2017 (print) | LCC HT168.S55 (ebook) |
    DDC 307.1/2160975284—dc23
LC record available at https://lccn.loc.gov/2016037980

Cornell University Press strives to use environmentally responsible suppliers
and materials to the fullest extent possible in the publishing of its books. Such
materials include vegetable-based, low-VOC inks and acid-free papers that are
recycled, totally chlorine-free, or partly composed of nonwood fibers. For further
information, visit our website at www.cornellpress.cornell.edu.

For the citizens and professionals who serve as trustees of the future and stewards of the environment

Contents

Figures and Tables

Preface

The idea for this book grew from my experience as chair of the Montgomery County Planning Board of the Maryland-National Capital Park and Planning Commission (M-NCPPC). I served twice in that capacity; first from 1972 to 1981 and again from 2006 to 2010. That position is a political, not a professional one, and I came to it initially from a career of a political scientist who specialized in metropolitan studies, a civic reformer, and sometime politician long interested in how theory and practice informed each other. I was recruited for the position by a newly elected council of liberal Democrats and charged with instituting a wide range of reforms in land use policy for one of the fastest-growing counties in the nation. With the council's strong support, a board of similarly motivated colleagues, and a professional staff led by a brilliant planning director, Richard Tustian, Montgomery County became a national leader in suburban planning, with innovations in development of new mass transit stations and corridor cities, linking zoning with master plans, staging development and growth policy, inclusive zoning, farmland and historic preservation.

Working with professional planners and politicians I was intrigued by the interplay of their different but complementary ways of approaching problems, and with the often conflicting interests of developers and residents as we wrestled to craft land use policies that served notions of the current and future public interest. I returned to academic life at the end of the decade, first managing the work of the National Research Council's Committee on National Urban Policy, then as a professor and administrator at the University of Minnesota and the University of Texas at Dallas. Even in venues as different in attitudes toward politics and planning as the Twin Cities and Dallas, lessons drawn and ideas adapted from Montgomery had resonance with local practitioners. Observations made in these places also helped me understand better some of the issues I had confronted in Montgomery County and to appreciate that unique localities can share common problems. Teaching and research provided opportunity to reflect and think more systematically about both the substance and process of planning politics than was possible when embroiled in its day-to-day practice.

I returned to Montgomery County in 1998 after an absence of fifteen years. Like Rip Van Winkle, I encountered a landscape transformed. I found some policies for which I was responsible produced outcomes much as intended and were well regarded. Others fared less well. Some were wisely abandoned for different approaches. I contented myself that most of the policies I had confidently declared to be in the public interest seemed to have met the test of ground proofing but a few had not. In either case, it took decades to tell. This was a lesson I took with me when the county council in 2006 asked me to return to chair the planning board, twenty-five years after leaving it, to help clean up a mess of planning and regulatory failures in Clarksburg, the county's last planned corridor city, and to resuscitate an organization that had lost its edge.

My second tour was more complicated than the first. The council was more divided than in my earlier tour and lacked a coherent approach to land use policy. A new planning director had to be found to rebuild a demoralized staff and to reinvigorate its intellectual energy. I was fortunate in having the support of my colleagues on the planning board and in recruiting Rollin Stanley to lead the planning department in formulating strategy for the county's transition from its era of suburban growth to one focused on a set of urban centers. This required an appreciation of how prior decisions and their results on the ground constrained some actions while identifying selective opportunities for innovation. The transition was not altogether smooth, but it was largely successful. New mixed-use redevelopment of obsolete commercial strips and centers are underway and there is an overdue emphasis on high quality urban design under Rollin's successor, Gwen Wright. The county is embracing its growing diversity and urbanity.

The rare experience of being a recidivist in the chair under two quite different governing regimes forced me to think harder about the role and responsibilities of professional and citizen planners in the democratic governance of their communities. A bookshelf in my office contained a copy of every master plan adopted by the commission. Several had received awards from professional societies. Some had been implemented with subdivisions and facilities as envisioned. Others were shelved in more ways than on my bookcase. The difference in their respective fates impressed upon me that understanding planning decisions and their consequences required a long historical perspective and an appreciation of shifts in community values and the organization of power. Upon retiring from the commission I resolved to use the century of county growth to explore the nature of suburban planning politics and the extent to which it produced policies that arguably served the public interest.

In telling the story of planning politics in Montgomery County I had the advantage of being deeply involved in many of the key decisions, and had access to the people and records necessary for research. The most difficult problem was deciding how to tell it. A conventional history risked losing the thread of important decisions in a detailed chronology and a sacrifice of analysis to description.

I finally chose to build a narrative around a few themes that could help explain how and why a line of strategically significant decisions that shaped the ultimate pattern of development were made. This approach necessarily excluded discussion of most master plans for predominately residential communities. Although they covered most of the county's land and some of them involved interesting issues or heated controversies over land uses or public facilities, few contained significant policy innovations or had profound impacts beyond their borders. Finally, in evaluating the extent to which the pattern of development served the public interest, I primarily used existing analyses. If readers do not find this altogether satisfactory, they can take some comfort in knowing I share that concern. My excuse is that the county's politicians did not take the advice to establish a set of indicators that could be used to measure effects of planning outcomes on public well-being. This is as unsurprising as it is unfortunate. I hope this book encourages Montgomery County and others to determine what should be measured and to do it on a regular basis.

Many people helped as I researched, wrote, revised, and rewrote drafts. Special thanks are due Hal Wolman, my George Washington University colleague; Richard Tustian, the long-time planning director of Montgomery County; and Rick Pruetz, a planning consultant and author with wide experience. All three read successive versions of chapters and the entire manuscript, offering helpful corrections and suggestions, debated ideas, and provided encouragement and advice. William Willcox, Gordon Lamb, and Harry Lerch were indispensable advisers in helping me reconstruct some of the early history of the General Plan and the politics of the 1960s and 1970s. Several staff members of the Montgomery County Planning Department closely read chapters for errors of fact and interpretation. In late 2014 and early 2015 I delivered five public lectures based on the draft. The fifteen discussants (three for each lecture) provided valuable insights and suggestions that have improved the work.

The entire effort would have been impossible without the assistance of Hilary Stryker, manager of the M-NCPPC Archives, which were critical, not only in reconstructing years when I was not involved in county affairs, but in serving as a corrective of my own recollections. I was chastened to discover how unreliable my memory was. It occasionally rendered vivid reconstructions of things that did not happen, or happened differently, and yielded blanks of things that clearly occurred. Therefore, I relied on documents as much as possible, and if documents were not available, secondary sources, interviews, and conversations with a great many people that were contemporaneously involved in the plans and decisions recounted. I am grateful for their help and absolve them of any blame for inaccuracies or injustices that infect these pages. I alone am responsible for things I still got wrong, and for the reflections, opinions, and lessons drawn. Because

I was a major actor in many of the decisions recounted in the book I have used the first person in discussing my role to avoid the conceit of referring to myself as a stranger.

Citizen and professional planners, land use lawyers, developers, and local officials in other growing communities will recognize familiar issues, responses, and themes in Montgomery County's experience. Since in making public policy, plagiarism is the sincerest compliment, the book's purpose will be well served if insights and lessons from its account of successes and shortcomings help others understand similar situations, avoid some problems and resolve others. For Montgomery County readers, I hope this account helps explain how it got this way.

SUBURB

LEARNING FROM A CENTURY OF PLANNING POLITICS

Suburbs are places we hate to love. From ancient Rome through the industrial era they were retreats where the metropolitan elite escaped the congestion, clamor, epidemics, and stresses of urban life and indulged appetites for grand villas, gardens, and horses. With the extension of rail and streetcar lines, they provided homes for an aspiring middle class with good credit. After World War II suburbs expanded as cities ran out of space to house workers or perform other specialized functions. They became locations of choice for the next two generations of Americans.

Governing Growth

Long disparaged as sprawling, bland, monotonous, and soulless, suburbs evolved into diverse places of growing interest to urban scholars and journalists.[1] By the beginning of the twenty-first century, suburbs were no longer mere appendages of their mother cities even though economic, cultural, amenity, image, and social connections remained strong.[2] They contained a majority of the U.S. metropolitan population and employment. A 2009 Brookings Institution paper reported that in the ninety-eight largest U.S. metropolitan areas only 21 percent of jobs were located within three miles of downtown while 45 percent were located more than ten miles from the central city core.[3] In the Washington metropolitan area three of every five jobs were located in the first tier suburbs of Maryland and Virginia. The District of Columbia contained only one-fourth of the region's jobs.[4]

The speed and scale of their growth and the rate at which suburbs changed in form, function, and demography made land development the most important component of the suburban political economy, placing its governance at the top of the local policy agenda. Suburbs differ in scale, governance institutions, and civic culture, but share common issues of growth and transformation of their landscapes, economies, and populations. They are engaged in continuous debate about how well individual development decisions and their cumulative effects advance the well-being of the community and its residents. That debate raises the question of how equitably the benefits and burdens of growth are distributed

1

across the suburb. Subdivisions built for relatively homogeneous markets can discourage integration of income classes at community scale even if the suburb-wide mix is fairly well balanced. Significant barriers to racial and ethnic integration of suburban housing are pervasive. Moreover, rapid and robust growth, which often creates an overall improvement in wealth and quality of life, frequently bypasses, overwhelms, destabilizes, or underserves some neighborhoods; especially those housing the poor or minorities.

Montgomery County—Typically Unique

While many American suburbs could serve as suitable places to explore those issues, Montgomery County offers some particular advantages. Its growth trajectory tracked that of most first tier suburbs in major metropolitan areas. With one million residents in 2012, Montgomery ranks ninth in population among U.S. counties that contain no major central city and eighth in density, with just under 2,000 residents per square mile. In 2014, *Forbes* ranked it the eighth best county in which to live, based on an average of household income (eleventh nationally at $94,965 in 2012), high school graduation rates (81.7%—third highest among the fifty largest school districts), employment (3.5% unemployment in 2015) and poverty rates (6.7% from 2009 to 2013), and the nation's highest percentage of adults with postgraduate degrees (29.2%). Although not included in most rankings, the county has the most honored local park system in the nation, as the only six-time recipient of the gold medal of the National Parks and Recreation Association. After discounting for luck, it would appear it got some things right, making examination of the policies that shaped it worthwhile. Even though Montgomery is no more typical of all suburbs than Dallas and Chicago are of all cities, each shares attributes and problems common to other suburbs and cities, and the things that make them different are what make them the more interesting.

Montgomery County's suburbanization began near the beginning of the twentieth century with modest streetcar communities on the border of the District of Columbia. It developed steadily following World War I. Like many American suburbs it grew exponentially after World War II, generating political conflict over the scale, pace, and effects of development. And like many older suburbs, parts of the county were urbanizing by the end of the twentieth century.

During the early decades of its growth, most Montgomery suburbanites commuted to work in Washington but by 1980 a majority were employed in the county, rising to 60 percent in 2010. A fourth still worked in Washington and the remainder were scattered across the metropolitan area. With a half million jobs, Montgomery had become the economic engine of Maryland and home to a wide range of institutions and enterprises of the advanced knowledge-based economy. County demography was transformed during the same period. Once with a fairly homogeneous upper middle class white population, the county gradually became highly diverse and multiracial. The 2014 *American Community Survey* reported that non-Hispanic whites comprised only 46 percent of the total population, a demographic shift from white dominance shared by 77 other U.S. counties since 2000. Blacks and Hispanics each accounted for 19 percent and Asians 15 percent of residents. Almost one-third of the population was foreign-born. As the 2015 academic year began, a majority of students in county public schools were not white Anglos. Once a suburb primarily of single-family detached homes, multifamily structures now provide one-third of the housing stock, although owners of houses and condos still comprise over two-thirds of all households. As vacant land for new subdivisions grew scarce, home values increased, tastes in living styles changed, and policy shifted from greenfield development toward redevelopment of obsolete commercial and mixed-use areas, producing a second reconfiguration of the landscape.

Although Montgomery County's growth and its economic and demographic transformation followed a pattern similar to many other suburban areas developed during the twentieth century, its planning politics involves some uncommon distinctions. The most important is that its planning organization, the Maryland-National Capital Park and Planning Commission (M-NCPPC), is a quasi-autonomous subregional state agency. Its Montgomery division, the Montgomery County Planning Board, prepares master plans, provides advice on zoning and special exceptions, regulates subdivisions and site plans, and administers laws relating to forest conservation and water quality. In addition, it operates one of the nation's largest local park systems. This organizational distinction results in a second variation from the usual suburban planning environment—a proliferation of municipalities, each with its own planning and zoning powers. With the exception of six municipalities whose planning powers were granted prior to countywide extension of M-NCPPC jurisdiction, and which collectively contain about 12 percent of the population, the planning board's jurisdiction includes all other municipalities in the county.

The commission's administrative system is independent of the two county governments and each county planning board is supported by large professional planning and parks departments. Its general counsel, executive director, and secretary-treasurer are statutory officers. Planning commissioners are appointed by the county council, which has jurisdiction, exclusive of the county executive, over final approval of plans and enactment of zoning regulations and maps.

The chair of the planning board is a full-time position, commissioners are salaried, and the board meets weekly to conduct its business. The commission's organic statute mandates minimum property tax rates to provide basic support for parks, planning, and administrative functions. The counties may increase but not decrease those rates. It also has bonded debt authority separate from the counties.

The commission's autonomy and power make it an outlier among the nation's planning institutions, as shown in Figure I.1. Most commissions draw their legal authority from local ordinances or charters pursuant to state enabling laws. The weakest provide advice only to elected officials on comprehensive plans and zoning. They are supported by planning staff that report to an elected executive or appointed manager. Regulatory functions, such as approval of subdivisions, site plans, and variances, are often performed by separate executive agencies. Planning commissioners are usually volunteers, meet monthly, and receive only a per diem payment for meetings.

Stronger commissions exercise regulatory functions, often subject to appeal to the council or the courts, although many places tend to limit the commission's role to hearing appeals from administrators' decisions. Some have a secretariat to manage the flow of business. A few are assigned control of planning staff. In larger jurisdictions commissioners may receive a modest stipend for their service.

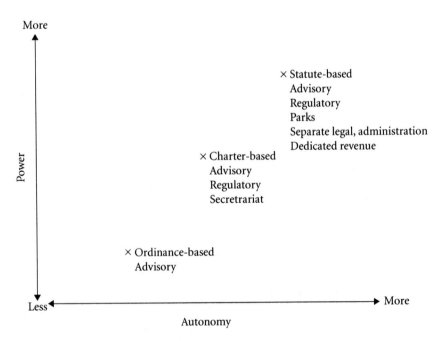

FIGURE I.1 A typology of planning commissions

They would be unlikely, however, to have dedicated revenue or separate legal staff.

Notwithstanding these organizational differences, during a century of growth Montgomery County coped with the tensions, pressures, and frustrations of rapid change common to most growing suburbs. Its planners and political leaders, like those of other burgeoning communities, struggled to understand the economic and political forces that drove and resisted development and to manage them in ways that might produce a desirable place to live and work. Whatever its similarities or differences with other suburbs, what makes Montgomery County worthy of close study is that in face of rapid change it has been a leading innovator in land use policies. Many of the policy tools it invented or adapted became models for others.

County planners, politicians, and lawyers invented hybrid zones that linked zoning effectively to plans and increased flexibility, reduced transaction costs, encouraged better design, and enhanced public benefits in areas planned for intensive development. Montgomery's pioneering approach to inclusionary zoning, the Moderate-Priced Dwelling Unit Ordinance, has been widely acclaimed in a number of well-researched commentaries.[5] It is discussed here in terms of its effect on development patterns and the character and cost of housing. Montgomery was among earliest fast-growing suburbs to stage development concurrently with the provision of public facilities. Its experience in fashioning a sophisticated growth management system provides insight into the effectiveness and limitations of such policies. Creation of an Agricultural Reserve through a combination of zoning, limitation of sewer service, and use of transferable development rights is one of the nation's most successful and widely emulated efforts to preserve farmland in perpetuity. Montgomery also made mistakes. Some efforts failed or fell short of their ambitions. These may be as instructive as the successes.

Approach and Organization

The invention and evolution of Montgomery's land use policies were efforts by the county's planners and politicians to solve practical problems in the public interest, which may be roughly defined as outcomes that result in a net benefit for the whole public of the county and equitable outcomes for its component communities. Consideration of how well policies served the public interest requires a two-track inquiry. The first consists of a descriptive history of particular policies that can provide practitioners with analogies and techniques they might apply in comparable situations. It can also help understand the dynamics of suburban planning politics and how, over time, they shaped the county's development pattern. Professionals interested in more details can follow the links provided to adopted plans and other documents.

The second track involves a prescriptive interpretation of that history and its consequences. It is both an argument about the character of planning politics and a commentary on the extent to which it meets or falls short of certain standards of public interest. That analysis and the questions it raises should be read critically for insight into the process of planning politics and for balance and fairness in evaluation of its outcomes. Its purpose is to stimulate debate and dialogue among planners, politicians, and all those interested in the quality of their communities.

This is not the first attempt to assess the impact of planning politics on the public interest. In their seminal study of planning for public housing in Chicago, Martin Meyerson and Edward Banfield illuminated the tension between the rational, comprehensive aspirations of planning, and the group and racial dynamics of that great city's political system.[6] Meticulous detailing of how that decision was made provided deep insight into the interplay of planners and politicians, but necessarily limited the ability to generalize from it. Meyerson and Banfield did not follow the outcome of the decision on the ground so they could only speculate about whether it served the public interest of the city. Because the case included the notorious Cabrini-Green public housing site there is reason to suspect that in the fullness of time their assessment of its service to the public interest might have been less benign.

Rather than a suburban replica of the Chicago study, which would take a snapshot in time and subject a single decision to minute analysis, this book explores a century of development and follows a chain of strategic decisions that transformed Montgomery County from a rural hinterland of the national capital into a socially diverse urbanizing county of a million people. This long view makes it possible to observe the separate and cumulative effects of those decisions on the natural and built environment and to assess the extent to which their outcomes met different tests of service to the public interest.

Chapter 1 introduces three themes that unify the narrative of strategic decisions. First, planners and politicians reason in distinctive but complementary ways that shape their respective roles in planning politics and the character of decisions they make. Second, the core conflict that pervades suburban planning politics reflects interests and values imbedded in two virtual republics—the miniature republic rooted in ideals of Jeffersonian democracy and progressive reform, and the commercial republic of a Hamiltonian political economy. Third, land use decisions reflected the "balance" struck between the reasoning of planners and politicians and the interests and values of the two republics represented in the four governing regimes of different eras of county development. Each regime left its imprint on the land, which constrained the choices available to its successors. A summary of their composition and key actions provides an historical context for later discussion of strategic decisions.

Chapter 2 is the first of eight case studies of strings of strategic decisions that cumulatively produced a distinctive pattern of development. It describes the decade-long political struggle for regime change resulting in adoption of the county's iconic General Plan, *On Wedges and Corridors*, which is among the best known comprehensive plans in America. As important as it is in planning literature, what makes it a model is less its particular provisions or basic form than how it evolved from a static document into an organic "constitution" for land use policy with enough flexibility to adapt to new conditions in suburban life, the development industry, and the planning profession.

One of the most complex problems of first tier suburbs is redevelopment of older commercial districts. Chapters 3 through 5 discuss the trials, tribulations, and results of planning and redeveloping four activity centers at key Metro stations in the urban ring. They describe and analyze a series of decisions made during the fifty years that followed adoption of the General Plan in 1964. Chapter 3 is devoted to the planning and development of Friendship Heights and Bethesda. These centers involved the first applications of new approaches to planning for intensive development of small areas. They provided tests of the legal theories underlying new hybrid zones and for balancing land use with the capacity of public facilities, especially transportation.

In chapter 4, the decline and revival of Silver Spring, the county's oldest commercial center, provide important lessons in the consequences of misdiagnosing a problem, applying approaches that worked well elsewhere, and expecting comparable results. The combination of a stagnant market, unrealizable ambition by developers, intransigent opposition from residents, and misjudgments by both planners and politicians stymied effective redevelopment for four decades. The case also illustrates the importance of effective political leadership in ultimately resolving what had seemed an intractable problem.

White Flint, a 400-acre obsolete commercial strip on the county's most congested roadway is the subject of chapter 5. The most recent of the county's efforts in planning for mixed-use, transit-oriented activity centers, it offers a number of important lessons in successful planning politics. It illustrates the value of careful economic analysis, engagement of major property owners and community groups in making plans, creativity by professional staff in working with disparate and frequently conflicting interests, and willingness to abandon old ideas for new ones that fit the circumstances at hand. White Flint also illustrates the problems of bureaucratic and political resistance to new ways of financing infrastructure.

Chapters 6 and 7 cover the planning and development of four corridor cities—Rockville, Gaithersburg, Germantown, and Clarksburg. The General Plan contemplated each of them would be developed as a complete, compact "new town." The municipalities of Rockville and Gaithersburg resisted the idea of becoming corridor cities. The problem of many governments obstructed development in accord with the General Plan, although Rockville eventually evolved in a way close to the vision. Germantown presented a different problem, that of many builders without a coordinating master developer. It provides lessons on the effectiveness and limitations of using infrastructure extension and regulations such as an Adequate Public Facilities Ordinance to manage the pace and character of development. Clarksburg remains a wicked problem in which errors in planning, development regulation, developer violations, public protest, politics, economic recession, and environmental impacts interacted to create the first major development scandal since adoption of the General Plan and complicated the county's last major greenfield development.

Montgomery County's Agricultural Reserve is the nation's most successful effort at use of transferable development rights for preservation of a working agricultural landscape within a major metropolitan area. Chapter 8 provides an analysis of the strategy and tactics of planning politics in its creation and in protecting it from fragmentation by exurban subdivisions and other incompatible uses. Its successes and problems provide lessons in policy design and methods of resisting incremental erosion of the critical mass of farmland essential to sustenance of a viable agricultural community.

Montgomery County was a pioneer in growth management. Chapter 9 examines the evolution and efficacy of county growth policy as a technique for staging growth in concert with the expansion of public facilities and in light of concerns for environmental, social, and economic sustainability. Recounting the difficulties of reconciling the rational ideas of planners with the exigencies of local politics allows an examination of the design, legal, and practical administrative problems of implementing growth management in a large geographic area.

The book concludes with a critique of how well the county's development pattern, as the cumulative result of its planning politics, satisfies different substantive and procedural notions of public interest. Chapter 10 also includes some reflections on the peculiar role of planning in democratic governance and on practical, organizational, and ethical issues planners and public officials confront in seeking the public interest. It ends with some thoughts about Montgomery's contribution to understanding planning politics and brief speculation about the county's future.

PLANNING POLITICS

Everything has to happen somewhere. That makes planning useful. Nothing happens by itself. That makes politics necessary. In Montgomery County, as in other burgeoning suburbs, pressures of growth were countered by efforts to contain and manage it. The county's natural systems and the buildings and infrastructure already in place imposed a few constraints on decisions. Watersheds draining to the Potomac determined the direction growth could move with the least resistance. The arterial road system was based on ridgeline trails used by the region's precolonial natives, old mill roads, and turnpikes leading toward Georgetown, Frederick, and Baltimore. The rail line bisecting the county once carried the products of 400 dairy farms and fostered several small planned suburbs in Takoma Park, Forest Glen, Garrett Park, and Kensington. The extension of streetcar lines from Washington facilitated residential settlements in Chevy Chase, Silver Spring, Friendship Heights, and Glen Echo. As World War I ended, only one in five of the county's 35,000 residents lived in towns. Just two contained over 1,000 people.

Spurred by pollution of Rock Creek and the Anacostia River from failing or nonexistent suburban sanitary systems and repeated typhoid epidemics, in 1916 the Maryland General Assembly created the Washington Suburban Sanitary Commission to provide public water and sewerage to Montgomery and Prince George's counties communities surrounding the District of Columbia. With ample land it was now clear that there could be a strong market for suburban homes as the federal workforce grew and the District of Columbia was built out.

Montgomery's leaders and landowners promoted growth. Developers enthusiastically responded. The new residents they attracted resisted additional development; demanded better planning, and rebelled against the established local regime. Land use controversies occupied the center of suburban politics as each generation of planners and politicians claimed its actions were in the public interest of the county. Developers and residents contested these claims and competed for influence in a cycle of planning politics, which over the course of a century produced a distinctive pattern of development.

A conceptual framework can help make sense of how and why that particular development pattern emerged from ten decades of land use decisions. First, understanding the distinctive ways in which planners and politicians—the central participants in those decisions—think can illuminate their respective and complementary roles in planning politics. Second, the decisions they made reflected and served some interests better than others. Thus, it is useful to identify and characterize the ideas and values that guide the principal interests that influence land use policy. Third, tracing the ebb and flow of political alliances that produce governing regimes can help explain eras of innovation, inertia, and transition in land use policy and the interests or values those policies reflected. Finally, land use decisions, uniquely, place facts on the ground, making it possible in due time to use empirical evidence to evaluate whether they have produced more benefits than burdens for the whole community and specific parts of it.

The Logic of Planners and Politicians

Planning is one of few arenas of local policy that is mandated by law to be comprehensive in approach. That mandate is carried out by two quite different actors. Planners and politicians use distinct systems of logic to arrive at and explain their decisions. Although they do not reason in the same way, the roles they play make their systems of logic complementary.

Planners are committed to the rational method and thinking comprehensively. Rooted in utilitarianism, theirs is the linear logic of consequentiality.[1] They ask: What is the problem? What are the alternative solutions? Which solution will most efficiently resolve the problem? Planners' value system is rooted in the belief that the physical environment and design have determinative influences on public well-being and happiness. Employing both science and art, planning requires special professional training and skills. Analytical models, mapping, design, and other graphic arts are important tools planners use to define and depict problems, frame issues, present solutions, and thus, influence the choices of policy makers. Ideally, the logic of planning achieves a balance or trade-off among different physical, economic, and social components, and then selects the most efficient means to achieve its goals. The logic of planning strives to impose a more rational order on the chaos of markets and politics. Plans are pictures of that more desirable future.

Politicians practice the art of the possible. They argue that doing what is feasible is as good as it gets. In the political world, problems, solutions, and politics are not sequentially organized but jumbled like refuse in a garbage can.[2] People with "solutions" search for "problems" to which they can be applied, individual and group interests may override more rational choices, issues may be reframed to fit suboptimal solutions, and symbolic responses may displace effective action. In a pluralist society, politics involves bargaining among various interests. Decisions tend to be satisficing rather than optimizing, incremental rather than comprehensive, and contingent rather than final.[3] Where planners strive to connect the dots to show interrelationships among interests; politicians prefer that they be compartmentalized to avoid inconvenient coalitions that upset established patterns of power and force or limit choices.

Politicians employ the logic of appropriateness, asking: Who am I? What kind of situation is this? What do I want or have to do? What is it appropriate to do?[4] Certain patterns of decision making become institutionalized through custom and usage, employing familiar "solution sets"—approaches that worked in the past—in settling similar matters.[5]

Where planners use graphics, conceptual models, and linear logic to explain ideas, politicians use stories, analogies, metaphors, and precedents as touchstones for action in a reasoning process that is less linear than dialectic; grounded less in data and deduction than experience and induction. A good anecdote can often trump a regression table. Politics at the county or city level operates at an intimate level of personal and political connections among elected and appointed officials, staff, and interested individuals and groups. If all politics is local, all local politics is intensely personal.

Neither the logic of planners nor that of politicians can retain its virginity if local development is to be governed with even moderate effectiveness. Politicians find the rational analysis and solutions devised by planners appropriate and useful in addressing situations and giving their actions legitimacy as products of sound professional analysis. Even when planning claims to be comprehensive it tends to be incremental as it responds to feedback from politics and exogenous forces such as demographic shifts or business cycles. This is especially the case for plans with long-term horizons that aspire to reshape the built environment. As planners gain experience they recognize the limits of omniscience and tweak or reverse earlier decisions. Planners, no less than politicians, do what seems appropriate, which, in their case involves presenting plans as products of the logic of consequentiality. In practice, planning politics is less an exercise in rational choices that maximize the aggregate "utility" of a polity than one of "bounded rationality"[6] achieved through ongoing negotiation and iterative adjustments celebrated as the Science of Muddling Through.[7] Public interest is a work in progress.

Suburbia's Virtual Republics

Suburban planning politics is commonly characterized as an ongoing confrontation between "the citizens" and "the developers." This oversimplified characterization of adversarial interests in land use decisions masks a complex and nuanced interplay of values and interests drawn from concurrent American political traditions. Two virtual republics are rooted in Hamiltonian and Jeffersonian ideals and contest different notions of property rights, democracy, community welfare, efficiency, fairness, governance, and the public interest.

Developers of the Commercial Republic

The interests and reasoning of developers are anchored in the Hamiltonian commercial republic, in which the market and government collaborate to foster a virtuous cycle of economic growth and prosperity.[8] In the commercial republic development is arguably the central function of the local political economy.[9] Because development is tightly connected to the tax base, it enjoys a special relationship to the fiscal health and governance of cities and counties. Heavy reliance on property taxes for both capital and operating budgets gives officials a strong predilection toward a rate of growth that keeps property values rising; ideally faster than the unit costs of services. The private interests of land owners, bankers, brokers, builders, and all their ancillary and supporting suppliers and consumers merge with the interests of local officials in provision of a politically satisfactory level of public services and facilities at economically and politically tolerable rates of taxation.

The local commercial republic celebrates individualism, a free market in land, and lightly regulated property rights. The good society allows markets to work their magic. Local public officials in the best of all commercial republics share these values (and often the hats) of the development sector. In this cozy and cooperative system, the private and public sectors are partners. Participants are likely to regard their self-interest as enlightened and indistinguishable from the public interest. The public partner's role is to promote growth; to foresee the need for and provide the infrastructure—water, sewers, roads, schools, and parks—that facilitates and serves the market. Policies should protect and enhance value, and encourage investment in homes and businesses. This sustains a virtuous cycle of growth, which generates revenues that can be invested to encourage more growth and more revenue. The system and the values undergirding it presume that a minimally constrained market will provide the broadest benefits for all in a commercial republic of producers and consumers.

Citizens of the Miniature Republic

Middle class suburbanites brought with them a more moralistic and communitarian value system anchored in homeownership and inextricably connected to the politics of land use. As Constance Perin observed: "In its legal instruments—zoning ordinances, deed restrictions—the American system of land use is defined into a hierarchy of uses at whose apex is the single-family-detached house."[10] Middle class suburban homeowners were not content to be consumers in a commercial republic or mere voters. Ownership conveyed moral authority as stakeholders, investors in the commonwealth. But like individual shareholders in great corporations, they had little voice in the commercial republic's management and owed it no loyalty. Boasting about the increase in the value of their homes could seamlessly segue into a diatribe condemning developers that converted open land into subdivisions with the connivance of local officials.

Home ownership alone was an incomplete moral and economic foundation for an alternative to the commercial republic. The new suburbanites, having rejected cities as domicile and polity, found answers in an idealized past and a planned future. They made themselves citizens of Jeffersonian republics in miniature,[11] which emphasized popular rule and grassroots decision making. Popular government gave them legitimate political power. The Progressive Movement taught them to use that power and expert administration to rein in the excesses of the commercial republic. Socially and environmentally inspired planning could ensure their neighborhoods would be harmonious "garden" communities where families could live safe, healthy lives and home values would appreciate. As a public philosophy of suburbia, the neo-Jeffersonian miniature republic fused popular rule, progressive reform, spatial determinism, and protection of property values. It resolved the paradox of citizens that regarded themselves as progressive on most matters, acting as conservatives when it involved land uses that impinged on their homes and neighborhoods.

The Republics' Values and Public Interest

The two republics offer different reasons for making decisions and different views of the public interest. The commercial republic found it in a robust market that produced revenues for public services and amenities. For the miniature republic it was secured when the will of the people prevailed to protect their homes and neighborhoods from adverse effects of growth. From time-to-time the values and interests of one republic tend to prevail over the other in a community's land use decisions. Neither holds an exclusive franchise in planning politics. That is because the commercial republic needs the legitimacy of popular approval and the miniature republic needs revenue. Land use decisions made in response to the interests of either put facts on the ground that successors in power cannot eradicate.

Taking a century-long view of the growth of a suburb makes possible tracking how values from these virtual republics influenced several generations of land use decisions and shaped the resulting development pattern. The reasons given for those decisions, knowingly or in innocence, reflect the logic employed and values and interests of the virtual republics of suburbia.

Regimes

Over time, land use decisions cumulate from generation to generation, each leaving a mark on the land its successors may alter but can rarely obliterate. These decisions reflect the relative influence of the virtual republics in the governing regimes then in power. Regimes are "the informal arrangements by which public bodies and private interests function together in order to be able to make and carry out governing decisions."[12]

A governing regime exists when officials and private or other interests have reached an accommodation that is sufficiently stable and lasting to enable them to govern, and make decisions that are binding on the people and property. The incentive to form regimes is strong because the limitations on and diffusion of power in the U.S. system of governance make it difficult for officials to achieve any substantial policy goals without the support and cooperation of private and public sectors.

Regimes endure when the cooperation of the partners yields mutually beneficial results and the positive feedback from the experience of resolving public issues builds civic capital that facilitates resolution of problems and reduces the ability of alternative coalitions to form and achieve success. A regime falters or dissolves when the benefits of cooperation are outweighed by its costs, or when other interests mobilize and displace one or more of its components. Regimes can fall if they cannot adapt to changing interests and conditions because their behavior no longer produces highly valued public benefits.

Suburban growth-oriented regimes tend to emphasize the values and interests of the commercial republic. Neighborhood and civic interests challenge growth regimes when they regard the principal burden of the amount or form of development as generating costs, congestion, and environmental damage, which will fall on them. Embodying the values of the miniature republic, they seek to coalesce with other groups to form an alternative partner with officials in a sustainable civic or progressive regime.

Four regimes presided over the growth of Montgomery County during its century of development. Two reflected the values of the commercial republic. One elevated those of the miniature republic and one showed no stable allegiance. This short history of their rise and decline provides context and reference for the case studies that follow.

The Lee Regime and the Birth of the Suburbs

By the end of the Great War Montgomery and Prince George's counties were positioned to receive a substantial share of the burgeoning population of Washington. The principal impediment to growth was the absence of public sanitary facilities. That was remedied in 1916 when the Maryland General Assembly created the Washington Suburban Sanitary Commission (WSSC) to establish a single system with exclusive jurisdiction over water, sewerage, and solid waste facilities in basins that drained to the Potomac through Washington.[13]

Sewers made suburban living possible. Automobiles made it feasible. E. Brooke Lee made it happen. Scion of generations of Lee and Blair statesmen, heir to hundreds of acres adjacent to the District of Columbia in Silver Spring, and a World War I hero, state party leaders nominated Lee for comptroller of Maryland as he returned from France in 1918. He also served as Maryland secretary of state, speaker of the House of Delegates, and state roads commissioner while developing the family's land. "The Colonel" skillfully leveraged his family's deep roots in the county, the loyalty of former comrades in arms, land ownership, political position and influence, business acumen, and a forceful personality to build and discipline with military efficiency a regime that seamlessly fused political power and private property in a growth machine that embodied the values of the commercial republic. It dominated county affairs from 1918 to 1949 and exercised waning influence for nearly twenty years more.

In the Lee Regime landowners, developers, and officials were often the same people. Officials of the formal governmental apparatus loyally followed the Colonel's leadership on matters of policy and patronage. With the single exception of defeat by a fusion slate of county commissioners in 1934, candidates endorsed by the Lee organization were always elected.

Two bi-county commissions were the linchpins connecting the development industry and the regime. The Washington Suburban Sanitary Commission financed water and sewer infrastructure with low-interest bonds. This allowed developers to price homes slightly lower than if they had to finance these facilities. The Maryland-National Capital Park and Planning Commission (M-NCPPC)[14] had extensive power to regulate development of new subdivisions in suburbanizing portions of the two counties bordering the District of Columbia, including municipalities. Lee created it in 1927 when serving as speaker of the Maryland House of Delegates. Lee and the boss of Prince George's County, Lansdale Sasscer—also a cousin of Lee's wife—controlled appointments to both commissions. During the ascendance of the regime, machine loyalists serving on the commission included Lee himself, a brother, a son, and several business associates as well as developers and landowners. When a civic organization proposed Louis Justement, a famous architect, for appointment to the commission, he was rejected for "conflict of interest." A machine opponent cracked: "How can that be? What Montgomery developer ever hired an architect?"

The law establishing the park and planning commission granted the two counties authority to zone land. This was critical to realization of Lee's vision for the county as a place for upscale homes in garden communities for the growing federal work force. It protected neighborhoods by separating residential from commercial and industrial land uses in accordance with planning doctrines of the time.

With responsibility for development of a park system and parkways, M-NCPPC's acquired parkland in stream valleys where flood plains and steep, wooded slopes were unsuited for homebuilding. A happy fusion of public and private interests, stream valley parks extended Washington's Rock Creek and Anacostia park systems into the suburbs and protected property from floods. They were the best locations for trunk sewers, opening opportunities for further development. Residential lots adjoining parkland sold at a premium, easily making up for any loss of potential home sites. The cost of improvement and care of parks shifted from developers to residents of the new park district. In 1930 Lee joined others to secure passage of the Capper-Cramton Act,[15] which provided $3 million in federal matching grants for stream valley acquisitions. By 1940 the park system had expanded from four to 920 acres. M-NCPPC paid cash for parkland, providing small but significant help for homebuilders during the Great Depression.[16]

Like WSSC taxes and fees, mandatory property taxes to support M-NCPPC functions applied only to property within the M-NCPPC district, shielding rural taxpayers from sharing the costs of growth and reinforcing their loyalty to the regime. The two commissions controlled permission to build while assisting developers by reducing costs of a high-level community amenity and assuring confidence in the stability of neighborhoods. M-NCPPC used its subdivision power to require dedication of land for streets, parks, and schools, reducing public acquisition costs. Zoning protected neighborhoods from unwanted uses, adding value to every home site. Including municipalities within M-NCPPC jurisdiction prevented balkanization and beggar-thy-neighbor zoning wars.

Between 1920 and 1930, 15,000 new residents increased county population by 41 percent. Recognizing the need for new and improved roads to handle growing traffic and support more development, Lee built East-West Highway in 1927–1929 connecting Bethesda and Silver Spring to Hyattsville in Prince George's County. Civil servants with paychecks immune from the Great Depression kept the housing market humming. Population grew by 35,000 (71%) between 1930 and 1940. Residential growth generated demand for local retail businesses. The first auto-oriented shopping centers were built in Silver Spring and Bethesda. Population continued to grow as the federal work force expanded during World War II.

The quality of development was high, and by the standards of the day, amenities and services were abundant. As one Lee critic conceded: "The Colonel wasn't greedy all the time." Indeed, he saw his enlightened self-interest as synonymous with the public interest. He was fiercely proud of his achievements, both political and material. The regime provided great parks, better roads, good schools, and an honest police force. Lee used his considerable influence to secure location of prized federal agencies. Bethesda Naval Hospital, the National Institutes of Health, and the Naval Research Laboratories created major employment centers, attracting more residents with good incomes and high standards for services and amenities, in what the regime regarded as a virtuous cycle of growth.

Charter, Reform, and Decline of the Lee Regime

The Lee Regime's growth machine built the base of its own demise. Affluent and well-educated newcomers, imbued with "good government" idealism of the Progressive Movement and New Deal, became the vanguard of a different regime—a coalition of civic or other nonbusiness interests and a new set of officials.[17] With federal employees barred by law from partisan activity, the Montgomery County Federation of Civic Associations became the voice of reform. It embraced the moralistic narratives associated with home ownership, the garden community, and the populism of the miniature republics. In 1938 the Federation and the League of Women Voters persuaded the fusion county board to commission a study of county government by the Brookings Institution. Published in March 1941, the study found wanting almost every aspect of county governance. It recommended adoption of a home rule charter and a council-manager form of government, with all administrative functions, including sanitation, parks, and planning placed under direction of a professional county manager appointed by a county council.[18]

The Lee Regime defeated a charter referendum in 1944, but in 1948 voters approved the first county home rule charter in Maryland with a classic council-manager government. Charter supporters won all seats on the 1949 interim council and in the regular 1950 council election. The Colonel executed a strategic flanking movement. He shepherded a state statute that required county officials to be nominated in party primaries and elected in gubernatorial election years. This effectively barred federal civil servants from running for council. Majorities elected in 1954 and 1958 were aligned with Lee Regime interests. The Colonel used his influence with the governor, the General Assembly, and his allies in Prince George's County to block legislation transferring jurisdiction over planning and parks to the county in four successive legislative sessions from 1947 to 1953.

Success for reformers had seemed at hand in 1953. Republicans controlled both the Montgomery and Prince George's delegations to the General Assembly. Governor Theodore McKeldin was a Republican and no friend of Lee's. The reformers formed a Coordinating Committee to present a united front in support of legislation introduced by Delegate Douglas Bradshaw (R-Montgomery) to abolish the M-NCPPC and transfer its powers and functions in Montgomery County to the county government.

Lee counterattacked. Bond Smith, the Commission's general counsel, set up shop in Annapolis where he and the agency's public relations officer managed a campaign against the "ripper" bill. Blair Lee III who was serving as secretary of the National Capital Planning Council, urged retaining the commission because of its sub-regional responsibilities. Responding to pressure organized by Lee and his allies, Montgomery's Republican Senator indicated he would no longer support the Bill unless it would save money. Bradshaw immediately released a draft report from the Sobeloff Commission, a legislative study group, which found savings. Smith and his allies produced a contrary study from the same commission. Neither had been approved by the commission, leaving the issue in doubt.

The civic coalition splintered. Reflecting the influence of the Sasscer machine in Prince George's County, the bi-county umbrella civic organization announced its opposition to Bradshaw's Bill, but the Montgomery Federation defected from that position. Bond and the Colonel mobilized a hundred M-NCPPC supporters to oppose the bill at the hearing before the House of Delegates' Bi-County Committee. Prince George's senator now defected along with two of that county's Republican delegates, joining one Democrat, splitting the Prince George's House delegation, 3–3. When the Bill came to the floor of the House of Delegates it was defeated 63–36. The only elements that survived were a reduction of the Administration Fund Tax and transfer of recreation programs to Montgomery County.

In 1957, Delegate Blair Lee III steered legislation through the General Assembly that extended M-NCPPC's Montgomery jurisdiction to the entire county, except for the six municipalities with their own planning powers. The commission was expanded to ten members; five appointed by each county government to serve as its planning board for matters affecting a single county.[19] These changes provided little solace to reformers, who failed to win council majorities in 1958 or 1962 and the Montgomery County Planning Board remained friendly to developers.[20]

The Builders and Bar Regime

The decade following World War II brought fundamental changes to the development industry. Merchant builders began to dominate the suburban housing market, responding to pent up demand and new federal home financing programs. They bought large tracts of land and mass-produced homes from a few standard models; a cultural shift in real estate marketing—from selling lots to selling homes. They shared the Lee Regime's enthusiasm for growth but were less dependent on its "friends and neighbors" system of patronage and mutual favors.

To build in a booming market the merchant builders needed changes in zoning to meet the demand for homes for newly forming households and to provide land for more commercial development. Suburbanites were certain to oppose such ambitions, creating uncertainties and increasing transaction costs. Presenting their cases to politically divided councils and crafting new policies required a partner with legal skills and political finesse.

Robert Linowes recognized an opportunity for a new kind of law firm that concentrated on land use. He resigned as assistant county attorney in 1956 to build a practice representing developers. Brash and brilliant, Linowes was a fierce, unrelenting advocate, ever ready to launch a withering assault on any challenger of a client's interests. A master of metaphoric disdain for master plans that displeased him, he characterized the preparation of one as "full of sound and fury, like copulating elephants, followed by a 27-month gestation period." A Linowes presentation of a development proposal was a dazzling spectacle, equal parts zoning law seminar, expert testimony, sheer hucksterism, and grandiloquent claims for its benefits to the public welfare. He put together some of the most important development deals in the county, including the first two regional shopping malls in Wheaton and North Bethesda. The firm he created with partner Joseph Blocher was the leading edge of an emerging land use bar that led a second-generation growth machine of the Builders and Bar Regime.

Representing multiple builders, the land use lawyers were the one constant player in the zoning game. With a compliant planning board populated primarily with the rear guard of the Lee Regime and an overworked staff consumed with processing rezoning and subdivision applications, the lawyers were the primary source of policy innovation as they advanced the interests of the merchant builders. Their involvement in all aspects of planning, development, and finance made them influential political advisers of their clients and other business leaders and intermediaries in financing campaigns for council candidates favoring robust growth.

The Builders and Bar Regime's growth machine was larger, wealthier, and even more aggressive than Lee's, but it lacked a governmental partner. With the Colonel's power fading, there was no dominant leader or strategist with the ability or even the inclination to coordinate public policy. Absent a public perspective, the new regime was less interested in a commercial republic that fused private and public interests than in simply advancing private interests. It was greedy all the time.

Twilight of the Growth Machine

In 1962 the council raised property taxes and both parties' primary elections produced mixed tickets of reform and antitax, progrowth candidates. Masterminded by two land use lawyers, a letterhead committee, "County Above Party (CAP)," was created and funded by developers. It endorsed a slate of the most prodevelopment candidates from each party. Just two weeks before the general election a tabloid "newspaper" was delivered to every household. Appropriating the nonpartisan rhetoric of the charter movement, it touted the CAP slate as fiscally prudent citizens dedicated to efficient government, selected without concern for party affiliation. The entire slate of four Republicans and three old guard Democrats was elected.

The CAP Council, willingly guided by zoning lawyers, discovered previously unrecognized changes in neighborhoods and considered few rezoning applications unworthy of approval. It regularly ignored recommendations of the planning board (itself hardly antagonistic toward development interests) and rezoned land so indiscriminately in so many places that its actions raised doubts about the viability of the Wedges and Corridors General Plan adopted in 1964 by the Park and Planning Commission. The general commercial zone was liberally granted for new businesses, apartments, and office space to be rented by federal agencies seeking suburban locations. The zone had traditionally been used for relatively modest retail and office buildings but it also permitted residential uses. Buildings were allowed maximum densities fourteen times the land area of a project and with no required setbacks they could cover an entire lot. Developers took advantage of this residential "loophole" to construct massive apartment and office towers that loomed above adjacent neighborhoods of detached houses on small lots in Silver Spring, Friendship Heights, and Bethesda.

In 1966 five of the seven incumbents were defeated. Undaunted, the lame duck council held "midnight sessions," at which it rezoned over 200 properties covering thousands of acres. Assistant county attorneys wheeled shopping carts

filled with rezoning application into the council chamber for a preliminary council vote, returned to the legal office where the applicants' attorneys wrote council approval opinions, then dashed back to the council for final approval. The
rezoning binge was stopped only when the circuit court approved a petition by
newly elected council member David Scull to allow the new council members
to be sworn into office as soon as their elections were certified. Undone by its
excesses, the CAP Council made politically toxic establishment of any new governing regime that included the development industry.

Scull, though Colonel Lee's son-in-law, was a reform Republican. In a deal
brokered by Richard Shifter, the reform chairman of the county Democratic
Party, he formed a progressive coalition with the new council's three Democrats.
The Democrats agreed to elect Scull council president for the first year, after
which he would support a presidential year for each Democrat. The arrangement collapsed following Scull's death in early 1968, shortly after Democrat William Greenhalgh succeeded him. The Republican Central Committee declined
to nominate Scull's wife, Elizabeth, to fill the vacancy. Instead it selected James
P. Gleason, a more conservative Republican. The council presidency returned to
Republican control the following year.

Although often divided, the council made three significant decisions with
long-term consequences for planning politics and county development. The first
of these was reform of the process for making decisions on individual rezoning
applications. On taking office it established a panel to review the zoning decisions of the CAP Council. The panel recommended reconsideration of about 180
cases. The council quickly realized that if it provided proper hearings it would
have time for almost no other business during its term of office. It asked Harry
Lerch, the general counsel of the planning commission and Rita Davidson, an
attorney who had represented civic groups in contested zoning cases and had
been narrowly defeated for council, to find a solution. Following their recommendations, the council created the Office of Zoning Hearing Examiner to hear
all individual zoning cases and recommend their disposition to the council based
on the hearing record and law.[21] The zoning examiner law prohibited all off-the-
record communications concerning a zoning case, ending lobbying of council
members by applicants and their opponents. These changes built public confidence that zoning cases would be reviewed and decided on their merits and
sharply reduced council time devoted to zoning.

The council's second, and in many ways its most important decision was to
approve in 1969 an updated version of Montgomery County's portion of the
General Plan: *On Wedges and Corridors*, which became the touchstone for land
use policy. Its third major decision was appointment of a charter revision committee, which proposed changing from the council-manager system to one with

an elected county executive responsible for administrative functions and political leadership.

After approval of the new charter by voters in 1968, legislation enacted to facilitate the transition to the new form of government transferred M-NCPPC and WSSC appointments from the council to the executive. Exclusive responsibility for zoning and approval of master plans, however, remained with the council because civic leaders, with vivid memories of the Lee machine, adamantly opposed granting the executive planning authority. The 1970 election set up an immediate power struggle over planning board appointments and the future of land use policy when the conservative James P. Gleason was elected as county executive and Democrats won all seven council seats.

The Rise and Fall of the Progressive Regime

The all-Democratic council elected in 1970 promised to implement the General Plan and accelerate planning for areas to be impacted by Metro stations, several of which were expected to be in operation before the end of the decade. County Executive Gleason did not share the council's planning philosophy and he had power under enabling legislation for the new charter to appoint members of the planning board. Its control was key to the establishment and maintenance of a governing regime.

The first appointment had to be a Democrat to replace M-NCPPC commissioner William Willcox, who was elected to the council. The council advised Gleason they wanted me to be appointed. I was closely aligned politically with the reformers on the new council, and had served on the Board of Governors of the Citizens Planning Association. Since 1966 I had been president of the Washington Center for Metropolitan Studies, an interuniversity think tank. I was the leading advocate for an elected county executive, a member of the Charter Commission, and had also served on the committee that recommended approval of the General Plan. When the Democratic and Republican Central Committees agreed on a bipartisan slate of delegates to the 1968 State Constitutional Convention, Gleason and I were the nonnegotiable demands of our respective parties. We were opposites in temperament and political philosophy but had agreed on the executive form of government and on the proposed constitution. The council assumed Gleason would make the nomination as a matter of interparty comity. He declined the honor, agreeing to nominate me only if the council withdrew its support for pending legislation to strip him of power to appoint planning board members and return it to the council.[22] When the council refused, Gleason negotiated directly with the county's state legislators. In return for a one-year study of the planning function, he agreed to nominate me and allow the council to select one of the next two appointees.[23] He forwarded my nomination but the council deferred confirmation for two weeks to demonstrate it would have no part of his deal with the legislators. Council members argued they should make all planning appointments because the charter and state law assigned them ultimate responsibility for zoning, master plans, and setting the commission's tax rate, exclusive of executive veto.[24]

The executive and council remained at loggerheads over control of the planning board for the remainder of 1971. They agreed the board needed a full-time chair, but disagreed on which of them should make that appointment and whom it should be. Gleason nominated former state senator Thomas Anderson to the planning board and as the board's chair. The council confirmed Anderson's appointment as a commissioner, but refused to approve him as chair. The council rejected two nominees to replace Gordon Lamb, a Republican commissioner Gleason disliked. Finally, Gleason demanded a vote on making Anderson the chair. The council instead persuaded the county's all-Democratic legislative delegation to restore its authority to appoint all planning board members and designate the chair. By the spring of 1972 the board had been reconstituted with a Democratic majority. The council appointed me as full-time chair.

A Progressive Regime was now in place. It had three principal components: a council of reform-oriented liberal Democrats; a cohesive planning board with a strong professional staff; and an electoral base among the miniature republics composed of civic associations, the reform Democratic precinct organization, and an emerging set of environmental groups. It had no business partner and the executive was not a central player in land use policy. The Progressive Regime's planning philosophy was forged fighting the prior regimes and the CAP Council. Council members expected the planning board to provide leadership in implementing and amplifying the General Plan.

The party, civic, and environmental groups were essential to the sustainability of the regime but they were its most fissile element. They were united less by a shared agenda than by opposition to any development that threatened their perceptions of neighborhood quality. Technically knowledgeable, rhetorically gifted, litigious, and capable of producing a mass turnout to denounce a disfavored decision as sellout to developers, they had few enduring loyalties since land use decisions invariably disappointed some members of a miniature republic.

The reconstituted planning board, with an enhanced professional staff, was even more critical to the Progressive Regime than it had been to its predecessors. Because the council was occupied with a broad range of issues, its attention was diffused, and because it was elected, short. Therefore, the board, and particularly the chair and planning director, Richard Tustian, became the leaders and lightning rods of land use policy as the regime moved from one highly controversial issue to the next. The planners' logic of consequentiality was well synchronized with the council's logic of appropriateness. Crafting master plans, zoning ordinances and other measures, the planning board seized the policy initiative from the land use bar, finally severing its umbilical attachment to the development industry.

With priority on preparing for the impact of Metro, the board devised and the council approved a new system of planning, zoning, and development for transit station areas to bring the scale of development in line with transportation capacity. These plans provoked developers with more ambitious interests and angered civic groups that wanted even greater reductions in development potential. Litigation blossomed.

Two measures heightened tensions with development interests and produced cracks in the regime's civic base. Developers bitterly opposed adoption of an Adequate Public Facilities Ordinance to "stage" approval of subdivisions concurrently with extension of public facilities.[25] Civic activists complained its administration was insufficiently aggressive. Both developers and some neighborhood activists disliked the Moderate-Priced Dwelling Unit (MPDU) law enacted by the council, which required all major development projects to offer 12.5 percent of its housing units at prices affordable for moderate-income households in return for a density bonus.[26] Developers denounced its effects on marketability and profits. Neighborhood activists decried the impact of the added density on their communities and schools. They feared possible effects on their home values of different housing styles and lower priced homes and their imagined occupants.

One of the most important achievements of the regime was placing one-third of the county's land in an Agricultural Reserve, implementing the "wedges" element of the General Plan.[27] A plan for preservation of historic sites and districts was also approved, protecting the county's significant historic and cultural resources.[28]

During the decade and a half of the Progressive Regime's ascendance, development interests remained influential, but insulation of most land use policy from executive control frustrated establishment of a governing regime composed of a strong political leader and a cohesive private sector partner. The ability of the Progressive Regime to maintain itself without a major business partner was aided by a slower pace of development for the first time in five decades. Several broad economic factors contributed to the decline in building. The most important factor, however, was a building moratorium imposed to correct violations of federal clean water regulations by the regional sewage treatment plant at Blue Plains and inadequate capacity in older WSSC trunk lines to handle flows from recent growth.

Growth slowed but did not stop. County population grew during the 1970s from 523,000 to 579,000. Housing construction in the 1960s and 1970s hovered at about 34,000 units each decade but multiunit development increased eight-fold to reach 9,500 units in 1979. Nearly 6 million square feet of shopping space was developed. For the first time, a majority of the county's work force was employed at jobs in the county, marking a shift from being a county of commuters to jobs elsewhere.

Each election, beginning in 1974, weakened council cohesion on land use issues. Every decision made by the board and council left some part of the progressive coalition dissatisfied. Newer council members had not been engaged in the long struggle against the older regimes. They had different priorities and interests. The council elected in 1974 maintained a majority of five strong progressives. In 1978 the reliable progressive majority was trimmed to four members. While other members usually voted for most of the policies recommended by the planning board, they were not fully reliable allies of the progressive majority.

When I decided to leave the planning board in 1981 to direct the work of the Committee on National Urban Policy of the National Research Council, the progressive majority agreed Norman Christeller, a former planning board and council member, should replace me. By the time the council scheduled a vote on the appointment, Elizabeth Scull was terminally ill. The council deadlocked in her absence. At the next council session Scull made a dramatic appearance in her wheelchair and in a barely audible voice cast the deciding vote for Christeller. She died a few weeks later and the council appointed her son, David, to complete her term. He was elected to a full term in 1982 and a progressive core sustained the working coalition with the planning board on development policy. Christeller, Tustian, and the planning staff methodically put flesh on the bones of the plans and policies produced by the Progressive Regime. The county experienced its greatest one-decade increase in housing in the 1980s, when over 60,000 single-family homes and 16,000 multifamily homes were built.

The Pure Political Regime

The three county executives serving between 1970 and 1990 were antagonists of the planning board. Each resented its independence of executive control and the fact that it ultimately exercised greater influence over development of the county than the executive. Moreover, the plans it proposed and the council approved tended to drive the county's capital improvement program for which the executive was responsible. The statutory requirement that all county capital projects must be subjected to "mandatory review" by the board was a continuing source of irritation, and occasional embarrassment when the board recommended major revisions, or declined to approve a project. Even though the board's recommendations were only advisory, agencies still had to endure a public hearing and occasional criticism that was politically hard to dismiss. Before he left office in 1986 County Executive Charles Gilchrist worked with State Senator Sidney Kramer and other legislators to weaken the institutional linkage between the council and planning board. Amendments to the M-NCPPC law limited planning commissioners to two consecutive four-year terms, forcing Christeller to retire in 1989. The amendments gave the executive authority to nominate two planning board members, revise master plans before their submission to council, veto plans approved by the council, and create a separate planning office in the executive branch.[29]

The transition from the Progressive Regime began with Sidney Kramer's election as county executive in 1986. Progressive council members were reduced to a minority for the first time since 1970. Elected with substantial support from the development industry, Kramer exercised his new appointment power to replace two strong Christeller allies.[30] He created an executive planning office and aggressively revised master plans before transmitting them to the council. This presented the council with dueling documents and undermined the role of the board's chair as the council's principal adviser on land use policy. In a council sharply divided over development issues, Kramer's allies argued they could not rely on Christeller for advice when the board and executive were in disagreement. Therefore, the council added staff to provide its own source of advice.

With the bond between the council and the planning board frayed, Kramer proposed his director of housing and community development to succeed Christeller. The council, in another four-to-three vote, instead chose Gus Bauman, a land use attorney and civic leader, who earlier served as the board's associate general counsel and then as counsel for the National Association of Home Builders. William Hanna, the chairman of the council's Planning, Housing, and Economic Development (PHED) Committee, cast the critical vote. Though generally allied with Kramer, he was wary of greater executive influence over planning. He disagreed with Bauman on a Silver Spring development proposal but agreed with him on housing policy and acquisition of an abandoned railroad right of way for future transit use between Silver Spring and Bethesda.

Kramer overplayed his hand on development issues, leading to his defeat in the 1990 Democratic primary by Neal Potter, the council's veteran progressive. Potter's election disrupted formation of a more prodevelopment regime led by the executive. He secured restoration of council authority to make all board appointments, and reduction of the executive's role in master planning to fiscal analysis and comment on board recommendations.[31] Only two consistent Kramer allies on the council survived the Potter landslide. Expanded to nine members (five elected from districts and four at-large), the council lacked the political cohesion or common goals of the earlier progressives.

The planning agenda in the early 1990s was occupied by contentious proposals for redevelopment of Silver Spring, updating several area master plans, preparing a refinement of the General Plan, and institutionalizing growth policy. A particularly delicate task involved using the planning board's Advanced Land Acquisition Fund to continue acquiring right-of-way for the Inter-County Connector (ICC), a link between I-270 and I-95, against efforts by some council members to delete it from transportation plans.[32] The board made headway on two other significant transportation objectives: designating a Bethesda-Silver Spring light rail transit route for the abandoned railroad right-of-way of the Georgetown Branch, and establishing an alignment for the Corridor Cities Transitway from the Shady Grove Metro terminal to Clarksburg.

The board lost intellectual leadership of development policy when the Bauman board forced Tustian's retirement as planning director in 1990. The first two replacements had short tenures and the board finally promoted Charles Loehr, the head of the Development Review Division. As director Loehr provided stable management of the department but no strong intellectual leadership or quality control. A divided board drifted. It was stunned when Commissioner Ruthann Aron was indicted for soliciting an undercover police office she thought was a hit man to murder her husband, who failed to succumb to poisoned chili she served him, and an attorney that had won a lawsuit against her. The council removed Aron from office after she refused to resign while awaiting trial in jail. She was convicted.

When Bauman resigned in 1994 to run unsuccessfully for county executive the council appointed William Hussmann, who served as chief administrative officer in the Potter and Gleason administrations, interspersed with experience as an executive in two local development firms. Douglas Duncan was elected county executive and Potter returned to the council. Even though council authority over planning was restored, its members no longer regarded the planning board as their partner in a governing regime, but more as a subordinate bureaucracy. Alliances formed and dissolved issue by issue. A Pure Political Regime emerged in which each council member was an independent political entrepreneur.[33]

The Pure Political Regime reflected a more complex and fragmented county political economy. The county's largest employers were public institutions, the largest corporations were regional or international in orientation, and many key local business institutions, such as banks and news media, had become branches of national firms.[34] Many residents that worked on national and international affairs had little interest in local policy unless directly affected. The entry of women into the labor force that began in the late 1960s depleted the leadership of the civic movement and political parties. After 1990 minorities and immigrants accounted for most of the county's population growth. A growing proportion of new households were renters. These newcomers had lower rates of voting participation and less interest in land use issues than older homeowners. With the withering of the Republican Party in the county and the disappearance of Democratic pre-primary endorsement conventions, unions representing public school teachers and county government employees became the most important sources of primary support for Democratic candidates for council and executive. Declining participation in primary elections enhanced their influence and shifted the policy agenda toward their concerns.

The Hussmann board's principal initiative was Legacy Open Space, a program designed to acquire or otherwise protect critical natural and cultural resources from development. The great contentious issues of transportation policy that had accumulated over fifty years were assigned for resolution to a thirty-five-member Transportation Policy Task Force. After ninety-three task force, workshop, focus group, forum, and work group meetings held over two years, progrowth and slow growth members remained divided over key projects such as the ICC.[35] It punted the tough issues to the planning board, which called time out "to work toward theoretical balance of land use and transportation planning within four subareas of the county."[36] Thus, resolution of the major controversies over the ICC and redevelopment of transit and other activity centers was deferred.

Derick Berlage, the council's PHED Committee chair, replaced Hussmann as the road war over the ICC reached climax in 2002. Seeking a third term, County Executive Duncan was determined to move the ICC forward. Council Member Blair Ewing was as determined to stop it. He led a primary slate of candidates aimed at purging Duncan's council allies and strengthening the anti-ICC faction. Instead, most of Duncan's "Anti-Gridlock" slate was elected, defeating Ewing, reducing the anti-ICC faction to three members, and assuring council support. Construction began in 2006 and was completed in 2012, providing the long planned strategic link for the knowledge-based firms of the I-270 Corridor to Baltimore-Washington International airport.

Beyond supporting Duncan's transportation improvements, the "End Gridlock" majority had no coherent planning philosophy. Berlage was a passive chair, providing little leadership to either the planning board or the council. This lassitude was abruptly challenged when a Clarksburg civic group discovered multiple site plan violations by builders. The ensuing publicity and the planning board's fumbling response reawakened council interest in planning. A generous amount of political flailing and blame-casting ensued. Berlage, seeing his council support evaporate, declined to seek reappointment. In 2006 the council asked me to return as chair of the planning board.

Isiah Leggett was elected county executive in 2006. Five incumbents and four new members were elected to the council but they shared no common goals for development policy. Council staff had become a separate power center. As the last voice the council heard, it replaced the executive staff's role as editor and reviser of plans and the planning board chair as its principal planning adviser. Clarksburg reinforced the shift. A regime based on council-board trust could not be resuscitated.

Despite these difficulties, a reenergized board and staff produced and the council approved a series of sector plans for redevelopment of obsolete commercial centers and strips. Plans were approved for transit-oriented redevelopment of the White Flint area, the Great Seneca Sciences Corridor, and the Germantown employment corridor. Final alignments were approved for a light rail line between Bethesda and New Carrollton in Prince George's County, and the Corridor Cities Transitway for Bus Rapid Transit linking the Shady Grove Metro terminus with Gaithersburg, a life sciences complex, Germantown, and Clarksburg.

In 2010 the county's population approached 1 million. It had become culturally and economically diverse. Development activity in the first decade of the twenty-first century was concentrated at opposite ends of the county. After languishing for decades in the shadow of Bethesda's booming resurgence as a business and housing center, the rejuvenation of Silver Spring finally began, transforming the county's first business district into an interesting, varied, and pleasantly quirky place. At the other end of the county, Clarksburg was growing as the county's final corridor city. Both reflected changing tastes in housing and communities. A new generation of homebuyers and renters were more interested in diverse, mixed-use communities. The surge in building coincided with a second significant shift in the character of the development industry. National development firms had become the dominant builders of housing and high-density mixed-use projects. A century of suburbanization was ending. A more urban future dawned.

Four Regimes and Planning Politics

Each of the four regimes imprinted its character and values on the county's landscape and its planning politics. The Lee Regime was anchored to a political economy based on extraction of value from land and deference to the county's benevolent boss system. Its decisions set the residential character of most of the urban ring and it conceived and initiated extension of the national capital's stream valley park system into Montgomery County. Its most important legacy, however, was establishment of a strong planning institution, the Maryland-National

Capital Park and Planning Commission. Colonel Lee designed it as a specialized organ of the state, fully equipped and empowered it to act independently of the elected governments of the two counties it served. This arrangement ensured its competence in furthering the interests of the Lee Regime and provided a structure of land use governance that enabled it to retain control of the development agenda for several years even after its electoral base was eclipsed.

Under the Lee Regime the initiative in land use policy lay with landowners and developers who moonlighted as public officials. Formal authority was dispersed but the power to exercise it was centralized. Public interest was privately held in a commercial republic. The logic of appropriateness exclusively informed planning politics.

In its struggle with the Lee Regime the charter movement followed the national trend and sought to integrate planning into a more comprehensive governing framework, but the Byzantine barriers to change Lee erected proved how sticky established structure could be. Ironically, the defensive adjustments that kept it intact facilitated its conversion from tool of development interests to land use policy innovator of the Progressive Regime. The county councils gradually gained control of appointments, budget, work program, and approval of master plans. Executive efforts to gain control over planning were repulsed. Although diminished from the Colonel's heyday, the autonomy and power of the planning board remain the most important structural features of Montgomery's planning politics.

The transitional Builders and Bar Regime shared its predecessor's interest in development without Lee's sense of stewardship. For it, land was a commodity. The regime formed as post war demand for housing, new forms of financing, marketing, and the greater scale and new techniques of homebuilding required financial resources, management skills, and legal innovations that exceeded the capacity of the Lee Regime. Ever in pursuit of the main chance, the Builders and Bar Regime seized the moment. The land use bar held the initiative in land use policy, but the regime's ultimate overachievement, the CAP Council, was its undoing.

Planning politics proceeded on two fronts during the Builders and Bar Regime. The first involved the case-by-case dispersion of development through rezoning, extension of sewers, approval of subdivisions, and the adoption of floating zones. The regime's approach to policy was short-term and tactical, focused on individual zoning changes and development projects. The second front was the largely symbolic adoption of the 1964 General Plan. This grand vision of how the county might be developed had no enforceable connection to the individual zoning cases being decided by the CAP Council, which steadily eroded its viability. Ironically, the commission's autonomous authority to adopt the General Plan kept it alive and made the Progressive Regime possible.

The fortuitous council coalition of David Scull and the three Democrats laid the foundation for the Progressive Regime by converting the General Plan from symbol to policy. The office of Zoning Hearing Examiner neutered the politics of rezoning. With consolidation of board appointments and other planning powers in the council after the adoption of the second county charter creation of an executive-centered regime was frustrated. The planning board, which had been the faithful servant and last redoubt for the rear guard of the prior regimes, was repurposed as the council's coalition partner and became the vanguard of the Progressive Regime's alliance of political reformers and civic activists of the miniature republics. The CAP Council created the position of full-time chair to be the loyal enforcer of its policies but Progressive Regime councils regarded the chair as the leader of land use policy and the planning board its principal adviser on planning and land use issues. An invigorated board led the regime in adopting plans that shifted the county's development pattern from aimless sprawl toward the wedges and corridors of the General Plan. The logic of consequentiality coincided with the logic of appropriateness.

Council cohesion on planning matters dissipated and its linkage to the board was compromised by the temporary enhancement of executive powers during the Kramer administration. The board's relationship with councils of the Pure Political Regime became more arm's length. Council members began to regard the chair more as a department head of a bureaucracy to be overseen than as a colleague trusted to guide their deliberations. As major and long-standing development issues were resolved, land use receded and other issues rose in electoral importance. Civic support retreated to neighborhood defenses as the miniature republics fractured over disputes about the appropriate scale of local development. Employee union influence in primary elections displaced the liberal precinct organizations and civic associations. Council cohesion on development policy dissipated. Election of a majority of the council from single-member districts, devolution of planning deliberations to committee, executive incursions, and the rise of the council's staff as its principal planning advisers combined to undermine the trust relationship with the planning board and its chair.

The Pure Political Regime had no common or consistent private or civic partner. No coherent strategic vision guided its decisions. Its approach to development policy was ad hoc, with alliances of convenience shifting with interests of the miniature and commercial republics. The planning board's leadership of land use policy was weakened but survived the transition to the Pure Political Regime. Council staff became the first responders to planning board proposals. As independent critics of board proposals and recommendations from executive and other sources, they were sensitive to council interests and gradually assumed some functions formerly performed by the planning board chair in guiding and advising committee and council deliberation on master plans and other land use policies. The initiative remained with the board to propose policy, however, because no other entity had the capacity to initiate long-range plans or perform the analytical tasks of policy making an increasingly complex and diverse county required. The chair's role in council deliberations shifted from chief adviser and affirmative advocate to defender of board proposals against council staff critique, with the PHED Committee and council adjudicating a quasi-adversarial process. The major innovations of the Progressive Regime were largely maintained with occasional modifications. Policy drifted, lurching from neglect to micromanagement with occasional disruptions. The logic of appropriateness dominated decision making.

Land use attorneys remained influential in the formulation of innovations at the project level and in helping craft special policies that occasionally had wide effects. As the private sector's institutional memory of planning and zoning issues, these experienced attorneys had an impact on the character of development that extended well beyond its legal dimensions. In the often adversarial, rule-dense atmosphere of Montgomery County, lawyers, rather than architects or designers, typically presented projects to the planning staff and the board. This practice placed the focus on whether a project met legal requirements rather than how well it achieved higher aspirations of form or function. With some fortunate exceptions, subdivisions and buildings were often as uninspired as they were legal.

Except for the short period when County Executive Kramer (1986–1990) had power to revise and veto plans, executives exercised little influence on the content of master plans. Executive initiatives and leadership focused instead on significant individual projects and public-private ventures. In most cases, these initiatives were consistent with master plans, but a few presented facts on the ground around which the board had to plan.

Developers shaped land use policy during the Lee Regime and were the force behind their lawyers in the Builders and Bar Regime. After the rise of the Progressive Regime their role became that of a major interest group rather than regime partner. Developers were consistently engaged in preliminary discussions leading to placing plans or other development policies on the agenda. Industry representatives populated advisory committees, council and board work sessions and hearings. Individual developers and their attorneys exercised influence though their participation in deliberations on issues that directly affected them and the industry remained a principal source of financing for campaigns.

Citizens of Montgomery's myriad miniature republics were the most numerous and vociferous respondents to land use initiatives. Through all four regimes, the League of Women Voters was the most respected civic voice on planning and other issues. It kept its members and a broader public informed of significant land use issues through weekly reports from its volunteer observers at planning board and council meetings. Its study groups became a training ground for a generation of women who served in elective office and on the planning board.

For five decades the Montgomery County Federation of Civic Associations was the voice of "the citizens." Through the first three regimes Federation membership and that of the parallel Allied Civic Group (ACG) included most communities, making their views highly influential. In general, the Federation practiced the paranoid style of politics.[37] While this was a reasonable perspective during the Lee and Builders and Bar Regimes, it was hard to abandon a habit of presuming that proposals by developers were suspect and if the board or council found them reasonable, they were assumed to be fruit of a corrupt bargain.

As development extended into the corridor cities and increasingly took forms that varied from conventional single-family subdivisions, Federation membership growth stalled. In 2011 its members included only 54 of the 1,337 civic and other associations registered with the Montgomery County Planning Board to receive notice of plans and regulatory matters pending in their areas.[38] It had few minority members in a county that had become over half non-white. Its member organizations included few condominium or renter associations. As the Federation declined, its leadership aged, became sclerotic and increasingly estranged from the mainstream of county affairs.[39] ACG expired in 2005, exhausted from several decades of battle over the redevelopment of Silver Spring.

During the Pure Political Regime, environmental organizations and other groups with particular geographic or topical interests began to play more significant roles in land use policy. Alliances increased among groups supporting "smart growth" objectives such as higher density transit-oriented development, which was not always favored by the traditional civic associations. The effectiveness of civic and environmental organizations was based on the expertise of their leaders, their tactical skills in generating mass protests and negotiating with public agencies or adversaries, and the voting power they could mobilize when aroused. Civic groups provided decisive margins in critical elections in 1950, 1966, 1970, and 1990 that changed the course of planning policies and politics.

From a general perspective, Montgomery County's history suggests the early phases of suburban growth favor establishment of a commercial regime due to the affinity of leaders of a traditional land-based economy for the economic and personal benefits of development. As development proceeds and accelerates, new homeowners perceive development's costs and inconveniences outweigh its benefits. Reform coalitions anchored in the values of the miniature republic provide the base for a new regime devoted to reigning in the excesses of growth. Reform regimes tend to be fragile and more difficult to sustain for a long time because the economic interests of coalition members are less intense and more diffuse and because specific land use decisions produce dissention among groups allied by generalities. As land use reforms take hold, their salience recedes. New concerns take their place on the public agenda, leading to dissipation of policy coherence and resort to the lowest common denominator in selection of policies and leaders.

Finally, the Montgomery experience suggests the transition from one suburban governing regime to the next is rarely abrupt. It may take several election cycles as the balance between the miniature and commercial republics shifts. Each emerging regime must cope not only with the defunct reasoning of its predecessors but the physical residue of their decisions.

Suburban planning politics blends the reasoning of planners and politicians. It reflects the relative weight of the interests and values of the miniature and commercial republics in the composition of governing regimes. And it occurs in a structured system in which some roles are assigned by law and others are assumed or acquired by custom, initiative, or default. Keeping in mind the history of the interaction of reasons, republics, and regimes helps in understanding how and why strategic decisions that shaped a county's pattern of development were more than discrete events. It links them to each other and the interests and values they served. It provides a framework for understanding them as elements in a continuous process of planning politics.

This broad and long view facilitates testing outcomes of land use decisions empirically as opposed to speculating about contemporaneous assertions that particular decisions served the public interest. This is because land use decisions result in buildings, infrastructure, conservation areas, and other land uses, that preserve or transform places. At a minimum this approach should make it possible to answer some important questions. Were the goals of a plan or policy realized? What were its consequences for economic conditions, environmental quality, housing costs, mobility, or social equity? Have the burdens imposed been offset by public benefits? Has the policy been accepted? Were the major decisions made with adherence to critical moral values of democracy?

It would be extraordinary for a proponent of a policy to declare it would harm the public interest. But it is reasonable to expect some decisions proclaimed as beneficial when made might be regarded less kindly by future generations. "What were they thinking?" is not an uncommon question raised about some plan or project, heralded in its time as essential to the well-being of the community. By the same token, decisions "right thinking people" regarded as grave errors when made may come to be viewed as treasured assets.

ON WEDGES AND CORRIDORS

The absence of a plan for the development of Montgomery County was a significant issue in the campaign for a home rule charter. After Brooke Lee frustrated its effort to incorporate the park and planning functions into county government, the first Charter Council created a separate Upper Montgomery County Planning Commission to prepare plans for areas outside the Maryland-National Capital Park and Planning Commission (M-NCPPC) district. As the Maryland General Assembly was enacting legislation in 1957 to expand its jurisdiction to the entire county and eliminate the upper county commission, M-NCPPC produced a General Plan for its original district. It was not an elaborate document but it provided a basis for the commission to require dedication of local streets and parks shown on the plan and prevented building in rights-of-way for major roads.

The 1957 plan was adopted at a time of substantial ferment about planning in the Washington region. The U.S. Congress, concerned with the effects of rapid growth in the National Capital Region on the functioning of the national government, established the Joint Committee on Washington Metropolitan Area Problems, chaired by Senator Alan Bible (D-Nev.). The committee staff, directed by Frederick Gutheim, the former chairman of the Upper-County Commission, conducted studies on transportation, water supply, sewerage, solid waste disposal, and regional planning. The staff reports and committee hearings stimulated broad discussion among local government officials about the future of the region.[1] Senator Bible sponsored legislation to establish a National Capital Transportation Agency to plan a rail rapid transit system recommended by his committee.[2] Local officials from the District of Columbia, Maryland, and Virginia organized the Metropolitan Washington Council of Governments and negotiated an interstate compact that created the Washington Metropolitan Area Transportation Authority (WMATA).[3]

The Year 2000 Plan

The election of President John F. Kennedy in 1960 brought heightened national attention to the problems of cities and to the Washington area in particular. Kennedy's appointments to the National Capital Planning Commission (NCPC) energized that somnolent body, and its regional appendage, the National Capital Regional Planning Council, composed of local planning agency representatives. William E. Finley, the planning director for both bodies, had been working on a policy plan for the region under the previous NCPC chairman, Harland Bartholomew. *A Plan for the Year 2000 for The National Capita Region* was released with the president's endorsement on May 8, 1961. It was not a detailed guide for the area's development, "but rather a set of policies to guide governmental decision-making and the preparation of physical plans. The aim is to inaugurate a process of openly arrived at decision and action which will shape the region in the years to come."[4]

Arguing the ability of the region to meet its needs depended to a considerable extent on the *pattern of growth* it followed, the plan was a classic example of rational planning as practiced at mid-century. It defined the problem as accommodating growth in a way that did not impede the functioning of the federal government and was "worthy of the fact that this Region is symbol and focus of free world aspirations."[5] The plan forecast with reasonable accuracy that by the year 2000 the region would contain 5 million residents. It laid out general goals for broadening choices for living, working and participating in the region, creation of an efficient pattern of growth, and providing a high quality living environment. Seven alternatives were presented for accommodating the growth and achieving those goals.[6] Following the logic of consequentiality, the plan found the Radial Corridor alternative provided the most efficient use of mass transportation, allowed the largest number of people access to employment opportunities in the metro center and a number of corridor cities, and provided for wedges of open space between the corridors.

The Year 2000 Plan was skillfully packaged and presented against the background of heightened interest in managing the region's growth and serving its burgeoning population and traffic. The Interstate Highway program enacted during the Eisenhower administration was reshaping metropolitan areas. Highway planners proposed three freeway loops for the Washington area: one circling the historic city core and passing at the foot of Capitol Hill, a second that became the Capital Beltway (already under construction), and a third outer loop with about twice the radius of the Beltway. In Montgomery County the two beltways were to be connected by three radial freeways: an extension of the future I-270 through Bethesda, Friendship Heights, and Glover-Archbold Park in northwest Washington to a new Potomac crossing to Virginia at Three Sisters Islands; a North Central Freeway through Silver Spring, Takoma Park, and the Metropolitan Branch Rail corridor to the inner loop; and a parkway along the Chesapeake & Ohio (C&O) Canal.

Planning Politics and the General Plan

The 1957 and 1960 amendments to the Regional District Act provided a legislative mandate for the M-NCPPC to plan for the entirety of the two counties. Commission Chairman Herbert Wells and Vice Chairman Donald Gingery were fresh from participation in the production of the Year 2000 Plan as members of the National Capital Regional Planning Council. Responding to the groundswell of interest in the regional plan, they launched preparation of a general plan for the enlarged Regional District that would follow the radial corridor concept. This was less an act of altruism or affection for planning than a practical judgment that a general plan for the bi-county area would do two politically useful things. It would mollify critics like the League of Women Voters, Civic Federation, and Citizens Planning Association that were demanding a plan to guide the growth of both counties. More important for Gingery, who chaired both the Montgomery Planning Board and the Regional Planning Council during production of the Plan for the Year 2000, a general plan would confirm the freeway network. A developer, he was a passionate advocate of the full freeway system, believing it essential for development of the county.

A Clear Vision—The Bartholomew Draft

The commission engaged the nationally renowned planning consultant Harland Bartholomew to prepare the plan. He was a logical choice for both substantive and political reasons. Bartholomew chaired the National Capital Planning Commission during the Eisenhower administration and had overseen production of the 1959 Mass Transportation Survey that stimulated the controversy over the relative roles of highways and transit. He was influential in the selection of the radial corridor alternative recommended by the *Plan for the Year 2000*, and was a proponent of a "balanced" transportation system for the region, which included both the full freeway system and mass transportation in the major corridors. Everyone was for balance. Highway advocates interpreted "balance" to include all the roads in the 1959 plan and possibly some transit. Transit advocates interpreted it to mean substitution of transit in major corridors for highways.

Bartholomew's 1962 draft offered a clear and powerful vision for the future of the two counties. It was faithful to the radial concept of the Year 2000 Plan. It accepted the National Capital Transportation Agency's recommendations for rail transit and retained all the proposed highways of earlier plans and studies, including the outer beltway and the Northwest and North Central freeways. The plan's three elements were the "urban ring" of suburbs in M-NCPPC's original Regional District, "corridors" that extended toward Frederick, Baltimore and

Annapolis, and low-density "wedges" separating the corridors. The draft's land use map clearly distinguished the corridors from the low-density residential areas and rural open spaces of the wedges.

Publication of the Bartholomew draft coincided with the pyrrhic triumph of the Builders and Bar Regime in electing the County Above Party (CAP) Council and with the bitter, seemingly endless regional transportation policy debate between transit advocates and highway enthusiasts. In Montgomery County, it pitted Gingery against Darwin Stolzenbach, the head of National Capital Transportation Agency. A long-time Montgomery civic activist and former chair of the Citizens Planning Association, Stolzenbach had led efforts to abolish the M-NCPPC and had loudly demanded that Gingery and other developers serving on the commission should be disqualified for conflicts of interest. To say the two men detested each other would barely do justice to the intensity of their enmity.

The CAP Council exhibited minimum enthusiasm, if not open disdain, for the plan. Civic groups were strongly supportive. Gingery and other commissioners had reservations about the sharp distinction the Bartholomew plan made between the wedges and the corridors, which seemed to place much of the county out of bounds for development. Prince George's commissioners were skeptical of the entire wedges and corridors concept, which unsettled some development expectations and fit its topography less comfortably than it did Montgomery's.

More than 400 people testified at the commission's eight public hearings on the plan. The Montgomery County Chamber of Commerce blasted it as relegating the county to a dormitory for the District of Columbia. Arguing that the proposed mass transit system was designed primarily to build jobs in Washington rather than to foster their location in the county, the Chamber proposed an alternative development pattern it called "ribs and spine." The ribs were to be a network of roads built at right angles to the I-270 spine to provide opportunities for building houses and employment centers. The Chamber said stream valley parkland and neighborhood parks would provide plenty of open space.

Homebuilders objected to the corridor scheme and its emphasis on rapid transit, which they felt benefitted only the District of Columbia. They favored a satellite community pattern—clusters of communities distributed across the county to accommodate population growth. The Farm Bureau denounced the open space wedges as reducing the value of farmland and the ability of farmers to sell at subdivision prices or for any other use they desired. Landowners and speculators were largely opposed to the plan, depending, of course, on where they had or were seeking to acquire property interests.

Civic groups generally supported the wedges and corridors concept, although many expressed reservations about the densities that might occur in the corridors. They also questioned the resolve and ability of the county and commission to restrain development of the wedges.[7] Given the extent of disagreement and the active disinterest of the CAP Council, the future of the General Plan seemed uncertain. It was rescued by a fortunate confluence of events and interests.

Fudging and Smudging—The Commission Plan

In the 1962 election that brought the CAP Council to power, David Scull became chairman of the Republican Central Committee. Scull and his wife, Elizabeth, the Colonel's daughter, were leaders in the civic reform faction of the Republican Party that had long cooperated with Democrats in the charter and planning reform movements. It was still customary for the party central committees to select nominees for the planning board. Scull maneuvered to select Caroline Freeland, a proponent of the General Plan. She joined Commissioner Everett Jones, who also favored its adoption. Blair Lee III joined Scull, his brother-in-law, behind the scenes in urging Democrats on the commission to adopt the General Plan as a way of forestalling efforts to disband the commission.

Freeland and Jones were appointed to a bi-county committee along with two commissioners from Prince George's to review the public hearing testimony and recommend changes to the draft plan. The committee's report resulted in the commission's adoption of *On Wedges and Corridors: A General Plan for the Maryland-Washington Regional District.*

It was a significant planning document, policy statement, and political achievement. As a planning document it accepted the wedges and corridors framework for the physical development of suburban Maryland. As a policy statement it blurred some of the distinctions made in the 1962 draft between the low-density residential and rural/conservation elements of the wedges. But it established—at least in Montgomery County—a foundation upon which subsequent land use decisions would be built for the next half-century. As a political achievement it accommodated the divergent interests of the growth machine and the planning reformers while establishing the reputation of the commission as a leader in regional planning. The key to all three achievements was in the way in which the conceptual core of the Plan—the wedges and the corridors—was reconfigured.

The wedges of open space were a necessary corollary of the corridors. They were designed both to limit urban sprawl and to reserve land for agriculture, mineral extraction (particularly sand, gravel, and Diabase stone), recreation, and protection of the region's water supply, which included an intake on the Potomac and two reservoirs on the Patuxent. The 1962 draft designated about half the county's land area for nonurban uses and clearly demarked the low-density residential component of the "wedges" from the much larger area that would protect agriculture and natural resources.

There was no consensus in the commission on where the corridors should end or the level of density that should be permitted in the wedges. Some commissioners were uncomfortable with the implication of the draft that precluded suburban densities in much of the county. Lewis Elston, the planner assigned the task of preparing the final map, bridged the impasse among the commissioners by using pastels instead of ink to prepare the land use map, gradually shading the "wedges" from yellow, representing residential uses along the corridors, to darker shades of green as one approached the county boundaries. This allowed each commissioner to interpret the density of residential development as he or she wished. Thus, consensus was achieved by rule of (Elston's) thumb.

Development interests took comfort in the fact that the CAP Council, which kept its distance from the plan, would not enact a comprehensive zoning map that conformed to it. The General Plan was essentially a guideline for master plans, which, in turn, were only guidelines for subdivision regulation and future zoning. Under Maryland's Change/Mistake Doctrine, individual rezoning applications would be referenced to the 1930 zoning map, not the General Plan.[8] Civic activists got a general plan; developers got no significant change in the rules of the game. Everyone won. Agreement required fudging some issues and was facilitated by Elston's artful smudging of the wedges. Because the reformers lost their fight to bring M-NCPPC under control of county government and the General Assembly had not yet granted the council authority to amend and approve master plans, the commission was able to adopt the plan without approval by the CAP Council, where attitudes toward it ranged from indifference to hostility.

The adopted plan accepted the professional conventions of the day. It assumed space should be made available to accommodate the Maryland suburbs' share of the long-range regional forecast of population and jobs. In so doing, it formulated a set of goals.[9] Most were innocuous platitudes. Among them, however, lay the foundation for staging development with the provision of public facilities. The plan was critical of rezoning land prematurely, recommending that zoning be "staged" by placing most land in large-lot "holding" zones until closer-in land developed and the county was ready to extend public facilities for more dense and compact growth. Only then should enough land be rezoned at densities recommended by master plans to allow a competitive market to operate, dampening both speculation and leapfrog development patterns.

The General Plan took a conventional approach to zoning, recommending that residential uses be excluded from all commercial and industrial zones, with the possible exception of "layered" zoning in major commercial centers. It was cautious about planned development zones, fearing they might be used in lieu of master plans and be approved in rural areas or wedges, contrary to the recommended pattern. It repeated the 1957 General Plan's recommendations for townhouse and high-rise apartment zones.

True to its inspiration—the Year 2000 Plan—the General Plan's four transportation corridors radiated from the District of Columbia as the region's core. The main corridor in Montgomery County followed I-270 and MD 355 from Rockville at the edge of the suburban ring, toward Frederick. New corridor cities were proposed beyond Rockville at Gaithersburg and Germantown, with another possible at Clarksburg after the Year 2000. A second corridor aimed toward Baltimore was proposed along the boundary of the two counties with new corridor cities located in Fairland and Laurel.

By spacing corridor city centers four miles apart, development could be compact to facilitate the use of mass transit. Density would be progressively tapered from high-rise offices and apartments in each of the corridor cities' centers toward residential estates and low-rise office and industrial parks at their edges. Greenbelts with regional parks encircled each corridor city. Transit stations were recommended at two-mile intervals to balance the need for high-speed train service with convenient access for riders. The two beltways connected the corridors.

In addition to the corridor cities, the plan acknowledged that it would be necessary to thicken the suburban ring to accommodate as much as 63 percent of the population growth forecasted for 2000. This would produce problems that the plan suggested could be addressed by applying some of the "refinements" used in the corridor cities. It did not, however, recommend creating strong urban centers within the ring like those proposed for the corridor cities. Arguing that the design of the suburbs had been set, the plan proposed instead that the necessary expansion of the housing supply could be achieved through careful development of passed over tracts and benign redevelopment of "blighted" areas. While the plan did not expect residents of the urban ring would use transit to the same extent as the new inhabitants of the corridor cities, it recognized that:

> Rapid transit and a few high-speed freeways will have to be painfully pushed through the ring, but once done this will keep through-traffic off the local streets and out of quiet residential neighborhoods. Constant road-widenings will cease and stability will be returned to the close-in communities.[10]

By the time the plan was published in 1964, only the North Central Freeway remained under consideration as a major road inside the beltway.[11] Lawsuits in the

District, public opposition, and congressional action killed the Northwest Freeway. In 1954 Justice William O. Douglas led the famous hike on the C&O towpath
from Washington to Cumberland and the supporters of that freeway capitulated,
although parkways were constructed on both sides of the Potomac from Georgetown and Arlington to the Capital Beltway. Transit stations would serve commuters in the suburban ring. They would be conveniently located in the most popu-
lous areas but the General Plan suggested that demand for pedestrian access would
be low and the stations should be designed primarily as park & ride facilities.

By 1960 some areas outside the urban ring and isolated from the planned
corridor cities, such as Olney and Damascus, had already experienced some residential and commercial development. The adopted plan retained the draft's recommendation for low-density development of both satellite communities but
the land use map indicated a substantially larger area and future population for
each than the 1962 draft had done. It suggested they would, however, be dependent on Washington, the urban ring, and the corridor cities for most services
and employment opportunities. The more remote communities of Poolesville,
Barnesville, Laytonsville, and Darnestown were expected to remain country villages due to lack of sewer and soils unsuitable for dense development on septic
systems. Large-lot estate housing was endorsed for the urban fringe in Potomac,
Upper Rock Creek, and Upper Northwest Branch.

An important goal of the plan was to retain about half of Montgomery County
in rural and open space uses to protect stream valleys and provide recreational
opportunities in regional and local parks that were readily accessible to suburban
neighborhoods. Even before the commission adopted the General Plan, John P.
"Jack" Hewitt, who was appointed director of parks in 1957, anticipated this recommendation and accelerated expansion of the park system. Under his leadership parks were transformed from an accessory to housing development into a
national leader in park management. In the decade from 1960 to 1970 the park
system grew almost five-fold, from 3,353 to 15,741 acres.

The recommendations of the commission that zoning should be consistent
with its newly adopted General Plan had little if any influence on the decisions of
the CAP Council. It merrily rezoned hundreds of properties as requested by their
owners and contract purchasers. Its zoning decisions occasionally conformed to
the General Plan; often they did not.

The Blue Ribbon Committee

The Wedges and Corridors concept gained broad support among community
organizations and advocates of managed growth. Developer opposition qui-

eted in light of the changes made in the commission-adopted plan and voter repudiation of the CAP Council in the 1966 elections. The new council majority of three reform Democrats and Republican David Scull were convinced that without a general plan officially endorsed by the council, development would continue to outpace planning, rather than the reverse. They quickly appointed a "Blue Ribbon" committee to advise whether the wedges and corridors concept was still valid or had been so vitiated by the CAP Council that it was no longer a useful guide. They asked Blair Lee III to chair the committee. Elected to the State Senate in 1966, Lee worked closely with Harry Lerch, the commission's general counsel, to revise the Regional District Act to require the council to approve plans before the commission could adopt them. Though the absence of council power enabled the commission to adopt the General Plan, the law now brought planning as well as zoning under council governance.

Lee was a shrewd choice. His prior service on the planning board (1949–1951 and 1965–1966) and as executive director of the National Capital Regional Planning Council (1951–1954) gave him an appreciation of the importance of a general plan to guide the region's growth. As author of the several revisions to the Regional District Act, he guarded the autonomy of the commission by skillfully engineering its adaptation to the shifting preferences of the county's political leadership. While his lineage made him suspect among some of the purists in the reform movement, he earned the trust of the new Democratic leaders by showing a deft combination of respect for and differences with his father. Because he was a bridge between generations and between the prior regimes and the progressives, his endorsement of the General Plan could be accepted, even if not welcomed by most prodevelopment groups. He steered the committee through its investigation, assigning key tasks to members he trusted to produce answers favorable to the plan.

After several months of discussion, the committee advised the council that while decisions of the CAP Council slightly widened the corridors and marginally thickened density in parts of the wedges, "wedges and corridors" remained a sound basis for detailed planning of the county. The committee recommended that the planning board revise and update the plan in light of decisions that had been made regarding alignment of the Metro lines and relocation of the outer beltway. In particular, it recommended defining and delineating different kinds of open space for parkland, long-term agricultural use, low-density residential uses, land reserved for natural resource protection, and permanent elements of local or regional development structure. The committee noted that some open spaces could serve more than one of these functions.[12]

Council Adjustments and Approval

The council accepted the committee's conclusions and directed the planning board to update the General Plan, incorporating irreversible decisions made since 1964. Two of those decisions required significant adjustments in the configuration of the plan's corridor and wedge components: the alignment of the Metro routes and station locations, and the extension of sewer to Olney.

Realigning Metro

The 1964 General Plan incorporated the Metro system's "fishhook" alignment of the Red Line in Montgomery County. The shank of the hook ran from the terminus at Shady Grove via the B&O right-of-way through Silver Spring, first curving west, then northwest through Washington before reentering the county at Friendship Heights and ending at Grosvenor, north of the beltway. The Washington Metropolitan Area Transportation Authority (WMATA), however, allowed each local government to determine the final alignment and station locations, within some cost constraints. Strong support developed among land and business interests to reverse the "fishhook," to provide a continuous western line, paralleling Rockville Pike from Friendship Heights to Shady Grove. The eastern branch of the line would leave the railroad right-of-way past Silver Spring at Forest Glen and proceed parallel to Georgia Avenue to Wheaton and Glenmont. The planning board recommended keeping the original alignment as more supportive of the corridors concept. The council, however, supported the Glenmont alternative in a 5–2 vote.

The council's debate revealed political cleavage on both interpretation of the General Plan and the state of Montgomery officials' understanding of the role of mass transit in the suburbs. Council Member Idamae Garrott, urged her colleagues to support the General Plan alignment, pointing out that the eastern "wedge" was already endangered by the extension of sewer service to Olney and the development of the Leisure World retirement community. She argued that transit service would make retention of low-density housing and open space infeasible. Scull and Rose Kramer advocated for the alternative. In explaining his preference, Scull expressed the view that the main use of Metro would be for workers from the District to have good transportation for jobs in Montgomery, and it was, therefore, important that the line in the Rockville Pike corridor be continuous.

Other council members pointed out that the alignment decision would have long-term effects on the county's development, and that development at Wheaton, a historically important commercial center, and other eastern county centers would be at a substantial disadvantage if there were no rail transit on the east side of the county beyond Silver Spring.[13] Although all council members were enthusiasts of transit, they assumed few Montgomery residents would walk to Metro. Echoing views expressed in the General Plan, debate focused on how much parking should be provided at stations. The changes in alignment added opportunities for more intensive development on both branches—in North Bethesda on the western route and at Wheaton and Glenmont on the eastern branch.

With alignment of the Red Line settled, the council took on the thornier task of selecting sites for Metro stations and their related parking, bus, and maintenance facilities. Location options were limited for the five stations adjacent to the railroad.[14] The most controversial station locations were Bethesda and Forest Glen. Bethesda civic associations favored locating the station in the Woodmont Triangle, placing it farther from single family neighborhoods than one located more centrally, at the intersection of Old Georgetown Road and Wisconsin Avenue, near the Edgemoor and Chevy Chase neighborhoods. The planning staff and board recommended the central location as better serving the business district. The council finally approved it, in part because the Woodmont location was too close to the next station at the National Institutes of Health and because access and circulation around the station could be better engineered at the Wisconsin Avenue site.

Forest Glen was about halfway between Silver Spring and Wheaton, just north of the intersection of the Capital Beltway and Georgia Avenue—a convenient location to intercept park & ride commuters. The area contained garden apartments within walking distance, single-family neighborhoods, Holy Cross Hospital and related medical offices. Residents opposed having a station in their neighborhood, dreading its impact on a congested intersection and fearing Metro could bring criminals to their community. The planning board and council concluded these fears were exaggerated and that the importance of the station to the overall system outweighed community concerns.

Once the Glenmont line was approved over her initial objections, Garrott, the self-proclaimed champion of "The Citizens," persistently urged the council to demand construction of the Glenmont Line in a deep rock tunnel after it left the railroad right of way north of Silver Spring. Her position reflected concerns that cut-and-cover construction would disrupt neighborhoods and ruin businesses—especially in Wheaton—as it had in the District of Columbia. She also spoke for the feelings of citizens on the Glenmont line that they should receive a system equal in quality to the Shady Grove line, which would be in tunnel until it crossed the Beltway.

Equipped with encyclopedic mastery of detail, photographic memory of everything she had ever said and any adversary's every error; garrulous, self-righteousness, and with the capacity to sit and filibuster for hours while the resolve and stamina of others wilted, Garrott sometimes prevailed by simply exhausting her opposition. But she was a shrewd politician who knew how to stimulate civic activists to launch gossip, phone, mail campaigns, and mass meetings in support of her causes. "The citizens of this county were screwed over for years. So, I will always be on the side of the citizens in a fight with the developers," she declared. Finally, the council and WMATA agreed to tunnel and placed the Forest Glen station on the west side of Georgia Avenue, farther from Holy Cross Hospital. At 196 feet, Forest Glen is the deepest station in the entire system and can be served only by high-speed elevators instead of escalators.

Sewering Olney

Both the Bartholomew draft and the 1964 General Plan placed the upper reaches of Rock Creek and Northwest Branch in a broad open space wedge. Leisure World, approved by the CAP Council, filled the bottom of the wedge but the lack of sewer beyond that point protected the remainder of it and delayed development in Olney, three miles farther out Georgia Avenue, where both the Bartholomew draft and the 1964 General Plan proposed a small satellite community at the crossroads of Georgia Avenue and MD Route 108.

Developer Albert Turner acquired the Olney Mill property west of Georgia Avenue and north of MD 108 in the early 1960s. It was zoned for residential development on half-acre lots. He applied to the sanitary commission for extension of sewer service to his property, which was located in the headwaters of Reddy Branch, a tributary of the Patuxent River that supplied Washington Suburban Sanitary Commission (WSSC)'s Tridelphia Reservoir. Leaders of the Planning Association and the Civic Federation vociferously opposed approval of sewer service, arguing it was contrary to the General Plan and posed a threat to the bi-county water supply. WSSC denied the request for service. Lacking sewer, the planning board would not approve the subdivision.

To gain the necessary approvals, Turner retained William B. Wheeler as his attorney. The CAP Council had just appointed Wheeler to the sanitary commission. Turner renewed his application, which the WSSC now approved, along with a pumping station on Reddy Branch to transfer the sewage across the ridge into the Rock Creek system. Wheeler recused himself from the vote but did not disclose his interest in Turner's application, as the law required. With sewer promised, the planning board approved the subdivision. In the meantime, another developer acquired a large property in the southwest quadrant of the Olney intersection. To secure sewer for it, he made a $100,000 contribution to the sanitary commission to extend the North Branch of Rock Creek sewer to his property.

Such contributions were legal and common under existing practice, and permitted land to be developed without waiting for the ordinary process of capital programming. This completed the connection necessary for both subdivisions to move forward.

These decisions by the sanitary commission along with a decision to build a second pumping station on James Branch in the Northeast quadrant of Olney to deliver sewage from Montgomery General Hospital into the Northwest Branch sewer provided opportunity for a substantially larger satellite community in Olney than had been contemplated. It also meant Olney developed sooner than otherwise would have been possible. While the pumping stations conveyed sewage out of the Patuxent Watershed, they allowed development that would produce a substantial increase in storm water pollution of reservoir tributaries.

The council initially rejected the Reddy Branch pumping station pending approval of a master plan for Olney, which the planning board was preparing. The sanitary commission, however, did not delete the pumping station from its capital program but moved its location downstream, where it could serve more homes. When the planning board completed work in 1966 on the Olney Master Plan it included the pumping stations, recognized the approved subdivisions, and accordingly increased the population forecast for Olney. This set up a confrontation at the public hearings pitting landowners and developers against civic activists and supporters of the wedges and corridors concept. The CAP Council approved the Olney plan, effectively reversing its earlier vote against the pumping station.

In updating the General Plan the planning board reorganized it, restated its goals, and added sections on environment and housing. The land use element reflected recently adopted area master plans and irreversible zoning and subdivision approvals. It recognized that the Olney sewer decision, along with Leisure World and the choice of the Glenmont alignment for Metro, created a second mini-corridor along Georgia Avenue. Concurrent zoning decisions of councils in both counties preempted the urban density necessary for the feasibility of the bi-county I-95 corridor cities, so they were eliminated from the plan. It accepted the low-density housing that had been approved in western and eastern county areas.

A possible future corridor city was indicated at Clarksburg and the development potential of Damascus was increased. The Germantown corridor city was altered to add industrial uses along I-270 and a greenbelt park, consistent with a recently adopted master plan. In a departure from the 1964 plan, the update called for mixed uses in employment centers and a wider variety of housing densities and types to create "life cycle" neighborhoods.

The updated plan revised population and job estimates based on the boom in development that occurred during the 1960s. No mention was made of the added impetus to migration of Washington residents to the suburbs following the urban riots in 1968 and the deterioration of the DC public school system. The planning staff reported that provision of infrastructure, especially transportation facilities, lagged behind development. No progress was made toward staging development.

The updated plan carried forward the goal of maintaining large areas of open space wedges, but except for park acquisitions, nothing was done to protect them

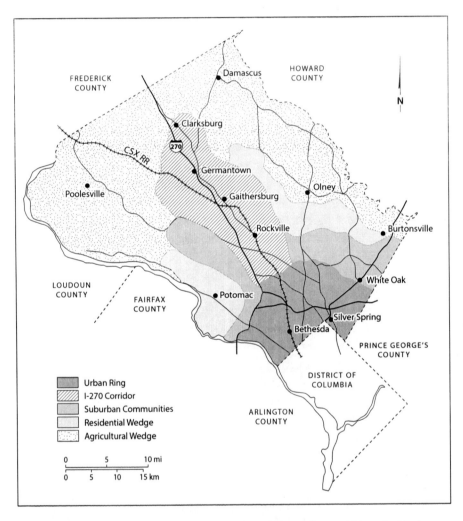

FIGURE 2.1 Schematic of the Approved and Adopted General Plan: On Wedges and Corridors 1969. Courtesy Montgomery County Planning Department M-NCPPC

from scattered subdivisions or to preserve their rural character. It proposed more consistent density for the rural wedges—less than the prevailing half-acre zoning—but was not specific about how much less. The wedges were smaller than in the 1964 plan due to encroachment from development already built or approved.

The plan's new conservation and environmental elements laid a basis for policies protecting historic and cultural sites as well as stream valleys and other important natural resources. It recommended strong protection of the Patuxent watershed, aquifer recharge areas, water quality of streams, and more effective storm water management. It also emphasized the importance of improved community design, amenities, and aesthetics. The council approved the updated plan in 1969.[15]

From Plan to Practice

The existence of *Wedges and Corridors*, the General Plan for Montgomery County, was a lucky incident of planning politics. Its creation can be explained on two interrelated levels. At a regional level it was a product of concern that continuation of the rapid growth experienced in the 1950s would overwhelm the capacity of the area's infrastructure and resources. The Bible Committee and the National Capital Regional Planning Council offered policy proposals and plans based in the logic of consequentiality. They occupied political high ground and were embraced by key leaders in national and state governments. President Kennedy's endorsement of the Year 2000 Plan and the initiation of planning for a regional rail transit system forced local leaders to contemplate its implications for their counties. The regional ferment made serious planning, or at least the appearance of it, an appropriate response to the situation at hand.

In Montgomery County the Lee and Builders and Bar regimes served a commercial republic in retreat before the miniature republics that rose from the subdivisions they built. The M-NCPPC had previously shown little interest in plans that would do more than preserve rights of way for roads and sites for parks and schools. Coopted into the regional planning system, the commission responded to civic pressure and hired Bartholomew to prepare a general plan for the Maryland sub-region. It seemed a relatively harmless and symbolic sop to miniature republics clamoring for a plan. Faced with strong opposition to the Bartholomew draft from their pro-development allies and enthusiastic support among reform groups, the commissioners took two years to adopt a revised plan.

David Scull's intervention in selecting Caroline Freeland for the planning board and behind the scenes nudging from Blair Lee III secured the necessary votes for adoption after adjustments were made and Lewis Elston's artful rendering of the land use map made the character of the wedges ambiguous enough for all interested parties to read their interests onto it. Upon adoption it was little more than a trophy for reformers with no practical effect on decisions of the CAP Council. Hostile toward planning and busily whooping the last hurrah of the growth machine, the CAP Council's rezoning excesses brought to power the bi-partisan coalition led by David Scull that was determined to rescue the plan.

Once more, Blair Lee played a key role in both giving the plan legitimacy through his leadership of the Blue Ribbon Committee and changing the law to require council approval of it and all subsequent master plans. There was relatively little controversy accompanying preparation of the updated plan by the planning board or its approval by the council in 1970. It had broad support among civic organizations, and the building industry did not strenuously object since its policy statements were vague enough to allow a wide range of interpretations. It was not self-implementing. It could have become another pretty picture filed on a shelf. But it did not.

The approval of the General Plan inaugurated a new era in Montgomery County development policy. Its basic spatial framework was never again seriously challenged. *Wedges and Corridors* became a planning icon and the land use constitution of Montgomery County. All subsequent planning decisions would be debated in the terms of their fidelity to it. Every area, sector, or functional master plan adopted since 1969 was an amendment of the General Plan and, thus, subject to debate about whether it was instrumental to its vision and goals. In this sense the General Plan became the trunk of a great decision tree that took root, branched, and was shaped by a half-century of derivative decisions. The most fundamental decisions were those that affected the form and pattern of development established by the plan. These included development of the suburban ring, the corridor cities, and measures to protect the low-density and rural wedges. Implementing *Wedges and Corridors* became the objective of the logic of consequentiality and the touchstone of the logic of appropriateness.

There are broader lessons to be gleaned from Montgomery County's experience in approving its general plan. First, a bold, clear vision, expressed graphically, can be critical in generating support for a plan. That vision, however, and the logic of consequentiality that buttresses it, must be tempered with the logic of appropriateness anchored in an acute understanding of the temper of the most influential interests in the commercial and miniature republics. Second, generality and ambiguity can paper over differences and permit adversaries to reconcile enough to adopt a plan, but generate later conflict over its interpretation and frustrate or delay smooth implementation of vague goals.

The emphasis on the substance of plans can obscure the importance of individuals, whether policy entrepreneurs, mediators, or technicians whose timely exploitation of an opportunity or strategic and timely intervention resolves a problem or impasse that moves the policy or political agenda in a particular direction. Structure also matters by creating the venues in which decisions must be made and reservoirs of authority on which alert officials can draw. Finally, achieving consensus on a transformative plan like Wedges and Corridors takes time, including political setbacks, accommodation of adversaries, persistence by advocates, and fortunate elections and political coalitions.

RETROFITTING SUBURBIA

Planning and managing redevelopment of built-up areas is among the most technically complex and politically challenging tasks in public planning. The dirty secret of land economics is that all owners do not seek the highest and best use of their property. Most are not in the development business. They do not view their land as a commodity but as an integral component of home or business. Once they establish a use, they are reluctant to change it to one an economist might regard as higher and better. Others may be willing to accept all highest and best uses suited to the entire area on their humble parcels.

To further complicate matters, property is more than a piece of dirt within a boundary defined by official survey or recital of metes and bounds in a deed. It is imbued with rights, burdens, and restrictions. The land and structures on it represent only a portion of its value. Public investments and regulations can create windfalls and wipeouts for property owners.[1] As any other investor, the government seeks a reasonable return on its investments in revenues to offset its expenses and in the wellbeing of its citizens. Elected officials are especially interested in public happiness and, therefore, anxious that land uses that disturb the status quo do not excite widespread hostility among constituents sufficient to endanger their careers.

When the first council of the Progressive Regime took office in late 1970, Metro, the largest public works project in the region's history, was underway. Four principal business districts—Friendship Heights, Bethesda, Silver Spring, and Wheaton—would contain Metro stations. From the beginning of suburbanization in the early twentieth century, these commercial districts slowly formed, parcel-by-parcel, along busy thoroughfares and at crossroads. Now, intense pressure was building from the commercial republic to capitalize on the value added by Metro and to grow up and out. Properties near stations were already targets of speculation among owners, realtors, and developers.

Speculative enthusiasms inspired dread in the miniature republics of single-family neighborhoods. In proof of Emerson's aphorism that foolish consistency was the hobgoblin of little minds, civic activists harbored two not always harmonious convictions. One ardently supported rational, comprehensive planning, of which mass transit was a major component because it held the potential of reducing the need for more roads. The other was a deep suspicion of any action that might benefit developers or disturb the serenity of their neighborhoods. Hardened by three decades of battle, they were poised for bitter political and legal combat.

Elected on promises to bring the grand vision of *Wedges and Corridors* to reality, the council would have to figure out how to balance strong market pressure to increase densities and change established uses and settlement patterns with constituent resistance to those pressures and demands for protection of their homes, neighborhoods, and way of life. The General Plan offered a benign vision but no strategy for the future of the urban ring, blithely asserting:

> Although the urban ring is substantially developed, it has by no means reached its ultimate population. . . . Planning in the urban ring will include new development as well as refinements to the old. As in the case of planning regulations for guiding growth in the corridor cities, improved zoning and subdivision ordinances will be needed in the urban ring to encourage greater flexibility of design in relation to natural views, terrain, and vegetation.[2]

This left the planning board and council with a chore but little guidance. They were expected to produce delicately balanced master plans and enforce a coherent strategy of development that could bend to its purposes the ad hoc ambitions of well-financed and politically connected interests. This presented challenges in both policy innovation and political skill.

Rethinking Development Strategy

Once the political struggle over my appointment to the planning board ended the council appointed a Committee on the Planning, Zoning and Development of Central Business Districts and Transit Station Areas to develop recommendations for managing development around the twelve Metro station areas under county jurisdiction.[3] The committee's nineteen members represented a wide spectrum of interests, ranging from the counsel for the builders association to civic leaders that were fierce critics of the planning and development history of the county. The council agreed that the committee, which I chaired, should report through the planning board, which needed to be invested in its recommendations since it would be responsible for administering any new system that was devised.

The committee quickly concluded that existing master plans and zones were inadequate to guide Metro-induced growth in central business districts. Land ownership was fragmented among hundreds of small lots that would have to be assembled for substantial redevelopment to occur. Existing policies provided few incentives to assemble land for redevelopment because permitted densities were high and tended to inflate land values. The zoning code prohibited mixed uses and provided no means of requiring commercial developers to provide the enhanced facilities and amenities needed in a well-functioning transit-oriented center.

The few area master plans adopted by1970 covered many square miles, a scale that precluded useful design guidance; essentially a moot issue since the planning department had no staff of urban designers and architects capable of producing design guidelines. The county's experience with site plans was limited to arrangement of structures and landscaping in floating zones and clustered residential projects. There was little coordination among projects; even those adjacent to each other.

As the committee worked through these challenges, it agreed to propose "sector plans"—amendments to area master plans that would contain detailed objectives for the design and functionality of development around transit stations, including public use spaces and consistent standards for landscaping and streetscapes. Density and height would be "tented"—greatest at Metro portals, then gradually decline to a scale compatible with neighborhoods at a sector's edges. The committee agreed sector plans should be updated on a six-to-ten-year cycle to account for changes in markets and tastes and to make other adjustments in light of experience. In a sharp break from traditional practice, it recommended that immediately following adoption of a sector plan the council should enact a "sectional map amendment" to rezone all land in the sector. This would make zoning consistent with the plan. It would also impede individual rezoning applications because it would be virtually impossible to show a change in the neighborhood for so recent a rezoning, thus protecting adjoining neighborhoods from the threat of a domino effect from rezoning—a legitimate fear of civic leaders with fresh memories of the CAP Council.

As the committee began discussing how to implement sector plans civic activists and builders on the committee could not agree on an approach to zoning. Civic members opposed applying a single Euclidean zone to an entire sector. High-rise buildings could be built "by right" anywhere in such a zone, frustrate the tenting concept recommended for sector plans, overshadow nearby homes, and induce homeowners to sell, leading to expansion of the boundaries of the district. Uniform height and density standards for every lot in the zone would provide no incentive to assemble parcels for major projects, discouraging coordinated development. Developers liked the certainty of Euclidean zones' uniform standards but disliked their inflexibility, which discouraged imaginative design that could add value and produce more marketable buildings. They feared both a cookie-cutter approach and excessive restrictions on land close to the edges of a sector, although they recognized the importance of providing neighborhoods with comfort from overbearing heights next door.

Civic leaders were also suspicious of floating zones, which were not required to conform to recommendations of master plans. They worried they might be crafted to float into their neighborhoods where land values would be lower.[4] Conversely, they liked the idea that each application would have to be individually approved by the council after review by the zoning hearing examiner. Builders were wary of floating zones because they entailed high transaction costs in navigating the hearing examiner process and there was a high probability of a favorable decision being appealed, adding one or more years before a project could start construction. They feared they might be forced to apply for floating zones if the Euclidean zones placed on the land made redevelopment financially unattractive.

After several weeks of fruitless discussion panelists agreed only that existing zoning tools were unsatisfactory. A committee member, Jack Neumann, in a conversation with me, proposed creating a new two-level hybrid zone with a low-density Euclidean "base" and a higher density "option" with attributes of a floating zone—except that it could not float. He argued it would be analogous to the cluster option available in some residential zones that permitted smaller lots in return for more open space and site plan approval.

I thought the approach might resolve the stalemate but if Neumann, a land use attorney, proposed it, some of the civic members would reflexively balk, even with my endorsement. I convened an ad hoc group to flesh out the proposal. It consisted of Neumann, Paul McGuckian (the committee's special counsel), William Green, and me. Although not a committee member, Green was an accomplished attorney who often represented civic associations and homeowners. As president of the Potomac Valley League, he had high credibility among the civic community and the respect of developers and the land use bar. The three lawyers agreed that although novel, the approach was in line with the general tendency of the Maryland Court of Appeals to allow innovation in dealing with complex land use issues. If it were successfully challenged, the county could fall back on the more cumbersome but clearly legal approach of applying conventional Euclidean zones by a sectional map amendment and hoping owners would apply for a recommended floating zone.

We refined the concept to propose three zones, to be called CBD-1, CBD-2, and CBD-3. The numbers represented the floor area ratio (FAR),[5] or density, of their respective Euclidean bases. The base zones contained uniform standards for height, setbacks, frontage, and other dimensions, which if met, allowed development to proceed as a matter of right under the "Standard Method." Each zone also contained an Optional Method of Development, which allowed greater density and height, and more flexible standards.

CBD-3, the most intense zone, was designed for use at Metro stations or other locations where sector plans recommended the greatest heights, densities, and mix of uses. The CBD-1 zone was designed to be compatible, in height and density with adjacent residential neighborhoods. The zones could be applied only by sectional map amendment as recommended by a sector plan. Each zone would contain a purpose clause, describing where it could be applied.

The planning board could approve an optional method project in two stages. First, a developer must assemble at least 22,000 square feet and apply to use the optional method. The applicant would present a development plan showing a schematic layout of the project demonstrating how it furthered the goals, objectives, and design guidelines of the sector plan. After approval of the development plan, a detailed site plan would be submitted for final approval. Both the initial development plan and the final site plan would be subject to staff review and public hearing before the planning board, but it would not be necessary to seek rezoning through the hearing examiner process.

Applying the CBD zones would require substantial down zoning of most of the land in the four central business districts, which was in the general commercial (C-2) zone that permitted building to 14 FAR without site plan approval. CBD-3, the densest of the new zones, would allow only 3 FAR under the Standard Method and a maximum of 8 FAR under Optional Method. It allowed greater height—up to 200 feet—near transit stations, exchanging height for using 20 percent of the site for public spaces such as streetscape, plazas, parks, fountains, landscaping, and other amenities.

While there were certain to be objections from owners and developers, few existing buildings in the CBDs exceeded the proposed standard method densities. They could be "grandfathered" so that they would not become nonconforming uses. The standard method "base" was well above the bar for a regulatory taking but low enough to encourage assembly and use of the optional method for development of high value land. Allowing the optional method to be approved without enduring the rezoning process was an additional incentive to build in a way that furthered objectives of the sector plan.

As we worked out the details, Neumann, McGuckian, Green, and I began discussions with members of the panel, explaining the concept and how it might work, testing its acceptability and making adjustments as we received comments from colleagues and constituencies. I met with council members, explaining the committee's approach and preparing them for its report.

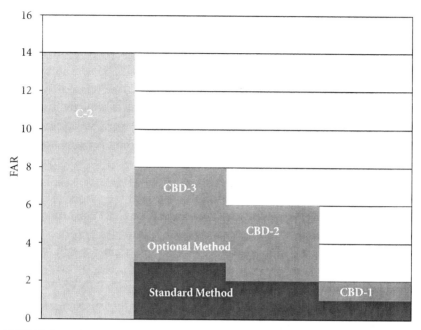

FIGURE 3.1 Comparison of CBD Zones with General Commercial Zone (C-2)

After several long work sessions, the committee accepted the CBD zones, but civic members insisted on a more conventional approach for the transit station areas that were not located in the four central business districts. A majority favored applying existing low-density Euclidean zones at these locations, with sector plans recommending a specific floating zone when they became ripe for development. Two zones were crafted: Transit Station-Residential (TS-R), for exclusive residential use; Transit Station-Mixed Use (TS-M), for mixed-use projects. To avoid the risk of these zones floating throughout the county, they were restricted to places recommended by sector plans. Both limited density to 2.5 FAR. Neither included a height limit, leaving it to negotiations involved in the zoning hearing process or site plan review.

Winning Council Approval of the CBD Zones

The committee submitted its report to the council in early 1972 with the unanimous endorsement of the planning board.[6] Council consideration became entwined with the intense debate over the future of Friendship Heights, where one of the first Metro stations in Montgomery County would be built and where the planning board, anticipating approval of the new zones, was preparing its first sector plan. Since sector plans and the CBD zones were untried, opponents and skeptics raised the specter of unintended consequences. They asserted the CBD zones would permit too much development; neighborhood protection was inadequate; and the optional method gave the unelected planning board power the council should exercise through rezoning.

Faced with incipient rebellion from their political base in the miniature republics of suburban neighborhoods, council members hesitated. Prolonged inaction or worse, rejection of the new zones, would leave the planning board without tools to plan for Metro's arrival in Friendship Heights and other CBDs. There was a need for evidence to refute the speculation that growth at Metro stations, once permitted, could not be effectively managed.

Evidence to quash the speculation was scarce. The San Francisco Bay Area Rapid Transit system was still under construction, Toronto was the only North American city to install and operate a new rail rapid transit system following World War II. Its metropolitan government had also undertaken an aggressive program of managing development around its stations, which extended into suburban communities. Richard Tustian, the planning director, was a native of Toronto, had practiced architecture there, and retained professional contacts. He suggested taking the board and council on a fact-finding trip to observe development around its transit stations and to meet with Toronto's political leaders, community representatives, and planning officials. Council members readily agreed, and all council and planning board members joined the tour.

The Toronto trip convinced council members that it was possible to use the CBD zones to "tent" development with greatest density and height at transit stations, then gradually reduce them as surrounding residential neighborhoods were approached. Upon returning to Montgomery County, the council adopted the three CBD zones and added two additional ones: a CBD-0.5 zone with an optional method density of 1.0 FAR for use adjacent to residential neighborhoods where some thought the CBD-1 might be too dense or high; and a CBD-R zone restricted to residential use. Some council members were worried that the market for office uses would be so strong that residential uses near transit might be squeezed out, reducing opportunities to increase pedestrian access to transit and provide a mixture of uses in the vicinity. The council also adopted the two Transit Station floating zones.

Redesigning the Planning Process

As important as the new approach to planning and zoning was, it would be for naught if the planning board lacked the resources to prepare the sector plans and administer the optional method. For many years two-thirds of the agency's budget and staff were devoted to review of development projects. Since the county had been growing at a rate of 7 percent a year, staff could not be diverted to plan preparation and the board needed permanent in-house expertise and an institutional memory of how and why planning decisions were made. The council agreed to expand the staff from about 60 to 100 members, reversing the ratio of resources devoted to planning and regulation. Tustian set about recruiting a strong staff. He established three community planning groups focused on eastern, western, and northern sections of the county, and four new specialized divisions for transportation, environment, research, and urban design.

The board agreed to establish citizen advisory committees, chaired by a board member, to review and comment on staff analyses and working drafts and offer ideas and insight from the perspectives of residents and property owners or builders in and around the planning area. The board also agreed to a set of management principles that distinguished the role of professional staff work from deliberations of the board. Commissioners agreed to leave staff free from board direction or intervention in conducting analyses and to support an environment in which staff was expected to offer its best professional advice to advisory committees and the board. The board would then exercise its judgment on any modifications of staff recommendations and take responsibility for the product it ultimately presented to the council. Staff reports and positions would be available to the public and all work sessions of committees and the board were opened to the public.

With the basic regulatory tools in hand, staff and technical resources being acquired, and better processes of public engagement put in place, the board could plan for the arrival of Metro, and more important, it would have the ability to implement its plans. The first tests of the new system and for the ability of the Progressive Regime to govern land use would be Friendship Heights. It would not go smoothly.

The Battle of Friendship Heights

Until 1950 Friendship Heights and the Hills, a thirty-two-acre special tax district, was a pleasant treed community of rambling Victorian homes on the Wisconsin Avenue streetcar line just across Western Avenue from the District of Columbia. In that year Woodward & Lothrop ("Woodies"), Washington's largest department store, built its first suburban store at the corner of Western and Wisconsin Avenues. Thelma "Tim" Edwards, a local resident and a realtor, recognized an opportunity for more commercial and apartment development and gradually assembled most of the land in the village into larger parcels.

The Hottest Piece of Real Estate in the United States

In 1964 the planning board recommended commercial use for all the land in Friendship Heights and parcels in Chevy Chase Village with frontage on Wisconsin Avenue.[7] The CAP Council obligingly rezoned the land. By 1971 Friendship Heights was being described as the "hottest piece of real estate in the country." Two high-rise apartments and an office building were constructed on land Edwards assembled. Neiman Marcus and Lord & Taylor opened stores just across Western Avenue in the District of Columbia. Saks Fifth Avenue opened its branch on Wisconsin Avenue, north of the Chevy Chase Center. Property owners pooled resources to employ architect Vlastimil Koubek to produce a plan for the overall development of Friendship Heights. The "Koubek Plan," unveiled in early 1971, proposed 16 million additional square feet in a high-density center that filled the C-2 zoning envelope in Friendship Heights and Chevy Chase, including redevelopment of the shopping center across Wisconsin Avenue from Woodies. The Donahoe Company acquired a tract on Willard Avenue where it proposed building a large structure. The largest project was the Taubman Company's proposal to redevelopment Woodies' property as a 900,000 square foot shopping mall; quadruple the size of the existing store.

The Bergdoll Tract

Adding heat and interest to the challenge before the planning board, on the north border of Friendship Heights the Bergdoll Tract was the site of an epic zoning battle between its would-be developer and the Town of Somerset. The case would rival *Jarndyce v. Jarndyce* for longevity and was wryly described in 1968 by Chief Judge Harold Hammond of the Maryland Court of Appeals:

> Within the [Somerset] Town limits and abutting on its southern and eastern boundaries lay the Bergdoll property, an undeveloped wooded tract of some 30 acres, traversed by a stream. This was not the sylvan idyll which it seemed, however. . . . Some 20 years ago, there had been an abortive effort to have it rezoned for apartments, and 10 years ago the Hecht Company had sought commercial zoning, but had been persuaded to withdraw its application.
>
> This was the situation in April of 1961 when Community Builders purchased the Bergdoll property for $1,100,000. On 31 May 1961, the purchasers filed an application for R-10 zoning and this set off a barrage of legal artillery which has to this day illumined the horizons of the Montgomery County Council, the Circuit Court for Montgomery County and this Court.[8]

Somerset's fierce opposition to the high-rise apartment (R-10) zoning resulted in its withdrawal. A few weeks after election of the CAP Council the owner filed an application for the high-rise residential floating (R-H) zone with the same density (43.5 units per acre) on twenty-five acres, The Somerset Council opposed the application and voted to condemn fifteen acres for a park. The Maryland-National Capital Park and Planning Commission (M-NCPPC) consented to the park acquisition, but Newton Brewer, the vice-chairman of the commission, suggested that the builder and the town enter negotiations to find an acceptable resolution.

An agreement was reached. The town agreed to support the floating zone, which required site plan review. The schematic design showed three buildings about 140 feet high, and the developer agreed to sell the town a two-acre parcel and over the course of several years convey an additional ten acres to shield the town's single-family homes from sight of the apartments. The developer further agreed to limit density on the site to the number of units that could be constructed on only sixteen acres.

Once the land was rezoned, Somerset prepared to issue bonds to purchase the two acres for a park, but the sale was frustrated by a citizen's lawsuit. The agreement was modified to donate the two acres in return for allowing the density of the project to be calculated on the basis of 18.2 instead of 16 acres, increasing the number of units by roughly 100 to a total of 793.

The controversy reignited when the developer altered the design of the project from three twelve-to-fourteen-story buildings to two thirty-story towers. Although surprised by this change, the mayor and council of Somerset felt obligated to accept it, since the towers had to be set back a distance equal to their height. Some townspeople, however, were outraged. They felt betrayed and insisted that the town fight the project anew.

Somerset retained counsel and petitioned the county council to impose a height limit of 143 feet in the R-H zone. After failing in that effort, the town enacted its own ordinance, of dubious legality, to limit the height of any structure within the town to 160 feet. Although it subsequently repealed the ordinance, the developer, in retaliation, sought to retract deeds for the parkland and applied to the county to start construction. When the county granted permits for buildings 210 feet high the town appealed their issuance. Suits and countersuits followed,[9] with multiple trips up and down the judicial ladder, culminating in Judge Hammond's 1968 opinion, which ordered the developer to file a rezoning application to return the entire tract to its original residential zoning, nullifying the deed of easement for the park, voiding further conveyances, and ordering the town to return any of the Bergdoll tract it had received. The court seemed to have had quite enough of the matter. That was not to be. As work began on the sector plan for Friendship Heights the owners of the Bergdoll tract saw a new opportunity to revive their project, using a new floating zone that had been crafted for a Silver Spring tract. They revived negotiations with Somerset and Chevy Chase to gain their support for a new and improved version.

Inventing Sector Planning

It would be an understatement to say the development proposals for Friendship Heights and the Bergdoll tract produced a state of heightened anxiety among miniature republics of Chevy Chase, Somerset, Brookdale, condominium owners in Friendship Heights itself, and other neighborhoods within range of their civic uproar. They formed the Citizens Coordinating Committee for Friendship Heights to fight its "Manhattanization."

Producing a new plan for Friendship Heights was complicated by the fact that work began before the Committee on the Planning, Zoning and Development of Central Business Districts and Transit Station Areas completed its work, so it was unclear what kind zoning would be available to implement a plan's land use recommendations. What was clear was that the various stakeholders would do their utmost to influence the character of those zones.

Thus, the planning board plunged into an important, high profile planning and development conflict uncertain about the tools that would be available to deal with its most important recommendations. In addition, staffing for the plan was in flux as Tustian was reorganizing the planning department and recruiting new staff, which meant that staff resources would shift as the plan progressed. The board was making it up as it went. The advisory committee honored the rule that everyone should get into the act, but citizens of the miniature republic and developers of the commercial republic exhibited very different interests in getting some action. The committee was more adversarial than advisory. Landowners and developers wanted ratification of the Koubek Plan. They viewed the community members of the committee as reflexive NIMBYs opposed to all growth. The community members distrusted the developers, seeing them as greedy despoilers of their quiet communities. Both groups opposed virtually all proposals made by the planning staff or board, albeit for opposite reasons.

The initial staff analysis of conditions in Friendship Heights indicated that even with heroic assumptions of Metro ridership and feasible roadway additions, the area could support only 1.6 million square feet of additional development. Developers denounced this finding as flawed and economically ruinous. Their transportation consultants used different assumptions and argued there was more room for growth. The Coordinating Committee declared an additional 1.6 million square feet was more than their neighborhoods could bear and demanded further reductions in density to prevent Friendship Heights from becoming another Crystal City (or Manhattan, depending on the simile of the day). They objected to a new road to allow some traffic to bypass the intersection at Wisconsin and Western. Their transportation expert found less capacity than the staff did.

After reviewing the opposing claims and arguments, the planning board accepted the staff analysis as the basis for the plan, the clear implication of which was that Friendship Heights would have to be down zoned, reducing by 90 percent the scale of development proposed by the Koubek plan. The board had limited experience with down zoning. Its new associate general counsel, Gus Bauman, advised that given the stakes involved for both developers and citizens, litigation was almost certain, regardless of the action taken. He prepared a memorandum for the board that emphasized the importance of basing decisions on careful study of the area and connecting decisions to the findings of the study. He also warned that while down zoning could reduce the value and potential use of land, the reduction could not deprive an owner of all reasonable uses.

The board agreed to base the development envelope in Friendship Heights on the transportation "capacity" analysis. By taking that position, it countered objections by developers that it was unreasonably restrictive by pointing out that there was no basis for a more generous allocation of density. The board also responded to the Coordinating Committee that reducing density below the transportation capacity threshold would be arbitrary and vulnerable to suits by developers. Both sides found this logic unpersuasive.

The decision to down zone set off a race, albeit at the stately pace commensurate with decision making in Montgomery County. Developers striving to entitle their projects and vest their rights to build under existing zoning were pitted against planners trying to craft the county's first sector plan, create a new form of zoning, and persuade the council to approve the plan and zoning changes before the facts on the ground mooted the effort. Coordinating Committee members continued to regard the scale of development proposed by the planning staff as far too dense and denounced it as a sell-out to developers.

Going with the (Sewage) Flow

In many respects, the key to success for either side, and for the future of Friendship Heights, was the fate of the mall project on the Woodies site. By early 1972, over a million dollars had been spent designing the project and preparing applications for permits. All that remained for the project to move forward was approval of the preliminary subdivision plan to consolidate two existing lots and dedicate rights of way for abutting streets, followed by approval of the record plat, normally a ministerial action. It could then apply for building permits and start construction. Once construction was underway, the right to complete the project under existing zoning would be vested.[10]

Woodies filed its subdivision application for the "Town Center" in December 1971 when work on the sector plan was still at an early stage. Approval required a planning board finding that it could receive adequate sewerage service. Because the area was under a building moratorium brought about by both limited trunk line capacity and overloading of treatment capacity at the regional sewage treatment plant, the board requested a special finding by the Washington Suburban Sanitary Commission (WSSC) that sewer service could be provided.

In its review of the preliminary plan, the WSSC noted that the project was suitable for service, but did not commit to installation. Pressed at the subdivision hearing for greater clarity, the commission staff refused to say that service would or could be denied. The planning board was frustrated by the WSSC's response, but absent a clear statement that service would not be available, there was no legally defensible basis for rejecting the subdivision. The board reluctantly approved it, recognizing that the project would use half of the total transportation capacity available for the whole area and require an even more severe down zoning of other properties. The Coordinating Committee vociferously denounced the board's action.

Before the record plat returned to the planning board for final approval at the end of March 1972 the sanitary commission imposed a moratorium on new sewer connections in the Little Falls basin, which included Friendship Heights. The moratorium specifically prohibited replacement projects that would generate greater sewage flows than those produced by existing facilities. In its initial review of the record plat, the planning board concurred with the staff's conclusion that the size of the project would likely violate the moratorium's restriction on flows. I wrote the WSSC chairman, saying that before the board would approve the record plat it would require further assurances that the project could receive service.

Woodies urged the WSSC to give that assurance and submitted information to the commission purporting to show that by use of water saving devices and delaying installation of high volume water users, such as restaurants, the new mall's sewage flows would be lower than those from the existing store. Based on Woodies' submission, WSSC replied to me on May 3 that "no additional sewage flows will be generated by the proposed buildings."[11]

After the board expressed doubt that this could be so, three weeks later the Sanitary Commission wrote again to say that although it had seen no construction plans for the mall, the information submitted indicated that, based on standard methods of determining flows from plumbing fixtures, there would be no greater flows. It promised to monitor the project at final construction plans to ensure that the flows would not be increased. Once again, the board felt bound by the WSSC's response and approved the record plat.

Woodies moved quickly to record the plat and made the required street dedications in June. It applied to the county for a building permit in September. It first, however, had to obtain a sewer hookup permit from WSSC, for which it applied on October 25. It expected to begin construction within ninety days of receiving the building permit.

Meanwhile, the planning board published the preliminary sector plan for the Friendship Heights CBD. Assuming construction of the mall would begin before the council could approve the plan and adopt a sectional map amendment, the board proposed placing the Woodies site in the pending CBD-2 zone. That zone permitted enough density for the mall to be built as proposed in the approved subdivision plan.

The Coordinating Committee representatives and I were now joined by council members in publicly criticizing the sanitary commission for acting on untested assurances from the developer. The WSSC staff took to its bunker, resenting the criticism as an effort to dissuade it from issuing the sewer permit. The commission was also under broader political assault for mismanagement of the sewerage system, which had resulted in moratoria on building in several basins, of which Little Falls was only the latest. Woodies continued to demand that the commission approve its hookup.

At the planning board's February 7, 1973 public hearing on the preliminary sector plan, a member of the Coordinating Committee suggested that if WSSC failed to act on the permit, and the council acted promptly to down zone the entire area, Woodies would not be able to vest its right to proceed under the C-2 zoning. Thus, he proposed that we instead recommend the CBD-1 zone.

A week later, the WSSC chairman and I convened a joint public meeting of our boards to discuss how to improve communication and cooperation. The discussion soon segued to concern about the scale of the Woodies project. At this point sanitary commission staff members revealed they had never read the meter at the existing store and, thus, had no direct knowledge of existing flows. This news was not well received.

Two days later, on February 15, WSSC staff met with Woodies' representatives and demanded additional sewage flow information before they could act on the hookup application. A series of submissions by Woodies ensued, each followed by requests from the commission staff for additional information. This continued until the end of June, when a new director of project planning for WSSC reviewed the information submitted by Woodies. He concluded that a new 16-inch water main would be necessary to serve the project. That would require an amendment to the ten-year Water and Sewerage Plan by the county council, a task that would take several months.

Desperate to save the project, its investment in planning and design, and its dedication of streets and pedestrian areas valued at $800,000, Woodies demanded a hearing before the WSSC. The commission did not schedule the hearing until August 29, but canceled it on August 22 because the Maryland Secretary of Health and Mental Hygiene issued a new sewer moratorium that prohibited provision of service to the site.

Woodies sued WSSC, alleging it was entitled to the permit, or at least a hearing and a decision. The case was not tried in circuit court until the following summer. By then, July 1974, the council had approved the sector plan with minor amendments and adopted the sectional map amendment, including CBD-1 zoning for the Woodies property. The circuit court decided in Woodies' favor, but was overruled by the Maryland Court of Appeals in 1977. Woodies also lost a companion case in which it alleged the planning board and sanitary commission conspired to deny them the sewer permit. The conspiracy allegation seemed a stretch since officials of the two agencies were barely on speaking terms. The Court of Appeals found that the public statements of members of the board and council were legitimate criticisms of the sanitary commission's performance.[12]

In all, Woodies and other frustrated developers filed thirteen lawsuits against the planning board and the county. Ten of them reached the Court of Appeals and were decided in the county's favor, upholding the validity of the CBD zones and their application in Friendship Heights. The U.S. Supreme Court declined to review the decision.[13]

A Plan with Nothing for Everyone

The planning board's five public hearings on the draft sector plan were dominated by a parade of witnesses organized by the Coordinating Committee, objecting to increases in density above existing levels of development, denouncing proposals for specific tracts, and demanding park buffers for adjacent residential communities. The group convinced itself that the proposed CBD zones, which allowed an increase in density over *existing conditions*, was an egregious up zoning, rather than the drastic reduction of the amount of development possible under *existing zoning*. At the last hearing, held at the local high school auditorium to accommodate the crowd mobilized by the Coordinating Committee, a flood of witnesses repetitively demanded more hearings in an effort to the delay action on the plan and bring council pressure on the board to reduce densities further. Finding little substantive content in the testimony, I announced that the board would sit as long as necessary to hear everyone. The last witness was called shortly before 3:00 a.m. the following morning, and I closed the hearing record.

At work sessions after the hearings, Coordinating Committee participants continued their objections to the densities recommended by the plan. Its volunteer planning consultant produced a sincere but hastily drawn alternative plan with such unremitting low density that Lester Bagg, the planning department's new chief of urban design, characterized it as the "plant it in petunias" plan. The committee requested that the parcel recently purchased by Donahoe be designated as a community center and purchased by the park system, although a larger tract a few hundred yards away from the site had already been acquired. It challenged hearing and work session procedure, arguing they should be allowed to cross-examine developers and planning staff, and that the CBD zones were illegal because they allowed the planning board to administer the optional method rather than require applications for floating zones that would be subject to the hearing examiner process. Developers, on the other hand, protested the down zoning of their properties was an unconstitutional taking. One developer retained as counsel a close friend of mine to try to persuade me and the board to increase his density. I explained if we increased density on his property it would have to be reduced elsewhere.

The planning board completed posthearing work sessions on the sector plan in June. Because of the limited transportation capacity, the board's final plan recommended no CBD-3 zoning in Friendship Heights. CBD-2 zoning was recommended for only a small area owned by the Chevy Chase Land Company at the Metro portal. Most of Friendship Heights, including the Woodies tract, was proposed for the CBD-1 zone. If the council approved the plan and sectional map amendment before construction got under way, Woodies' project could not be built as proposed.

The GEICO building retained its Commercial Office (CO) zone and the remainder of the twenty-six-acre tract was left in the residential (R-60) zone, as it was used primarily for parking under a special exception. The same approach was used for the parking lot bordering the Village of Chevy Chase. Eighteen acres of the Bergdoll tract were confirmed for the high-rise residential (R-H) zone. The board recommended that the Donahoe tract be acquired by the Village for its community center, or if retained by a private owner it should be developed under the CBD-1 zone at one-seventh of the scale originally proposed by the developer.

Friendship Heights had a plan. No one liked it.

Politics of Plan Approval

At the council's three hearings in early February 1974, Coordinating Committee leaders, landowners, and developers agreed on only one thing: the council should not approve the plan as submitted. Although the planning board's revisions to the preliminary sector plan met many of its objections, the Coordinating Committee reprised its claim that the plan would Manhattanize Friendship Heights, notwithstanding the 90 percent reduction in zoning density. The height limits were denounced as overwhelming adjacent neighborhoods and destroying them with traffic. Coordinating Committee Chairman Norman Knopf, speaking for its fifteen civic association members, captured the civic mood:

> The Citizens Coordinating Committee on Friendship Heights firmly believes that concept of a regional central business district, with its incredibly dense development and massive traffic generation, will result in further deterioration of the quality of life of the residential communities adjacent to Friendship Heights and may well result in the actual destruction of those residential communities. The decision to be made is thus clear; either the intensity of development in Friendship Heights is to be severely restricted or all of the adjacent residential areas are to be written off as desirable places to live. To view the situation as posing any other alternative is to deceive ourselves.[14]

The Coordinating Committee proposed small-lot single-family residences for the Bergdoll tract, with a possible option for town houses or for low-to-mid-rise garden apartments. Their preference, however was that the planning board condemn the entire thirty acres for a park.[15] On this matter, however, there was dissention in the civic ranks. The Bergdoll tract owners reached a new preliminary agreement with the Town of Somerset and the Village of Chevy Chase to rezone eighteen acres of its acreage in a CBD-Residential zone in return for limiting traffic access to Wisconsin Avenue and local streets. Instead, traffic would have access to the project from Friendship Boulevard, the planned new "bypass" street through Friendship Heights connecting Western and Wisconsin Avenues. The newly elected Friendship Heights Council, composed of Coordinating Committee members, unsuccessfully sued Bergdoll's developer and the planning board in an attempt to prevent it from recommending the road.[16]

During its work sessions the council agreed that the county, rather than the Friendship Heights Village Council should acquire the Donahoe site for a community recreation center, as proposed by the Coordinating Committee.[17] It made no other substantial changes, except to remove the Bergdoll tract from the CBD and split the zoning on the Chevy Chase Shopping Center, leaving CBD-2 on the triangle at Wisconsin and Western but reducing the old strip shopping center to CBD-1.

As the council prepared to vote, my discussions with individual council members indicated there were five votes for the plan. As the vote proceeded, Idamae

Garrott announced that she would vote against the plan because it was too dense. Elizabeth Scull also voted "no." At this point, William Sher and Norman Christeller, appointed to the council after William Willcox resigned, switched their votes to "no," denying council approval. I was obviously distressed, but Christeller left the council table to tell me to remain calm. He and Sher were convinced that Garrott, in particular, was pandering to the Coordinating Committee, counting on her colleagues to ensure approval. They were correct. Both Garrott and the Coordinating Committee were visibly flummoxed that the plan had been rejected.

Christeller then told Garrott that he and Sher would move reconsideration only if they could be assured the plan would be approved unanimously and if the Coordinating Committee would become supportive. The alternative was no plan and retention of the existing zoning that allowed developers to proceed under the Koubek plan without any site plan regulation. The following week, Christeller moved reconsideration and the council approved the plan without dissent. It then proceeded to enact the sectional map amendment to implement it. The Coordinating Committee filed an amicus brief in support of the plan and the zoning in the appeal of the *Woodward & Lothrop* case.

Redevelopment slowed following adoption of the sector plan and rezoning. Two major projects were built in the 1980s. The Metro Center building in the triangle of land at Wisconsin Circle was approved in 1981. Construction began on the 18 acres of the Bergdoll tract in the mid-1980s for Somerset House, an 1100-unit condominium complex. In March 1988 voters in Somerset voted 486–110 to de-annex the eighteen acres under development, leaving only the twelve acres of parkland in the town limits. Even though the apartments would have generated more than $500,000 in annual property tax revenues, town residents feared their new neighbors could outvote them and destroy the town's identity. "We like the green space and the small town felling," a town council member told the *Washington Post*.[18] In an interesting turn of events, the Village of Friendship Heights, all residents of which lived in high-rise apartments, expressed interest in annexing the new complex.

In the 1998 update of the sector plan, Transit Station zones were recommended for the Chevy Chase and GEICO parking lots adjacent to single family neighborhoods that had retained R-60 zoning in the 1974 Sector Plan. A project was approved and built replacing the Chevy Chase Shopping Center. The Woodies site was rezoned CBD-2, and was finally redeveloped in 2006 as a mixed-use project anchored by Bloomingdale's department store. A development plan for the GEICO tract was approved, but no redevelopment had occurred by 2016.

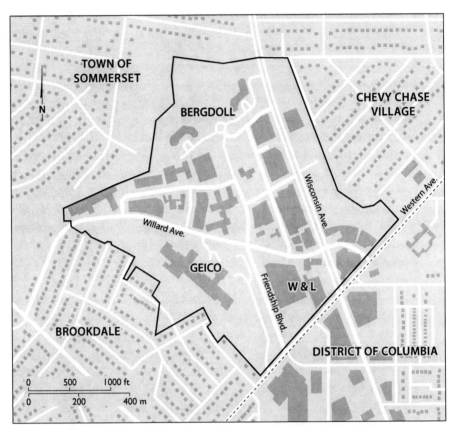

FIGURE 3.2 Friendship Heights sector plan area and buildings at Wisconsin Place and Wisconsin Circle. Courtesy Montgomery County Planning Department M-NCPPC. Photos by author

Planning Politics in the Progressive Regime

A key lesson to be drawn from the creation of the CBD zones and the Friendship Heights Sector Plan is that they required application of the reasoning methods of both planners and politicians. The logic of consequentiality was critical in crafting an approach to planning and zoning that could withstand internal challenges to its consistency and external assault on its legality. Artful application of the logic of appropriateness made the rationale of the CBD zones politically acceptable to opposing interests of the miniature and commercial republics on the advisory committee by engineering its sponsorship by respected supporters from each camp. Securing approval of the zones required not only persuading council members of their internal logic, but also convincing them by the trip to Toronto that they were appropriate for Montgomery County.

The planners' logic of consequentiality hardly resolved all matters, as debates over the Woodies, Donahoe, Barlow, Bergdoll, and other sites demonstrated. The planning board, and finally the council, acted in accordance with the logic of appropriateness as it bargained with stakeholders to resolve these issues within the constraints of the sector plan. The board doubted the sanitary commission's finding on sewerage service for Woodies but approved its subdivision and record plat because it concluded it was inappropriate to substitute its judgment for that of the responsible agency (and there was no legally defensible basis for doing so). It changed its decision on the zoning for Woodies when the situation changed. Finally, to secure unanimous approval of the plan, Christeller used raw power to force Garrott and Scull to abandon their symbolic opposition, thus strengthening its political legitimacy and preventing—at least for the time being—a breach in the progressive regime.

The battle of Friendship Heights was a microcosm of the long struggle for ascendency in the governance of land use between forces of the commercial and miniature republics. It epitomized the tension between the visions and values of a sylvan suburbia and those of relentless growth. The Progressive Regime that came to power in 1970 as stewards of the miniature republic promised rational planning, balanced transportation and growth, and to protect, preserve, and defend neighborhoods. It was not as easy as it sounded. Progressive council members won election without alliances with commercial interests. Elected, they assumed fiduciary responsibilities for providing the facilities, services, and amenities demanded by their constituents. Growth from development and appreciation of property values was the principal source of revenue to support those public goods. Rational planning left the commercial republic less than it wanted but more than the miniature republic preferred. But by devising land use policies that sustained reasonable growth for the commercial republic in a way that satisfied its political base in the miniature republic the Progressive Regime consolidated its electoral victory. Through trial and error, serendipity, force of circumstances, luck, and occasional guile, the progressives held together and in the process changed the character of planning politics.

The creation of sector planning, the hybrid CBD zones, and the use of transportation capacity to limit the zoning envelope in Friendship Heights were consistent with the miniature republic's progressive ideology of rational decision-making. The ideal of experts as disinterested problem solvers was reinforced by the new planning board's policy of protecting the independence of staff analysis as the foundation of board deliberations. The use of advisory committees established new rules of civic engagement that broadened participation in planning politics and ensured that all significant stakeholders were heard—at length. Advisory committees became a civic rite without which presumptions of legitimacy for land use decisions would be weakened.

These changes, begun in Friendship Heights, became standard practice and were employed for almost every master plan during the following forty years. Staff analyses framed issues master plans had to resolve. Debate in advisory committees, board, and council hearings and work sessions tended to focus on the reliability and interpretation of the information the staff presented. With enhancement of their analytical capacity, all parties had to use the planners' numbers, forcing deliberation onto their turf. As their analyses withstood challenges to accuracy and reasonableness the issues narrowed to the equitable distribution of available capacity among properties and how best to address boundary, design, and amenity issues. Henceforth, decisions on virtually every contested plan and project turned on the capacity of facilities to accommodate the amount or kind of development contemplated and the standard by which capacity was to be determined. These changes shifted the initiative from developers and the land use bar to the planning board and its professional staff. The timing of critical decisions moved from rezoning or subdivision of particular sites to comprehensive planning for a whole area. The Koubek Plan was the last major effort to continue the old practice. The Friendship Heights Sector Plan was the vanguard of the new order.

Approval of the Friendship Heights plan was a critical first step in the incremental urbanization of strategically important centers served by Metro. Blending the methods of planning and politics, it illustrated the virtues of bounded rationality.[19] The development allowed in Friendship Heights may not have been optimal from the perspective of either the Coordinating Committee or the landowners but it established the new approach to planning and zoning advanced by the advisory committee on CBDs and transit stations. It established, and the Maryland Court of Appeals confirmed, the ability of the county to zone land based on careful analysis of the carrying capacity of its transportation and sanitary systems.

Most important, it worked on the ground. The fears of the residents in adjoining communities that the CBD would expand did not materialize. Proximity to the region's highest-end retail center at the border of the District of Columbia resulted in exponential increases in residential property values. Chevy Chase, Somerset, and Brookdale remained stable communities with convenient pedestrian access to Metro. Both took measures to restrict overflow parking and through traffic. And they remained ever vigilant against further development.

From an institutional perspective, the plan built the confidence of the planning staff, the board, and council that it could use its new tools effectively to make and implement plans, which, if not always immediately popular, could ultimately be accepted. For Tustian and the planning staff, approval of the sector plan was vindication of over two years of analysis, meetings, public clamor, and abuse as they improvised as they worked.

The Friendship Heights Sector Plan was a turning point in the history of the planning board, transforming it from enabler of the development industry to manager of growth. A progressive governing regime was established in the land use policy arena: an alliance of reform Democratic politicians on the council and a planning board with enough political autonomy to protect professional staff integrity and balance competing interests. Civic support for the regime would continue, but always with loud reservations about the amount or rate of growth allowed in any given place, and fierce defense of residential communities.

Remodeling Bethesda

Friendship Heights was the strategic breakthrough for the new approach to planning and zoning. It created both a method and political confidence it could be applied in other central business districts. Consequently, the next set of decisions for the Bethesda CBD generated less controversy even though the economic stakes for the county were greater because, with ten times the land area of Friendship Heights there was much greater potential for growth. Bethesda's principal contribution to the evolution of planning politics was demonstrating that better urban design and attention to the public realm could add coherence and value to urban development. It also reinforced the importance of attending to the present interests of existing communities to gain room to provide for the future interest of different kinds of communities.

In 1975 Bethesda was a well-established but not densely developed wedge of commerce between the settled neighborhoods of Edgemoor, East Bethesda, the

Town of Chevy Chase, and the National Institutes of Health campus. Lot-by-lot conversion from residential to commercial uses had occurred over fifty years. Speculation was less fevered than in Friendship Heights and most land was not assembled for development. The merchant-owners of small commercial parcels were not developers and did not expect to sell to one. Thus, fewer investment-based expectations were unsettled by the planning staff's finding that Bethesda's roads and transit could handle only 12 million square feet of new development at an acceptable level of service, instead of the 63 million theoretically possible under existing zoning. That seemed enough room for growth to satisfy the Bethesda market for many years. Of course, those with significant holdings made clear their interest in having CBD-3 zoning on their land.

Bethesda presented three major issues. The most difficult political problem was calming the concerns of the bordering neighborhoods that looming towers would overshadow their homes and gardens, compromise their privacy, and growing traffic would turn their streets into alternative routes for commuters, workers, and shoppers. The most challenging technical planning problem was providing adequate access to Metro without inducing excessive congestion at the constricted intersection of three state highways at the Metro station. The key land use and design problem was figuring out how to generate high-density development at the Metro site and, thus, foster the coherent transformation of the entire business district.

Boundaries and Barriers

The planning board's experience in Friendship Heights taught that opposition from neighborhoods surrounding a business district could delay completion of a plan and endanger its approval by a council responsive to citizens of miniature republics. The residents of Bethesda's communities were as vigilant and skilled as those in Friendship Heights in opposing further density and tall buildings. They expected the plan to reconfirm single-family residential zoning for their neighborhoods and demanded physical barriers to commercial encroachment.

The planning board responded in two ways. For the few edge areas where residential integrity was irreparably compromised by previous changes in use, a new Commercial Transition Zone was proposed to encourage conversion of existing residential structures to low intensity commercial and office uses.[20] The more important response was to provide parks to buffer neighborhoods from business district expansion. On the CBD's western border with Edgemoor, a park joined an elementary school and a public library to establish a solid barrier of public facilities. Creating a park on the southeast side in the town of Chevy Chase presented one of the most difficult problems for the plan. It required acquisition and demolition of an entire block of rental houses.

Without assurance of the park, opposition to the sector plan by the town and its residents was certain. The rear of a ten-story building confronted the neighborhood and speculators had shown interest in expansion. A park was shown as a "floating symbol" on the 1968 Bethesda-Chevy Chase Master Plan, but its location was not fixed. In 1972, Nicholas Read, a local community leader, showed slides of the deteriorating homes behind the building and persuaded the county council to approve funds to design the park, running north-south along the CBD boundary, perpendicular to the railroad along the northern boundary of the Town of Chevy Chase. The school board intervened to propose reorienting the park east-west to connect it to Leland Jr. High School, a change that would have divided the neighborhood. After the community defeated that effort, the county executive in 1974 impounded funds for half of the park, leaving the half-block nearest the business district available for development. After the council overrode the executive and restored the park to its full size, the Maryland Board of Public Works cut off all state funding for local park acquisition and development.

By the time the Bethesda CBD Sector Plan was nearing completion, the park had become an important symbol of whether the community could trust the planning board and the county, and consequently, whether it would oppose or support the sector plan. The planning board used park bonds for acquisition and development and accelerated acquisition and demolition of houses. This secured community acceptance of the sector plan.

Following council approval of the plan, construction of the park continued to encounter obstacles. The last tenant refused to move. To avoid his eviction during the Christmas season, the parks department moved the family to a house it recently acquired for another park that was not scheduled for development. Then, just as design work was beginning, the county executive proposed converting the now vacant block into a parking lot. Without waiting for final design, the board ordered the parks department to plant grass and install benches and picnic tables to establish its use as a park to prevent further takeover efforts.

Elm Street Park was finally completed and dedicated in 1981. It became one of the most used neighborhood parks in the county, attracting both community residents, office workers from the CBD, and resting cyclists on Capital Crescent Trail built in the 1990s on the abandoned railroad right-of-way. Its completion became an important symbol of the planning board's good faith in dealing with communities and was critical to building public confidence in the planning process.

Getting to Metro and the Beauty Contest

The Metro access problem was addressed by converting several streets encircling the Metro station and parking garages to one-way traffic. The planning board proposed an additional one-way north-south couplet on the east side of Wisconsin Avenue, but the council did not accept it for its full length and the rights-of-way of other streets were not widened after objections were raised by residents from the East Bethesda neighborhood. Once again, pacification of the progressive regime's civic constituency was critical to securing council support for the plan. The other one-way streets affected no residential neighborhoods. The logic of appropriateness prevailed.

Metro's plan for the Bethesda station and its bus facilities occupied a large chunk of the CBD core fronting Wisconsin Avenue at its intersection with Old Georgetown Road and East-West Highway. Combined with a county parking garage behind the below-grade station, there was a strong possibility that the core of the business district would become a vast dead zone instead of a vibrant focal point of the new Bethesda envisioned by the sector plan. If this area did not develop as the plan envisioned, Bethesda was likely to remain a sprawling, inchoate place—only denser everywhere but at the center.

The sewer moratorium was still in effect in 1976 and transportation capacity was limited until Metro opened. Thus, the plan restricted the first 1.5 million square feet of development in Bethesda to the Metro site and adjacent parcels. A second stage for an additional million square feet could commence in two years, assuming sewer capacity became generally available and there was adequate traffic capacity.

This did not work out as planned. Metro's opening was delayed. Only one of the projects approved by late 1981 was at Metro center. Others were on the periphery of the area, leaving too little of the density allocated in stage 1 available for effective development of the core. The planning board and Metro staffs warned that without a change in the staging element, the center of Bethesda would be a large hole in the ground. There would be no plaza or signature buildings. The one building approved for the core included both privately held land and air rights over property acquired for the station. Both the board's urban design staff and the developer recognized that the project would set a standard for the way in which optional method applications under the new CBD zones would be viewed, and for the quality of design that would be expected for projects in Bethesda and other CBDs. Although the project included an iconic building and an attractive fountain at the Metro portal it provided only a portion of the plaza called for in the sector plan, leaving much of the station area an uncovered bus-to-subway transfer area. If the buildings for the entire core could not proceed as the station facilities were being constructed, Metro operations would be severely disrupted by future construction that might continue for years, making building far more costly. Metro was beginning station construction and had to know if it would have private partners. There was just enough time for joint development to occur before the station was to be in operation in 1983 or 1984.

Using new peak hour traffic counts, planning staff estimated there was capacity for another 2,100 trips, especially if development was coordinated with the opening of Metro. Tustian and John Westbrook, the chief of the Urban Design division, recommended an amendment to the staging element of the sector plan to allocate that capacity to the core, subject to a "beauty contest." Projects would compete for approval based on the quality of their design and provision of public benefits and amenities rather than in the order they were filed. To expedite a decision, the board and council held a joint public hearing on the amendment. Representatives from the surrounding neighborhoods, joined by the Montgomery County Federation of Civic Associations, strongly opposed it. The council, however, approved the amendment.[21]

Ten projects were submitted by the deadline set by the board. The planning staff ranked them on building design; provision of benefits and amenities, such as streetscape and public art; plans for management of trips and facilities; and capacity for timely performance. Sufficient transportation capacity existed for eight projects, including several that would complete Metro Center. A significant result of the contest was creation of an inviting public realm with common streetscape standards that were extended throughout the CBD as development proceeded.[22] The quality of design also quieted the fears of civic groups. During two days of hearings before the board to approve winners of the "beauty contest," none of the civic associations that initially opposed it commented.[23] The Bethesda Coalition, an umbrella group representing area civic associations, supported project plans for buildings at Metro Center when they came to the board for review.[24]

The beauty contest established a standard for building design and public realm. Even more important, by coordinating several projects it created a sense of place and identity for Bethesda. This not only added value to the buildings of Metro Center but to development in the rest of Bethesda. High standards of design and amenity, metro access for businesses and residents, and pedestrian activity helped generate business, higher rents, and more revenue.

Bethesda is widely recognized as a successful transit-oriented center. Metro Center, while aesthetically striking, did not become the gathering place that was anticipated. Its heroic scale left it pretty but rather barren when the low-rise retail pavilion at the plaza's center did not enjoy success and, therefore, did not help

FIGURE 3.3 Bethesda Metro Center and Bethesda Row. Photos by author

activate the plaza. An effort in 2008 to replace it with a fourth tower failed due to design flaws and issues of plan and ordinance interpretation. It also faced intense opposition from the owners of other buildings on and near the plaza, producing the rare and delicious spectacle of senior partners of three of the county's major land use law firms fighting a project championed by a fourth, claiming, among other objections, it would impair their respective clients' views from penthouse offices.[25]

The most successful development did not occur at Metro Center. Bethesda Row, a 600,000 square foot new urbanism district on some thirteen acres at the southern edge of the core, is widely cited for its design and functionality.[26] Its shops, restaurants, cinema, and apartments comprise a unified pedestrian district that comes to focus at the small plaza in front of a bookstore welcoming bikers entering Bethesda from the Capital Crescent Trail exiting the tunnel beneath Wisconsin Avenue.

When the sector plan was updated in 1994 it focused on boundary adjustments and urban design issues. Responding to concerns of Bethesda community groups, it gave particular attention to building heights to be permitted near single-family neighborhoods and included a diagram specifying heights in the plan rather than leave that determination to the planning board at site plan review.[27] As projects came before the planning board for approval in later years, differing interpretations of the diagram by developers, civic activists, and planners produced disputes that attained almost theological proportions. A new revision of the sector plan, begun in 2013, focused on improvement of the public realm inside the district.

Planning Politics of the Suburban Republics

The planning struggles of Friendship Heights and Bethesda belie the hope of James Madison (a county resident for three days in 1814 after the British burned the White House) that republics would be natural allies. He, of course, had no experience with the commercial and miniature republics of twentieth-century suburbs. The Bethesda central business district became the urban capital of Montgomery's commercial republic only after allaying the fears of the suburban miniature republics surrounding it. The planning board's planners and attorneys provided the economic and legal foundations for the transformation of suburban commercial districts into new urban centers by calibrating scale and allocating densities, crafting the policies and zones, and enforcing design standards. Their work withstood competing expert critique and legal assault and met the tests of market experience and fiscal benefits. The consequences justified the logic.

The great planning battles of the first waves of urbanization, however, were not fought over issues of density and design within the districts, but at the boundaries where the two republics met. Here the hard linear logic of consequentiality gave way to the more malleable logic of appropriateness. Parks and floating zones, height limits, ambiguous language, street closings and speed bumps provided barriers to expansion of the new centers and helped calm neighborhoods, making transformation of the CBD interior palatable. The politics of planning Friendship Heights and Bethesda for futures as mixed-use, transit-oriented activity centers involved side payments and compromises with present interests to sustain the Progressive Regime, and later, to build support for the individual entrepreneurs of the Pure Political Regime.

Bethesda's scale and, ultimately its economic and aesthetic success made it more important than Friendship Heights in establishing the credibility of the new CBD sector planning and zoning system. Together, they established the planning board as the forum of first impression for resolution of conflicts among developers and residents. The council became the forum of last resort, where the disgruntled and unsatisfied, in hope of palliation, reprised unrequited claims, fears, and implicit or overt threats of electoral retaliation. Judicial appeals became less frequent after the Friendship Heights cases settled most substantive and procedural issues favorably to the county and the planning board. Litigation, therefore, became more tactical than substantive, inducing delay and providing further opportunities to negotiate for additional advantage or to discourage or exhaust the opposing party.

The development of a strong professional staff allowed the board to frame issues and effectively forced all parties to use its information as the basis from which their cases were argued. Developers could be counted on to argue that density ceilings were too low, the estimates of traffic generation were too high, and too little credit was given to future improvements for mobility. They regularly produced transportation consultants to dispute the data and forecasts of the staff. Residents brought their own experts (both volunteer and paid) and abundant detailed anecdotal experience, including examples of county and state failure to deliver promised roads and schools. They could be expected to claim the densities and heights were too great and dispute the accuracy and integrity of the data used to support them. They could pack a hearing room with citizens warning of impending urban doom. Their arguments were often accompanied by assertions that insufficient notice was provided to respond to a proposal, that developers had special access, insufficient time was allowed to make a full presentation, or that decisions were being rushed (or delayed) to clinch a predetermined deal.

This Kabuki performance was usually bracketed with genuine deliberation that strengthened the legitimacy of the plan through reduction of disagreements about overall density and heights to a few contested parcels and policy issues. Board decisions about these matters became subjects of protracted discussion once the plan reached the council as one or more members sought to champion causes of the unhappy. Once agreement was reached by the council on the plan even the largest projects tended to excite relatively little controversy unless they involved some much loved building or space.

THE DEATH AND LIFE OF
SILVER SPRING

While Bethesda experienced robust urbanization, becoming one of the most successful uptown centers on the Metro system, the Silver Spring business district
first languished and then declined during the last three decades of the twentieth
century.

Silver Spring grew from a railroad suburb on the B&O's Metropolitan Branch
to become the first significant commercial area in Montgomery County. Industries such as the Giant Bakery and Canada Dry Bottling Company clustered near
the railroad. Business establishments were strung along Georgia Avenue by the
late 1920s as the Lee Regime revved its growth machine. When the first zoning
ordinance was adopted in 1928, the frontage on Georgia Avenue between the
District of Columbia boundary and Colesville Road was zoned for general commercial uses.

The growth of Silver Spring followed a trajectory common in Montgomery
County. Large tracts were subdivided for homes, followed by commercial development along highways and at major intersections. Small shops spread from
the main roads to back streets as residential lots were incrementally rezoned
from residential to commercial uses. Redevelopment was relatively rare. Landowners and developers led the first fifty years of Silver Spring's development.
A 1957 report by the Maryland-National Capital Park and Planning Commission
(M-NCPPC) succinctly captured its zoning and development history: "[Zoning]
additions were made by local map amendment, each of which would be judged
on its own merits but without regard to the overall development of a business
district."[1] Like other commercial centers in Montgomery County, Silver Spring
was not planned; it just happened.

The Hecht Company built the region's first suburban department store on
Colesville Road in 1947. Other major retailers followed, making Silver Spring
the second largest and most profitable commercial center in metropolitan Washington. Even after much of its retail business migrated to Wheaton Plaza and
Montgomery Mall, Silver Spring businesses remained prosperous throughout
the 1960s. Apartment complexes at Summit Hill west of 16th Street and on the
Blair estate on East-West Highway added customers for local shops. Expansion
of its parking lot district, financed by parking meters and a tax on businesses that

provided no on-site customer parking helped it compete with the strip centers proliferating across the county.

Even after major retailers on Colesville Road shut their doors and decamped for the regional malls, Silver Spring's economy remained resilient for a time. A number of Washington merchants displaced by the race riots of the late 1960s along Washington's Georgia Avenue corridor moved their businesses to Silver Spring, producing a spike in demand for commercial and office space. Apartment construction flourished in the 1960s, taking advantage of the residential loophole in the general commercial zone. A couple of office buildings were built at either end of the district, and a hideous hotel was erected on Georgia Avenue overshadowing the M-NCPPC's offices, an omnipresent reminder of the agency's impotence in inspiring better design. By the mid-1970s, Silver Spring still generated a high level of retail sales, but its peak had passed. Decline, imperceptible at first, had begun.

Falkland, Round 1

It was in the spirit of the time that in 1936 the heirs of Montgomery Blair developed a garden apartment complex of some 400 units on twenty-eight acres straddling East-West Highway at the western edge of the Silver Spring commercial area and the 16th Street portal to the District of Columbia. One of the first garden apartment projects built in the Washington suburbs; it was a prototype of affordable housing for working families. Taking its name from the Blair manse, Falkland was financed by the New Deal's Federal Housing Administration. Architect Louis Justement designed it with sensitivity for its natural setting. Eleanor Roosevelt attended its opening in 1938.

In 1966, the Blair estate leased Falkland to D.F. Antonelli, Jr. and Kingdon Gould, Jr., developers and co-owners of PMI, a DC parking firm. They retained attorney Robert Linowes to manage conversion of the much-loved community to a mixed-use high-rise project. Linowes commissioned architect Edwin Weihe to design the new Falkland. His design proposed twelve high-rise buildings containing 2 million square feet of office space, 1,500 apartments, a convention center, a 400-room motel, 100,000 square feet for local businesses, underground parking for 5,000 cars, restaurants, a cinema, sidewalk cafes, tennis courts, and indoor and outdoor swimming pools.

This plan was kept under wraps as decisions were being made on the location of the Silver Spring Metro station. Linowes quietly lobbied officials to relocate it from the Silver Spring B&O station to the rail crossing at Colesville Road, adjacent to Falkland. In April 1968 the planning board and council concurred.

Two months later, consultant Martin Rody, presented a proposed master plan for Silver Spring to the planning board. He recommended confining the business district to the traditional retail core area east of Georgia Avenue to encourage its redevelopment. When the board invited comment, Linowes dramatically unveiled the Falkland project, declaring it "By far, the most ambitious project ever undertaken in the entire District metropolitan area."[2] Using diagrams of the project, Linowes laid on a dazzling show, complete with testimony from the architect and other consultants. He asked the planning board to expand the boundary of the central business district to include Falkland, the first of his three-step strategy for approval. The second step was a zoning text amendment to create a floating Residential-Office Central Business District Zone designed to permit the project. The third step would apply that zone to the Falkland site.

The planning staff and Rody, caught by surprise, recommended against CBD expansion. Rody pointed out that the sort of redevelopment contemplated at Falkland would absorb the Silver Spring office market for many years and chill interest in redeveloping the traditional retail district. In effect, Linowes's proposal would shift activity from the center of the area to its edge, although it would be closer to Metro than the old retail core.

When the Falkland project formally came before the planning board in May and June 1969 the planning staff and Rody again recommended denial of the boundary extension and the new zone Linowes proposed. They argued the project was contrary to the master plan and would result in a second center that would frustrate revitalization of the traditional commercial area. The Silver Spring Chamber of Commerce embraced it. The chamber's small business owners saw the project as good for them. It removed any immediate threat of displacement by the redevelopment envisioned in Rody's plan and would provide a new source of higher income customers for local business and consumer services. Colonel Lee warmly endorsed the project, proclaiming it was just what Montgomery County needed to compete with Arlington's Crystal City and Rosslyn.

The board approved expansion of the CBD in a 2–1 vote; one commissioner for it and one against it were absent. Linowes promised to help current residents resettle. Two weeks later the council approved the expansion of the CBD by a vote of 5–1. Council Member Idamae Garrott raised questions about the project and the zone. The only opposing testimony came from the Montgomery County Civic Federation. In September, the council added Linowes's proposed zone to the county code.

Linowes had completed two of the three steps. Rezoning remained. He hired Richard Arms, the former planning director of Arlington County, to redesign the project and deal with issues raised by the planning staff. Arms had overseen the redevelopment of Rosslyn and Crystal City and was skilled in dealing with the regulatory environment the project had to navigate. The planning staff recommended approval of the revised zoning application, but at only 85 percent of the proposed density because of its expected traffic generation. The planning board concurred and the zoning hearing examiner initiated formal hearings in April 1970.

As the hearing proceeded substantial opposition emerged for the first time from Falkland residents. They pointed out that it was a much-loved community of modest-income renters. Despite a relatively high turnover among residents, many had lived there for years. As home prices rose in the county, Falkland remained a community of increasingly rare moderately priced rental units.

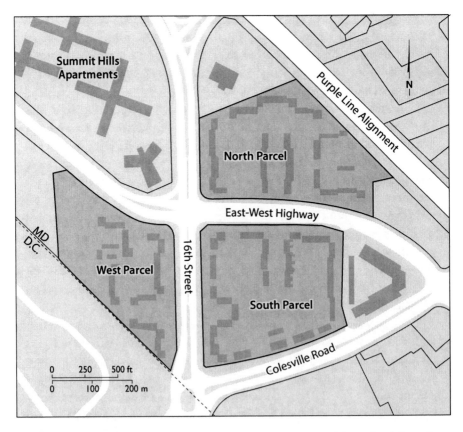

FIGURE 4.1 Falkland. North parcel ultimately was approved for redevelopment. South and West Parcels are to be restored as historic sites. Courtesy Montgomery County Planning Department M-NCPPC

The District of Columbia government made an unprecedented appearance in a Montgomery land use case, opposing the height and proximity of proposed buildings adjacent to a single-family neighborhood bordering Falkland, and insinuating that if approved, Falkland would strengthen the case for construction of the North Central Freeway, which both Montgomery and DC officials opposed.

On October 6, six months after the hearing began, Zoning Hearing Examiner Richard S. McKernon issued his report to the council. He recommended approval of rezoning for only the south and north parcels. He withheld decision on the west parcel pending changes to reduce the impact on DC neighborhoods. Since the 1970 elections were at hand, the council deferred action on the case. The council elected in November did not seem likely to look as kindly on the Falkland project as the one it replaced. On February 3, 1971 Linowes asked that the application be remanded to the hearing examiner to allow revisions to address issues raised by the opposition.

After further hearings, in September 1972 McKernon again recommended approval. Residents continued their fierce opposition in oral argument before the council. After mulling a decision over the holidays, at its first meeting in 1973 the council remanded the case to the hearing examiner until after it held its public hearing on the Silver Spring CBD Sector Plan. Four and a half years had passed since Linowes unveiled "the most ambitious project ever undertaken in the entire District metropolitan area." It had moved two steps forward and one step back, twice.

Plans That Moved Little Earth

The Planning Board began work on a sector plan for the Silver Spring CBD approximately the same time as it had for Bethesda. The area encompassed over 300 acres, split by Georgia Avenue, Colesville Road (U.S. 29) and the railroad. Land ownership was fragmented among hundreds of small lots averaging about 3,000 square feet. The largest parcels of land were owned by car dealerships. NBC news anchor David Brinkley exaggerated only slightly in his characterization of Silver Spring in a 1975 article:

> There's a suburb of Washington named Silver Spring, Md., and it's perfectly hideous—rampant, unplanned, uncontrolled, postwar growth. It's horrible. There's a Chevrolet dealer's building on one of its main corners called Loving Chevrolet. They have a commercial on radio with a little jingle that goes: "The prettiest thing in Silver Spring is Loving Chevrolet." The sad part is, it's true.[3]

As in Friendship Heights and Bethesda, general commercial zoning allowed a level of density many times the capacity of the transportation system. It provided little incentive for assembling land as its allowable density of 14 FAR (floor area ratio) inflated the value of small tracts. When assembly did occur, the hulking buildings erected offered compelling evidence of its deficiencies in site and building design or in providing an amenable public realm.

Unlike Friendship Heights and Bethesda, the Silver Spring Metro station was not at the center of the district, but at its edge. Because it would be the terminus of the eastern leg of the Red Line for a decade or longer, the station included a large bus-to-rail transfer area and Kiss & Ride lot. The county planned to build a huge parking garage just south of the station. Building over the elevated station was impracticable.

In many respects, the new CBD planning, zoning, and development system was invented with Silver Spring in mind. The planning board now tried to apply it. As in Friendship Heights and Bethesda, highest densities were proposed near the Metro station and in the traditional retail core east of Georgia Avenue. Densities and heights tapered downward and more residential uses were proposed where single-family neighborhoods adjoined the CBD. Parks were added to harden northern boundaries and prevent CBD expansion into Woodside. East Silver Spring was to be protected by low-rise buildings along Fenton Street, although a large apartment building had already been built on the neighborhood side of the street.

The plan retained Falkland in the CBD and recommended redevelopment under the optional method of the CBD-2 zone for the north parcel and a section of the south parcel nearest Metro, allowing densities of 4–6 FAR. The CBD-1 zone, with maximum densities of 2 FAR under the optional method, was proposed for the remainder of the south parcel. The existing garden apartment zone was retained on the parcel west of 16th Street.

When the sector plan reached the council in 1975, representatives of the commercial and miniature republics opposed it for different reasons. As in Friendship Heights, civic leaders regarded the density recommendations involving the CBD zones as increases rather than decreases from existing zoning. They objected to redevelopment that would replace the small community-oriented businesses that dominated Silver Spring. Housing advocates opposed redevelopment of Falkland. Property owners and speculators disliked the minimum lot size requirement for use of the optional method under the CBD zones. They complained that their properties were being down zoned from C-2 densities, even though the ultimate zoning envelope proposed by the plan would accommodate 42 million square feet of commercial and residential buildings. Colonel Lee insisted that his property on the prime corner of Georgia and Colesville should be designated for CBD-3 zoning.

Council Member Elizabeth Scull recused herself from voting because of Lee family interests in various properties throughout Silver Spring, including Falkland, so the council deadlocked 3–3 and, thus, failed to approve the sector plan. The following week, former Council Member Idamae Garrott announced the formation of the "Save Falkland Coalition" of anti-development, environmental, low-income housing, Falkland residents, historic preservation, and other advocates. Finally, on July 12, the council approved the sector plan with an amendment postponing any redevelopment of Falkland before 1980.[4]

Falkland, Round 2

Following adoption of the sector plan, the Antonelli group cancelled its long-term lease of Falkland. The Blair estate sold the property in 1985 to a Washington area firm that expected to keep the apartments as rental units. Within a year, however, the council called a hearing on the fate of the property in the wake of residents' complaints that the owner was allowing buildings to deteriorate to justify their demolition. The property, except for two acres east of Draper Lane was sold to Trammel Crow Co. for just under $10 million. To ensure Falkland's preservation, a deal was worked out between the new owner and the Housing Opportunities Commission to fund renovation of the apartments with $28 million in tax-exempt bonds in return for the owner's agreement to maintain 385 units as rental property for fifteen years.[5]

Opponents of redevelopment opened a second front in their effort to preserve Falkland. In 1980 a Master Plan for Historic Preservation and an ordinance establishing procedures for protecting historically significant properties were adopted. Special regulations restricted demolition or substantial alteration of designated properties. Falkland's advocates urged the planning board to recommend adding it to the historic preservation master plan even though it was not quite fifty years old, a rule of thumb for eligibility for historic designation. The board, however, declined to do so, and sent the council a negative recommendation. The council decided to place only one building on the master plan—the Cupola Building on the south parcel. In the mid-1980s, the two acres east of Draper Lane were sold to developer F.C. Harris, who demolished the 34 units on the site. The Lenox Park apartment project, containing 408 units was nearing completion as the sector plan was being revised in 1993. Thus, that parcel retained its CBD-2 zone.

The 1993 sector plan continued to recommend redevelopment of the north parcel but down zoned most of it from CBD-2, which had encouraged mixed uses, to CBD-R1, restricting it primarily to residential development. A section nearest the Metro station retained CBD-3 zoning. Except for the Lenox

Park property, the south parcel was restored to garden apartment (R-20) zoning to reflect existing use and reduce the opportunity for redevelopment. No change was recommended with regard to historic designation. Quiet resumed in Falkland.

The Silver Triangle Collapses

Neither the 1975 sector plan nor the imminent arrival of Metro stimulated revitalization of Silver Spring. Public efforts to resuscitate its economy and improve its appearance proved too little or simply misfired. In an attempt to provide some amenity at the Metro station, the Parks Department built a tiered hardscape park and a fountain. The park was little used and the fountain was a design disaster. Wind whistling through the railroad overpass of Colesville Road converted the fountain's cascading water into a fine spray across the station entrance in summer and a sheet of ice in winter. It was turned into a planter that often contained more rubbish than foliage.

The county made an effort to stimulate Silver Spring development by offering a county-owned parking lot near the Metro station property for the U.S. Nuclear Regulatory Commission (NRC) headquarters. At the same time he was lobbying Congress and the General Services Administration for the NRC relocation, County Executive Charles Gilchrist, frustrated by its autonomy from executive control, was trying to force the M-NCPPC to move from its building in Silver Spring to the new Executive Office Building in Rockville. That effort failed after the chair of the U.S. Senate's Public Works Committee, Jennings Randolph (D-WV), questioned locating a federal facility where the county proposed moving the major local agency with deep roots in the community. Gilchrist quickly backpedaled on moving the commission. An NRC move was soon mooted due to an appropriations rider by Senator Daniel Patrick Moynihan (D-NY) banning relocation of federal headquarters facilities from the District of Columbia.

A few private office buildings were constructed on scattered sites in the 1980s and 1990s. To try to change the bleak image of Silver Spring the county installed distinctive sidewalk pavers, planted street trees, and hung brightly colored banners from lampposts. They did little to brighten the increasingly bleak streetscape fronted by closed shops. After the ban on suburban federal offices was lifted, the National Oceanic and Atmospheric Administration (NOAA) built its headquarters next to the Metro Station, bringing a sizeable workforce into Silver Spring, but it was located too far from the moribund commercial center to spark its revitalization.

Several factors inhibited redevelopment. The area was large and land owner-ship was fragmented. Two busy highways and a railroad divided it. Its transit station was elevated at the edge of town rather than below grade at its center, and was the terminus of the eastern branch of Metro's Red Line for well over a decade after it opened in 1978. Silver Spring's banks and businesses provided no leadership. The local chamber of commerce essentially served the interests of its small business members. Commercial property owners were passive rent takers. The Hecht Company moved to Wheaton Plaza and sold its large, important site with deed restrictions prohibiting a directly competitive business.

The sites developed under the CBD zones' optional method were relatively small and widely scattered, compared to the concentration in Bethesda around the Metro station. The public spaces and amenities often were not individually well executed or integrated into a coherent public realm. Revolving business les-sees on both sides of Colesville Road struggled to survive during recession in the 1980s. Banks and insurance companies closed during the savings and loan crisis at the end of that decade.

Even though Silver Spring was in obvious decline and disrepair, development did not stop. It was just scattered and its sum was less than its parts. In June 1988 the planning staff reported that 1,755,000 square feet of building had been com-pleted in the CBD since adoption of the 1975 plan and another 675,000 square feet were under construction. The planning board had approved an additional 1,860,000 square feet, including City Place, a renovation of the Hecht site. Appli-cations were pending for over 4 million square feet, including 2.2 million for a regional mall-office complex.[6] Except for government buildings, vacancy rates were high, raising doubts that new projects would be built. By the mid-1980s Silver Spring was entering its "see through" era as buildings lost old tenants and new ones did not arrive.[7]

Hopes for revival were raised when the owner of the Art Deco shopping cen-ter and most of the block fronting Colesville Road, including the Silver Theater, signed an option contract with Lloyd Moore, the developer of one of the new office buildings in Silver Spring. Moore also obtained ownership of the "triangle" adjacent to the Metro station bounded by Colesville Road, Georgia, and Wayne Avenues. He proposed a large office-retail mall—named "Silver Triangle"—with a store-lined skywalk spanning Georgia Avenue connecting its two sections, each anchored by a major department store.

County Executive Sidney Kramer, a businessman and former state senator, elected in 1986 with support from the business and development communities, endorsed the Silver Triangle project. His staff began the studies required to estab-lish an urban renewal area to allow the county to acquire some additional parcels that would be necessary for the project to be achieved. After intensive lobbying by

Kramer, a bare majority of a bitterly divided council endorsed the Moore scheme and the urban renewal project.

The key to Kramer's majority was Council President Rose Crenca. As a civic activist in the 1970s, she had opposed intensive redevelopment in Silver Spring, but as a council member she often supported developer initiatives. Her support of the project caused a break with the Allied Civic Group (ACG), of which she had once been president. ACG and other civic groups opposed the project as too massive in scale and likely to damage local businesses. Opposition was further aggravated when Moore began demolition of the vacant Silver Theater to prevent its designation as an historic site. This action outraged preservationists and mobilized community activists. They persuaded the county to withdraw the demolition permit, but only after much of the interior décor and the marquee had been removed. Moore also proposed demolition of the Tastee Diner, making preservation of it and the theater catalysts for formation of the Silver Spring Historical Society.[8]

In October 1988, following two days of emotion-charged hearings, the planning board approved Moore's application to develop Silver Triangle under the Optional Method of Development, along with a preliminary subdivision plan that consolidated the several lots he had acquired. Opponents appealed the decision. They argued that a 1987 amendment to the sector plan was invalid, and therefore, the project plan covered by it was void. The circuit court agreed and reversed the board, which appealed the decision.

In February 1988 the planning board began work with a citizens' advisory committee on a comprehensive revision of the 1975 sector plan. In addition to the controversy over Silver Triangle, a major issue surfaced concerning the lack of capacity of existing or planned transportation systems to support the volume of traffic that would be generated if development reached the maximum density allowed by the zoning envelope. Recent history provided little evidence this was an imminent danger. The mismatch of transportation capacity and zoning, however, had become a set piece in planning politics. Opponents of intense development seized the issue and the board responded by reducing densities in several areas of the CBD, inflaming property owners whose dreams of development potential were as unrealistic as the fears of it among residential neighborhoods.

As the council was considering the sector plan in 1989, Nordstrom, one of Moore's rumored anchor tenants, announced that it would not locate a store in Silver Spring.[9] The resulting uncertainty about the viability of the Silver Triangle project led Kramer to recommend disapproval of the sector plan. The council concurred and sent it back to the planning board with instructions to consider alternative approaches to revitalization of the retail core and to increase its housing potential.[10]

While appeal of the Silver Triangle case was pending, Moore refiled his application based on a clarification of the circuit court's ruling. In early 1990 the board approved it again, contingent on Moore obtaining commitments to the project by at least two anchor tenants by June 29, 1990. He obtained one apparent commitment by the deadline from Macy's, and the board extended the time for him to obtain the second.

In 1989, Planning Board Chair Gus Bauman, who had opposed the Moore project, worked to save the Silver Theater. A film buff, he urged acquaintances at the American Film Institute to consider it as a local venue for showing classic films. Local civic groups initially opposed this idea. Moved by nostalgia more than economic reality, they wanted the theater to return to its traditional role as a community movie house.

Kramer by now had earned the enmity of the county's miniature republics, especially as a result of his backing of Silver Triangle, and more broadly for his efforts to take control of planning and the perception of indiscriminate support of development during the building boom that ended with the national savings and loan crisis. Civic activists and liberal Democrats searched frantically for a candidate to oppose him in the 1990 Democratic primary. Veteran council member Neal Potter reluctantly decided to oppose Kramer, filing as a candidate on the last day. Though greatly outspent, Potter trounced Kramer in the primary campaign and was easily elected in November, along with a supportive council majority. Only two council members that supported the Silver Triangle project were re-elected. Crenca was defeated in the Democratic primary. Potter's staff continued work on the urban renewal plan and acquired properties while owners and the Chamber of Commerce complained that uncertainty about redevelopment was driving out tenants and undercutting land values.

In January 1991 the Court of Appeals reversed the Silver Triangle decision of the circuit court, reinstating the original project approvals just as the planning board was starting public hearings on revisions to the sector plan.[11] Although the draft plan assumed Silver Triangle would be built as approved, Potter and many citizens demanded that the board consider alternatives. In its work sessions reviewing hearing testimony the board concluded that Silver Triangle was unlikely to materialize as approved. It instructed the staff to prepare an alternative and consider changes to zoning on parcels with approved projects but on which building had not commenced.

The board reconstituted a citizens' advisory committee for the plan and charged it with seeking consensus on an alternative vision for the retail core and a realistic plan with achievable goals. Consultant HSG/Gould Associates was retained to evaluate alternatives for retail development if the Silver Triangle project did not go forward.[12] Bauman persuaded Moore and the project's opponents to agree to mediation, which produced an agreement incorporated into the 1993 Sector Plan. The entire project was reduced to 1.4 million square feet. A 750,000 square foot mall would be located east of Georgia Avenue in the traditional retail district. A 650,000 square foot office complex would be located in the triangle west of Georgia Avenue. The hotel and the skyway across Georgia Avenue were eliminated.

The sector plan included an alternative approach to redevelopment of the core in the event the revised Silver Triangle did not materialize: a "mini-anchor mall" featuring off-price retailers with a closer economic and physical connection to City Place, the off-price center on the redeveloped Hecht site. An Urban Land Institute Technical Assistance Team examined the alternative and pronounced it acceptable.[13]

In addition to the changes in Falkland zoning, discussed above, the plan made a number of other significant changes. It reduced some of the density permitted by the 1975 plan outside the core area. Several new zones were established and applied to tracts at the periphery of the CBD. Properties along Fenton Street facing the East Silver Spring neighborhood were down zoned from a base density of 1.0 to 0.5 FAR. Flexibility in choice of uses was also limited by the plan, which aimed to provide a strong incentive to commercial redevelopment of the core and to discourage it elsewhere. With most interests appeased or exhausted, the council approved the sector plan.

The Silver Triangle was not built. Both Macy's and Penney's withdrew or declined to make firm commitments to become anchor tenants. The U.S. Securities and Exchange Commission, which had selected the triangle site for its new headquarters building, also reversed its decision. Moore was left with a large property, no viable development plan, and a legacy of community distrust. The Silver Triangle dealt an additional blow to redevelopment because its approval under the Adequate Public Facilities Ordinance captured all available traffic capacity in Silver Spring, preventing any other development from going forward so long as it remained in the "pipeline."

Bad Dream

When Douglas Duncan was elected county executive in 1994, he asked for a briefing on Silver Spring. He discovered nothing was happening, there was no real renewal project, and the retail area was continuing its shambling decline. He canceled the county's contract with Moore and issued a Request for Expressions of Interest (REOI) to determine if a private partner could be found to participate in the project. The county would acquire some necessary parcels, and build parking facilities, a transportation center at the Metro site, a new county services center and park, and make other infrastructure improvements. Duncan empaneled a new forty-eight-member citizen advisory board to help select a partner. In a key move to end the acrimony between the civic and business communities, John Robinson, the new president of the Allied Civic Group met with Bruce Lee, the president of the Chamber of Commerce. They agreed Silver Spring was running out of time and that civic and business leaders should work for a common objective.

Among the responses to the REOI was one from Moore and Bryant Foulger, the developer of the NOAA site, and another from Triple Five, the Canadian firm that built the Mall of America in Bloomington, Minnesota. The county dismissed the Moore-Foulger proposal, based on community antipathy toward Moore and his history of being unable to produce a viable project. The advisory committee was intrigued with the Canadian proposal to construct a $585 million, 2.1 million square foot "American Dream" urban entertainment mall containing an ice skating arena with seating for 1,000 spectators, wave pools for 3,000 swimmers, an indoor roller coaster, IMAX and a multiplex cinema, a hotel, restaurants, nightclubs, and high-end retail stores. Triple Five's owners, the Ghermezian brothers of Edmonton, Alberta, also promised to restore the Silver Theater, provide underground parking for 2,000 cars and create several park-like areas for public use.[14]

Their initial bombastic presentation before a crowd of 800 was not well received. Local residents had opposed the Moore project as too massive and insensitive to neighboring communities and much-treasured local merchants. They were now vocally skeptical of the Ghermezians' extravagant claims and dismissive assurances. With Moore's loss of anchor tenants and failure to find financing fresh in their minds, county officials were dubious of the grandiose scale of the proposal. But enough members of the advisory board remained interested to justify its further consideration.[15]

The Ghermezians, realizing they needed local champions, hired Bauman, who had community credibility as an early critic of the Moore scheme and as a former planning board chair, and Stephen Kaufmann, a Linowes and Blocher partner, to lead a concerted campaign to persuade the community and the advisory committee. Traffic studies were conducted and other consultant reports were issued to satiate Montgomery's civic and official appetite for detailed information to deconstruct and contest. An excursion was arranged for committee members and county officials to visit the Mall of America in Minnesota and the firm's original mega-mall project in Edmonton.

The effort resulted in a 41–4 vote by the advisory committee recommending that the county enter an agreement with Triple Five to determine the feasibility of the American Dream Mall. Committee members from both miniature and commercial republics were impressed with the Ghermezians' track record. Even those with doubts about the feasibility or desirability of the proposal were convinced that if it was rejected Silver Spring would soon be hollowed out. Office vacancies were so high that owners were offering prospective tenants a first year of free rent and lowered rates for an extended period. Stores were closing. Home values were at risk.

The county entered into a memorandum of understanding with the firm but, doubting its ability to perform, Duncan required it to secure financing before establishing a binding partnership. As they sought financial backers, it became clear potential investors were far less sanguine than the Ghermezians that the mall would be profitable and that Silver Spring was a good venue for it. In May 1996 Duncan gave the firm 100 days to come up with a concrete financing plan. By November they could offer only "expressions of interest." Adding to official displeasure, they proposed a bundle of direct public subsidies and tax breaks valued at $235 million, which Duncan, members of the council, and the county delegation to the General Assembly considered financially and politically unrealistic. Duncan terminated the county's agreement with Triple Five, citing the failure to obtain private financing and its request for public financing "at levels that cannot be reasonably achieved."[16]

Revival

The community and officials awoke from their bad American Dream and confronted reality. In the prior decade well over 200 businesses had closed their doors in Silver Spring. A fourth of storefronts were empty, and the office vacancy rate hovered at 40 percent. Still, there were glimmers of hope. A new townhouse project near Metro was economically successful, providing evidence of a strong residential market.

In early 1997 Duncan decided to change strategies. Rather than try to find a single "home run" project that could solve Silver Spring's problems, he decided to increase efforts to support projects that could "hit singles and doubles." He concluded that if one big project failed, the place was in deep trouble, but if eight of ten small ones succeeded, there would still be significant gains. He selected a joint venture development team led by Bryant Foulger and the Peterson Companies. Foulger had acquired Moore's remaining property interests in the Silver Spring shopping center and the theater. He had a track record of high quality development in the NOAA complex and had built successful projects elsewhere in the county.

Under an exclusive agreement, Foulger and his team agreed to work with the county and a new thirty-one-member Silver Spring Redevelopment Steering Committee Duncan appointed to craft a new town center plan over a six-month period. Foulger met with community groups to listen to what they wanted. He told them that he would try to provide it with the understanding that if he did, they would support the plan. The steering committee also served as the advisory committee for new sector plan. It followed a streamlined process, using focus groups to test issues and concepts. Consensus emerged for a "new urbanism" approach that was pedestrian-scaled and focused on the twenty-two-acre area east of Georgia Avenue that the county had acquired under its urban renewal authority.

The completed Foulger-Peterson project maintained the low-rise scale of the retail heart of Silver Spring between Colesville Road and Wayne Avenue. The art deco shopping center at the corner of Colesville and Georgia was renovated and became the portal to "Downtown," a remade Ellsworth Avenue as a pedestrian-oriented street, lined with restaurants and shops centered on a splash fountain. A land trade was arranged with M-NCPPC by which the historic National Guard Armory could be demolished and the land incorporated into the redevelopment plan. A new Veteran's Plaza would be constructed with a county civic building. A multiplex cinema, bookstore, Whole Foods grocery, and Strosnider's Hardware—treasured by generations of Montgomery households—were persuaded to join the row of restaurants and shops lining Ellsworth Avenue and Fenton Street.

The county restored the Silver Theater, which the American Film Institute made its East Coast headquarters and venue for showing historic, documentary, and other significant films. Space was provided next door for a second stage of Round House Theater, a local acting company that had originated in the Silver Spring area. To ensure coordination of the public and private elements of the plan and facilitate navigation through the regulatory and budgeting processes, Duncan established an on-site Silver Spring office, headed by Assistant Chief Administrative Officer William Mooney.

As the Downtown project was coming to fruition, Duncan was actively wooing John Henricks, the CEO of Discovery Communications, which had outgrown its Bethesda offices, to keep its headquarters in the county. In the fall of 1998 Hendricks agreed to build the firm's new headquarters in Silver Spring and acquired the triangle site from Moore. To accommodate Discovery's need for land, and assuage the local historic preservationists, the county moved the Tastee Diner from its site on Georgia Avenue to a new location on Cameron Street. Discovery agreed with the county that its new corporate complex would have no cafeteria, thus encouraging its 1,500 employees to patronize local shops and spark revival of daytime business activity. The county planned to redevelop the Metro station area into a multi-modal transportation center serving transit, commuter trains, and buses. Foulger-Pratt expected to develop high-rise offices and other uses on the remaining Metro land that had been used for parking and commuter drop-off.

Ultimately, the county and state invested over a half-billion dollars in Silver Spring for land acquisition, public facilities, and tax credits. Direct private sector investments exceeded \$2 billion. The General Assembly designated the core area an Arts and Entertainment District in 2002 and a the county declared a slightly larger area an Enterprise Zone, making development of property within the respective districts eligible for public financial subsidies and tax benefits.

The sector plan took three years to complete. As approved in February 2000, it was more than a refinement of the 1993 plan. Unlike its predecessors in 1975 and 1993, it could build on concrete accomplishments rather than aspirations and ideas. It restored much of the density and flexibility in uses the 1993 plan had reduced, finding that the zoning restrictions had inhibited redevelopment. The CBD was divided into four principal districts for distinct treatment and emphasis was placed on improving the pedestrian environment throughout the area.

The completion of Downtown, restoration of the Silver Theater, and the opening of Discovery Communications headquarters began the transformation of Silver Spring. United Therapeutics built its headquarters buildings a block north of City Place. A new residential tower was built next door. Apartments were built along East-West Highway and others were approved in the Ripley District south of the transportation center containing Metrorail, bus, and commuter rail stations.[17] The county built the new civic center and Veteran's Plaza, including an ice skating rink, to replace the Silver Spring Armory. A new district court house was built in 2005. A public library with a future Purple Line transit stop at the edge of the downtown district was completed in 2015. Ethnic restaurants were lining Georgia Avenue and side streets, joining Silver Spring traditions like Crisfield's seafood restaurant and providing dining options to the national franchises on Ellsworth.

After forty years of trying and missing markets and opportunities, redevelopment strategy shifted from seeking a silver bullet to jump start revival, such as opening Metro, capturing a huge federal installation, or conjuring a mighty mall from developers' bluster (and copious public subsidies). Instead, the new approach honored local sensibilities and strategically used public powers and investments to leverage private capital. Duncan spent political capital making hardheaded decisions, sweet-talking business executives, and creating an enduring management system to oversee implementation of plans and projects.

FIGURE 4.2   Redeveloped Downtown Silver Spring: Views of Ellsworth Avenue and Discovery Communications Headquarters. Courtesy Montgomery County Planning Department M-NCPPC

Silver Spring turned around. The population was becoming younger and more diverse. A vibrant arts and entertainment community was stimulated by rejuvenation of the Silver Theater and installation of the Round House Theater. Both enlivened the south side of Colesville Road but the north side remained economically moribund and culturally dead. To brighten Silver Spring's historic main street Duncan secured a $4 million bond bill from the General Assembly and a matching subsidy from the county to provide a live music venue on the long-vacant site behind the historic façade of the J.C. Penney store. Birchmere Music Hall expressed interest but withdrew after protracted negotiations between the county and the Lee Development Group (LDG), the owner of the site and adjacent property, had not concluded by the time Duncan left office in December 2006.

It took the administration of County Executive Isiah Leggett an additional four years to work out a deal and bring Live Nation's Fillmore to a 23,000 square foot space at the Penney's site. The county acceded to a series of demands from LDG in return for its donation of the site to the county. The grand bargain included amendments to zoning and subdivision laws that prohibited the planning board from enforcing a sector plan recommendation for a mid-block pedestrian way on LDG property. The amendments also stipulated the donation of the Penney's site satisfied all public space and amenity requirements for any development on the remainder of the Lee's adjacent property. Since LDG was not ready to develop the remainder of its property, the deal extended its entitlement to develop for eighteen years and the county agreed to reimburse the company for the cost of complying with any new regulations that might be adopted before they began development.

The planning board opposed these changes as contrary to a strong master plan recommendation to improve pedestrian circulation in the superblock and as unwise policy that gave one developer advantages over others by reducing its requirement to provide public space and amenities that would benefit both building occupants and the general public. In addition, the extension of entitlement far beyond the normal period of seven years could prevent ready projects from going forward during that period if transportation or school capacity in the area were constrained. The executive countered that the special provisions were a reasonable tradeoff for donation of the site, valued by LDG (but not appraised) at $3.5 million, and that the music hall (although leased to a private, profit-making company) was a good substitute for the public spaces and amenities that would otherwise be required when the remainder of the LDG property developed. Leggett also argued that rent, taxes, and fees from the operation of the project would far exceed the debt service on the bonds.[18] The council concurred, and approved the changes in law by a vote of 7–2. Within a few months after the deal was signed, a local newspaper reported that the public subsidy would actually be $11.5 million instead of $8 million. Leggett transferred the additional funds from the Recreation Department's capital budget. The Fillmore opened in the fall of 2011.

Falkland, Round 3

The 2000 sector plan retained the 1993 zoning for Falkland. There was strong evidence that the housing market in Silver Spring was picking up along with its commercial revitalization, and the planning board reasoned that mixed-use development was preferable to housing alone. That would be possible because although the north Falkland parcel was zoned for residential uses, it was adjacent to a tract in the same ownership that retained CBD-3 zoning. The two parcels could be developed under a single mixed-use design with a strong pedestrian orientation to Metro.

Home Properties, a builder and manager of rental properties—based in Rochester, New York—acquired Falkland in 2001. The new owners changed its name to Falkland Chase and invested in long overdue improvements to the buildings. It also announced that it planned to redevelop the north parcel and in 2006 filed a mixed-use development plan including over 1,000 units and a Harris-Teeter grocery store.

The Silver Spring Historical Society (SSHS), which had organized to protect historic resources from demolition by Silver Triangle and other projects, revived the effort to have all of Falkland, now more than fifty years old, placed on the Master Plan for Historic Preservation. At a hearing lasting several hours, SSHS and Home Properties presented dueling experts, who, respectively, extolled and dismissed Falkland's historic and architectural significance. Affordable housing advocates opposed designation and favored redevelopment. The board concluded that all three parcels should be considered for preservation and referred the matter to the Historic Preservation Commission (HPC) for its recommendation.

The HPC promptly recommended placing all three Falkland parcels on the master plan. The board's historic preservation staff, which also served as staff to the HPC, strongly supported designation. Planning director Rollin Stanley, however, was convinced that development of the north parcel under a well-designed plan could provide a substantial public benefit to Silver Spring if accompanied by restoration and environmental enhancement of the other two parcels. He persuaded Home Properties to revise its initial plan to create a more pedestrian oriented project, increase the number of affordable units available on the three parcels, improve the environmental quality of both the new project and the other two parcels, and agree to placing the south and west parcels on the Master Plan for Historic Preservation.

Both Stanley and I were convinced the council would not approve designation of all three parcels and that if the board recommended it the council probably would designate none of them. In a recent case, the council had resisted designating properties if their owners were opposed. I estimated that there were only two council members that would surely vote to place all three parcels on the master plan. I counted five as unwilling to place them on the master plan and favoring redevelopment.

At the second planning board hearing, each side reprised its case. The board accepted Stanley's recommendation. After one more hearing of the same arguments, the council concurred. In 2010 Home Properties received approval for redevelopment of the north parcel, forty-four years after Linowes first presented his redevelopment plan. Home Properties sold the property in 2013 to JBG, which announced that it had no immediate plans to redevelop.[19]

Planning Politics and Redevelopment

Silver Spring was a school in humility for planners, civic and business leaders, developers, and politicians. Redevelopment is hard in the most favorable circumstances. It was immensely more difficult when forces of the miniature and commercial republics were locked in combat over whether, where, and how it should be done. That is because redevelopment is a revolutionary act, replacing a built environment to which people have become accustomed, even if they have no particular affection for it. It substitutes new property interests for ones long established, produces windfalls for some, wipeouts for others, and redistributes power and wealth within the commercial republic.

For the fifty years before 1970, land use policy for Silver Spring resided with the growth machines of the Lee and Builders and Bar Regimes. Linowes's initial Falkland proposal fit the established pattern of parcel-by-parcel expansion of the business district through rezoning at the initiative of developers. Quick approval was the appropriate action under then existing practices of planning politics. The objections of the board's consultant and staff were based only on a pending master plan. Even if adopted it would have been merely a guideline that would not override the market's wisdom, revealed through the Falkland proposal.

The Falkland project foundered on changes in rules and regimes. The time consumed in the detailed and laborious review by the hearing examiner prevented a decision by a lame duck council that had clearly signaled its inclination to approve it by expanding the CBD boundary and adopting the new zone. The long hearing allowed time for opposition to form. None of the council members elected in 1970 was a certain supporter. While a revised proposal returned to the hearing examiner, the council adopted the CBD zones and work began on the Silver Spring sector plan, making it appropriate to delay a decision further, effectively killing the project for years to come.

The Progressive Regime's changes in planning process empowered Silver Spring's civic activists to voice their concerns in advisory committees and mobilize to defend their neighborhoods from perceived threats from increased density, traffic, and other ills of urban development.[20] The policy tools the planning board fashioned in Friendship Heights and Bethesda were designed to influence and regulate development projects initiated by the private sector in a robust market.

The same techniques employed in the 1975 Silver Spring CBD Sector Plan proved inadequate to the challenge of creating a market for assembling land and redeveloping a moribund commercial center.

Failure to analyze fully the problems unique to Silver Spring resulted in an inadequate strategy to address them. Unlike Bethesda, the arrival of Metro was not enough to set off a land rush. For one thing, the transit station was off-center and its location at the elevated railroad crossing of Colesville Road precluded the sort of intensive air rights construction that occurred in Bethesda. Land ownership was not only fragmented, but many owners held unrealistic expectations that each parcel should be valued at the maximum level the CBD zones permitted even though it could not qualify for development under the optional method.

Even if the land assembly problem could have been overcome, redevelopment of the area faced formidable extrinsic obstacles. The office market was soft in Silver Spring, except for projects built for institutional tenants such as NOAA. Although Silver Spring's older buildings and relatively low rents provided refuge for small businesses displaced by the race riots in the District of Columbia, its location at the top of a corridor of urban unrest was no boon to investor interest. The residential area surrounding the business district was older and had a larger proportion of moderate-income households and renters than the western side of the county. These neighborhoods were beginning to experience significant turn-over and demographic change, which raised the level of homeowner anxiety as it further dampened investor interest in the CBD. Disinvestment was exacerbated by historically high interest rates during the late 1970s and early 1980s.

If the planners' logic of consequentiality misdiagnosed the problem and prescribed an inadequate remedy, the politicians' logic of appropriateness also failed repeatedly in Silver Spring. As the assessment of the situation was repeatedly inaccurate it was not possible for officials to fashion an appropriate response to it. Developers, such as Moore, withheld critical information about their proposed projects, and did not possess commitments from anchor tenants or for financing. This led to improvident official support for the Silver Triangle project and allocation to it of all the CBD's transportation capacity, which blocked other projects from moving forward until its fate was determined.

Civic fury was unleashed when the developer began demolition of the Silver Theater. Response to growing civic unrest and disaffection, combined with the undead mall, contributed to a 1993 plan that necessarily, under the conventions now well established for sector plans, restricted development elsewhere in Silver Spring. The state of planning politics for Silver Spring at the end of the century reflected the title of Lindblom's sardonic response to criticism of his championship of incrementalism: "Still Muddling, Not Yet Through."[21]

The first two sector plans for Silver Spring were strongly influenced by solicitude for the residential neighborhoods adjacent to the CBD. The 1993 plan, in particular, might be considered a lesson for civic leaders on the consequences of getting what they wished for. Rather than protecting their neighborhoods and residential property values, the studies conducted for the 2000 sector plan found that the earlier plan's restrictions on density probably contributed to stagnation in growth and the further decline of the business district.

Civic interests made significant contributions to plans, however, first achieving revision, and then abandonment of the Silver Triangle proposal. The advisory committee's endorsement of the American Dream Mall may have been the hallucinatory effect of too many meetings, but it brought the issue to a head. The consensus reached by the commercial and miniature republics to embrace the pedestrian scale of the ultimate redevelopment of the core area suggests that persistent public engagement does, in fact, build civic capital and result in social production—power to solve problems rather than simply exercise power over others.[22]

Activists that participated in the serial planning exercises developed expertise in both planning and politics. Each of the planning cycles produced significant new public leaders that began their careers in advisory committees or as advocates for the interests of their communities. Participants in the long struggle to revive Silver Spring gained a better understanding of economic realities and played constructive roles in selecting a viable approach to redevelopment. They also developed skills in political strategy and tactics that informed subsequent participation in planning exercises and review of projects. In Falkland, for example, mobilization of civic and preservation interests contributed to defeat of earlier proposals for its redevelopment and facilitated the final compromise that allowed redevelopment of the north parcel while assuring historic preservation and improvement of buildings and landscape for the other two.

After displacement of the Progressive Regime by the Pure Political Regime the policy initiative shifted back toward the commercial republic as the Silver Triangle, American Dream Mall, and town center projects galvanized politicians, civic activists, and public agencies. Power shifted toward the county executive. Kramer imprudently endorsed Moore's Silver Triangle without either economic or political due diligence. Although he refused to use urban renewal powers to acquire land to allow a comprehensive approach to redevelopment, he bulldozed through council a change in growth policy to add trip capacity for the project and backed a parking garage to support it. Both were vociferously opposed by civic organizations. These actions helped mobilize opposition and were principal causes of his defeat in the 1990 Democratic Primary. By the end of Potter's term in 1994, the Silver Triangle proposal had collapsed from its own deficiencies.

It is reasonable to conclude that but for County Executive Douglas Duncan's actions, the revival of Silver Spring would not have occurred, or would not have occurred with as good a result. His determination to find an alternative to the Silver Triangle working with community and business leaders eventually led to consensus between Silver Spring's miniature and commercial republics. Despite having reservations, he acceded to their initial fascination with the American Dream Mall, then killed it when it became clear the developer could not find the necessary financing and was demanding unattainable public subsidies. This gave him the opportunity to work out the arrangement with Foulger-Pratt and Peterson, who worked closely with the community to design a project that all could support, even if some of the support was based on exhaustion. Reaching agreement on demolition of the armory and persuading Discovery Communications to locate its headquarters at a strategically critical site required intensive executive involvement. He made redevelopment a major priority of his administration and assigned William Mooney to coordinate public and private projects and facilitate action. He also pushed tax incentives for redevelopment through the council and General Assembly.

Duncan and his staff learned to be wary of grandiose claims by developers with stronger public relations offices than tenant commitments. They also learned that given the political culture of the county and the ability of aroused civic associations to influence elections—especially party primaries—a major planning enterprise was more likely to achieve success if community leaders were invested in the public deliberations that produced it.

The planning board played a supporting rather than a leading role in the 2000 sector plan by removing many of the constraints that had been imposed in 1993. The plan endorsed the "downtown" concept and made an important contribution to the quality of the redevelopment by embracing historic preservation for the Silver Spring Shopping Center and the Silver Theater. By removing rigidities in use and scale established in the 1993 plan, the 2000 plan allowed the market to respond to a strong new demand for residential development that brought new vibrancy to Silver Spring.

Shifts in regime politics and attenuated processes clearly delayed the redevelopment of the Falkland tract. It is debatable whether its early approval could have sparked new interest in redevelopment of the retail core or would have further sapped its vitality. Although it took more than four decades to settle Falkland's future, its resolution will provide additional housing—including more low-income units—with easy access to jobs and Metro, while preserving most of that historic garden district. The redevelopment of the retail core stimulated transit-oriented housing in the adjacent districts. The completion of the transportation center should establish Silver Spring as a major regional transportation hub and open a stronger market for housing and office development, which will add strength to the commercial district.

THE END OF SUBURBIA?

Between 1980 and 2010 Montgomery County's demography was transformed. The percentage of non-Hispanic whites declined from 83 to 49 percent, and was aging. The black population increased from 9 to 19 percent, Hispanics from 4 to 17 percent, and Asians from 4 to 14 percent. In addition, the percentage of married households dropped from 62 to 53 percent while nonfamily households increased from 27 to 31 percent.

The market shifted with the population and moved toward more attached and multifamily housing. A bubble in condominium construction deflated in the Great Recession of 2008 and the demand for rental housing grew. The recession arrested the ability of the county to expand services. Inflated value was wrung from residential property values, contracting the assessable base for the first time in a century. Budgets were cut. Resumption of rates of exponential growth that had allowed the county to finance expansion of services and facilities seemed unlikely.

There was neither the land nor a demand to return to old patterns of growth and development. A new strategy was necessary. The successes of Bethesda, Friendship Heights, and Silver Spring suggested that transit oriented redevelopment of obsolete centers could serve important niches in the housing and commercial markets. The planning staff in 1989 recommended such a strategy.

The independent political entrepreneurs of the Pure Political Regime paid little heed. Sharing no common vision, they lacked the collective will even to debate the proposals of a report they commissioned. Development policy was governed by inertia, occasionally enlivened by skirmishes in Silver Spring or Germantown, disputes over boundaries and heights in new master plans, and arguments about roads and forest conservation. Many of the county's new minority and immigrant residents did not become citizens of miniature republics. They were more likely renters than homeowners, less likely to work for federal agencies, and they had not weaned on the reform ideology of the progressive era. They voted less regularly and were less concerned with land use issues than with educational opportunities, public safety, recreation facilities, and other social services. Aside from an affluent professional class, most were workers rather than business owners. Although large numbers worked in the construction industry, almost none were developers and few were members of the commercial republic even if they were entrepreneurs.

With few new entries, traditional cleavages persisted, but were largely site and project specific, symbolic of fears and unsatisfied appetites but devoid of strategic context. They could be loud and produce electoral consequences, as in the 1990 defeat of Sidney Kramer by Neal Potter, and the 2002 insurgency of Blair Ewing against Douglas Duncan and the End Gridlock slate. A quarrelsome council temporized, alternatively seeking to pacify the commercial and miniature republics they uneasily governed. Members crafted ambiguous provisions that would employ a cottage industry deconstructing their meaning. A county that made its national reputation planning its future reverted to obsession with the present, using techniques of the past. The council sleepwalked into the twenty-first century and innovation was essentially dead at the planning board.

Market forces turned inward to meet the growth in demand for more opportunities to live and work in higher density activity centers. Moreover, the synergy of housing, office, and commercial uses yielded a high ratio of property tax revenue to services. Moving from the abstract to the practical, few areas provided opportunities for meeting a new generation of housing and employment demands without abandoning the vision of the General Plan. Of places within the urban ring, White Flint, halfway between Bethesda and Rockville was the prime target for the best place to create a model for a new generation of land use policy.

Getting to White Flint

The ambivalence of the county toward development of non-Central Business District (CBD) Metro areas was reflected in the 1978 sector plans for the three stations between the Capital Beltway and Rockville. Over time, each assumed a unique function. The Grosvenor-Strathmore station, just north of the Capital Beltway on the east side of Rockville Pike, provided a massive commuter parking lot surrounded by apartments, campuses of private and parochial institutions, and Strathmore Hall—eventually, the county's music and arts center. The 1978 sector plan for Grosvenor recommended multiunit housing above the station and its parking area. Residents of Grosvenor Park, one the densest apartment complexes in the county, bitterly opposed this idea, as well as the pedestrian tunnel under Rockville Pike connecting them to Metro. The president of the tenants association, Harriet Archawsky, told the planning board at its public hearing on the plan: "We all moved to the suburbs to escape from urban confusion. We do not want intensive development, with its attendant traffic, noise, air pollution, crime and other undesirable attributes."[1]

No private development occurred on the Metro site, even though the revisions made by the 1992 North Bethesda-Garrett Park Master plan recommended planned development with a density of twenty-five units per acre. A new apartment project was built on vacant land south of the site, and town houses replaced the campus of the American Speech and Hearing Association north of Strathmore.

Tryout in Twinbrook

The Twinbrook station at the southern edge of Rockville is adjacent to the railroad tracks that separate commercial clutter along Rockville Pike from an old light industrial area dominated by the hulking Parklawn building occupied by federal agencies. The few residences that existed in 1978 had vanished by 1993 when a new plan proposed a mixed-use development near the station. A new urbanism project, Twinbrook Station, was approved, annexed by Rockville, and completed in 2010. United States Pharmacopoeia built offices and laboratories near the Parklawn Building. The planning board began preparing a third sector plan for Twinbrook in 2007. The plan's significance lay not in the modest changes recommended, but the role it played in testing two ideas that would come to fruition in White Flint.

The first involved responding to a council request for a flexible approach to zoning that allowed a mixture of uses at a wide range of densities and heights, which could be applied to other areas where plans were being prepared.[2] Experience with the floating zones that were designed for transit station areas in the 1970s proved to have high transaction costs for approval and rigidities that had complicated their use for complex projects that could involve adjustments during the development process. The second issue arose from the report of an ad hoc Working Group on Agricultural Preservation that recommended providing density bonuses for development that acquired Building Lot Termination (BLT) easements extinguishing residential development rights remaining on land in the county's Agricultural Reserve, where owners held a Transferable Development Right (TDR) for each five acres but zoning allowed only one house for each 25 acres. Landowners usually sold the four "excess" TDRs and retained the one "buildable" right.

After trying to adapt existing zones to meet these objectives, the staff and board agreed to start from scratch with a new zone that might satisfy the council's request for a single approach for all new sector plans and include provisions for use of BLT easements to increase both residential and commercial densities. A single Transit Mixed-Use (TMX) zone was proposed, with standard and optional methods of development. It set a maximum density limit of 3 FAR for the optional method, but left it to master plans to set the height and density ceilings for specific properties within that envelope. A strong emphasis was placed on site plan review by the planning board to achieve better project design and coordinate individual projects to meet sector plan standards for the public realm. Preliminary analysis of other areas for which planning was beginning suggested that 3 FAR might be adequate for their potential new growth.

The Building Lot Termination Puzzle

Figuring out how to address BLT easements, however, was more difficult. It presented three technical problems: (1) estimating the average market value of a BLT easement, which could be translated by a developer into a cost to the project; (2) determining the amount of bonus density that should be added to a building for each BLT easement acquired; and (3) deciding whether to treat acquisition of BLT easements as an exaction or an incentive.

Since "buildable lots" in the Agricultural Reserve were selling for $300,000 to $750,000 in the years leading to the Great Recession, easements terminating building rights would probably cost $200,000 or more. This was approximately five times the current price of "excess" Transferable Development Rights (TDRs). Since the average dwelling unit built in projects using TDRs was 1,800 square feet, Jacob Sesker, the planning department's economist, recommended that each BLT easement a developer acquired should allow it to construct either an additional 9,000 square feet of residential space or 7,500 square feet of commercial/office space. Developers participating in staff and board discussions agreed that these estimates were reasonable because the marginal cost to a project, including transaction costs, was exceeded by the marginal return on investment from the additional density the easement allowed. The board accepted them as the basis for the amount of incremental density to be awarded for each BLT easement in a new Transit Mixed-Use (TMX) zone.

If purchase of BLT easements were exactions required as a condition of project approval, to avoid being considered a regulatory taking they must have a nexus with the project, meaning they must directly benefit it or ameliorate the direct impact of the project on other property, facilities, or the local environment. Because builders could build "by right" under the standard method an exaction designed to save farmland several miles away was unlikely to survive legal challenge. But without requiring BLT easements developers would be unlikely to participate in the program and it would fail. The board decided to require purchase of BLT easements in return for 12.5 percent of the additional density granted for development under the optional method. This avoided the legal issue because developers had to apply for the optional method and, therefore, voluntarily accepted its requirements. In cases where an easement purchase could not be arranged, developers could make an equivalent contribution to a special BLT fund established in the county's Agricultural Easement Purchase program.[3] The 12.5 percent figure number was selected because it was the same as the requirement for Moderate Priced Dwelling Units and trial analysis of hypothetical development scenarios for Twinbrook sites indicated that the marginal cost per square foot to a project was at the top of an acceptable range.

Loss Leader

The board completed work on the TMX zone and sent it to the council. The Planning, Housing and Economic Development Committee accepted the BLT requirements with little disagreement. Instead, controversy focused on linking the zone to the sector plan to establish heights and densities of particular parcels within permitted maximums. This approach, while not entirely novel, allowed a single zone to be applied to the entire planning area, using the sector plan to tailor density and height for particular parcels within the maximum of 3.0 FAR (floor area ratio) permitted by the zone, instead of using separate zones for each change in height or density.

This enhancement of the regulatory authority of the plan was too great a break from tradition for council staff, which argued that it would be safer to create a separate zone for each variation in density and height. Although the council had asked for a zone that could be applied in other areas, a majority of the committee and council accepted its staff's recommendation and limited the density of the TMX zone to 2.0 FAR, since that was the maximum needed in Twinbrook. This decision allowed the Twinbrook plan to be approved with a few tweaks to road alignments and other minor changes from the board's draft.

Limiting the TMX zone's maximum density to 2.0 FAR, however, made it inadequate for use in White Flint where substantial variations in density and height across this large area would be needed. Creating a separate zone for each situation could add pages to the zoning code for little benefit. In addition, White Flint developers were challenging the scale and mandatory character of BLT easement provisions as economically infeasible and of questionable legality, even if limited to optional development projects.

One of the inherent problems of the TMX requirement for BLT easements was that while the marginal cost, standing alone, was not onerous, its effect on return to investment could discourage developers from using the optional method. If that happened it would frustrate the goal of producing higher densities and mixed uses within walking distance of a Metro station. As the staff delved more deeply into analysis of the issue it became clear that the cost of a BLT provision could not be considered in isolation, but as one more layer in the "parfait" of regulations, each of which carried a cost. This insight led to a different approach for White Flint and other redevelopment areas.

Reimagining White Flint

The White Flint Metro station is roughly halfway between Grosvenor and Twinbrook, in the two-mile long commercial strip fronting both sides of Rockville Pike, the most cluttered, pedestrian-hostile, reviled, and heavily congested roadway in the county. When the location decision was made in 1968 the immediate area's sole residential building had no convenient pedestrian access to the station. Sixty-three percent of the land within a 2,000-foot radius of the station portal was undeveloped, one of the largest amounts near any station in the county. White Flint Mall, built in late 1975 before the station opened was just beyond a comfortable walking distance. The 1978 sector plan for the station, therefore, stated: "The Nicholson Lane area is envisioned as a unique opportunity, present nowhere else in Montgomery County, to provide new mixed uses including office, retail, and residential development on what is still vacant land, in close proximity to a rapid-rail station."[4] It recognized the major factor limiting the area's potential was the capacity of the road system to handle additional traffic.

A Slow Start on Rockville Pike

To increase traffic capacity the plan recommended a number of street and intersection improvements, plus Marinelli Road, a new access from the west. Eastern access was limited to only two crossings of the railroad and transit line—by Randolph Road to the north, and Nicholson Lane/Parklawn Drive south of the station. The sector plan left in place most of the existing commercial, industrial, and single-family residential zoning on land recommended for redevelopment in the 200-acre sector plan area. Based on a trip generation analysis, the plan estimated the maximum amount of additional development the area could accommodate under the recommended floating transit station zones, including an air rights building over the station, was 1,600 residential units, 600 hotel units, and 1,070,000 square feet of office and retail-commercial space. Design guidelines generally followed conventions of the time, recommending fifty-foot setbacks from Rockville Pike with buildings clustered and oriented away from the street in park-like settings rather than meeting a build-to line to create an active pedestrian streetscape.

Representatives of civic associations testifying at the board and council hearings on the plan generally objected to the increases in density, expressing fears that it would be accompanied by crime, and repeatedly deplored the anticipated increase in traffic congestion. The complaint of Thomas Broderick, representing the North Bethesda Congress, was typical: "The North Bethesda sector plan should be revised to serve the citizens of Montgomery County, not the future citizens of Grosvenor City, and Nicholson City [White Flint], at transit stations now shown in the plan."[5]

Although the 1978 sector plan envisioned White Flint developing as an uptown center, relatively little growth occurred prior to its revision in 1992 as part of the master plan for North Bethesda-Garrett Park. The most significant projects included a large condominium apartment building and the headquarters of the U.S. Nuclear Regulatory Commission. The thirty-five-acre Metro site remained undeveloped.

The 1992 plan continued to recommend that White Flint be developed as the main urban center of North Bethesda. The base zoning applied in 1978 was left in place, with transit station floating zones recommended when redevelopment occurred. The plan generally separated residential and business uses, recommending residential development of the west side of the Pike and primarily office and commercial development on the east side. It went into considerable detail concerning FAR and height limits in each sub-area where transit station floating zones were recommended.

A county conference center was proposed for the Metro parking lot west of Rockville Pike.[6] The $36.5 million conference center was completed west of the Pike in 2004 with funding from the county and $23.1 million in Maryland Stadium Authority revenue bonds. An adjoining Marriott Hotel was concurrently developed. Three major residential projects were built in the following years. Two large mixed-use projects were underway in 2006: North Bethesda Market on ten acres west of Rockville Pike near the mall, and the thirty-two-acre North Bethesda Town Center at the Metro station. Other projects were coming before the planning board for approval. While most were reasonably well designed, there were significant exceptions, and they were not adding up to produce a well-integrated urban center. The 1992 sector plan area retained the 1978 boundaries, which excluded two significant tracts: the twenty-acre Mid-Pike Plaza, an obsolete strip mall, and the fifty-acre White Flint Mall, suggesting that no change was anticipated in these properties during the life of the plan. Owners of both properties were becoming interested in redevelopment, which would be difficult under the general commercial (C-2) zone governing them, which had long since been amended to allow a maximum density of only 1.5 FAR.

The Last Best Opportunity

White Flint offered the best and perhaps last opportunity in the county for a new high-quality Metro-oriented urban center. Competent, financially strong development firms with substantial holdings could carry forward a well-designed plan. It also provided an opportunity to transform Rockville Pike from an unsightly, inefficient, and obsolete commercial strip into an exemplary boulevard, uniting an uptown urban center that could substantially add strength to the county's economic base and, conceivably even reduce traffic congestion by colocating homes and businesses.

Situated about half-way between Bethesda and Rockville, the expanded White Flint sector plan area of about 430 acres was over a mile long, stretching from Montrose Parkway-Randolph Road on the north to White Flint Mall on the south, and from Old Georgetown Road on the west to the railroad tracks on the east. Aside from the large projects mentioned above, it was populated with small strip malls, car dealerships, and a smattering of other small business sites. Over a fourth of the area was covered with surface parking lots. It was situated between two large, politically active and sophisticated single-family communities: Luxmanor on the west, and Garrett Park Estates on the East. A third, Randolph Hills, was across the railroad/Metro tracks, east of the planning area.

Executives of Federal Realty Investment Trust, owners of Mid-Pike Plaza, met with me in 2006, reporting that most of their leases would soon expire and they would renew them if redevelopment were not possible in the foreseeable future. Four other national development firms owned significant tracts of land: The Lerner Corp., owner of White Flint Mall; JBG, constructing North Bethesda Market; LCOR, building North Bethesda Town Center; and Washington Realty Investment Trust, owner of a smaller tract on the east side of the area. Jack Fitzgerald, who owned an automobile dealership at Nicholson Lane put together a short-lived consortium of adjacent landowners interested in the coordinated redevelopment of their properties, and there were a number of other individuals and firms that owned various tracts scattered along the Pike and cross streets. All these owners were interested in a new plan for the area and lobbied the council to add a sector plan for White Flint to the board's work program. The initial hope was that the plan could be completed in a year. The council added the sector plan to the Board's FY 2008–9 work program.

Assaying its task, the board decided against appointing a traditional advisory committee. Because of the large number of stakeholders, it established a larger, open membership group of some fifty people to work with the staff in a series of charrettes and forums to produce an initial draft plan. All landowners were invited to join, as were representatives of the civic, environmental, condominium, and neighborhood associations. At the initial meeting of the group, I urged them to think boldly about the area.

Adjusting Ambitions to Reality

It was not surprising when staff analyses indicated that even an enhanced transportation system could not support the aggregated ambitions of the developers and landowners. Commissioner John Robinson, who was closely following the discussions and had held one-on-one conversations with the major developers, confirmed that their combined ambitions far exceeded the total development potential of the area. He told them competition among the developers could torpedo a successful plan. I agreed, and at a meeting arranged with the largest developers, Robinson and I emphasized that if they could not cooperate it was likely that there would be no plan that could be approved by the council.

New sources of financing would be required to achieve some of the infrastructure improvements necessary to support increased density. These improvements would be costly but add value to projects in the area by enhancing both access and amenity. They included a second Metro portal, reconstruction of a major intersection and creation of a street grid to handle local traffic. The most significant need was to transform Rockville Pike into a multi-modal boulevard that could unite the development on either side of it rather than continue to be a barrier and unsightly mess. Commissioners Robinson, Gene Lynch, and I expressed the view that a special funding mechanism, such as a tax district, would be necessary to fund projects that could neither be exacted through the subdivision process nor financed in the regular course of capital budgets.

As the staff worked on the technical problems associated with transportation, land uses, densities and heights, public facilities, environmental improvements, and design standards, the developers worked with residents of the area and civic stakeholders to form alliances. Ultimately, the proredevelopment interests coalesced into three principal bargaining groups. The most comprehensive was the White Flint Development Partnership, consisting of several of the major property owners and development organizations.[7] Evan Goldman, the local Federal Realty executive, served as the principal spokesman and lobbyist for the group, although the executives of the member corporations were also frequent participants in work sessions and contacts with staff and board members. The Partnership financed a consultant's transportation study that recommended a scheme for reconstruction of Rockville Pike as a boulevard with bus rapid transit lanes in the median, and proposed a surtax on development to finance the improvements. LCOR, which was building North Bethesda Town Center was loosely affiliated with the Partnership, but maintained its independence. Nicholson Lane Properties included several smaller property owners represented by planning consultant Perry Berman.

As the plan took shape, Barnaby Zall, an energetic local resident and blogger, with help from JBG executive Rod Lawrence, organized Friends of White Flint to support the plan. Modeled on Rosslyn Renaissance in Arlington, Virginia, Friends brought together citizens, property owners, and businesses to educate residents about the plan and advocate transformation of White Flint into a walkable, transit-oriented "new urban" district. The organization was a particularly effective advocate because it transcended the traditional divide between the commercial and miniature republics. Moreover, the developers and community members cooperated to resolve issues and conduct an aggressive outreach program, using social media and conducting over eighty community presentations over a nine-month period to build support for the plan's vision.

The two adjacent single-family neighborhoods, Luxmanor and Garrett Park Estates, were represented primarily by Paula Bienenfeld and Natalie Goldberg, but other community members were in frequent attendance at forums and work sessions. Goldberg was particularly effective in extracting transitional land uses to buffer her neighborhood. Bienenfeld tended to be less effective; in part because other residents of her community were more favorably disposed toward the vision for the area and because Luxmanor was not as heavily impacted as Garrett Park Estates. Their civic associations were eventually joined by a few others to argue for less density and were especially concerned for protection of their neighborhoods from increased traffic, impact of added residences on schools, and the effect of tall buildings on the serenity of their communities.

The large collection of builders and citizens working with staff reached early consensus on the reconstruction and transformation of Rockville Pike. Civic leaders urged the board to require that it be rebuilt before any of the development proceeded, understandably concerned that if not placed at the head of redevelopment it might not get done. It took some time to persuade them that this was not feasible, since reconstruction would have to be done concurrently with redevelopment of private property fronting the Pike and that alternative road improvements would have to be made first to allow through traffic to bypass the Pike during its reconstruction.

Aside from agreement on the importance of the central boulevard, the other usual planning conundrums for redevelopment of older districts persisted as the planning process entered its second year. Overall density had to be balanced with transportation capacity. A housing-jobs ratio needed enough flexibility to allow adjustment for market cycles. Density had to be allocated among tracts to provide an efficiently functioning center while treating landowners equitably and limiting adverse impacts on adjoining residential neighborhoods. A zoning system had to be designed to implement the plan's vision of well-designed buildings and a gracious and active public realm, transforming an auto-oriented area into a pedestrian-oriented place centered at the transit station. Since much of the area developed before the county had storm water management or forest conservation requirements there was opportunity to improve the area's environmental quality. Finally, it was clear that the ultimate success of any plan would depend on creation of a mechanism that could finance a variety of public facilities—especially a remade Pike.

Resolving Key Issues

The planning board published the White Flint Sector Plan public hearing draft in December 2008. A model of the logic of consequentiality, it proposed a total density ceiling of 42 million square feet, including 9,800 housing units. The highest density, 4.0 FAR, was centered at the Metro station and decreased in one-eighth mile concentric rings to 2.0 FAR at the edges. The "ring" approach was modified to allow 3.0 FAR for properties with frontage on the Pike that would have otherwise been allowed only 2.5 FAR. This placed the highest densities within one-quarter mile of Metro and continuous density along the Pike to provide a busy pedestrian environment. Building heights of 300 feet were proposed at the Metro center but declined to 36–50 feet adjacent to residential neighborhoods. Since the council had not yet acted to limit the TMX zone, it was proposed for the entire area, with density and heights set by the plan.

The Partnership and other developers objected to the concentric circle approach and proposed an alternative elliptical configuration, which stretched the higher densities in a north-south line along the Pike. Coincidentally, the ellipse gave each developer the density it desired. The board abandoned geometric symmetry and instead approved a distribution of the higher densities based on estimated five and ten minute walking times to Metro on the new street pattern the plan proposed. This approach eschewed arbitrary distance gradients (whether circular or elliptical) that assumed people could walk through walls and would experience no delay at street crossings. The resulting pattern was somewhat irregular but provided an empirical basis for density allocations. It disappointed some developers but co-opted their argument that density should be based on proximity to Metro by measuring the actual rather than the theoretical time required to walk to it.

A New Approach to Zoning

The board began work sessions on White Flint just as the council completed action on the TMX zone. It was immediately apparent that White Flint needed a greater range of densities than the zone permitted. Intensive discussions with owners of large tracts in White Flint and staff analyses of their pro forma financing plans, convinced the board that requiring purchase of BLT easements to obtain 12.5 percent of optional method density was so costly it would cause developers to build under the standard method or not redevelop their properties at all. The result would be underdevelopment of an area of immense economic importance to the county and simultaneous frustration of the goal of terminating a large number of buildable development rights in the Agricultural Reserve.

Furthermore, the open-ended character of the TMX zone with regard to the kind of public benefits and amenities to be provided raised concerns among both builders and civic leaders. Both wanted more certainty about what had to be done so the range of disputes could be narrowed and a developer could make a better estimate of cost and return on investment. Reviewing the situation, planner Piera Weiss, planning director Rollin Stanley, and I concluded a different kind of zoning was required for White Flint and other areas that should undergo intensive mixed-use redevelopment.

Stanley began work on a new Commercial-Residential (CR) zone based primarily on incentives that awarded increments of density in return for provision of public benefits and amenities. The architecture of his draft addressed two central concerns raised by the Twinbrook discussions: uncertainty about the mixture of residential and non-residential uses, and vagueness about the specific public benefits and amenities that a development must or could provide.

Stanley's draft zone had four basic elements: Total density (CR), Commercial Density (C), Residential Density (R)—each expressed as FAR, and Height (H)—expressed in feet. Thus, if a plan called for a total density of 3 FAR for a tract, divided equally between commercial and residential uses, and a maximum height of 200 feet, the zone would be expressed as CR3, C1.5, R1.5, H 200. Instead of leaving public benefits unspecified, the zone contained several categories of public benefits, such as street-level interest and connections to transit or other uses, diversity of uses, high quality design, environmental improvements and services, and energy efficiency. A project could proffer benefits from three or more categories in justification of the density it proposed above a standard base density of 0.5 FAR.

The approach had a number of advantages over the TMX zone and Stanley and I, along with Associate General Counsel David Lieb, began to rework and vet it with key stakeholders. Consultations were conducted with participants in the White Flint work sessions, key zoning attorneys, a subcommittee of the Zoning Advisory Panel appointed to assist in a comprehensive revision of the zoning code, and the council's zoning advisers—a committee composed the council's legislative counsel, an assistant county attorney, the zoning hearing examiner, and the People's Counsel. Most were intrigued. A few were enthusiastic. Others were suspicious or hostile. The latter feared that it threatened neighborhood stability because it could be applied through individual rezoning cases. This was a legitimate, if somewhat overblown fear and the board agreed to amend the draft to require that a CR zone could be applied only by sectional map amendment in conformance with an approved plan.

Another critical feature of the zone was accepted without controversy: development under it must be consistent with the recommendations of the appropriate master or sector plan. Under Maryland law this linkage gave the plan regulatory status. Thus, the plan could suggest or require preference for certain public benefits at a particular site or establish a lower density or height than the maximum permitted by the zone. This made it possible for the plan to establish common building lines, height gradients across several properties, and standards for streetscape and other features of the public realm that otherwise would be difficult to achieve as development proceeded parcel by parcel over many years with several changes in ownership and in staff and planning board membership.

One objection involved the question whether, as proposed, the zone ran afoul of the "uniformity" rule requiring all property in a given zone to be subject to the same requirements. Strict adherents of the uniformity rule argued that a separate zone should be created for each variation in density, use, and height. That could require hundreds of zones, each with repetitive language except for the specific dimensions. An alternative was fewer zones but greater dependence on language in sector plans to fine tune provisions within the maximums allowed. This brought back the uncertainty issue. Others thought that requiring specific exactions would provide greater certainty than a smorgasbord of density incentives from which developers could choose as proffers of benefits and amenities. The uniformity issue was resolved by providing that each combination of uses and heights was a distinct zone. This allowed zones to be created as they were being applied through sectional map amendment in conformance with an approved plan.

A group of citizens involved in development issues in Friendship Heights and other areas over the years objected to procedure for approving use of the optional method and specifying the categories of benefits that could be proffered by a developer. The zone required an applicant for optional method to present a "sketch plan" showing the basic arrangement, bulk, and massing of structures, location of streets and public spaces, distribution of uses, a description of the public benefits and amenities to be provided, and a statement of how it advanced the objectives and policies of the sector plan. The group argued that greater detail should be provided and that the benefit package should be more open ended to provide more opportunity for civic leaders participating in the review process to negotiate for things they wanted. Developers felt that absent the specific benefit categories their projects were often held hostage to unreasonable demands that could kill a development deal.

Stanley and I argued that there was ample room to negotiate the benefit package, since the planning board was not required to accept a developers' proffers, and requiring greater detail at the sketch plan stage imposed unnecessary costs for detailed architectural and site studies that should not be done until the project

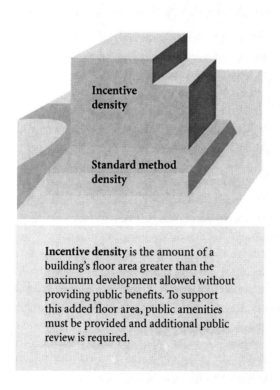

Incentive density

Standard method density

Incentive density is the amount of a building's floor area greater than the maximum development allowed without providing public benefits. To support this added floor area, public amenities must be provided and additional public review is required.

FIGURE 5.1   Structure of the CR Zone

Source: Montgomery County Planning Department M-NCPPC.

returned for public site plan review. After months of bargaining, hearings, deliberations by board and council, and a few substantively inconsequential but symbolically appropriate amendments, the council unanimously adopted the CR zones in March 2010.[8]

The CR zones relied primarily on incentives in the form of density increases in return for provision of public benefits and amenities. The one exception was a requirement that 5 percent of the additional density granted for development using the optional method must come from participation in the BLT program. The board decided on this level of exaction after repeated tests of financial models and discussions with owners of the large tracts with high potential for extensive redevelopment. Five percent was low enough to be absorbed in overall project costs without discouraging redevelopment of old, though still profitable shopping centers and surface parking lots. Because of the scale of redevelopment in White Flint, it was high enough to result in termination of a large number of buildable development rights. The density bonus for each BLT easement was increased to 20,000 square feet of either commercial or residential space. This more generous allotment reduced the per-foot cost and simplified the process. Each BLT easement purchased in addition to the mandatory 5 percent added 30,000 square feet, up to a maximum of 30 percent of a project's optional method density.[9] Builders agreed to accept the BLT requirement in return for improvements in the county's workforce housing requirement to make it less expensive to include affordable units as part of a project.

Commuter Rail and Schools

Once the zoning approach was settled and the zoning envelope was reconciled with a transportation system designed to support it, including public transit and a new street grid, two issues remained: locations for a commuter rail station and an elementary school.

Redevelopment of White Flint provided an opportunity to add a commuter rail station between Silver Spring and Rockville. A new White Flint station could involve closing an historic station in Garrett Park, but generate far more usage. Staff proposed locating the new station at a site parallel with the Metro station, reasoning that although the two stations would be several blocks apart, transfers between the two systems would be facilitated. The Nicholson Lane property owners favored a site where that road crossed the tracks and offered to provide land for a station. Residents of Randolph Hills also supported that location because it provided access from their community. The Town of Garrett Park preferred no new station, but supported the northern site, which posed less danger to retention of its station. The board decided the Nicholson Lane site was the better option because of its access from both sides of the tracks and concluded that Rockville, where the train and Metro stations were close to each other, was a better place for transfers between lines for the few commuters that would switch systems.

Middle and high schools serving White Flint could accommodate the additional students but an additional elementary school might be needed. Staff initially recommended two potential sites in the planning area. Both were about five-to-six acres, about half the size of the standard suburban elementary school campus. School officials were cool to the idea of a site that did not meet traditional suburban acreage standards. As alternatives to a more "urban" campus, the staff draft suggested meeting the elementary school needs of the area either by reopening one of several former elementary schools in the vicinity that had been converted to other uses, or by adjusting attendance boundaries to send the new White Flint students to a school with excess classroom capacity.

Civic leaders from Randolph Hills urged reopening the elementary school in their neighborhood. Garrett Park Estates representatives opposed one suggested site they felt infringed on the small neighborhood park that buffered their community from the mall and placed the new school near their own elementary school. The Luxmanor Parent-Teacher-Student Association was horrified at the idea of redistricting, which could place them in a high school cluster they considered less desirable than the status quo.

During planning board work sessions Robinson and I argued that if an elementary school was needed, it should be at a site within the planning area to which students could easily walk. Our three colleagues, however, felt that it was important to have a standard campus and favored reopening the closed Randolph Hills School, which became the recommendation of the board.

The Politics of Council Approval

While the council debated the CR zone and the board finished work on the plan, Barnaby Zall and Evan Goldman mobilized Friends of White Flint supporters to testify in favor of the sector plan at the council's hearing. As a result, in contrast to past sector plan hearings at which community groups provided repetitive testimony denouncing the impacts of density, heights, and traffic on their neighborhoods, seventy witnesses—including residents of every age, ethnic, and income group praised the plan—expressed excitement about the focus on the pedestrian environment, mixture of uses, and opportunity for an active urban environment.

Only twenty-five witnesses appeared in opposition. Goldberg supported many aspects of the plan but reprised her community's concerns about traffic.

The most strident opposition dealt with the elementary school. School officials and some council members complained that the planning board should not recommend a site the school system opposed or even hint that it might be appropriate to redraw cluster boundaries. That hint was enough to mobilize Luxmanor and other parents from the Walter Johnson Cluster. They turned out in large numbers at the council's hearing, wearing tee shirts emblazoned with "Save Our Schools" and demanding salvation from future redistricting into the Einstein Cluster. The matter was amicably resolved when planning staff brokered a deal in which the owner of White Flint Mall and civic leaders of Garrett Park Estates agreed on a site of some five acres on the southern boundary of the mall property. The property owner could provide the site as a public benefit proffered when it redeveloped under a CR zone.

Two material matters remained in contention: transportation capacity and a method of financing necessary infrastructure and facilities. The most protracted discussion centered on traffic generation and flow through the area when fully developed. Although the transportation models used by the planning staff indicated an acceptable level of service, auto speeds on the reconstructed Rockville Pike would be slowed to urban rather than suburban standards. Public transportation would be enhanced by a second Metro portal and greater regional and local bus service, including a possible Bus Rapid Transit route on the Pike. The county's Department of Transportation objected to allowing higher levels of congestion, and therefore, slower speeds, in areas like White Flint that had better transit service. Consequently, the county executive recommended a reduction in the overall density of the plan.

Council Member Marc Elrich supported neighborhood and civic interests in questioning the plan's traffic analysis and density recommendations, arguing that Metro would be overcrowded and higher congestion levels and slower roadway speeds should not be tolerated. In response, I pointed to the experience of Arlington County where density in one of its major transportation corridors increased, pedestrian and Metro travel grew but auto traffic and roadway congestion declined as people relied less on cars for commuting. Fortunately, council staff concluded that the land use and transportation systems of the plan were in appropriate balance. As a sop to the opposition, the council provided for a monitoring committee to review progress in implementing the plan.

A Financing Mechanism

From the outset of work on the plan it was clear that a special financing mechanism would be necessary to produce the needed transportation infrastructure and some of the other public facilities in a timely manner. Studies by the planning staff and Partnership consultants agreed that a levy of an additional 10 percent on nonresidential property could finance facilities that could not be obtained through development exactions or incentives, particularly the transformation of Rockville Pike into a boulevard. Developers indicated a willingness to accept such a tax because it would facilitate development and add value to their projects that could be recovered in rent and return to investment. Both studies indicated that development of the White Flint area would generate a net revenue benefit for the county in the range of $6–$8 billion over its thirty-five to forty-year build out period.

Accordingly, the planning board suggested a tax increment district and/or a special tax district should be considered, pointing out that:

> Excessive reliance on piecemeal private sector delivery of capital facilities can result in haphazard, "Swiss-cheese" development patterns. Excessive reliance on public sector capital improvement programming can often result in infrastructure delivery that is slowed by politics or bonding capacity, and which favors projects that add lane capacity over those that improve aesthetic qualities of place. As such, finding the proper balance between public and private sector financing and delivery of infrastructure can prove critical to successful implementation of complex redevelopment plans.[10]

Representatives of the county executive objected to any discussion of financing in the plan, arguing that such matters were beyond the jurisdiction of the planning board.[11] Sesker's preliminary discussions with the county Finance Department were not productive. In November 2008, as the plan was being published for the board's public hearing, I called Tim Firestine, the chief administrative officer of the county and asked for a meeting with the appropriate department heads to discuss with them an appropriate financing mechanism. I outlined the importance of White Flint to the future of the county, our estimate of the costs, and asked that the executive branch work with us on a financing mechanism.

There was no movement from the executive, so the board included in the plan sent to the council a proposal to create a Redevelopment Implementation Authority empowered to levy taxes, issue bonds, condemn property, program and build facilities. This was a stalking horse, designed to get a response from the executive, which it did. But instead of proposing an alternative, the executive simply opposed the authority and urged that the proposal be reworked.[12] Basically, the finance department opposed a tax increment district as that would allow White Flint to recapture some of the increased revenue from its development, preventing the county from using that additional revenue wherever it pleased.

FIGURE 5.2 Redevelopment in White Flint. Top: 1960s-era Mid-Pike Plaza before redevelopment. Bottom: Model for Pike and Rose. The first phase was built and occupied by 2015. Courtesy Montgomery County Planning Department M-NCPPC

Frustrated by the executive's intransigence, I urged the property owners to meet with county executive Isiah Leggett to stress the importance of a viable financing system and emphasizing their willingness to participate. I met with members of the council to build support for a special tax district. Still there was no movement from the executive as the council hearing and work sessions proceeded in early 2010. Council members were now expressing frustration at Leggett's reluctance to arrive at some funding approach other than the ordinary capital budget process. Several council members met with him to find a solution, but none was forthcoming by the time the council was ready to take final action to approve the plan. In deference to Leggett, the council removed references in the plan to anything smacking of tax increment financing. Instead it noted that the council and executive would develop a financing mechanism. To spur action by the executive, the council amended the staging element of the plan to require that a financing mechanism had to be established within six months after adoption of the sectional map amendment.

Leggett was finally persuaded of the economic importance of White Flint and agreed with the property owners on a special tax district, similar to one of the alternatives initially proposed by the planning board. The council established the White Flint Development Tax District in November 2010, and levied a 10 percent property surtax to pay for a set of specific infrastructure projects that developers could not be required to provide as conditions of project approval or that involved expenditures unique to the area, such as the conversion of Rockville Pike.[13] The tax exempted projects from the traffic tests of Adequate Public Facilities Ordinance and displaced the usual transportation impact taxes and fees. Once the financing issue was resolved, developers began filing sketch plans for substantial redevelopment projects. Forty-one years after approval of the General Plan, the last major planning project to retrofit the "urban ring" began to take shape.

Continuity and Change in Planning an Urban Future

It is too soon to tell how well White Flint's redevelopment will serve the public interest. Approved sketch plans and site plans for major tracts and construction underway in 2016 suggest considerable promise of achieving the goals of the plan. Experience teaches that some modifications to the plan will be needed as development progresses. What is clear is that White Flint represented a generational shift in the county's planning politics, much as Friendship Heights had thirty-five years earlier.

Friendship Heights and Bethesda initiated a sharp break with past practice, as the planning board took control of the policy agenda from the land use bar. It established infrastructure capacity as a limitation on the volume of development in an area. Planning took precedence over individual zoning and subdivision cases. Linking the application of zones to sector plans and requiring projects proposed under the zones to be consistent with plan recommendations gave plans regulatory authority rather than function merely as guidelines. The redevelopment of Silver Spring, although it occurred a generation later, followed the same pattern and used the same basic policy tools, plus urban renewal land acquisitions, subsidies, and negotiated development agreements.

Despite their significance the planning and regulatory measures were products of their time, crafted to accommodate the *suburban* sensibilities of the Progressive Regime. Their legitimacy ultimately rested on the perceptions of the people of the miniature republics who lived outside the business districts and station areas, not on those that might live and work within them. They aimed to tame and manage the commercial republic, first by down zoning to remove the specter of overpowering development, then allowing a more modest increment of density, circumscribed by elaborate public review.

White Flint maintained continuity with the established planning and zoning structure but made subtle shifts in emphasis and technique. The sector plan and the new CR zones accommodated the *urban* sensibilities of the people that would live and work inside the planning area; a population with weak ties to the values of the established miniature republics of suburban Montgomery. Young, newly forming, and nontraditional households; newcomers to the county and nation; mobile professionals and prospective merchants; empty nesters escaping lawn care and two cars—these new urbanites lacked a common ideology or organization. They were more likely to meet on Facebook, at Starbucks, or the health club than at the PTA or the Chamber of Commerce, and to govern their residential communities through a condominium or renters association. More autonomous of each other than citizens of the suburban miniature republic and less inclined to collective action, Zall and Goldman proved they could be mobilized to support a shared interest in the convenience, amenity, and activity of an urban village.

These new urbanites altered the political environment and opened a window of opportunity for changes in policy. For the first time in memory, more residents praised a plan than disparaged it at the council's public hearing. Their powerful support provided the independent entrepreneurs of the Pure Political Regime an alternative constituency to traditional neighborhood activists. This made endorsing the increased density of White Flint responsive to urgent public demand rather than truckling to developers. Without it, it seems unlikely that the plan and the CR zones would have ultimately received unanimous council support.

The common cause of the developers and the urbanites also allowed a conceptual shift from fixation on congestion and the capacity of infrastructure toward consideration of how organization and design of the built environment could affect builder, resident, and worker behavior. Thus, incentives were designed to enhance connectivity among uses, energy conservation, non-auto travel, and to create a public realm of interest, amenity, and activity. The density necessary to support these public benefits generated a handsome return on investment for the private sector and fiscal surplus for the county treasury. This justified, indeed necessitated, an economic element in the form of a special tax district and a mechanism for coordinating the production of public infrastructure with the progress of private development. The aggregate effect was a shift in land use policy from its traditional obsession with capacity toward an emphasis on sustainability.

Casting the plan in terms of sustainability helped the county come to terms with its long- standing difficult relationship with the commercial republic. It recognized the county's ability to accommodate the growth of its population and economy required redeveloping areas that had grown functionally obsolete or were poorly or inadequately developed to meet emerging needs. The plan and the zones tailored to implement it called attention to the fact that the county could no longer rely on exponential growth in the value of single-family homes to support the services demanded by a growing and increasingly diverse population. The future fiscal health of the county would depend ever more heavily on high value commercial and multiunit residential property and on a decline in the proportion of households with school-age children.

The forty years between the Friendship Heights and White Flint sector plans encapsulate the evolution of planning politics in Montgomery County. Each iteration built on previous experience. At each step, professional development and changes in public attitudes and political support were mutually reinforcing in some policy arenas, mutually limiting in others. Until White Flint, the basic array of interests remained remarkably stable. Neighborhood protectors, developers and their attorneys, planners, and politicians played their well-rehearsed roles. There was little innovation in plan production or zoning until White Flint.

The tension caused by conflicting interests in certainty and flexibility among both developers and community groups was reflected in the debate over the CR zones. Developers wanted certainty they could proceed if they met clear standards and provided specified benefits. "Just tell us what we have to do," they insisted. But they also wanted enough flexibility to adapt to market trends and gain timely approval to modify a project's design based on better information about site conditions or for other reasons both the builder and regulators agreed were desirable. Civic activists wanted the certainty that what the master plan showed was what they would eventually get and that the public benefits and amenities of development would strike a favorable balance with real and perceived adverse effects. But they wanted enough room in the project approval process to allow them to negotiate better outcomes for their communities.

Approval of the White Flint Sector Plan and agreement on a new approach to zoning and financing of its infrastructure represented a maturation of planning politics. Consensus had been forming since the first sector plan in Friendship Heights favoring mixed-use development at strategic Metro stations. Development of Smart Growth policies at the state level reinforced this consensus. The evolution of zoning from the CBD and transit station zones of the 1970s to the CR zones of 2010 were exercises in organizational learning as planners, builders, and citizens experienced both the processes and outcomes of the earlier policies. Ironically, as the gulf between "citizens" and "developers" narrowed to provide strong public support for the White Flint Plan, the CR zone, and a novel (for Montgomery) approach to funding the necessary infrastructure, the principal resistance came from council and executive bureaucrats uneasy with changing established ways.

Some Lessons from the Urban Ring

The forty-year process of reimagining the urban ring's auto-oriented commercial districts and rebuilding them as coherent transit-oriented downtowns of "Edge Cities" illustrates the challenges of moving a place's planning politics from a suburban to an urban orientation. Planning institutions are as susceptible as other bureaucracies to the inertia of going concerns. They tend to do what they know how to do. Breaking the suburban mold is not natural or easy. Spurts of innovation, as in the creation of the CBD zones and sector plans, were succeeded by long periods of repetition of past techniques even as conditions changed and experience accumulated that they were not performing adequately. As Christensen pointed out in *The Innovator's Dilemma*, the tendency is to make marginal improvements on a widely used product rather than replace it with something different and better, in part because its producers and consumers haven't discovered they need it until it is invented.[14]

Innovation in land use policy occurs in an environment of suspicion by both miniature and commercial republics. The former fear change; the latter increased regulation and higher transaction costs. Elected officials elected on promises to "think outside the box" find being outside it disorienting. They want assurance that a proposed unfamiliar policy has succeeded elsewhere. What is being done may not be working, but it is being done better than ever.

The experience of Montgomery's mixed-use centers demonstrates that plans without markets cannot succeed. This fact of life makes it imperative that plans include careful economic analysis and address the institutional as well as the physical infrastructure needed to redevelop older, obsolete districts. Both the use of renewal authority to consolidate land and establishment of an office to coordinate public and private activity in Silver Spring, and the creation of a special taxing district to fund transportation infrastructure in White Flint were critical to their successes.

Finally, as painful as it sometimes is for planners and politicians, broad participation of the miniature and commercial republics in the development of plans and policy tools is essential to reaching appropriate, and thus, legitimate decisions. In some cases, public participation and deliberation reverses the order of the logics of planning politics. Settling at least tentatively on an appropriate response may be necessary before the logic of consequentiality can be put to work.

6

TRIALS IN CORRIDOR CITY PLANNING

The distinctive development policy of the General Plan was its recommendation that a large portion of the future growth of Montgomery County should occur in four planned new cities built along the I-270/MD 355 transportation corridor while preserving "wedges" of low-density housing and open space. Each corridor city was to be "self-contained," with a balance of housing and jobs, served by both roads and transit, and encircled by greenbelts of public parkland. All but Rockville would be built mostly on raw land. They would contain a nested hierarchy of homes, neighborhoods, villages, and town centers with commensurate levels of governance, facilities, and services.

The idea of corridor cities melded the interests of the county's miniature and commercial republics—a rare consensus in land use policy. Suburban civic activists strongly supported the idea of vast open spaces and placing much of the county's future growth a respectable distance up the freeway. Landowners in the corridor welcomed the prospect of exponential increases in land values. Developers saw opportunities to serve increasingly diverse housing and commercial markets without local opposition. Officials expected growth in the tax base.

The corridor cities concept shared enthusiasm for the nation's second new towns movement.[1] Robert Simon had begun building Reston in Fairfax County and James Rouse was getting Columbia underway in Howard County. Kettler Brothers assembled land on the edge of Gaithersburg for a planned community. Each project was initiated, planned, and managed by a private developer dealing with a single government. Creating Montgomery's corridor cities would require coping with the problem of many governments for some and the problem of many builders for others.

The Problem of Many Governments

The General Plan imagined Rockville and Gaithersburg as the first corridor cities. Neither municipality was party to the General Plan. Each resisted the destiny *Wedges and Corridors* prescribed for it and had its own ideas of how it should

130

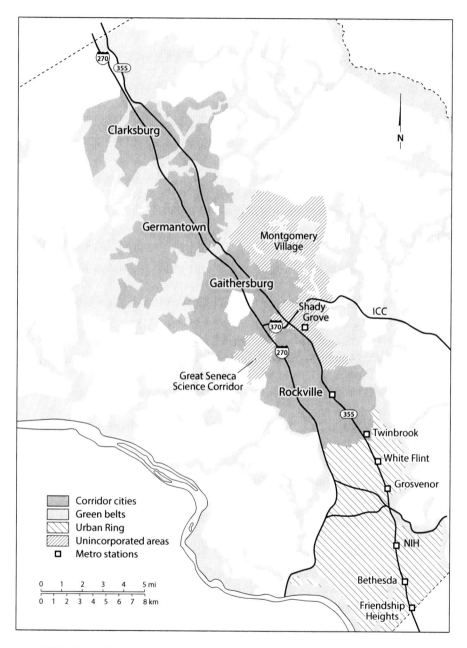

FIGURE 6.1 The I-270 Corridor. Courtesy Montgomery County Planning Department M-NCPPC

grow. Each had planning authority exclusive of the Maryland-National Capital Park and Planning Commission (M-NCPPC) and could follow its own preferences. Both used its annexation powers to frustrate county plans it disliked and to enfold high value projects it liked. Competing interests of the county and the two cities resulted in a pattern of development in the lower corridor that contains islands of well-executed communities and centers in a sea of lightly cabined sprawl.

Rockville

Rockville was already a suburban town of 42,000 in 1969 when the General Plan was approved. Postwar annexations had added large residential subdivisions, a long commercial strip on Rockville Pike, and office parks along I-270. Its 1970 plan acknowledged the wedges and corridors plan, but unequivocally declared: "Rockville is principally a residential community."[2] It annexed more residential and industrial land over the ensuing forty years, built city parks and trails connecting its neighborhoods, and after two failed efforts finally succeeded in redeveloping its historic core with a mixed-use new urbanism town square; welcome relief from the forbidding brutalism of county and court offices.

By 2010, Rockville was largely built out. Almost despite itself, it gradually acquired attributes envisioned for corridor cities while retaining an overall suburban "feel." It had expanded to nearly 9,000 acres. Just under half of its land area was devoted to housing. Forty percent of its 62,500 residents were minorities. Single-family detached homes made up 47 percent of the housing stock and contained slightly over half of the population. With 75,000 jobs and 25,000 homes, the city's 3:1 jobs-housing ratio was double the countywide average. Its neighborhoods, like those of the urban ring, reflected the subdivision conventions of the period in which they were built, ranging from the street grid of its historic core, to the curvilinear streets and modest homes of post-war subdivisions, modernist New Mark Commons, and the new urbanism of King Farm, Twinbrook Station, and Town Square. Having its own local government gave Rockville's residents a miniature republic of political and civic coherence that overcame the occasional incoherence of the development that occurred within its elastic boundary.

Gaithersburg

In contrast with a largely developed Rockville, Gaithersburg in 1960 was a sleepy village of 804 acres and only 3,847 residents. The General Plan envisioned it as a "satellite community," relatively compact in form, separated from Rockville by an extensive industrial park, and surrounded by rural wedges devoted to agriculture and open space.

The Gaithersburg city council, awakened to prospects for growth, aggressively annexed and rezoned adjacent land for higher density residential and commercial uses. Following opportunity rather than a coherent strategy, the city declined to embrace even the rhetoric of *Wedges and Corridors*. Some of its annexations were transparently calculated to frustrate county plans, precipitating legislation that prevented changes to the zoning of annexed land for five years. To some degree, M-NCPPC's lack of realism contributed to the fraught relationship with the city. The 1971 Gaithersburg Vicinity master plan declared rapid transit was the key to development of the corridor city but Metro terminated at Shady Grove, well short of a station proposed for a new central business district at the county fairgrounds near an I-270 interchange.[3] The cumulative effect of Gaithersburg's unplanned growth was short of the plan's vision.[4]

In 2010 half of the city's housing stock was apartments with a high proportion of rental units, giving it one of the highest concentrations of affordable housing in the county and making it attractive to both young and immigrant households.[5] Townhouses comprised another 30 percent. A few exemplary projects relieve the sprawl of residential subdivisions, conventional garden apartments, and office parks. The city preserved its historic "Olde Town" adjacent to the rail station. It fostered Kentlands, an emblematic 400-acre new urbanism community designed by Andrés Duany, cofounder of the Congress for the New Urbanism. The Washingtonian Center, annexed in 1991, was transformed from a failed golf course surrounding a single apartment tower into a well-designed lakeshore mixed-use life-style center. Economically and socially successful in isolation, neither of these "jolly bits" of urbanism brought coherence to the city's 6,600 acres, or to the broader vicinity, divided by city and county planning jurisdictions.

Montgomery Village

Montgomery Village was the one part of the lower corridor that arguably embodied the vision of the General Plan. The land lay in the county, under M-NCPPC jurisdiction.[6] In 1962 Kettler Brothers purchased a 412-acre dairy farm on the northern edge of Gaithersburg, initially intending to build a subdivision of single-family homes. Publication of the General Plan and location of the National Institutes of Science and Technology (NIST) and IBM on nearby tracts induced the firm to rethink plans for the property. Kettler quietly acquired over two dozen adjoining farms and decided to build a planned community containing a wide variety of housing types, business and employment opportunities, large open spaces, and recreation facilities.

No zoning category allowed the variable densities and mixture of housing types and land uses, private streets, and flexibility in design necessary to produce a genuine new town. Kettler's attorney, Norman Glascow, worked with project consultants and M-NCPPC planner Lewis Elston to write a new "Town Sector" (TS) floating zone, which applied the logic of appropriateness to reconcile interests of the commercial and miniature republics. It permitted all of the uses necessary to make the town reasonably self-sufficient, except for "major employment and central business district shopping."[7] A regional mall would be built on adjacent land annexed by Gaithersburg. To avoid opposition to the unconventional zone from the ever-vigilant miniature republics in the urban ring, it required a minimum of 1,500 acres and was restricted to land "lying principally within a corridor city." Subject to approval of site plans, the zone allowed broad flexibility in design, types of units, building heights, and relationships among uses. Residential density was not preassigned to specific tracts but the entire project was limited to an average of fifteen persons per acre, based on the average number of persons occupying different types of housing in 1960.[8] Private streets and common open spaces were required to be held in perpetuity by the developer or a successor homes association, with an easement granted to the county. Land in the TS zone could not be rezoned for fifty years, preventing the developer or subsequent owners from seeking a change and leaving the community unfinished.

Making a rare enlightened decision, the CAP Council adopted the TS zone in May 1965. Kettler immediately applied for rezoning of 1,767.3 acres. The council unanimously approved the zoning for Montgomery Village three months after adoption of the text of the new zone. Construction began in 1966 and the first homes were occupied two years later.

As sole developer and builder, Kettler designed and built everything, including public infrastructure and community facilities. The TS zone required the developer and successor homes associations to own and maintain common property—pedestrian pathways, open spaces, and private streets, and a system of lakes designed for storm water management and recreation. Covenants and deed restrictions created homes corporations for community facilities and the Montgomery Village Foundation to manage village-wide resources and serve as a private government for the village. The developer controlled them until the communities were fairly well settled. Kettler transferred common property debt free to the Foundation and corporations. Moreover, a portion of the proceeds from each home sale was invested in a fund that left each homes corporation a financial nest egg when it assumed control.

As development proceeded over thirty years, shifts in housing demand induced reductions from original plans for multifamily units, rental apartments, and town houses. Implementation of the density bonus under the Moderate-Price Dwelling Unit ordinance resulted in a slight increase in the number of housing units. At the end of the twentieth century Kettler sold the village's commercial and office centers and several rental apartment complexes to other real estate management firms. This resulted in substantial variation in the quality of property management, particularly among rental properties.

Montgomery Village is the largest planned community in Montgomery County developed as a single entity. Additional acquisitions brought it to just over 2,500 acres. Its 2010 population was approximately 35,000. Its development followed the original plan with relatively minor adjustments. The advantage of having a single developer-builder is reflected in a coherent system of interconnected neighborhoods and a high level of consistency in building quality and community amenities. The disadvantage of planning jurisdiction divided between the county and Gaithersburg is that from its inception it could be only a sector of a corridor city. Its approach was replicated only on a small scale in a few places in the city. The overall result was a missed opportunity.

As the village approached its fiftieth anniversary in 2016, the Village Center and related office complexes were financially troubled and relatively obsolete by current standards. Its privately owned golf course, never part of the common lands of the Village, closed and was sold to a developer that reached an accommodation with the Village Foundation to build additional homes on part of it but retaining most as open space. The adjacent regional mall was experiencing problems common to enclosed shopping centers around the country. The planning board prepared a new master plan for the Village and the surrounding land but the division in jurisdictions made a unified plan including the mall, much less for the entire Gaithersburg area, unlikely in spite of their interdependence. Here, Montgomery's planning politics resembled many other places where planning authority is distributed among multiple cities, towns, and counties.

Filling in the Gaps

Rockville, Gaithersburg, and Montgomery Village together occupied 18,000 acres—most of the area the General Plan designated for the first two corridor cities. The cities annexed toward each other but significant space between them remained in county jurisdiction. Initial county land use decisions in these areas contributed to the incoherent development of the lower corridor.

In 1972 County Executive James Gleason, located the county's service park on 300 acres at the terminus of the Shady Grove Metro line. From the singular perspective of logistics for county vehicles, central services for schools and parks, and the county liquor warehouse, the location made sense. There was quick access to I-270 and the then-planned Outer Beltway. However, it precluded establishing a transit-oriented community at the station.

The 1977 *Shady Grove Sector Plan* accepted the fact of the service park and focused on ameliorating its impact on surrounding communities.[9] In 1990, a revised Shady Grove plan, recommended shifting land uses west of the Metro station, including the 440-acre King farm, from industrial uses to "a major employment and housing center."[10]

By the beginning of the twenty-first century, the thirty-year-old facilities in the service park were overcrowded and obsolete. Finally, there was recognition that maintaining a county service park within walking distance of the Shady Grove station was not the best use of the land. Development of King Farm as a new urbanism community at the edge of Rockville demonstrated a strong market for housing near the station. A new Shady Grove sector plan, approved in 2006, recommended relocation of service park facilities and redevelopment of the land with a mixed-use urban village containing a range of housing types and locally oriented businesses.[11] In 2008 County Executive Isiah Leggett announced a "Smart Growth Initiative," and acquired land to move county facilities from the service park to three other locations in the Gaithersburg area. Redevelopment as a mixed-use community began in 2014.

In the late 1970s, County Executive Charles Gilchrist, supported locating Adventist Hospital's mid-county medical center on Shady Grove Road west of I-270 between Rockville and Gaithersburg. The decision followed the county's economic development strategy of concentrating bioscience and other information-based industries along the I-270 corridor. But it established a major employment "center" at the edge of both cities. When the Planning Board revised the Gaithersburg Vicinity Master Plan in 1985 it re-labeled the complex centered on the hospital as the "Research and Development (R&D) Village," but the zoning and transportation decisions produced nothing resembling a village; just sprawling office parks amidst major roads.[12]

During the next twenty-five years the R&D Village was narrowed by annexation of residential land by Rockville and Gaithersburg. Medical offices, bioscience research firms, and branches of the Johns Hopkins University and the Universities of Maryland at Shady Grove (USG) were built in the area. Hopkins also acquired the 138-acre Belward Farm for a future research center. Because local commercial uses were separated from the office and science facilities and there was virtually no housing within the R&D Village, all sectors, including the hospital, depended on automobile travel. An alignment for the Corridor Cities Transitway (CCT), a future transit line linking the Shady Grove Metro station to King Farm, Washingtonian Center, R&D Village, NIST, Germantown, and Clarksburg was approved in 1996 but no funding was provided.[13]

In 2006 David McDonough—Hopkins' director of real estate development— began promoting more intense development of the Belward property and transformation of the R&D Village into a "science city" that could compete with leading international centers of scientific research and industry. Leaders of the commercial republic, County Executive Isiah Leggett and some council members became enamored of the idea. In October 2008 the council directed the planning board to prepare a sector plan for the area for council action in 2009.

The planning challenge was to give the area more coherence to foster agglomeration of life science institutions and businesses by ameliorating a development pattern based in auto-centric conventions of the 1980s. Seven million square feet of existing development limited options. The hospital and related buildings occupied the center of the area, precluding a pedestrian-oriented core. The USG campus and private research institutions were located around the periphery. Conversely, two large office parks that were only half built out and relocation of the county's Public Service Training Academy (PSTA) provided opportunities to introduce more housing into the area.

The plan emphasized mixed-use development and structured parking to reduce the acreage devoted to cars. New streets were introduced to break superblocks, although established development patterns precluded a comprehensive grid. The CCT was realigned to serve the hospital, the PSTA housing site, and Belward. A proposed "green" loop road and pedestrian/bike path connected six districts distinguished by their primary functions: health care, residences, and research. No new major arterial roads were proposed, although the staff and board drafts proposed a new freeway interchange on the northern boundary, which Gaithersburg strongly opposed.

The zoning plan increased the maximum non-residential density of the area from 13 million to 20 million square feet. Belward was limited to 4 million square feet, instead of the 6 million requested by Hopkins, and almost half of it was designated for open space uses to protect the historic farmstead and confronting residential neighborhoods. Residential uses were increased from 3,800 to 9,000 units. Development was staged to coincide with funding of CCT segments.

Two miniature republics arose to oppose the plan. Residents for Responsible Development, an alliance of transit advocates, environmentalists, and civic groups, objected to more density than the 13 million square feet allowed under the existing plan. It opposed CCT realignment to serve Belward and urged concentrating development near the hospital and Hopkins' existing campus. The Gaithersburg-Rockville-North Potomac Coalition decried "Montgomery's Science City Monster." The coalition's president, Donna Baron, asserted the proposed development would be the equivalent of four and a half Pentagons and listed twenty objections to it.[14] Increased density for Belward was denounced and the prospect of increased traffic deplored. Heirs of Elizabeth Banks, the former owner of Belward, joined the opposition to Hopkins' plans for the property, contending it violated the terms of her sale to the university.

County Executive Leggett praised the plan's vision, but recommended reducing non-residential development level to 18 million square feet.[15] The council ultimately left the development ceiling at 20 million, but devised a staging element that allowed only 17.5 million; a reasonable outcome since many existing structures were unlikely to be redeveloped. This symbolic reduction in scale justified removing two highway interchanges, ameliorating concerns of Gaithersburg. With these amendments and 36 pages of other changes that tweaked zoning recommendations for some parcels and added planning poetry to the plan's environmental and sustainability goals, the council unanimously approved the renamed Great Seneca Science Corridor Sector Plan.[16]

Shortly after the plan was approved, the National Cancer Institute began construction of a new facility on the original Hopkins campus. The planning board approved a subdivision plan for the Belward tract that was consistent with the sector plan. The heirs of Elizabeth Banks sued Hopkins but the Maryland Court of Special Appeals held the use restrictions in the sale did not limit the scale of development.[17] The logic of appropriateness smoothed the rough edges of the logic of consequentiality.

Many Governments and Corridor Cities

The division of the lower corridor among Rockville, Gaithersburg, and the county frustrated planning and building the kind of corridor cities proposed by the General Plan. Lack of a common vision and coordination precluded comprehensive application of the logic of consequentiality. Each jurisdiction acted on the logic of what was appropriate for it without addressing broader consequences. Competition resulted in eventual location of a major employment center between the cities on county land rather than at the center of either. That much of the growth in corridor employment occurred during the ascendency of planning doctrines favoring office and industrial parks exacerbated the tendency toward separation of uses and sprawl. Delay in building the CCT contributed to the auto-oriented development pattern but allowed the alignment to be modified in 2010 to serve better the redesigned "Science Corridor."

The cities' lack of enthusiasm for the density and diversity implied by the corridor cities concept was reflected in their decisions, as they annexed vacant or developing land. Some annexations frustrated county policy; others merely moved existing or county-approved projects onto city tax rolls. County executives' preemption of areas remaining in county jurisdiction for a central service park and to create a life sciences complex could be justified by their internal logic but prevented a more comprehensive approach involving county and cities. Facts on the ground then constrained retrofitting the strung out area between the two cities.

There were notable exceptions to this record of planning underachievement: Montgomery Village, Kentlands, and King Farm represented their eras' state-of-the-art in community planning and development. They demonstrated what inspired developers could produce, working with supportive regulators. Each, in its own way, also demonstrated how hard it is to plan, finance, and build complete communities, even when the entire project is under single ownership and management. They were ultimately fragments rather than complete cities, compromised by the amount of land their builders could assemble and by being surrounded by land developed in conventional ways.

It seems unfair to apply too severe hindsight to the shortcomings and disappointments of the past. Planning and development in and around the two cities at the base of the corridor produced some quite desirable communities along with some that provide little beyond shelter. But it is worth noting that the municipal governments of the two cities and the private governments of Montgomery Village and the other planned communities played significant roles in building a sense of place and civic identity that helped overcome some of the deficiencies of their circumstances. The cities are genuine miniature republics with full powers. As such, it is reasonable to assume that each acted in the democratically determined interest of its current public. As for the private governments, the voice they provided was heavily tilted toward homeowners. Renters must find their voices through voluntary organizations when, as often is the case, their interests are not congruent with those of their landlords.

The Problem of Many Builders—Germantown

A decade before the General Plan was adopted the Atomic Energy Commission (AEC) sought a site for its headquarters at least twenty miles from the

White House, assumed to be the range of a twenty-megaton bomb—the largest conceivable at that time. AEC selected a 109-acre farm in Germantown, at the intersection of I-270 (then called U.S. 240) and Germantown Road (MD 118). President Eisenhower dedicated the 516,000 square foot facility in 1957 and it was built in eighteen months. Surrounded by dairy farms, it stood alone until 1966 when Fairchild-Hiller built a research center north of the interchange.

The 1966 Master Plan

Following its adoption of the General Plan, M-NCPPC in 1966 adopted a master plan for Germantown as a corridor city straddling I-270. Both sides of the freeway were reserved for future industrial parks. A town center was located west of the AEC at the historic village served by commuter trains and a proposed extension of the Metro system. High-rise residential uses were proposed south of Germantown Road (MD 118), separated from the commercial and office uses recommended north of it. This "center" was surrounded by residential uses of gradually declining height and density. Neighborhood shopping centers were planned to serve these suburbs. Several lakes were recommended for storm water management and recreation. A greenbelt of parkland surrounded the corridor city. The transportation plan contained a ring road encircling the central core, crossing I-270 and connecting two community centers. Widening the interstate freeway and construction of two new parallel highways were proposed to permit through traffic to bypass Germantown. A dense system of additional roads and other improvements was also recommended.[18]

By the time the Progressive Council elected in 1970 was seated several problems with the 1966 plan were apparent. A review of development activity in Germantown found that fifty-four randomly scattered rezoning applications had been approved for over 2,600 acres of residential development and about 300 acres of industrial and commercial development. Nothing had been done to stage development in an orderly sequence. As a result, the county could face demands for costly extensions of roads, sewers and for school construction well before sufficient development occurred to pay for them. Most of the residential zoning (1,505 acres) was for the Churchill Town Sector, envisioned as a planned community similar to Montgomery Village. While preliminary subdivision plans had been approved for 5,991 housing units, only 239 building permits had been issued.[19] The Metro system was planned to end at Shady Grove, miles short of Germantown. Separation of residential and commercial uses was unlikely to produce a vibrant town center.

The 1974 Comprehensive Amendment

Before my appointment to the Planning Board I had directed Virginia Tech's Center for the Study of New Communities. Based on what I learned from the experience of the second generation of American new towns, I was concerned that the county was on the verge of losing the opportunity presented by Germantown to develop a well-conceived new town. The council approved my request to revise the master plan.

A consultant reported significant problems if Germantown continued to develop as planned. Its transportation system paradoxically included a local road network with more capacity than needed, but left I-270 over-congested and all of Germantown served by a single interchange. Reliance on mass transit was unrealistic since the Metro system would terminate at Shady Grove. No provision was made for a pedestrian system, a critical element in new town planning. Two to three times more land was recommended for commercial and industrial uses than the market could generate. Environmental issues were inadequately addressed. No specific means of implementation or staging was provided.[20]

Staff working on the new master plan raised additional issues. Most of the housing built or approved was townhouses, frustrating the goal of a diverse housing stock. A recent Seneca Creek watershed study emphasized a need for better storm water management facilities. Current population studies forecast a slowing growth rate, which would result in a longer build-out than previously contemplated. Montgomery College had an option to buy land for its third campus in a proposed greenbelt on the southwestern edge of the area, far from the proposed town center and with poor access. This would deprive the center of a source of activity and require early extension of sanitary and transportation facilities to a sector of the planning area that logically should develop in later stages, if at all. The county's decision to locate the hospital center on Shady Grove Road precluded achieving the goal of placing a hospital in Germantown in early stages of its development.

The most significant problem with Germantown, however, was that unlike Reston, Columbia, or Montgomery Village, there was no single owner or master developer. Aside from Churchill, no single property was large enough to meet the minimum acreage requirement for the Town Sector zone, and no other existing zone permitted the variety of housing or the mixture of uses needed to produce a reasonable approximation of a new town. The remaining 9,500 acres were divided among over 100 landowners. Builders in the Germantown market specialized in a single product—homes or commercial buildings. Few, if any, had access to the long-term capital needed to bear the front-end costs of infrastructure and land development for large-scale development. For the corridor city to develop as a coherent, complete new town, the county government would have to be more intensely involved in Germantown's development than was the case for Reston or Columbia.

The planning challenge was to produce a plan to guide creation of a new town by multiple developers over several decades. It had to do more than address the deficiencies identified in the 1966 plan and lay the foundation for production of a complete, coherent, and functioning "town." Following prevailing approaches to new town planning, this involved creating a hierarchy of communities, starting with neighborhoods organized into villages containing a variety of housing opportunities, and capped by a town center for intense urban activity. Community services and facilities and employment opportunities would be provided at appropriate scale for each village and the center.

Putting in place policies to achieve such a pattern required redirecting the nature and timing of development, aborting the ad hoc rezoning and subdivision process. Such a plan had to be more than guidelines landowners and officials could ignore if inconvenient. It required invention of new planning and regulatory techniques, and the political will to install and use them. A large number of subdivisions had been approved but little actual building had occurred due to the sewer moratorium and a soft market. Thus, the staff was working with open land as it shaped a draft plan that would frame the debate among stakeholders and the decisions of the board and council. The principal constraints were the landform and transportation capacity.

Great Seneca Creek on the south and its principal tributary, Little Seneca Creek, on the north, largely enclosed the planning area in a greenbelt of stream valley parkland. Smaller tributaries ran roughly perpendicular to both creeks from the ridgeline of Germantown Road. Delineation of floodplains and steep slopes provided the basis for recommendations for conservation, storm water management, and active recreation areas threaded throughout the new town. Buildable areas were based on the suitability of soils for development. An inventory of historic and cultural resources was conducted to identify those that should be preserved.

The road system and the railroad provided boundaries for six villages. The Town Center was relocated to the northwest quadrant formed by I-270 and Germantown Road. Staff recommended relocating Montgomery College nearer the town center in the southeast quadrant. Based on this recommendation, the planning board, exercising its mandatory review authority, recommended against the college's proposed site at the edge of Germantown. Although the board's action was advisory, I made sure members of the council, which would have to appropriate funds for site acquisition, understood the board's reasoning. After several intense discussions with college trustees and administrators, they agreed to the new location. This was not ideal from a planning perspective as it was still some distance from the town center, but it had excellent access, the parcel was available and large enough to accommodate future expansion of the campus, and it was *near*, if not *in* the center.

The transportation analysis found the road system could serve no more than 120,000 residents at an acceptable level of service. It also provided the basis for staging private development in coordination with the major roadway and other transportation improvements. The internal road network was changed from a loop to a "ladder" and land use densities were reallocated to be in balance with the roadway system. A second full interchange was recommended on I-270. The western and eastern arterials were retained. Transit recommendations were vague. Internal and external bus service was proposed, pending extension of a transit line from Shady Grove.

The plan devoted detailed attention to the six villages and town center. The objective was to create coherent neighborhoods by connecting separate subdivisions and to ensure provision of public and private facilities and amenities. Neighborhoods were aggregated into villages, with schools, parks, shops, and other services. Town-wide facilities and services such as the college, regional parks, a central library, and a hospital were planned for the town center and other specialized locations. The staff draft was a model of the rational method embodied in the logic of consequentiality.

The Staging Element

The most controversial element of the plan was its recommendation to develop Germantown in four stages to enable the county to provide public facilities in an orderly, efficient, and timely fashion. One set of villages would be the relatively complete before moving on to the next. Zoning and land development in each stage were to be coordinated with "the provision of publicly financed capital improvements for sewer, water, storm water management, transportation, education, parks and recreation, and other public services."[21] The plan called for the county to rezone land in successive stages to provide a competitive market. Euclidean zones with densities pegged just above the taking threshold and applied by sectional map amendment would function as "holding zones," producing strong incentives for owners to apply for a new Planned Development floating zone recommended to achieve the full density.[22] This mimicked the technique recommended for transit station areas outside of central business districts in the urban ring, but it was a sharp departure from the long-established practice in which developers essentially determined the sequence of development by buying land as opportunity arose, applied for rezoning on their timetable, and worked out an agreement with the sanitary commission for extension of water and sewer lines. Once homes were under construction and being occupied, the county responded to demands for roads, schools, and other facilities; often playing catch-up.

Two policy tools would manage provision of public facilities concurrently with development. Water and sewer extensions would be controlled by the Ten-Year Water and Sewerage System Plan, which designated time intervals for extending water and sewerage service. All other county facilities were scheduled through the six-year Capital Improvements Program (CIP), which the council revised and adopted annually after receiving recommendations from the county executive and the planning board.

The state presented a special problem for the plan. The CIP did not control state roads. The acting administrator of the State Highway Administration opposed "any additional interchanges with I-70-S [I-270] in the Germantown Master Plan Area until I-70-S is widened to eight (8) lanes and the Outer Beltway is constructed."[23] The State Highway Administration's support for two interchanges was contingent on the planning board and county council supporting the construction of a Western Arterial to freeway standards from Germantown to the Outer Beltway, and locating it so that it could be part of a continuous route from Rockville through Germantown to Frederick County.

A new Adequate Public Facilities Ordinance (APFO) was the linchpin for enforcement of the staging program. It required the planning board to deny a subdivision unless it determined that public facilities were adequate to support and serve it.[24] In a newly developing area like Germantown, roads and sewers were facilities without which a subdivision could not be built. Finding insufficient road capacity or that water and sewer were not available provided a solid basis on which to deny approval of a subdivision.

The landowners in Germantown and the development industry adamantly opposed APFO-enforced staging—especially since it looked like it could work. One landowner charged:

> The proposed staging plan, if adopted, would create unconstitutional discrimination, denial of equal protection of the laws, denial of due process, and could result in confiscation of property rights in the proposed village of Neelsville for a period of twenty years or more.[25]

The developers of the Churchill Village argued that with over $2 million already spent on land development: "There cannot be arbitrary and artificial staging policies superimposed on our development schedule." They decried staging policy as "only one step from dictating exactly which buildings and homes will be built and in which order. Private industry will soon suffocate under this supposed blanket of public protection."[26]

In the occasionally heated exchanges during the public hearing and work sessions on the plan, I reminded developers that there were two major investors in their projects. Their bankers provided loans and lines of credit to finance land acquisition and construction. Public-financed infrastructure was as essential as the bank loan. The cost of facilities was not borne solely by the developers or the buyers of the homes they built. Rather, they were added to the capital budget of the county and, thus, shared by all county taxpayers. Just as a bank was entitled to a reasonable return on its private investment, taxpayers were entitled to assurance that their investment would not result in excessive costs due to premature expansion and extension of facilities into new areas. The builders were unmoved. They regarded infrastructure and other facilities as public utilities that should automatically be extended wherever they built homes.

The planning board made one significant change in the staff's staging plan recommendations. Rather than set specific dates for moving from one stage to the next, it opened successive stages on the occurrence of certain events, such as the end of the sewer moratorium, funding of certain facilities in the CIP of the county or state, and completion of a portion of development in earlier stages.

The council accepted the staging approach of the Germantown plan, and with it, established staging as a regular element of master plans and growth management policy. The approved and adopted plan also created a monitoring process to provide for the initiation of amendments to the plan and other measures such as CIP changes as they became necessary or useful to achieve plan objectives. This also became a common feature of subsequent master plans.

Homes without a City

A 1976 study of the social and institutional development of Germantown found that 90 percent of its 6,600 residents were unaware they lived in a new town and neither developers, the county, nor the planning board were taking steps to build the institutions necessary for development of a self-conscious community.[27] It noted that "Although building is well underway in Germantown, there is no indication that villages exist and the neighborhoods are perceived to be entities unto themselves with no relationship to each other, to a village, or to the new town."[28]

Several factors explain lack of a "Germantown" consciousness. Marketing of homes was disaggregated, so there was no common "branding" of the separate subdivisions as part of a larger New Town. Each subdivision had its own homes association but there was no umbrella organization to manage common property, provide community services at the village or town scale, or provide a community voice. Many households were renters, for whom there was no compulsory association. Two-earner households had little leisure time for community meetings.

The monitoring committee kept track of changes in the physical development of Germantown and made adjustments in the staging of development and facilities, but institutional development was no one's job. County agencies were not organized to promote and serve Germantown as a distinctive community apart from the county as a whole. The absence of a municipal government or the presence of an umbrella organization such as the Columbia Association or the Montgomery Village Foundation stunted civic development.

Energy costs and soaring interest rates of the late 1970s and early 1980s contributed to difficulties in diversifying the housing stock. Higher monthly mortgage payments meant many buyers could not afford larger detached homes. Foreclosures and bankruptcies among builders increased and property ownership churned. Churchill's developers sold off sections so that the largest single project in Germantown was no longer being built to a common vision. At the same time, the demand for starter homes was at a historic peak, which further dampened the market for both more expensive detached houses and apartment living. This led developers with approved plans for apartments and detached houses to revise them to build townhouses instead. Further contributing to the tilt toward townhouses, most housing in low-density residential zones was built using the cluster option to comply with the Moderate Priced Dwelling Unit (MPDU) ordinance and to maximize open space and protect environmental resources. As it gradually recognized the extent of the problem, the planning board started approving increases in attached units only where environmental problems were severe.

Because approval of subdivision plans occurred piecemeal, it was not until the planning board began a general revision of the Germantown plan in 1987 that the cumulative effects of its decisions were fully appreciated. Planning Board Chair Norman Christeller reported to his colleagues that single-family detached housing accounted for only 18 percent (3,545 units) of all housing that had been built or approved in the planning area. Attached single-family dwellings—primarily townhouses—accounted for 51.3 percent (9,843 units). The remaining 30.2 percent (5,811 units) were in multi-family buildings.[29]

By 1987 as the county began transition from the Progressive to the Pure Political Regime, only a third of the land in Germantown (3,500 acres) remained uncommitted for development. Two villages were largely complete. Two had experienced little development. To that extent, staging worked. As the planning staff began to revise the master plan, they reported that the basic concept of a "new town" remained valid. However, implementing the assumption that the county could guide development by multiple owners, they confessed: "we soon found was tough to do." They added: "We learned a lot about community development and corridor city development. . . . And so we've realized over the years that community identity is an issue here."[30] Gene Brooks, the planning department's urban design chief emphasized six elements for which guidelines should be enforced: a pedestrian-bikeway system; transit accessibility; concentration of development in activity centers; screening parking from streets; improved signage; and development of gateway features.[31]

Town without a Center

The town center remained underdeveloped. To create a livelier "downtown" and sense of place, the staff proposed merging the village center for Churchill Village into an expanded town center that would include regional comparison shopping along with multifamily housing and offices. Two convenience shopping areas had already developed to serve Churchill Village. Most of the town center was in the TS zone, which permitted only convenience commercial uses. Staff recommended replacing it with a new Mixed-Use Planned Development (MXPD) zone that would allow more intensive housing, commercial and office development.

The future of the town center was placed in doubt by two other projects in Neelsville Village. The Marriott Corporation proposed building its international headquarters on 157 acres in acquired. Developer Jay Alfandre proposed a regional shopping center adjacent to the Marriott tract on land that had been designated as the Neelsville Village Center. County Executive Sidney Kramer enthusiastically supported both projects as boons to the county economy. The planning board could approve neither of them under the Adequate Public Facilities Ordinance because road improvements called for in the master plan had not been made.

Council Member William Hanna proposed amending the rules governing administration of the APFO so both projects could go forward. He complained: "We find ourselves totally immobilized. We're here to exercise judgment, not to have a set of rules so rigid that a computer could give you the answer." His colleague, Isiah Leggett, agreed, saying a majority of the council held the key to whether large new projects could go ahead despite moratoria. "It places us in no worse position than in the past in terms of land use," he added.[32] The council concurred, provided the developers contributed to the cost of necessary road improvements.[33] The Pure Political Regime's independent political entrepreneurs began eroding the Progressive Regime's commitment to coherent new town planning.

In August 1988, before work on the staff draft plan was completed, a divided board, now with two commissioners appointed by Kramer, approved Alfandre's project, rejecting contrary warnings from its staff as well as the executive's planning office that it undermined the ability to create a strong town center.[34] The board's final draft of the plan, therefore, included the mall, while continuing to recommend comparison shopping for the town center.

As Table 6.1 indicates, the planning board modified the housing mix. It increased the proportion of single-family units from 18 to 31 percent and reduced attached units from 54 to 41 percent of total at build-out. These changes were to increase opportunity to achieve a "full life cycle" community. They reduced the "build out" population from the 1974 plan's estimate of 110,000 to 91,000. The board recommended creating two "urban villages" in the employment corridor by adding multi-family housing to the commercial and industrial uses, arguing it would reduce trip generation and relieve the monotony of the great swath of office/industrial parks stretching the length I-270 as it traversed Germantown. Finally, it proposed realigning the Corridor Cities Transitway (CCT) to serve the industrial/office corridor and Montgomery College.

Kramer objected to the proposal for the urban villages and asked the board to delay action on the plan.[35] Using the enhanced powers granted the executive by the 1986 amendments, Kramer revised the board's draft, expanding the employment corridor by 100 acres, eliminating the proposed housing, and limiting uses to industry and offices. He accepted the realignment for the CCT, added a middle school, and eliminated one park. He also recommended that a transportation study be conducted before the third stage of development began to determine the

TABLE 6.1   Comparison of drafts of 1989 Germantown Master Plan, selected issues

RECOMMENDATION	STAFF	BOARD	EXECUTIVE	COUNCIL
Build-out population	91,000	85,000	n.a.	91,000
Total dwelling units	27,600	35,000	35,000	38,000
Single-family detached	28%	30%	30%	29%
Single-family attached	41%	34%	34%	31%
Multi-family	31%	36%	36%	40%
Transf. devel. rights	497	1,600	1,600	2,300
MXPD or TS in town ctr.	MXPD	TS	TS	TS
Mixed uses in empl. cor.	O/R/I	O/R/MF/I	I/O	O/R/MF/I
Storm water management	Wet ponds	General	General	General
Historic sites preserved	General	8	8	10
New local parks	16	18	17	18
CCT alignment/stations	West/2	West/3	East/3	West/?
New schools	5E/1M/1HS	6E/1M/1H	6E/2M/1H	6E/2M/1H

Sources: Montgomery County Department of Planning. August 1987. Staff Draft Germantown Master Plan; Montgomery County Planning Board. October 1988. Final Draft Germantown Master Plan; Montgomery County Executive. December 1988. County Executive Draft Germanton Master Plan; MNCPPC. July 1989. *Approved and Adopted Germantown Master Plan*; Montgomery County Council. June 13, 1989. Resolution No. 11-1498.

feasibility of transportation improvements or mitigation measures to support further growth of the employment corridor.

The council, however, accepted only his recommendation for the additional middle school. A major departure from board recommendations added 3000 housing units. The council also increased to 2300 the number of transferable development rights (TDRs) available for projects in Germantown. This decision was a well-intended effort to increase competition for TDRs and, thereby, help preserve farmland in the Agricultural Reserve. The combination of this policy with MPDU requirements increased density for each residential subdivision. This made clustering desirable if not mandatory to achieve the maximum yield of units and still meet requirements for open spaces and conservation of environmental resources. The conjunction of these regulations—each commendable standing alone—with high interest rates had the perverse effect of making detached housing infeasible and furthered the imbalance of attached housing in Germantown.

Rethinking the Employment Corridor

In the two decades following adoption of the 1989 Germantown master plan residential development continued at a brisk pace. By 2010, 86,000 residents populated 32,000 housing units. The town center finally began to take shape. A new regional library and the adjacent Black Rock Center for the Arts provided a focal point for a pleasant low-density pedestrian-friendly main street lined with consumer-oriented shops.

Development of the employment corridor continued to lag behind housing, however. Instead of the regional mall, Alfandre built an auto-oriented big-box center on the Neelsville site. The planning board approved Marriott's subdivision for a 3.1 million square feet international headquarters. The company balked at the substantial contribution the county demanded for roads serving the project, even after Kramer gained state support for $18 million in road improvements. After the council failed to approve rezoning for mixed uses allowing some housing, Marriott abandoned the site, selling it in 1997. Marriott's new international headquarters was eventually built in the North Bethesda office park adjacent to Montgomery Mall, with $44 million in state and local subsidies.[36]

A 2006 report by an Urban Land Institute (ULI) panel found that "The single-use zoning of the employment corridor is not the form that will best serve the market of the next five to ten years for higher-density- employment users."[37] Industrial zoning resulted in its underdevelopment and signature sites with high visibility remained undeveloped. The ULI team recommended revision of the

1989 plan to introduce an urban street grid to break up superblocks, encourage mixed uses, and foster a more pedestrian-oriented environment.[38]

In 2009 a new sector plan was approved. Covering roughly 2400 acres, it recommended mixed-uses and higher densities for the corridor and town center, served by five transit stations. The new plan established stronger design policies for development of vacant tracts and redevelopment of some underutilized properties in each sub-area. A street grid was introduced to break up the superblocks, and increased housing densities were proposed for areas close to transit stations and the commuter rail station in the historic district.[39]

Taking Stock of the First Corridor Cities

Rockville, Gaithersburg, and Germantown exemplify the challenges of resolving the tension between public disdain for sprawl and objections to increased density. From the perspective of the planners as stewards of the General Plan, there could be no wedges without the corridor. Translating a design concept into operational policies was daunting, particularly in coping with many governments and many builders. Persuading politicians with shifting and uncertain constituencies to adopt, pursue, and enforce policies consistent with the plans over many years in a resistant, diffuse, and changing market compounded the problem. At a number of points when it mattered, decision makers took the short rather than the long view, a tendency that grew in the Pure Political Regime. Given the competing political and economic interests involved, it is remarkable that fifty years after it was proposed, the corridor can be identified on satellite imagery of the metropolitan area.

At the outset of corridor development in the mid-1960s, there was a strong market for single-family attached homes. High interest rates in the 1970s and 1980s, combined with demand for starter homes, skewed the corridor market heavily toward townhouses. Even in recessionary periods and in spite of high financing costs, the market for homes in the Gaithersburg area and Germantown remained robust. This was a function of relatively low land costs due to distance from major employment centers, small lots, and lower per-unit construction costs of townhouses. Meanwhile, low values for commercial and industrial land, reinforced by office and industrial park zoning, produced a proliferation of single-use low-rise buildings surrounded by vast expanses of surface parking.

Unlike Rockville, Gaithersburg, and Montgomery Village, Germantown had neither municipal powers nor a private governance institution with access to resources and a mandate to serve the interests of the entire "town." The homes associations established for each subdivision lacked substantial resources and were not affiliated through a larger organization that could promote a common identity or enforce any consistent standards of design or services. Germantown lacked a miniature republic at its conception. As it developed, no institution took root that could mobilize its residents to bring a civic voice to policies affecting its development. Thus, developers had more influence and their projects less scrutiny than might otherwise have been the case.

The planning board's site plan authority did not extend to the establishment of architectural standards common in other new towns and planned communities, and it was not until a later time that the board began to establish guidelines for such features as street lighting, sidewalks, and tree cover. Subdivision and site plan approvals were, at best crude tools for enforcement of a New Town vision when the horizons of most developers and builders were circumscribed by the call dates on their loans. They built houses, not villages; commercial buildings and strip malls, not business districts and town centers.

Creation of a strong town center in Germantown was frustrated by both market and policy failures. The opening of Lakeforest Mall next to Montgomery Village preempted any near term opportunity for making Germantown the up-county regional comparison shopping center. Although Montgomery Collage was persuaded to move near the center of the new town, its location across the interstate highway and the college's commitment to a traditional suburban campus did not contribute to activation of the center or joint use of its facilities with the community as the planners hoped. But bringing the college into the Germantown employment corridor facilitated its engagement with the local business community. It formed partnerships with a developer for a technology business incubator and with Holy Cross Hospital for an up-county facility on the campus.

When a divided planning board approved Alfandre's shopping center in Neelsville Village against the advice of both planning and executive staffs, Germantown was dealt a double disappointment. The town center's development was stunted for two decades. And instead of becoming the regional mixed-use center initially proposed, the project devolved into a collection of big box stores ringing a vast expanse of surface parking. While these emporiums served important up county consumer demand, they made no contribution to distinguishing Germantown from conventional suburbia. On the other hand, the town center was spared eighty acres of asphalt and, thus, retained a chance to become a business district oriented to transit and pedestrians.

The 2009 sector plan provided some measures to strengthen the town center, which was slowly developing as an amenable business district. Much depended on timely construction of the Corridor Cities Transitway (CCT). The plan's initial recommendation to concentrate the highest densities nearest the center was undercut by council amendments that allowed greater densities and earlier development for peripheral tracts in response to appeals from landowners and lack of countervailing public support for the board's recommendations. Without a common sense of purpose for planning a new town, the logic of appropriateness for the politicians of the Pure Political Regime led to decisions based on appeals of owners of individual parcels without aggregating the results to see if they produced a desirable outcome. Ultimately, the town center became a tragedy of the commons. Its creation was in the interest of all, but no one had an interest in building it.

As the 1974 plan recognized, realization of a new town with many builders would require the county to act as more than a regulator; to assume an affirmative and entrepreneurial role usually performed by a developer, for which neither the planning board nor any executive agency was equipped. It also required creative and aggressive use of existing and newly crafted policy tools to guide and coordinate private development and public investments over several decades.

The extent to which Germantown was a moderate success is perhaps more significant than the shortcomings detailed above. In contrast to the diffused and ad hoc growth of Gaithersburg, Germantown was contained, first, by the greenbelt of parkland surrounding it, and after 1980 by establishment of the Agricultural Reserve. Creation of its park system was largely within control of the planning board. Through purchases and dedications, parks protected the stream valleys and key historic sites. Local parks were developed for each village. In addition, M-NCPPC developed major facilities in the greenbelt at South Germantown and North Germantown Recreational Parks, and Black Hill Regional Park.

The staging element was a qualified success. The Ten-Year Water and Sewerage Plan was managed to prevent scattering of subdivision projects across the entire area during the first decades of Germantown's growth. Phasing roadway projects concurrently with development was less successful. The politics of the county CIP regularly placed amelioration of congestion in the urban ring ahead of projects for Germantown. The shortfall in road improvements was exacerbated by the fact that some of the most important improvements were the responsibility of the state. Legislators representing the Germantown area were strong supporters of its transportation needs but they were a minority in the county delegation, which was struggling to move all county projects toward the top of a statewide program strapped for funds. The decision to terminate Metro at Shady Grove meant that well into the 21st century both residential and business development in the corridor would be automobile-dependent.

Under APFO regulations, developers facing disapproval of subdivisions for lack of roadway capacity could elect to provide the necessary improvements themselves. Owners of property along some planned but not programmed projects formed "road clubs," through which they shared the cost of improvements based on the number of trips their respective projects were forecast to generate. This device helped, but in some cases the first developer bore the full cost of the improvement and had to resort to begging or ultimately suing for reimbursement from club members that developed later.

Although the 1974 plan called for a special tax district for Germantown to fund various public facilities, including an internal transit system, none was established. Such a district could have helped keep improvements on track, either by levying a special tax on all property or by reserving an increment of the revenue resulting from the increase in property values as development proceeded. All the increased revenue from Germantown's development went into the county's general fund.

Germantown's planning and development was an exercise in organizational learning for the planning staff and board. Each iteration of policy drew lessons from previous ones as well as from the broader changes that were occurring in branches of the professional world of planning—especially community design, transportation, and environment. The continuity of the staff provided an institutional memory for success and failures and for the vicissitudes of markets and actors. Some of these lessons were applied and others were lost as the planning and arrested development of Clarksburg, the last corridor city, produced a crisis in planning politics.

ERRORS IN CORRIDOR CITY PLANNING

Originally the home of Seneca Indians, Clarksburg was first settled by whites in 1735. William Clarke, from whom the village would take its name, built a trading post where the Sinequa Trail, which evolved into the Georgetown-Fredericktown Pike (MD 355), crossed another trail that became Clarksburg Road (MD 121). Stagecoaches regularly stopped at the several taverns gracing the crossroads. General Edward Braddock rested at Dowden's Ordinary before leading his troops to slaughter on the Monongahela River. It became a regular meeting place for local Sons of Liberty, whose objections to taxes imposed on the colonies led to the Frederick County Court repudiating the Stamp Act in 1765. For the next two centuries Clarksburg's tranquility was interrupted only when Andrew Jackson dined there on his way to his inauguration as president.

The 1968 Clarksburg Master Plan

The 1964 General Plan suggested that another corridor city might be needed at Clarksburg after the turn of the century. The Maryland-National Capital Park and Planning Commission (M-NCPPC) paid two consultant firms $29,500 to prepare a master plan that provided for 13,800 dwelling units and 4.3 million square feet of industrial and commercial space.[1] It assumed a cross-county freeway, a western expressway, and a rapid transit line from the District of Columbia to Germantown would be in place when Clarksburg eventually developed.

At the commission's public hearing local residents raised concerns about the densities proposed and the location of a proposed bypass of I-270 through a stream valley. There was strong support for light industrial zoning along I-270 rather than heavy industrial uses. The Seneca Creek Watershed Association proposed a large lake. The Montgomery County Citizens Planning Association argued that the plan was too ambitious and would place Clarksburg, where speculators and developers owned most of the land, in premature competition with Germantown.[2] William Hussmann, then serving as program coordinator in the office of the county manager, questioned the need for the plan, pointing out its recommendations for roads parallel to I-270 were not based on traffic studies.

Nonetheless, the council approved it with minor changes but did not rezone land to implement it.[3]

A major land use issue arose in the 1970s when the county executive proposed locating an emergency landfill in the headwaters of Ten Mile Creek. The site was selected without public hearing after several other sites were rejected. In the face of fierce local opposition and strong scientific evidence of the site's problems, the county abandoned the landfill initiative and pursued alternative approaches for disposing of its solid waste.

Clarksburg experienced little change during last third of the 20th Century. In 1990 fewer than 1,600 people occupied its 560 homes. Its thin soils covering fractured rock were hostile to septic subdivisions and sewers did not penetrate the area beyond the site of the COMSAT headquarters built alongside I-270 north of Germantown. M-NCPPC continued to acquire land for Little Bennett Regional Park north and west of Clarksburg. In 1984, Little Seneca Lake in Black Hill Regional Park, on Clarksburg's southwest edge, was completed. This 505-acre reservoir, fed by Little Seneca Creek, Ten Mile Creek, and Cabin Branch, served both as a recreation resource and emergency water supply for the Washington region. Headwaters of all three streams were within the Clarksburg planning area. The Council designated properties clustered around the crossroads as an historic district.

What had changed while Clarksburg had not was the nature of planning politics. It became more transactional, short range, and opportunistic in the Pure Political Regime; less comprehensive in scope and ambition. At the same time the sophistication of the planning staff grew with experience and advances in planning theory, methods, and technology. And after seventy years of growth few large tracts remained available for development.

The trends in politics and the profession were mutually reinforcing. There was growing emphasis on mitigating the direct and indirect effects of development on the environment. Computerized modeling of transportation-land use interaction, unavailable when the 1968 plan was prepared, reached an advanced state. Transportation analysis guided the overall distribution and scale of development for master plans. It informed county growth policy that parsed the number of dwelling units and jobs that could be approved based on the capacity of existing and programmed transportation facilities. The New Urbanism movement influenced community design, bringing increased emphasis on traditional street grids, mixed uses, and the pedestrian experience. The landfill controversy sensitized area residents and the county's environmental activists to water quality in county streams. New state and county forest conservation legislation adopted in 1991 required developers to protect on-site forested areas and to replace forest cut to facilitate building.[4]

A New Urbanism Vision

In preparation for a new master plan, the planning staff in 1988 conducted three focus groups of local residents. Each group expressed preference for retaining the small town and rural character of Clarksburg. In 1989 a citizen advisory committee was empaneled, including local residents, landowners, business owners, developers, historic preservationists, and environmentalists. The committee met thirty-five times over the next two-years, commenting on staff and consultant studies and debating three alternative scenarios: conventional suburb, a transit-oriented town, and high-density urban nodes located at transit stations. Local residents continued to favor the light footprint of a rural hamlet and a conventional suburban development pattern. They adamantly opposed Clarksburg becoming "another Germantown," and insisted that if there was to be a more significant "town," its center should be adjacent to the historic village crossroads. Landowners sought a dense city and business leaders proposed more industry along I-270. As a staff draft was being readied for planning board review its approach was reinforced by new state legislation directing localities to concentrate new development in compact patterns where public facilities existed or were planned and to protect environmentally sensitive and rural areas from development.[5]

The planning board's environmental staff pointed out that Little Seneca Lake presented a new, major physical constraint on Clarksburg development. Ideally, its feeder watersheds would have been left undeveloped. But the General Plan suggested another corridor city at Clarksburg might be needed as Germantown built out. Contradicting the sacred text of *Wedges and Corridors* was not contemplated, even in the face of formidable environmental constraints. The challenge was how to create a corridor city, employing advances in planning practice and technology. Whether it should be done was not questioned, thus, bounding the logic of consequentiality.

Studies of the watersheds tributary to Little Seneca Lake established that protecting them and the lake from degradation drastically reduced the amount of land available for development. Ten Mile Creek had the best water quality of any county stream and it was the most vulnerable. The staff recommended protecting the entire western side of the watershed by adding it to the county's Agricultural Reserve, limiting residences to one per twenty-five acres. Most of the eastern side of the watershed was recommended for rural residential (five-acre) zoning, preserving a maximum amount of open space and limiting impervious cover of any site to 15 percent of its area. No sewer service was proposed except for the small portion of the headwaters east of I-270 included in the town center. Institutional use was retained for the long vacant 300-acre landfill site, where the county proposed building a new jail. These proposals were acknowledged as a compromise of the objective of protecting water quality to provide sufficient density for a transit-oriented town center and meeting a countywide need for the jail.

Development in the Little Seneca and Cabin Branch watersheds was to be permitted only with installation of "best management practices" to control storm water, erosion, and sediment. Stream valleys and steep slopes were to be added to the park system, providing forest buffers for the streams and creating a system of greenways with trails that extended throughout a "new urbanism," pedestrian-friendly town and connected Black Hill and Little Bennett Regional Parks.

The draft plan provided a maximum of 15,400 dwellings—12 percent more than the 1968 plan but half the number in Germantown—and 8.5 million square feet of commercial, office and industrial buildings. Development on the east side of I-270 was organized into neighborhoods and districts bounded by the greenways and arterial roads. The mixed-use town center district was assigned the highest densities. It wrapped the eastern boundary of the historic village but was not integrated with it. The Town Center District and the employment corridor were to be served by an extension of the Corridor Cities Transitway (CCT) connecting Clarksburg with the Metro terminus at Shady Grove via Germantown. Even with transit, the planners recommended widening I-270 to ten lanes to serve full development of the town and handle increased traffic from points west. A bypass highway would improve mobility for the eastern-most sector of the new town, provide a boundary between the town and the Agricultural Reserve, and eventually connect to a planned mid-county highway parallel to Frederick Pike (MD 355).[6]

The planning board made minor changes to the staff draft and conducted two evenings of public hearings in March and April of 1992 on the preliminary draft.[7] Testimony focused on the degree of protection for Ten Mile Creek, and the scale and density of the town center. Landowners in the sensitive watershed tended to oppose restrictions on development. Environmentalists either supported the preliminary plan's recommendations for agricultural and rural zoning of the watershed or urged placing both sides of it in the Agricultural Reserve. Some proposed the same treatment for Cabin Branch, bringing the Agricultural Reserve all the way to I-270. Local civic leaders seemed largely unconcerned with development of Ten Mile Creek if done at low densities with single-family residences. All parties opposed the county's proposed uses for the former landfill site. Testimony about the town center was predictably divided between community representatives who argued for less density and lower building heights and developers who sought greater densities and fewer restrictions and design standards.

After work sessions over the ensuing year, the planning board agreed on a final draft in June 1993. It recommended the five-acre rural zone for the east side of Ten Mile Creek and against extending sewer into the watershed west of I-270.

It left open the eventual uses for the county-owned landfill site. The board retained the staff's density recommendations but limited mixed use, office, and apartment building heights in the Town Center district to four stories.

The Politics of Plan Approval

Planning, Housing and Economic Development (PHED) Committee and full council review of the plan stretched through the next year. After public hearings in September 1993 where the issues raised before the planning board were reprised, the PHED Committee held seventeen work sessions between October 1993 and April 1994. The full council held seven sessions in the final month of deliberations.

The scale of development for Ten Mile Creek and the Town Center remained sticky issues. The council made several significant amendments before approving the plan. It reduced and redistributed the number of housing units, removing 1,200 units from the Town Center and three other neighborhoods, but adding 700 in the Ten Mile Creek watershed. Increases in density above "base" zoning in many neighborhoods were made contingent on use of transferable development rights (TDRs), making Clarksburg a major new TDR market to protect farmland in the Agricultural Reserve. The base for employment was increased slightly from 8.5 to 8.6 million square feet, but 10.3 million square feet would be permitted if transit service became available.[8]

The other significant changes involved staging development and financing of public facilities. The staging recommendations were extraordinarily detailed, in comparison with the rudimentary staging provisions of the 1974 Germantown Plan. Drawing lessons from two decades of experience and experimentation, each stage covered a fairly compact subarea where approval of plan-recommended floating zones or optional methods for private development of homes and businesses could be coordinated with the efficient provision of public facilities. In an attempt to avoid the problem that occurred in Germantown, where early retail development in the villages delayed maturity of the commercial market for the center, the staging element required 90,000 square feet of retail space to be underway in the Town Center before it could be approved elsewhere.

The Ten Mile Creek watershed, except for the small portion east of Frederick Pike in the Town Center district, was placed in the fourth and final stage. Responding to landowners, the council allocated 1,240 residential units and 960,000 square feet of commercial, office, and industrial uses, including up to 400,000 square feet for the jail. Instead of the conventional five-acre rural zoning proposed by the planning board, the council designated about half of this area for residential development at an average density of approximately three units per acre (with TDRs). The remainder was recommended for Rural Cluster zoning.

Development at the recommended density would require sewer, which would likely result in permanent degradation of Ten Mile Creek. Thus, in an effort to mollify the environmentalists and council members objecting to increased density in the watershed, the majority made initiation of its development contingent upon subsequent council approval of the extension of water and sewer service. This was to occur only after 2000 building permits had been issued in earlier stages and the council had reviewed an assessment of the effects of best storm water management techniques used by those projects on water quality in the Little Seneca and Ten Mile Creek.[9]

The county executive's fiscal analysis of the plan predicted revenue from new development allocated to infrastructure would fall $75-$126 million short of requirements.[10] Except for Frederick Pike, Damascus Road, and Clarksburg Road infrastructure did not exist. Those roads were already operating at capacity. Under the Adequate Public Facilities Ordinance the planning board could not approve new subdivisions if facilities were not available or programmed to serve them. As a practical matter, given the backlog of need in settled areas, Clarksburg would be in moratorium for decades. Yet it offered an opportunity to relieve pressure to house a growing population without greatly increasing infill development in the urban ring.

Responding to complaints from builders claiming they were ready and eager to build in Clarksburg, Council President William Hanna sent a memorandum to Robert Marriott, the director of the planning department, requesting a staging plan that would permit those ready to "develop and ready to fund the necessary infrastructure to proceed."[11] The planning staff and board recommended the creation of "Development Districts" to finance facilities that developers were not required to provide as a condition of subdivision approval.[12] Development Districts addressed both the problem of concurrency and the revenue gap by providing a way for developers to produce the public facilities as subdivisions were built, financing them with county bonds secured by a special property tax on the homes and businesses in the district.[13]

The PHED Committee embraced the idea, but developers objected that the master plan should allow other financing options, including "the private sector simply writing a check."[14] The council agreed. The approved plan provided development districts and "Similar Alternative Financing Mechanisms," without specifying what those mechanisms might be.[15] But a development district or an alternative financing mechanism had to be in place for subdivisions to be approved.

With the Ten Mile Creek, staging, and development district amendments, the council approved the master plan on a 6–3 vote. Those voting against the plan doubted the effectiveness of the staging provisions, but more importantly, they thought the plan provided more density than the environment could sustain, particularly in the Ten Mile Creek watershed.[16]

Development District Legislation

Following the plan's approval, council staff and developers' attorneys drafted legislation that created a three-step process for establishing development districts.[17] First, the council had to adopt a resolution declaring its intention to establish a district in response to a petition by owners of 80 percent of the real property and 80 percent of the assessed value of the property in the proposed district, the council's own motion, or a request from the county executive. The legislation was unclear whether a district could be created for a single subdivision or developer. This presented a problem in collective action that almost ensured each developer would seek a separate district. Competitors with fewer infrastructure requirements for their subdivisions would have little interest in joining a common district if they could be free riders on the facilities another district produced, leaving the homes they built subject to a lower tax, providing a marketing advantage.

The second step required the council, after a public hearing, to enact a resolution creating the district and setting the tax rate to fund part or all costs of specific facilities designated by the planning board and approved, with cost estimates, by the county executive. The listed facilities would be ones developers could not be required to build as conditions of subdivision approval.

Finally, after a third hearing, the council had to approve issuing bonds to finance the designated facilities. The district would then become operational, enabling the developer to use bond proceeds to finance infrastructure, with property owners paying the debt service.

If the council acted on the first resolution before building commenced, a development district would contain no residents. The petitioning developers would be the sole owner and holder of all assessed property. Only they would be immediately affected by the special tax but it would likely be lower than interest payments on private construction loans. The burden would shift to new homeowners as lots were sold. They would be informed of the tax at settlement, too late to have a voice in setting the rate.

Establishing a development district was cumbersome and time-consuming but it potentially avoided some of the frustrations encountered in Germantown by both developers and the county. Successful employment of the concept in Clarksburg, however, depended on the county taking the initiative to establish a comprehensive development district and assigning to each developer its proportionate share of infrastructure production. This alternative made the most sense, since some critical facilities—schools, a library, fire stations, and community centers, as well as arterial roads—served the entire town. It would be inequitable to impose on future residents of a single subdivision the debt service for projects serving the entire town. The council, however, did not establish a comprehensive development district and there is no evidence it was considered.

Instead, the council and executive assumed a passive posture, waiting for developers to petition for districts covering only their projects. Some submitted petitions, others did not, blithely assuming districts would be established if they needed them. Absent a development district, the planning board could approve a subdivision under the Adequate Public Facilities Ordinance only if the developer agreed to finance the necessary infrastructure by other means.

The Town Center Fiasco

Clarksburg Joint Venture, the owners of land planned for the 268-acre town center district, moved quickly after adoption of the master plan and comprehensive rezoning of the area. The planning board in 1995 approved an optional method project plan for a neo-traditional town center. It included 1,300 dwellings, 150,000 square feet of retail space, and 100,000 square feet of office space. Because a development district was not established, the board required the developer to fund necessary infrastructure estimated at $12.6 million, dedicate land and rights-of-way for sewers, parks, an elementary school, and roads, and construct of a number of specific facilities that served more than one subdivision.[18]

The board approved the site plan for the first residential phase, consisting of 768 housing units in March 1998. Before development got underway the property was sold for $15,000,000 in 1999 to Terrabrook, a Dallas-based development company that built the Reston Town Center. The new developer sought and obtained several amendments to the site plan to reduce the overall number of units, increase the variety of housing types, and make layout changes to enhance the new urbanism character of the community. Its home sales advertising emphasized the amenity-rich neo-traditional character of the community.

Realizing the extent of the financial obligations it assumed for infrastructure when it acquired the property, Terrabrook petitioned the council to create a Town Center Development District. Although the developer still owned most of the land, a few homes had been sold. The only witnesses at the public hearing, however, were the developer and a spokesperson for a countywide taxpayers organization. In September 2000 the council adopted a resolution stating its intention to create the district. This set in (slow) motion planning board and executive reviews to designate and estimate the cost of the facilities the developer was originally required to fund, but could now be shifted to the district. The council adopted the second resolution identifying those obligations in 2002.

Home sales in Clarksburg were robust, with prices ranging from $300,000 to $500,000, which made them highly competitive with homes of similar size further down county. Even so, the *Washington Business Journal* reported that Clarksburg homes carried a 10 to 15 percent premium over traditional subdivisions because of the community amenities that were to be provided.[19]

In 2002 the planning board approved Terrabrook's site plan for the second phase of Town Center's residential development. The following year the property was sold to California-based Newland Communities, which continued the neo-traditional marketing strategy initiated by Terrabrook. With sales brisk, in 2004 Newland prepared a revised site plan for the market/civic square at the heart of the community. Its proposal was met with outrage when it was presented at a meeting of residents. Rather than the pedestrian-oriented market square they had anticipated, the new homeowners were shown a conventional suburban auto-oriented shopping center. It was anchored by a large grocery/drug store flanked by smaller shops arrayed around a parking lot. A freestanding restaurant and a drive-through bank were also proposed, as well as a small office building. Newland representatives exhibited little interest in accommodating community objections and concerns.

Scandal

Within a week, a new citizens' organization, the Clarksburg Town Center Advisory Committee (CTCAC,) was formed. Officers of this new miniature republic shot off a letter to Derick Berlage, the planning board chair, demanding no action on the site plan without hearing from residents. Arguing that the site plan was inconsistent with requirements of the original project plan, CTCAC's co-chairs wrote:

> Although its configuration is in the shape of a square, Newland Communities' proposed change is the very antithesis of the 'Town Square" concept that is a defining characteristic of neo-traditional communities, and that was at the heart of the Clarksburg Town Center plan that the Board approved. It simply replaces the pedestrian-friendly, community-oriented Town Center concept with a regional strip mall, but with one important difference—Newland Communities' proposed regional strip mall will be located in the heart of a high-density residential community.[20]

The turnover in ownership of the town center project had already heightened frustration and created a perception of blame shifting by successive developers instead of addressing the normal problems encountered in a new subdivision. Now, residents sensed Newland was dismissive of their concern that the commercial heart of Town Center should reflect the new urbanism vision of the master plan and the approved project plan. They had literally bought more than a home; they bought (and paid a premium for) the community Terrabrook and Newland sold them—a pedestrian-oriented, amenity-rich, neo-traditional town. They bought their homes at the peak of the regional housing market, some paying $400,000 for a townhouse facing the vacant field from which the market square was to rise. They were unmoved by Newland's lament that the market did not support the sort of mixed-use center they were promised.

As their protests were rejected, CTCAC's leaders became convinced Newland was not dealing with them in good faith. They began compiling complaints and checking their observations against site plans and other documents that were supposed to govern the development of the community. They found significant differences between approved building plans and what was on the ground or scheduled for construction. Some buildings exceeded the 45 feet height specified in the data tables of approved final site plans signed by the developer. One exceeded sixty feet. Other documents, including the master plan, called for "four story" buildings in these locations without specifying height. Moreover, there were discrepancies between documents dealing with the same sites and structures.

In December 2004 the leaders of CTCAC brought their findings to Berlage. He told them he checked with staff and that the buildings were consistent with approved site plans, which included no measurements in feet, simply limiting the number of stories. He admitted that alternative interpretations of the standards were possible and advised them to request a hearing before the full board. CTCAC demanded the hearing, determined to force a developer they were convinced intended to evade the spirit of the master plan to at least adhere to the letter of it.

The core technical and legal issue was which documents in the regulatory chain controlled building heights—the master plan, the project plan approved under the zoning ordinance, the preliminary plan of subdivision, the site plan, or the "signature set," which was the final, detailed site plan signed by both the commission and the developer. Each of these sequential regulatory actions was linked to the one preceding it. The project plan, which described the general layout and character of the entire Town Center, was required by the zoning ordinance to conform to the master plan's recommendations. The subdivision plan must also be in substantial conformance with the master plan and the project plan. The site plan was required to conform to the subdivision plan and the project plan, and the signature set contained engineered drawings to implement the decisions embodied in the approved site plan. There were often minor changes between the site plan and the signature set due to more detailed engineering. In approving site plans, the board frequently delegated authority to staff to approve minor changes that were consistent with its action.

In preparation for the April 2005 hearing, the planning staff reported the site plans and buildings in question constructed under them were "consistent with the Clarksburg Master Plan and implement the vision of the Plan."[21] The evidence presented to the board at the hearing showed the master plan, project plan, site plan, and signature set all described building heights in "stories," rather than "feet." Although the signature set had contained a table showing "proposed heights" in feet, a staff member reported that she altered the table soon after its submission, replacing specific heights with "stories," so it conformed to prior plans in the chain. The board voted 4–1 that no violations of building heights had occurred.

CTCAC considered this response unsatisfactory and redoubled its examination of regulatory documents. Their suspicions were confirmed when they discovered a copy of the signature set the county Department of Permitting Services used to govern issuance of building permits. It contained an unaltered data table and signatures of acceptance from the developer. The staff member who altered the signature set now admitted she misled the board; she changed the document after CTCAC made its complaint.[22] CTCAC retained an attorney and aggressively pushed for a planning board hearing to air their findings and allegations of widespread violations of development regulations. They also contacted members of the council and took their findings to the news media.

What began as a complaint that the developer was not fulfilling the new urbanism promise made to homebuyers now expanded to charges of multiple violations of regulations by the developer and builders in Clarksburg. CTCAC also raised questions about the effectiveness and integrity of the planning board in enforcing its own decisions and managing the development process.

For Montgomery County, ever mindful of its reputation for squeaky-clean government, Clarksburg was a serious scandal. Everyone scrambled. The planner who altered the data table resigned, followed by the planning director. The board voted to reconsider the matter and scheduled a violation hearing. CTCAC assembled its evidence. Newland's attorneys argued that everything had been properly approved. Council members met with CTCAC leaders and pressed the board to clean up the mess.

The development review staff, now under new leadership, issued a report recommending the board find 433 town houses, twenty-six "two over two" buildings, and thirty multifamily units in violation of height limits specified in the sig-nature sets signed by the developer. The master plan described buildings only in terms of the number of stories they contained. The project plan carried forward this description but also included specific "proposed" heights in the data table, which the staff concluded were intended as limits on height made in response to concerns of local citizens that the new development should not overwhelm the adjacent historic district. Subdivision plans were silent on heights, and the site plan for Phase 1 contained no numerical standard, but incorporated the previous documents by reference. Finally, the signature set and enforcement agreement included the specific height standards of the project plan. The staff found 102 violations of setback standards required by project and site plans. In addition to these violations, locations of building types were switched, with apartment buildings built on sites the board approved for townhouses. Streets were not con-structed as required, and one was eliminated. Alleys were narrower than county standards and landscaping and other amenities shown on site plans were not provided.[23]

Members of the council reacted to these events and the findings of violations with outrage that such things could have happened in Montgomery County. The council ordered its Office of Legislative Oversight (OLO) to investigate what went wrong and to recommend changes to prevent a reoccurrence. Members that had supported the appointment of their former colleague, Berlage, to chair the planning board began to be concerned about his stewardship. Blame was liberally cast; responsibility was conservatively accepted. The council adopted a resolution containing measures to assure compliance with site plans and required the chair of the planning board and the director of county's Department of Permitting Services to provide the council with bi-weekly reports of progress in implement-ing the resolution.[24]

As the OLO assembled documents and interviewed participants and observ-ers, the board held further hearings. It found a pattern of developer violations of building heights, setbacks, roads, alleys, and parking, unauthorized unit changes, community amenities, environmental protection, and lot sizes, as CTCAC alleged. Berlage struggled for damage control. He hired a public relations spe-cialist and, at the suggestion of the commission's executive director, appointed Faroll Hamer, the chief of development review for the Prince George's County Planning Board, as interim planning director. In response to council urging, staff from the community planning division were reassigned to development review to try to clear out the backlog of cases filed during the peak of the housing boom.

In November OLO reported it found inconsistencies and ambiguities in the standards in the chain of documents that governed development of projects; inadequate record maintenance; no system for tracking and approving changes to approved plans; and an absence of sound practices for assuring compliance with board decisions in subsequent stages of the regulatory process. The board was faulted for ineffective and unfair responses to complaints about the project, inadequate compliance with requests for documents, and failure to carry out a timely and thorough investigation. It found Newland contributed to the problem by submitting documents and drawings containing errors or that were inconsistent with planning board decisions. Neither the developer nor staff brought these matters to the attention of the board. Legal issues included lack of clarity distinguishing major and minor amendments to a regulatory decision, leaving ambiguous the limits of staff authority to approve changes. It was also unclear where responsibility lay for assuring that building permits complied with site plans.

The release of the OLO report triggered a new round of frenetic activity by the council and planning board as the *Washington Post*, local newspapers, and television stations focused attention on Clarksburg. The board was preoccupied with hearings in which it had to sort out responsibility for violations among developers, staff, and its own lax management. Its staff was coping with disruption and demoralization in the wake of the charges, resignations, and reassignments, while earnestly trying to reconstruct the record of decisions, respond to demands for documents from CTCAC, OLO, and news reporters. In the process it confirmed or discovered additional site plan violations and issued stop work orders that halted projects that were underway.

In light of these findings, the council ordered the board to audit all recently approved site plans to see if the Clarksburg violations were only the tip of a deeper problem. The audit found very few violations beyond Clarksburg. Acting on OLO recommendations, the council directed the board to improve its internal management, and report regularly on its progress. The board retained a management consultant that produced a standard list of procedural changes, ranging from the obvious to the impossible. The beleaguered chair struggled to install them fast enough to report progress to the council at the biweekly inquisition. Council legal staff began drafting revisions to the zoning ordinance and subdivision regulations to require tighter scrutiny and better enforcement of decisions.

Violation Hearings, Mediation, and the Plan of Compliance

In November, the staff presented a comprehensive review of the situation and made recommendations for board action. Because a number of the homes with height or setback violations had already been sold, it was infeasible to require them to be torn down or modified. The board approved them as built to prevent them becoming nonconforming uses, impairing their owners' ability to finance, modify, or sell them. The developer or builders were required to correct violations of property that was still in their hands. Staff recommended fining the developers and builders $3.2 million for the violations and ordering them to present a comprehensive compliance program that would correct or remediate violations, address improvements in the design of the project, involve the community in development of the plan, and establish development standards for the project.[25]

The prospect of fines focused minds. Developers feared damage to their reputations (already in tatters), and more important, their credit ratings. Extensive litigation and prolonged suspension of development activity seemed likely. Before the board meeting on December 1, 2005, when the staff's recommendations were scheduled for hearing and decision, Council President Tom Perez suggested that CTCAC and Newland submit to mediation, with binding arbitration of differences, to see if they could agree on a settlement agreement and a plan of compliance that could be submitted to the planning board. CTCAC initially resisted, feeling that it had no regulatory authority, but ultimately agreed on assurance of support through the process. The planning board suspended the compliance hearing to await the outcome of the mediation.

About the same time I received a call from Steve Farber, the council's chief of staff, asking if I would be willing to advise the council on what needed to be done to restore the effectiveness of the planning board. After meeting with Perez, I agreed to undertake the project, but only pro bono, to assure that my recommendations were independent of any political influence, and with the understanding that I would not be a candidate to chair the board. It was obvious that Berlage had lost the council's confidence. His term was to expire in June and I did not want my involvement to be interpreted as an effort to replace him. I was seventy-four years old and had already retired twice.

With those understandings, I conducted an inquiry over the next two months and in February 2006 told the council that Clarksburg's problems were symptoms of failures in institutional and intellectual leadership at both board and staff levels. This resulted in loss of quality control in planning and development review. These conclusions reinforced dissatisfaction with Berlage who announced he would not seek reappointment. The council agreed to most of the recommendations I made, but ignored my insistence that I would not be a candidate for the chair, and persuaded me to return to the planning board in August 2006.

Newland and CTCAC agreed on a plan of compliance in June 2006. The planning staff recommended board approval, noting enhanced amenities and facilities, valued at $14 million, justified accepting them as an alternative to the fines previously recommended. The plan included a mixed-use, pedestrian-scaled retail core with a town plaza, library site, grocery, shops, and live-work housing lining structured parking, rather than the conventional shopping center and surface-parking proposal that had precipitated the initial community uproar. A community center, swimming pool, outdoor amphitheater, enhanced street trees, and landscaping were also proposed. The total number of housing units was reduced from 1,300 to 1,221.[26] Landscaping and amenities were to be augmented by $1 million to be used by a residents' association to mitigate the appearance of the height and setback violations of existing units and to improve the overall appearance of the neighborhood.

The board approved the compliance plan and the stop work order was lifted to allow construction of some additional residential units. A staged approach for the approval of additional sections was established. Newland was ordered to submit revised project, preliminary, and site plans, consistent with the plan of compliance, by October 26, 2006.[27]

The Development District Diversion

As CTCAC and Newland resumed mediation to comply, the nation's financial sector and housing market collapsed, the Great Recession began, and a series of collateral issues further eroded the relationship between Newland and CTCAC. Chief among them was Newland's effort to gain council approval for the issuance of bonds to activate the development district, which would allow Newland to shift facilities financing to it, and ultimately, the homeowners. The county executive, eager to end the stalemate in Clarksburg development, supported funding a revised list of facilities costing about $15 million.

At the council hearing CTCAC and its attorneys argued that the developer had responsibility for financing those facilities as a condition of planning board approval of its subdivision plans in 1995. Although Terrabrook applied for a development district after acquiring the property, it had not been funded when Newland assumed control with all the obligations of the original owner.

Resident opposition grew in intensity when the executive estimated the average special tax levied on each residence to pay debt service on development district bonds would exceed $1,000 annually for as long as twenty years. A number of people testified they were not made aware of the possibility of the special tax when they purchased their homes. Some, however, signed documents at settlement acknowledging the possibility of such a tax but those notices contained only the minimum required information that a future tax was possible—no statement of the rate or how the revenue would be used. Residents argued they should not bear the whole burden of financing facilities serving a wider community and that they had already paid for the facilities and amenities in premium prices for their homes.

The planning board had advised the council in 1995 that flaws in the law made it questionable whether development districts could be created for a single developer. It now pointed out that "The concept of development districts is not well suited to single-developer projects. . . . Such infrastructure should be provided, if feasible, through the cooperation of several developers, or through a fee or tax . . . on all users or all property owners."[28]

Council Member Mike Knapp, whose district included Clarksburg, introduced a resolution terminating the district, but a majority of the council would neither terminate it nor agree to issue bonds to make it operational. Instead it revised the development district law, strengthening notice requirements and measures to ensure the presence of a district or the potential for one would be disclosed to homebuyers.[29] This solved no existing problem but demonstrated the precedence of process over substance.

Builders protested they had counted on districts to help finance facilities, even though they agreed to finance them when their subdivisions were approved. The council appointed a Clarksburg Infrastructure Working Group to prioritize infrastructure projects and propose "suitable mechanisms" for financing them.[30] Its report rejected establishing a special tax district for the Town Center's two subdivisions, but narrowly agreed that districts should be created for two other subdivisions where developers had imposed property assessments through deed covenants that would be more onerous than a district tax.[31]

The Site Plan Decision

Newland missed the October 2006 deadline for the submission of subdivision and site plans required by the compliance order. It remained at odds with CTCAC on various issues, but claimed progress was being made. The board granted an extension. As the mediation process continued, Newland began to make changes CTCAC could not accept. Newland then invoked compulsory arbitration. After a series of acrimonious sessions, the arbitrator accepted Newland's changes over CTCAC's objections that they violated the compliance plan and the settlement agreement.

Plans filed in April 2007 differed substantially from the original compliance order, allegedly reflecting rulings of the arbitrator in support of the changes Newland made. CTCAC strenuously opposed them. After staff and agency review and comment, the developer did not respond until May of the following year. This required a new round of reviews. Newland did not respond to revisions proposed by staff and other agencies to meet requirements of the compliance order, arguing it was bound by the arbitrator's rulings and could make no changes. Newland and CTCAC were locked in perpetual disagreement about what they had agreed to, whether CTCAC was bound by the arbiter's determinations on the site plan, and even what the arbiter had ruled.

Exasperated by the long delay in resolving the matter, the board ordered a November 2008 hearing at which it would decide the issues. Rather than recommend denial, which would have resulted in further delay if the board concurred, the staff recommended approval with conditions that conformed to the 2006 compliance order so the Town Center could move toward completion. Recommendations included a new staging program to assure timely completion of community amenities and provide certainty for residents.[32]

I anticipated Newland would claim it could not deviate from the plan approved by the arbitrator and that under the terms of the binding arbitration CTCAC was required to support it as submitted. Therefore, I opened the hearing by ruling the board was proceeding under its July 2006 compliance order, and although Newland's submission was governed by binding arbitration, the board was not a party to that agreement. It had an independent responsibility to assure that the proposal before it reasonably conformed to the compliance order. This ruling supported the position that the plan of compliance was not, as Newland claimed, purely conceptual, but binding, since it had ordered Newland "to comply strictly with each of the elements, terms and conditions of the Compliance Program."[33] I ruled that variations from the plan of compliance would have to be found to be in the public interest.

Two full days of hearing illuminated the complex interplay of legal, political, technical, environmental, design, economic, procedural, and regulatory issues that had to be resolved before the project could be completed. Newland came prepared with design, retail, and parking consultants, its lawyers, and the company vice president. CTCAC was represented by counsel and board members but threatened with a lawsuit by Newland, said little. To the four planning commissioners participating in the hearing, it seemed as though Newland had learned nothing and CTCAC had forgotten nothing.[34] This did not foster an amiable hearing.

The character and design of the market square remained the central issue. Newland proposed major deviations from the Plan of Compliance. The depth of retail space was reduced. Buildings were changed, and brick paving for walkways was eliminated. Reconfiguration of the retail center encroached into a stream valley buffer, sidewalks were narrowed, retaining walls expanded and office space was reduced. Parking was reduced 40 percent below code requirements, double the reduction allowed in the compliance plan. Newland proposed meeting this lowered requirement by counting on-street parking in a residential neighborhood across a greenway and a substantial distance from the stores. A public street was converted to a private street with diagonal parking. A surface lot replaced one of two parking garages and the remaining one was reduced from three to two levels.

Newland claimed it had solicited proposals from thirty commercial builders, but none expressed interest in the retail development due to the structured parking. It argued retail could become viable only by eliminating one of the garages. Apparently prospective builders were not informed that the plan of compliance obligated Newland to build the garages as part of the improvements it agreed to provide in lieu of multimillion dollar fines.

The new plan failed to comply with the board's order regarding landscaping and special paving for common areas, claiming they were grandfathered along with structures conveyed to third parties and its substandard treatment of these spaces was not subject to the current review. The staff disagreed, as did community representatives. The community and developer failed to reach agreement on the design of the community center, leaving the issue for the board to resolve.

The Clarksburg master plan called for a public library in the town center and the compliance order required dedication of a site and structured parking for it. The configuration of the library remained unresolved. CTCAC demanded strict enforcement of the plan of compliance. During the mediation process, the library department sought a larger site and opposed structured parking. The larger site and surface parking would eliminate some residential units from the plan. The developer agreed to dedicate enough land to achieve the library's objective.

Two issues remained. The plan of compliance required additional road access from MD 355 to the center. The road alignment passed through the historic district and involved property the developer did not own or control. Also, CTCAC had not agreed how to use the $1 million the compliance order required the developer to provide for landscape enhancements over and above those required as conditions of site plan approval.

The board's resolutions on the amended project, subdivision, and site plans were specific and detailed. Parking was reduced by 18 percent, taking into account the pedestrian orientation of the retail center, but rejecting the developer's argument for more, apparently premised on access to transit, which the board considered likely only in the distant future. Structured parking, to be built by the developer, was required for the retail areas. The developer was required to dedicate a larger site for the library and construct shared surface parking for it. The retail center was configured so that stores fronted on the street rather than set behind parking. Some store depths were reduced. The community center was redesigned and the site for the civic building was shifted to accommodate a change in configuration. A landscaping fund was established to place any unspent funds from the $1 million in escrow for the homes association once residents had control of it. The access road alignment was established. Determined to avoid further delay by Newland, the board required submission of a certified site plan for staff review within 90 days, with a fine of $500 for each day of delay.[35]

Newland submitted a plan consisting of over 200 sheets by the deadline, but in reviewing it the staff found over 400 departures from board decisions. Some were significant, such as replacing the required brick walkway paving with asphalt, which the board specifically rejected. The board held an enforcement hearing and fined the developer $22,000 to defray the cost of staff time and required submission of corrected documents before the certified site plans could be approved, making it possible to apply for building permits.

Flipping Town Center and Final Resolution

Despite an approved certified site plan for the completion of the Town Center, Newland sued CTCAC for violation of the arbitration agreement, but lost when the arbiter testified she had not approved the plan submitted by Newland.[36] Newland started some of the required improvements in landscaping and completion of streets, but some installations violated the certified site plan. Then, in 2011 it sold its interest for $1.00 to Elm Street Development, which was building an adjacent Clarksburg district. Elm Street, with support of residents in the neighborhoods it built, persuaded the council to amend the staging element of the master plan so that a shopping center could be built outside the town center.[37] David Flanagan, Elm Street's president, declared that building the town center would not be economically feasible for twenty years unless the planning board approved a different plan for it.[38]

As the recession ended and interest in development revived, the new owner, sardonically named Third Try, produced an amended neo-traditional plan with community involvement. The principal changes were the elimination of structured parking, a slight reduction in residential units, a small increase in commercial space, and replacement of the library with a community building. With the endorsement of an exhausted miniature republic, the planning board approved the changes in July 2015.[39] It appeared the Town Center would finally be completed.

As the mills of the planning gods ground Clarksburg Town Center plans slowly and fine, development proceeded in other parts of eastern Clarksburg. A developers' consortium in Cabin Branch acquired most of the land and proposed a mixed-use development featuring a new branch of Adventist Hospital that would serve western Montgomery and adjacent areas of Frederick County. A site plan for the street network of the area was approved, but development plans were set back when the Maryland Health Care Commission approved a competing proposal for Holy Cross Hospital to build in Germantown on the

Montgomery College campus. In 2013 the planning board approved an outlet mall for the hospital site.[40]

Nothing Ever Ends

In 2009 the issues left by the prior council's equivocations on the development of the Ten Mile Creek watershed came home to roost as conditions were met for reviewing the fourth stage of Clarksburg's development. The key "trigger" was the report by the county Department of Environmental Protection and an inter-agency working group on the impact of development in Clarksburg on water quality and the ecosystems of Little Seneca and Ten Mile Creek watersheds. The function of this report was to provide up-to-date information the council could use to determine if changes should be made to the master plan to prevent degrading the special qualities of Ten Mile Creek.

The working group's analysis of data collected on the impact of development in Clarksburg concluded that current storm water management practices had been ineffective in preventing degradation of water quality in the streams; and the level of development the master plan proposed for headwaters areas of Ten Mile Creek could produce over 25 percent impervious cover and seriously degrade the stream's water quality.[41] Although the master plan limited impervious cover to 15 percent in part of the watershed, that was a less rigorous standard than evidence-based research would recommend.

These findings placed in immediate doubt the wisdom of a county proposal to build its North County Maintenance Center, with parking for heavy road equipment and 250 buses, on land adjacent to the jail. The board proposed preparing an amendment to the master plan based on a careful study of the watershed to determine the extent to which development could be permitted if it used the most advanced environmentally sensitive design practices. County Executive Leggett supported the master plan amendment process, and ordered a new effort to find another site for the maintenance center.

The council balked at initiating a master plan amendment. Instead, it appointed an *ad hoc* working group to examine the water quality issues and make recommendations to minimize development impacts on water quality.[42] The group held ten meetings over the next several months. It reviewed extant information on the Ten Mile Creek watershed, scientific literature, and regulations affecting water quality, storm water management, and sediment control. A five-member majority, comprised of the environmentalists and agency representatives on the working group, supported a limited master plan amendment, arguing the master plan's recommended zoning presented too great a risk to Ten

Mile Creek's sensitive ecology. Three members associated with the development industry recommended letting development proceed as planned, contending the combination of existing and new regulations would provide adequate protection for the stream. The chair of the group filed a separate statement recommending that the town center portion of the watershed be allowed to go forward but placing the remainder of the watershed in the Agricultural Reserve, pointing out that development in the watershed west of I-270 "cannot reasonably be characterized as contributing to compact, transit-oriented, mixed-use, town center development. . . . The challenges of protecting water quality developing parcels west of I-270 increase dramatically."[43]

The PHED Committee tabled the report and did not entertain further review of the 1994 plan. The council took no action that would allow development of Stage 4 to proceed, preserving the status quo, but only day-to-day.

The council's hand was forced in 2012 when two developers proposed projects in the Ten Mile Creek watershed. Peterson Companies began meetings with council members, other officials, and community groups promoting a large development of about 500,000 square feet at the top of the watershed east of I-270. Pulte Homes proposed a residential subdivision on over 500 acres west of I-270. Both argued their projects would help complete Clarksburg. Peterson claimed its project would provide the retail market that had been envisioned for the town center, albeit at a location across MD 355, three-quarters of a mile from the community, and in the form of a regional outlet center. These proposals generated swift and broad opposition from a compound miniature republic of community and environmental groups. They besieged the council with over 1,000 email and phone messages decrying the damage these developments would inflict on the watershed and Little Seneca Reservoir. The council agreed to amend the planning board's work program to prepare a plan amendment.

In the course of deliberations on the Ten Mile Creek Amendment, the board and council reversed their usual roles. Instead of following the logic of consequentiality, which would have framed the problem as one of protecting the water quality of the stream and reservoir, the planning staff and then the board sought a "balance" of water quality and development interests. The result was a plan that allowed a level of development and impervious surface in the headwaters that consultant and staff analyses found would degrade the stream. Staff recommended substantial reduction of development potential on the Pulte site from over a thousand dwellings to 200 and an 8 percent impervious limit, but increased the zoning potential on the Peterson tract to approximately two million square feet and recommended a 25 percent cap on imperviousness.

The planning board tripled the density on the Pulte tract and increased the impervious recommendation to 10 percent. On the Peterson parcel, it retained the 25 percent impervious limit but increased potential density by 50 percent, responding to interests of the commercial republic and following the logic of appropriateness.[44]

When the amendment reached the council the Ten Mile Creek Coalition, representing over two dozen environmental and civic groups, Livable Clarksburg, an organization of residents, and the Montgomery Countryside Alliance, a policy and advocacy organization based in the Agricultural Reserve, organized strong civic pressure and expert testimony in opposition to the board's recommendations. Initially, only three of the nine council members clearly supported reducing the scale of development and lower impervious limits. By completion of the public hearings a fourth council member had committed to the objectives of the coalition. But securing a crucial fifth vote remained in doubt. Craig Rice, the council president, represented the Clarksburg district and had encouraged the Peterson project.

Because the amendment involved both land use planning issues and major environmental concerns, the work sessions on the plan were conducted jointly by the council's PHED and Transportation, Environment, and Energy (TEE) committees. Participation in the work session by county, state, federal, and university experts on water quality provided the three proponents of stream protection comprising a majority of the joint committee (one member served on both committees) strong evidence for substantially reducing imperviousness in the watershed. The majority (TEE chairman Roger Berliner, TEE member Hans Reimer, and PHED member Marc Elrich), initially proposed an impervious limit of 8 percent for all development projects in the watershed, comparable to that imposed on other watersheds designated as special protection areas. Watershed experts, however, recommended reducing imperviousness to 6 percent on the Pulte parcel, but allowing up to 15 percent on land east of I-270, since those sub-watersheds were already somewhat degraded. The county executive concurred, and so did George Leventhal, providing the fourth vote in the joint committee. This assured passage of the changes, since Phil Andrews was one of the original three proponents of revising the board's recommendations. When the amendment came before the council, all opposition to the joint committee recommendations evaporated. Although he expressed dissatisfaction with the reductions in density and imperviousness, Rice joined his colleagues in approving the joint committee's changes to the plan amendment 9–0.[45] The council followed the logic of consequentiality, having discovered it was both appropriate and, to its delight, popular.

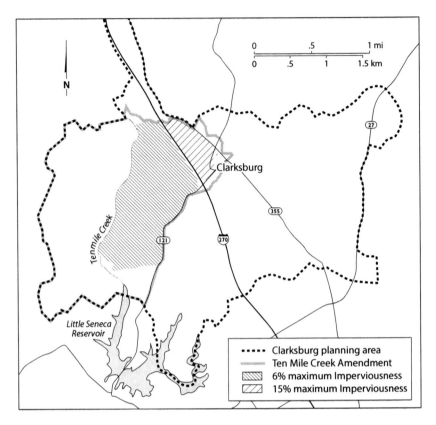

FIGURE 7.1   Impervious limit overlays in Ten Mile Creek Watershed. Courtesy Montgomery County Planning Department M-NCPPC

Lessons of Clarksburg

Clarksburg was bit by diverse snakes: cultural, political, technocratic, bureau-cratic, legal, corporate, and economic. In retrospect it is easy to see errors that were harder to appreciate as each decision was made, reducing options for the next. The original error was uncritically to add Clarksburg as the last "pearl on the string" of corridor cities. This was less a deliberate decision than policy iner-tia. It was expected. The General Plan, venerated for a generation, was not ques-tioned. The county needed to accommodate a growing population. It seemed preferable to channel growth into another compact corridor city than to accept greater suburban sprawl. Politically, it was far more acceptable to build on open land than increase densities in built up areas that were experiencing increased congestion and would surely organize to resist it. The planning board and council agreed it was the thing to do. The logic of appropriateness overwhelmed the logic of consequentiality. The question was not whether, but how to do it. It was a mistake.

Compounding a Mistake

Clarksburg would be built in the headwaters of a regional emergency water supply reservoir. The planning staff acknowledged the fragility of this environment and potential consequences for the lake. Its role was not to challenge the decision to produce a plan but to overcome the obstacles using the arsenal of planning techniques and policy tools that had been fashioned in the last third of the twentieth century. Within those bounds the staff's draft master plan was a technically adroit and rational exercise of the logic of consequentiality. It protected the most vulnerable resource—Ten Mile Creek—although explicitly compromising part of the headwaters for the "greater interest" of creating a large enough town center to support future transit service. Best Management Practices in storm water management and sediment control were expected to ameliorate the impacts on water quality of development in other watersheds. Development was limited to lands best suited for building and a garden city environment was envisioned, enclosing homes in an extensive system of greenways. Long-planned but unrealized roadway and transit facilities would be extended to balance transportation capacity with land uses. The staging plan was designed to establish a strong town center early in the development process.

As committee and council review of the plan proceeded, the broad politics of fulfilling the blurry vision of the General Plan for Clarksburg was displaced with the narrow politics of trimming and padding to assuage and "balance" the interests of landowners, developers, community leaders, historic preservationists, businesses, and environmentalists. As the time for council action approached, so did positioning for the 1994 elections. Council Member Bruce Adams, preparing to run for county executive, voted for approval of the plan against the urging of his environmental allies. Ironically, the three votes against final approval were from down-county members elected from single-member districts.

In approving the plan the council made two fateful decisions. First, it left ambiguous the future of the Ten Mile Creek watershed. On the one hand, it accommodated landowners by boosting density. On the other hand—to mollify environmentalists—it placed the watershed in the final stage of development and made it subject to approval by a future council based on analysis of the impact on water quality of building in Clarksburg watersheds. This produced conflicting expectations. Landowners expected eventually to develop at suburban densities. Environmentalists expected stream monitoring would demonstrate such densities were not feasible. Council members expected the decision would mercifully be made by their successors.

Second, the PHED Committee realized that administration of the Adequate Public Facilities Ordinance would foreclose any significant development in Clarksburg for the foreseeable future. Hanna's demand for some way of financing facilities so developers that were ready to build could do so led to the idea of development districts. Such districts were attractive to council members. They offered a way of financing facilities required to service growth from a tax on the growth itself. Clarksburg's facilities would not have to compete with other communities for capital improvement dollars. Development Districts were attractive to developers because they could bypass the vicissitudes of the county's capital programming by building the facilities themselves using proceeds from county bonds, with debt service passed on to the buyers of properties in their projects. If created well before homes were occupied there would be no need to seek approval of new residents who might object to higher taxes than homeowners in the rest of the county paid for the same services.

The lesson from Germantown that coordination of large-scale development involving fragmented land ownership required active engagement by the county government was not learned. In approving subdivisions, the planning board alerted the council that the law might need clarification if development districts were eventually proposed for individual subdivisions. Instead of establishing a single development district covering the entire "town," or at least the eastern side, the council left the initiative to developers, who apparently assumed districts could be set up at their convenience. This assumption lulled them to accept responsibility for financing specific facilities beyond those directly attributable to the impact of their subdivisions.

When Terrabrook requested establishment of a development district, the attenuated process bogged down. In the meantime, people bought homes and Newland acquired the unfinished project with its unfunded obligations. When it revived the request for the district in the midst of the unresolved issues over site plan violations and design of the market square, residents reacted with outrage at being taxed for facilities the developer had agreed to build when its subdivision was approved and that they had already paid for in premium prices for their homes.

Confronted with the snarled development district situation, the council delayed, temporized, declined to float bonds, and finally repealed the district authorization.[46] Still unsure how to proceed, it took appropriate action under the rules of planning politics and appointed a working group on what to do. The group gave them choices instead of answers, none of which found five votes.

A Wicked Problem

The Town Center imbroglio is a fine example of a wicked problem.[47] Each stakeholder defined it differently, and there was no agreement on its solution. The developer saw it as problems in economics, marketing, and excessive regulation. The residents saw it as a breach of implied contract, fraud, and inadequate enforcement. The council saw it as a management problem with large political consequences if they were blamed. The planning board saw it as a problem of its integrity and effectiveness. Each definition was a symptom of a deeper problem. The failure of staff to notice the site plan violations and stop them was a symptom of inadequate staff resources. That was a symptom of a higher-level failure in institutional quality control and leadership, which was a major contributor to the unauthorized change made to the signature set by a staff member.

As the property flipped from developer to developer, commitment to the plan was discounted along with the price. By the third transfer, Newland decided it could not meet the commitments of its predecessors to build the neo-traditional market square its sale brochures promised homebuyers. When it brushed off residents incensed by its proposal to build instead a conventional local shopping center it transformed them into an instant miniature republic with CTCAC as its voice. Mishandling CTCAC's initial complaint to the planning board set in motion a series of events that led to resignations, investigations, changes in board leadership, reorganizations, legislation, compliance agreements, negotiations and arbitration, more compliance hearings, fines, lawsuits, and another change in ownership. Diligent efforts by council, planning board and various staff to correct process and enforcement issues were promptly settled. The core issue of the market and civic center remained unresolved. Unraveling the reasons requires tracing the path of decisions, each of which produced new problems.

The problem metastasized from a straightforward matter of site plan enforcement when the December 2005 enforcement hearing was canceled so Newland and CTCAC could begin mediation to prepare a plan of compliance. It seemed like a good idea. The developer could avoid a heavy fine and admitting the violations. CTCAC participated in a more comprehensive revision of the site plan to protect its interest in the completion of the community. The planning board could avoid the risk of a prolonged legal battle over the fines and its authority to levy them. The council could look as if it had solved the problem.

The initial results seemed to justify the decision. CTCAC and Newland agreed on the June 2006 plan of compliance, which provided for a neo-traditional market square and an enriched program of amenities in lieu of a fine. The board, in its compliance order, however, did not require a bond to ensure the delivery of the $14 million package to which Newland agreed. And permitting the delay in bringing a final site plan to the board for approval left parties to negotiate the details. They were soon deadlocked in an uneven match of a volunteer citizens' group having to respond to proposals prepared by Newland's consultants. Newland used the time and rulings by the mediator to make substantial changes from the plan of compliance and then failed to respond to staff and agency comments for over a year after submitting its plan. When the exasperated planning board ordered a hearing for the plan its discretion was limited by its own compliance order. Further, the arbiter's restrictions on CTCAC to not oppose Newland's plan left the board to infer the interests of a key party. Though the board was not bound by the arbiter's decisions, it was obliged to weigh the evidence before it and decide how far, if at all, changed conditions justified deviation from the compliance order. Even after it approved a revised site plan, it had to require Newland to correct the final submission and impose a fine for staff time required to police the submission.

The board imposed strict and explicit conditions on the project but mistakenly relied on the good faith of the developer to act on the certified site plan and did not require a performance bond to assure that the prescribed facilities and amenities would be built. When Newland failed again to comply with the approved plan and then sold the project to Elm Street the problem did not become less wicked. As the market square approached its second decade in limbo, Elm Street claimed compliance was not feasible and suggested it might submit a new plan for a neighborhood-scale center instead. CTCAC's leadership was emotionally drained, financially exhausted, and criticized by other residents of Clarksburg—with encouragement from Elm Street and other developers—for retarding the provision of commercial services by fight with Newland. Responding to the genuine need for such services, the council approved the plan amendment that allowed retail development in other districts to proceed. It took another five years for Third Try to produce a consensus plan for the market square the board could approve. Only two council members serving in 2005 when the Town Center issue erupted remained in 2015. None of the planning board members that struggled with the issue from 2004 to 2009 remained in office.

Clarksburg provides important lessons. The master plan's presumption that by forcing retail development in the town center before allowing it to proceed elsewhere was questionable, since retail tends to follow residential development and is scaled to its market. Clarksburg's planners probably drew the wrong lesson from Germantown and should have paid closer attention to Reston. In the Virginia new town, the land for the town center was kept vacant until the final stages of development. Counterfactual argument is always hazardous, but if a more compliant developer had been willing to take a receptive community into its confidence, a mixed-use center might have been achieved. That is a big *if*, and depended on another: if there had been no egregious violations of development regulations.

That leads toward a second lesson: the resolution of the dispute over the future of Town Center should not have been outsourced to unequal parties and a mediator, but undertaken by the board. The staff prepared a compliance order that could have worked in 2005, three years before the onset of the Great Recession. A more forceful and definitive order on the 2006 compliance plan might have saved the project. Leaving details to later was an understandable decision, since Berlage felt a strong obligation to do as much as possible before he left office because the problem had arisen on his watch. But timing is important in development. The 18-month delay that ensued while CTCAC and Newland haggled enhanced Newland's position, weakened CTCAC's, and created a situation that inhibited the discretion of the board.

A third lesson for an enforcement action is to resist the temptation to assume the violator, when ordered to comply, will do so without a strong financial inducement. It was difficult for the board to imagine that its order would simply be ignored. This was contrary to its prior experience. It had not adjusted to dealing with a national builder rather than a local firm that expected to do nearly all its building in the county. Reputation matters only if people are aware of it.

It is premature to reach definitive conclusions about the extent to which Clarksburg's development will serve the public interest. Absent the presence of a special tax district, its cost to the county in terms of facilities and services will exceed substantially the revenues it generates. It captured a substantial portion of the county's population increase in a relatively compact community, consistent with smart growth principles and the General Plan. That, however, begs the question whether it was smart in the first place and whether the same level of growth absorption could have been more beneficially achieved in places where less new infrastructure would have been required. Once begun, the task confronting the planning board and county officials, the growing population of Clarksburg, and its developers is how to finish the town in a way that produces a livable and pleasant community that ultimately achieves the vision of its master plan.

Markets, Politics, and the Limits of Planning

The General Plan's vision of corridor cities was its most ambitious element. As exercises in the logic of consequentiality, the master plans for Germantown and Clarksburg were faithful to the vision. The number of governments involved in Rockville and Gaithersburg frustrated their coherent development as corridor cities. There was greater success in creating the corridor than in producing cities.

As a natural experiment in the limits of local planning politics, useful lessons can be drawn from Montgomery's experience.

Planning for "new towns" such as the corridor cities requires planners and politicians to engage in thinking comprehensively about the interrelationships among the components of a community. Because the planning horizon is so long, it can at the same time tempt them to make unrealistic assumptions about rates of growth of housing and employment, distribution of housing types, and the future provision of infrastructure, such as transit, that may be needed to balance facilities with land uses. Plans usually call for regular updates and revisions within six to ten years, to account for shifts in markets, tastes, and financing but competing demands for agency time tends to push revisions out to twenty years or longer.

Absent a private master developer such as the Rouse Company in Columbia, Mobil in Reston, or Kettler Brothers in Montgomery Village, with deep pockets of patient money and a pecuniary interest and psychic investment in success, there are limits on the extent to which public policy can guide development projects that take three or four decades to complete. That is enough time for a half-dozen business cycles. In a fast-growing suburb, it spans ten elections and may involve a change of regime. The building industry will have undergone at least one restructuring.

In contrast to a private or public development corporation with a sole mission to build a complete town, once a master plan is adopted the attention span of practitioners of the logic of appropriateness is short, episodic, and piecemeal. Planners, with limited resources, will be occupied preparing other plans. Elected officials focus on the problems of existing residents and their communities; not future ones. Government will engage with the development process of its planned communities when budgeting or acquiring land for a public facility, or taking a regulatory action such as approving zoning, subdivisions, or site plans. Its basic power is negative. By withholding public investments or project approvals it can prevent or delay development. It can place conditions or impose standards on a project but it cannot fully control its design. Staging mechanisms determine the order in which various sections of a planned new community or corridor city develop, but not the sequence applications for development are presented. And, especially, it cannot require a parcel to be developed.

As time passes and planners and politicians are replaced, institutional memory of the initial goals decays. Projects that range from slightly to profoundly contrary to the ancient plan come before new eyes and viewed in isolation, seem appropriate, and gain approval. Gradually, almost imperceptively, the grand design erodes and the vision fades.

Failure to pay attention to the institutional development of a new town as well as its physical elements can be a problem, even for its physical development. This soft infrastructure can be essential to the financing and coordination of facilities, from neighborhood amenities to timely installation of parks, roads, and libraries, as well as to the creation of either public or private governments that can be instrumental in creating community identity and fostering civic capital.

These observations suggest that one of the most important lessons is that government is an imperfect master developer even when it has done a reasonably good job of planning. That does not mean it should not try. Mindful of G.K. Chesterton's aphorism that "anything worth doing is worth doing badly," it seems incontestable that Montgomery's corridor developed more coherently because of its corridor city plans than it would have done without them.

THE AGRICULTURAL RESERVE

The recommendation of the General Plan to organize development in corridors separated by wedges of rural landscape, open spaces, and low-density suburbs was more aspiration than policy. Corridors were imprecisely defined. Density in the wedges was described in planning poetry and depicted with graphic ambiguity.

Realizing the plan's vision was complicated by reality. Most of the land designated as wedges was zoned for one dwelling for each half-acre. An effort by the Charter Council to downzone much of the area to ten acres in a 1954 lame duck session was undone by the "Harmony" Council that succeeded it. The 1969 General Plan recommended a rural zone but Maryland's preferential tax assessment for agricultural land was the principal policy tool for delaying conversion of farmland into subdivisions.[1] It allowed landowners and speculators to hold land at low cost for future development because, unlike states that imposed a substantial tax penalty when a farm was subdivided, Maryland only imposed a modest transfer tax at the time of sale for subdivision.[2]

Wedge Issues

The sewer moratorium stalled development in most of the county in the early 1970s but building proceeded on the suburban fringe where large lots could be served by well and septic. These scattered subdivisions were fragmenting the rural landscape. Ending the moratorium required expansion of the regional sewage treatment plant on the Potomac or construction of a new facility, or both. Desperate to end the moratorium, the Washington Suburban Sanitary Commission proposed building a 60-mgd advanced wastewater treatment plant on the Potomac River at Dickerson, approximately twenty-five miles west of the Capital Beltway and upstream of the commission's water intake. Sewage would be pumped by force main from the Beltway to Dickerson. County Executive James Gleason endorsed the proposal. The development industry enthusiastically supported it.

A Sewer Saves the Wedge

The force main posed a threat to the viability of the General Plan's western wedge by creating opportunity for development, which landowners and builders would be unlikely to ignore. Planning Director Richard Tustian saw the situation as an opportunity to draft and apply a rural zone to the wedges, as the General Plan recommended. He proposed a zone with a minimum lot size of five acres. This was near the average size of recently approved lots using septic tanks. There was no area master plan on which the board could rely to justify the downzoning but Arthur Drea, general counsel of the Maryland-National Capital Park and Planning Commission (M-NCPPC), concluded that the General Plan's recommendation for rural zoning provided sufficient justification for creating and applying such a zone. A detailed study was needed, however, to delineate the boundaries of the area to which it would be applied.

The board agreed to proceed and I informed the council of the proposal we would bring them, pointing out the danger to the integrity of the western wedge if they took no action. The council agreed to preparation of a zoning sectional map amendment. It was clear that the work would have to be done quickly because the county, the sanitary commission, and the state were moving as fast as possible to build the plant and end the moratorium.

With help from Drea, a planning team led by Perry Berman worked feverishly for several months to compile, overlay, and analyze zoning, land use, tax, property, municipal, soils, and other maps to identify properties that should be included in the amendment. They drafted the Rural Zone and a sectional map amendment covering more than a third of the county. To ensure everyone potentially affected was aware of it, the board mailed notices to every owner of record, notified all area civic and business associations, and placed prominent display ads in county newspapers in addition to the required legal notices. In addition to oral testimony at the board's hearings, over 100 written comments were received.

Landowners complained that downzoning reduced the value of their land, and thus, their equity in it as collateral, sale for retirement, or legacy for heirs. A few charged the amendment discriminated against minorities either by downzoning properties in the wedge that were owned by African-American families or by making it harder for them to acquire a small lot on which to build. The map amendment, however, confirmed existing zoning for the small, scattered black settlements in the area. Some of the more strident witnesses denounced Berman, a bearded, casually attired Brooklyn native, variously as a communist, a racist, a liberal, a fascist, or all of the above.

The planners responded that the land's value for development was not determined by the maximum density permitted by its zone, but by the number of lots that could actually be developed on septic. Recent experience averaged about one house per five acres. Such homes tended to be large and expensive. They were not additions to the county's affordable housing stock. The board argued that the proposed zoning recognized the reality of what the land could support without sewer service, which no one seriously suggested should be extended throughout the wedge.

The council approved the Rural Zone in October 1973. At the same time, it amended the Ten-Year Water and Sewerage Plan to deny access to the proposed force main beyond the boundaries of the Germantown and Gaithersburg corridor cities. The proposal for applying the zone to a wide swath of the General Plan's wedges remained hotly contested. To reinforce the board's recommendations, I called Lieutenant Governor Blair Lee III for help. He arranged for Governor Marvin Mandel to send me a letter expressing support for protecting the wedge concept of the General Plan, endorsing limited access to the force main, and stating: "It would be wise for the County to confirm its low-density development policy with rezoning that is clear in conformity with that policy." He added that a rural zone, "seems to be most appropriate as an important means of discouraging requests to develop land by making connections to the limited access sewer."[3]

The Sectional Map Amendment (SMA) covered 112,688 acres, of which 96,522 acres were placed in the new Rural Zone.[4] At the council's hearing on January 16, 1974, the views expressed at the planning board were replayed at full volume. The SMA was adopted on August 3 with no significant changes from the board's recommendations. The Rural Zone effectively ended interest in extending sewers into areas it covered but it soon became clear that it did not dampen pressure to covert farms to subdivisions. During the first eight years of the 1970s almost 19,000 acres were removed from the tax assessor's farm classification, and the annual conversion rate did not decline after introduction of five-acre zoning. The number of homes constructed on septic systems increased from 253 in 1974 to 575 in 1978. Subdivision activity increased from an average of twenty-two per year before 1973 to forty-two during the next five years. Fifty-one preliminary plans were filed in 1979.

The Dickerson wastewater treatment plant and force main were rejected by the U.S. Environmental Protection Agency in 1977 and were never built. Federal and local agencies agreed to expand and improve the regional facility at Blue Plains and the council approved a 20-mgd facility on Rock Run in Potomac.

Amputating the Outer Beltway's Western Leg

The General Plan included an outer beltway. It crossed the Potomac River near Great Falls, intersected I-270 south of Rockville and arced through the eastern half of the county to meet I-95 in Prince George's County and crossed back into Virginia south of Mount Vernon. Political priorities and resources were focused on construction of the Capital Beltway in the early 1960s, but soon after its completion county business and civic groups began agitating for relocation of the Outer Beltway. Potomac's affluent exurbanites objected to a freeway disrupting their tranquility. Highway advocates thought it was too close to the Capital Beltway to serve the growing businesses along I-270 north of Rockville. Plans for Metro suggested the need for a connection from I-270 to the Shady Grove station between Rockville and Gaithersburg. M-NCPPC's alignment hearing produced disagreement about whether to retain a "desire line" for the outer beltway, but if kept, the weight of testimony favored the new alignment.[5] The commission, however, took no action.

The issue resurfaced after the 1970 elections. In April 1971 the Montgomery County Planning Board conducted two alignment hearings. Almost a year passed before it sent the council a highway plan amendment moving the river crossing farther west and intersecting I-270 at Shady Grove. The council approved the new realignment east of I-270 but only the part of the western alignment from I-270 to a point east of Darnestown.[6] The segment from there to the Potomac River remained undetermined. The board and council held further work sessions and the council toured the area with citizens before approving the full alignment in 1973.[7]

Opposition to a Potomac crossing continued, led by environmentalists and residents on both sides of the river. In Virginia, development in western Fairfax and Eastern Loudoun County was obliterating the rural landscape[8] and Virginia reduced its plans for the section of the Outer Beltway approaching the Potomac to a partially controlled-access arterial highway. The Maryland Department of Transportation removed the Potomac crossing and the alignment west of I-270 from its highway program in 1974 as gas tax revenues sharply declined.

The 1980 Potomac and Vicinity Master Plan removed the western section and bridge from its transportation recommendations. Instead, it blandly noted that the outer beltway and a remnant of the original route—renamed the Rockville Facility—were regional in character and inappropriate for consideration by a local area plan.[9] All that remained of the Outer Beltway was the eastern section, renamed the Inter-County Connector (ICC).

The western section achieved a persistent vegetative state but highway advocates maintained hope of resuscitation. Some Montgomery business leaders sought better and faster access to Dulles International Airport. In January 2000 a business-backed group, the Washington Airports Task Force produced a report, "The Case for a New Potomac River Crossing between Montgomery County and Northern Virginia." It recommended a six-lane parkway/toll road in a landscaped 400-foot wide right-of-way but proposed no specific alignment. A Montgomery committee, Marylanders for a Second Crossing, was organized to support the

"Techway." *The Washington Post*, long a supporter of highways, endorsed a second crossing somewhere between Darnestown and Harper's Ferry.

Frank Wolf (R), Northern Virginia Congressman and the chairman of the U.S. House of Representatives Appropriations Subcommittee on Transportation, earmarked $2 million in the U.S. Department Of Transportation budget to study a second crossing. Virginia's governor pledged $400,000 to supplement the federal study and both parties' 2001 gubernatorial candidates expressed support, as did Wolf's two Northern Virginia congressional colleagues. Montgomery County residents opposed to the Techway formed a new organization, the Montgomery Countryside Alliance, to protect the rural landscape and its communities. No Montgomery County or Maryland elected official supported a river crossing.

As the federal study got underway, opposition grew among Virginia residents. Within a few months, Wolf asked that the study be terminated. All alternative routes would take dozens, perhaps hundreds of homes of affluent constituents in western Fairfax and eastern Loudoun counties. Undeterred, the Washington Board of Trade, AAA, and other Techway enthusiasts continued their advocacy but with all available highway funds committed to construction of the ICC, the Techway had no political support in Maryland.[10]

In 2012 Virginia's Commonwealth Transportation Board resurrected the idea of a belt road running through eastern Loudoun County, designating a broad swath of Loudoun and Prince William Counties as a "corridor of statewide significance." Loudoun County officials, environmental and civic groups denounced the idea. Maryland opponents mobilized again, fearing that if the idea survived in Virginia it could revive proposals for a river crossing and a connection to the ICC. Given the history of the idea and the paucity of transportation funds for the region, it seems reasonable to conclude the Techway has joined the Northwest Freeway, North Central Freeway, Three Sisters Bridge, and the Potomac Parkway in the Metropolitan Washington Mausoleum of Unbuilt Freeways.

Creating the Agricultural Reserve

By the second half of the 1970s both urban and rural interests were expressing alarm at the accelerating conversion of farmland on the fringes of metropolitan areas. Development patterns that consumed large land areas and required long commutes gained more urgent national and local attention in wake of the 1978 oil embargo imposed by the Organization of Petroleum Exporting Countries and the resulting spike in gas prices.[11] Across the country, agricultural interests joined urban planners and conservationists to find ways to protect farmland. The Maryland General Assembly enacted the Maryland Agricultural Land Preservation Foundation (MALPF)[12] and the Maryland Environmental Trust (MET).[13] MALPF purchased long-term easements on farmland to prevent it from being developed. MET acquired perpetual conservation easements, with a particular focus on areas of high environmental quality, including farmland.

Reframing the Issue for a Functional Master Plan

The commodity market contributed to interest in farmland preservation. Corn and soybean prices reached historic highs in 1979 and dampened enthusiasm among farmers for selling their land to developers. The local Farm Bureau, which had long opposed any restrictions on subdivision urged the council to complement state laws and take measures to help preserve farmland in Montgomery County. The council appointed an Agriculture Preservation Advisory Committee (APAC). Planning Commissioner George Kephart, who operated an historic Poolesville farm, Tustian, and I saw this as a window of opportunity to fashion more effective policies to realize the General Plan's vision by reframing the issue as preserving farming in the county rather than merely creating a wedge of passive open space.

The planning board urged the council to authorize it to prepare a Functional Master Plan for Preservation of Agriculture and Rural Open Space (AROS), using APAC as its advisory committee. To emphasize the urgency of acting, the board noted the recent filing of a preliminary plan for a large residential subdivision at the foot of Sugarloaf Mountain, which, if approved would consume a farm and change a treasured historic landscape. The council agreed and with a view toward Sugarloaf, set a deadline of a year for completion of action on the plan, which allowed the board to impose a moratorium on subdivisions in the area it covered. Tustian assigned Berman and another young planner, Melissa Banach, to develop the plan. General Counsel Drea again worked closely with the planning team to help them avoid issues that could complicate defending the plan or its implementation.

The Impermanence Syndrome

The great barrier to saving farmland was as much psychological as economic or political. As farms sprouted subdivisions neighbors began to regard suburban development as inevitable. The question was not whether to sell to a developer, but when to do it for the best price. Many considered the Rural Zone merely a "holding zone," certain to yield in time to the inexorable march of growth. This logic was driving growth across the river in Virginia. It was the historic experience in Montgomery.

Arresting this "impermanence syndrome" was the core challenge for the planners. It involved three critical elements that were simultaneously technical and political. The first was distinguishing the parts of the Wedge containing a "critical mass" of contiguous farmland and rural villages that should and could be protected primarily for agriculture. The second was devising a zoning scheme that might actually save that critical mass and have enough support to secure its adoption. Third, a means had to be found to address the issue of equity for farmers, which was tied to the value of their land.

Identifying the Critical Mass of Farmland

Keeping a large contiguous area of farmland intact was crucial to sustaining farming. Farmers' experience taught once an area was fragmented by residential subdivisions, farming became less viable. New residents often had slight, if any, interest in farming. Some were even hostile to its continuation, considering its activities noisy, odiferous, and inconvenient. Having paid a premium for a view of the bucolic landscape, they wished the land left undisturbed by those that had husbanded it, and the rustic roads unobstructed by slow-moving farm equipment.

Establishing the boundary for this critical mass of farmland—the rural component of the wedges—started with the area that was not scheduled for sewer service within ten years. Since the service envelope would inevitably be expanded, the study area was narrowed to the eleven planning areas where little development had occurred. Within this broad 163,000-acre area—about half the county—the staff mapped prime soils, working farms, and land subject to farmland assessment, existing and future parkland, floodplains, areas of critical state concern, such as land bordering the Potomac River and C&O Canal, the Patuxent River's water supply reservoirs, the electric power generating plant at Dickerson, and conservation areas adjacent to Sugarloaf Mountain.

Overlaying these maps, two distinct areas were identified. A 110,000-acre area containing most of the county's contiguous farmland arced across the upper county from the Potomac River on the southwest to the upper Patuxent River on the northeast. It encompassed the towns of Poolesville, Laytonsville, and Barnesville, and rural villages such as Damascus, Boyds, Dickerson, Woodfield, Unity, and Sunshine. These country towns and villages played an integral role in the rural economy, providing necessary commercial and community services.

A smaller 26,000-acre area had already succumbed to exurbanization. A few working farms remained, but the landscape was so fragmented with subdivisions that sustaining farming was problematic. The staff and advisory committee agreed it would be difficult to prevent further development, but by clustering homes more open space could be preserved and some farming might continue. Soils in much of this area could support septic systems on lots of two-to-five acres. Recognizing this reality neutralized opposition from most landowners in this area to zoning for clustered housing and open space.

Zoning for Agriculture Preservation

Deciding which land to protect required a rigorous application of the logic of consequentiality. Devising a regulatory scheme that could preserve farmland had to be defensible by that logic and win enough support from the farming community, developers, and environmentalists to gain council approval. This required application of the more subtle logic of appropriateness, and a great deal of listening and mutual adjustment—politics. The conventional approach to protecting farmland was large-lot zoning. The Farm Bureau had traditionally joined speculators in opposing any increase in the minimum acreage required for a residential lot. They calculated the value of their land by its potential yield of houses rather than crops, whether using it as collateral for a loan or as future income for retirement. Farmers and other landowners had successfully fought off the proposal for ten-acre zoning twenty-five years before, and vociferously opposed the imposition of the rural five-acre zone in 1973 even though it had not slowed conversion of farmland to subdivisions.

What had changed since 1973 was the growing concern among Montgomery farmers that agriculture in the county was in danger of being obliterated as a way of life. They wanted to preserve *farming* as well as farmland. The obvious technical question in crafting a credible agricultural zone was how much land was needed for a successful farm enterprise in Montgomery County? Farmers on the advisory committee had confidence in the judgment of Rene Johnson, the county's Agricultural Coordinator. Commissioned to estimate the amount of land needed for an economically successful farm, Johnson concluded that 25 acres was "*a feasible size acreage for a productive agricultural business in Montgomery County.*"[14] The staff, accordingly, recommended that a new zone with a twenty-five-acre minimum lot size for the critical mass of farmland.

Landowners and some members of the advisory committee strenuously protested. Their land had been downzoned five years earlier from one-half acre to five acres. They argued that this further drastic reduction in density would reduce the value of their land, whether for collateral, development, or retirement. Reaching agreement on zoning depended on solving the "equity" problem, which was about both fairness and money.

Solving the Equity Problem

Many farmers considered the "equity" in their property to be represented by its development value, less any debt secured by it, rather than the net value of the land and improvements as a farm. They further pointed out a twenty-five-acre minimum lot size meant they would have to break up a farm if one or more children wanted to build a home on the farm and eventually take over its operation. This had disadvantages from both operational and tax perspectives.

It seemed clear that while five-acre zoning had a negligible, if any, effect on land values, a twenty-five-acre zone would reduce the development value of a farm. Thus, to gain landowner support, or at least reduce the intensity of opposition, an effective farmland preservation program had to address land values and the equity those values represented for farmers and their estates. Whatever its merits, landowners would oppose a straight downzoning. There was a corollary problem of deflecting opposition to the plan from affordable housing advocates. They were concerned if a substantial segment of county land were removed from the development envelope it would cause a general increase in the cost of housing.[15]

At this point, I suggested to the advisory committee that transferable development rights (TDRs) might be an appropriate solution to both problems. Fortunately, a model for this approach was readily at hand. The planning staff was completing its draft of a new area master plan for Olney. Although it had a large area of active farms, Olney was excluded from the Rural Zone because it had an adopted area master plan that recommended more dense zoning. Working with the Greater Olney Civic Association, and two highly regarded farmers in the area planners Lyn Coleman and Perry Berman proposed a unique approach to farmland protection. Undeveloped farmland in the northern sector of the Olney area was downzoned to the five-acre Rural Zone. Landowners in the zone could build on well and septic or sell a development right for each five acres to homebuilders in other Olney locations planned for suburban densities, enabling them to increase density of their subdivisions.[16]

This TDR scheme did not increase the total density planned for Olney. Farmers could "cash out" the development value of their land without having to leave farming and the village's residential areas would be more compact. The farmers' interests in protecting their farms from development converged with interests of Olney's new residents. They envisioned Olney as a small village set in a landscape of farms and open space—an embodiment of the ideals of garden city and miniature republic. This appealed to the economic interests of the farmers, landowners, and developers, and to the aesthetic and community interests of the suburbanites, so long as the added density in the area receiving TDRs did not include attached dwellings.[17]

The proposal for the AROS plan differed significantly from Olney, in that the critical mass of agricultural land would be zoned to permit only one dwelling for each twenty-five acres but a landowner retained one TDR for each five acres, the maximum allowed under the existing Rural Zone. An owner could retain a development right for each twenty-five acres for existing or future houses and sell the "excess" TDRs to builders of subdivisions in designated "receiving areas" in other parts of the county. Because of soil conditions many landowners could not achieve the maximum density permitted by the five-acre zone, but they could sell their full allotment of TDRs regardless of a farm's ability to "perk." Because builders would buy transferable development rights without the land attached, they would be less expensive than additional lots, thus reducing the average cost ratio of land to housing.

The proposal was, in many respects, born of desperation. The five-acre Rural Zone had not slowed development pressure on the agricultural areas of the county. It actually increased the conversion of the best soils, which could support septic systems. There was no assurance larger lot zoning alone would save farms because pressure to rezone and connect to public water and sewer would probably increase over time. Thus, some means had to be found to protect the land in perpetuity from a level of residential development that would imperil the viability of farming. Land values on the urban fringe had already reached levels that made purchase of substantial conservation easement acreage beyond the fiscal reach of local and state governments.

The novelty of the approach was in its application to tens of thousands of acres and in allowing the transfer of development rights to sites miles away in other planning areas. Previously, development rights had been transferred to adjacent or nearby properties, as in Olney. That would not meet the goals of the AROS plan, since it would simply shift density from one farm to the next or to rural villages, such as Barnesville or Laytonsville, which had no interest in becoming suburbs.

Part of the appeal of TDRs was that the market would determine their value. Transactions would be between private buyers and sellers. Government's role was limited to accepting and recording perpetual easements that extinguished the rights severed from a parcel that limited forever the number of units that could be built on it. Participating in the TDR market would be voluntary, but because the twenty-five-acre zoning was mandatory, the incentive for rural landowners to participate was strong.

Agreement depended on working out the details. The staff and committee recommended a new Rural Density Transfer (RDT) zone to be applied to some 96,000 acres—the "critical mass" of farmland and the "sending area" for TDRs.[18] Following adoption of the AROS plan the planning board would designate "receiving areas" where densities allowed by existing zones could be increased by specified amounts upon purchase of TDRs. Landowners worried that council deference to local opponents of increased densities would result in too few receiving areas to create a competitive market for their development rights, thus depressing their value. Alternatively, they doubted builders would buy TDRs or that in periods of economic downturn farmers ready to retire or needing to liquidate their TDR assets for other reasons would have buyers, making the equity represented by TDRs worthless.

To address these concerns, the staff and I proposed establishment of a TDR "bank"—a fund to ensure a buyer for development rights for an interim period while the private market was being established. The bank could also serve as a purchaser of last resort for farmers needing to liquidate their development rights but could find no buyers and also operate as a guarantor of farm loans that used TDRs as collateral. Legislation was drafted to establish such a county funded bank at the same time as the sectional map amendment was enacted.[19]

The farm leaders gradually overcame their initial skepticism and accepted the approach, Some were persuaded of its merit; others were convinced a majority of the council was prepared to impose twenty-five-acre zoning by sectional map amendment with or without TDRs. One Farm Bureau official later told me: "You made us an offer we couldn't refuse."

Fine Tuning and Building Support

Agreement was reached that the zone would not require a minimum lot size of twenty-five acres, but instead establish a density of one dwelling for each twenty-five acres and allow lots to be as small as 40,000 square feet—roughly an acre. To facilitate the intergenerational transfer of family farms a provision was added to allow an owner of land when the RDT zone was applied to create a lot for each child, similar to rules for MALPF easements. Lots created prior to the adoption of the plan were "grandfathered" so their size, use, improvement, and subsequent transfer to new owners would not be impaired.

Once the elements of the draft plan were firm but before the board's public hearing, Berman and Banach toured the area, meeting with local groups and a number of individual farmers at their kitchen tables to explain the plan, its objectives, and how the zoning and TDR system would work. Key members of the advisory committee helped build acceptance of the plan within the farming community, although some landowners and developers remained strongly opposed.

The final touch was to give the area a distinctive name: the "Agricultural Reserve." The term was chosen to convey the notion that the area was being per-

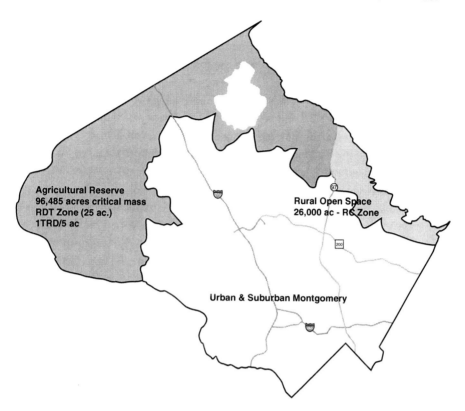

Agricultural Reserve
96,485 acres critical mass
RDT Zone (25 ac.)
1TRD/5 ac

Rural Open Space
26,000 ac - RC Zone

Urban & Suburban Montgomery

FIGURE 8.1   Montgomery County Agricultural Reserve 1980. Adapted from
M-NCPPC. 1980. Functional Master Plan for Protection of Agriculture and Rural
Open Space. Courtesy Montgomery County Planning Department M-NCPPC

manently set apart from the march of urbanization as a place for active farming,
to distinguish it from being merely a zoning classification, and create an image
of uniqueness justifying continuing stewardship. Like *Wedges and Corridors*, the
Reserve was a cause that could capture public imagination and mobilize political
support for a special place that not only provided food and fiber, but also sustained the county's rural heritage and provided critical environmental services.
Later, when the council approved the plan, I praised their decision as protecting
"the green lungs of the county."

The planning staff met the twelve-month deadline for production of the
sectional map amendment. But before it could move through the planning
board hearings and work sessions and reach the council for final action, the
legal time limit for a moratorium on subdivision approval expired.[20] The board
could no longer delay approval of the subdivision at the foot of Sugarloaf

Mountain that threatened to alter radically the view of the dominant natural and historic feature of the western wedge. I used the prospect of its imminent development to urge council members to promptly approve the sectional map amendment.

The council held only two hearings before approving the AROS plan with few changes in September 1980. The resolution approving the plan required the planning board to identify additional receiving areas within six months.[21] The council quickly adopted the sectional map amendment, placing 96,485 acres in the RDT zone. The Agricultural Reserve contained 11,134 TDRs, exclusive of land in public ownership or subject to other limitations on development.

Four landowners and developers sued the county, claiming their right to develop under prior zoning was vested. They further contended the downzoning was a regulatory taking, for which the TDRs were not "just compensation" required by the Fourteenth Amendment to the U.S. Constitution. The court, however, held the downzoning did not constitute a taking, so it was not necessary to address the question whether TDRs were compensation—whether just or not—and reminded the plaintiffs it was well-settled law in Maryland that no one had a vested right to prior zoning unless substantial construction was clearly underway before the rezoning occurred. The court noted, however, the county should move expeditiously to create receiving areas.[22]

Making the TDR Program Work

Area Master Plans completed in 1980 and 1981 recommended receiving areas for 4,014 TDRs. In 1982 the planning board identified twenty-seven more sites in various planning areas and submitted amendments to area master plans indicating the additional density for which each receiving area would be eligible upon purchase of TDRs. Civic associations that applauded the open space of the Agricultural Reserve saluted with a single digit creation of receiving areas to ensure its permanence. They feared the "bonus" density for TDRs would produce more homes on smaller lots and different types of houses than in established neighborhoods, overburden schools, and increase traffic congestion.

Establishing Receiving Areas

As each new master plan identified receiving areas, existing residents complained they were unfairly and disproportionately burdened with TDRs. They argued that the council was breaking faith with them by allowing more density without the facilities needed to serve their communities. A spokesman for the Columbia

Road Citizens Association, testifying on the master plan for Eastern Montgomery County made a typical argument:

> [TDRs] . . . have no place in the Eastern Montgomery plan. They yield no permanent protection to open space, and they reduce zoning protection in the receiving areas. Just because they are legal at present does not mean they must be used. Don't use them.[23]

Because receiving areas were identified in master plans and the TDR Zones were applied by sectional map amendment, civic groups might succeed in marginally reducing the number of TDRs allocated to a planning area but generally lacked the ability to prevent them entirely, which they might have done if they had to be established through individual rezoning cases.

The 984-acre Avenel Farm in Potomac included the site of the proposed Rock Run sewage treatment plant. Designated a receiving area, TDRs could increase its density from 379 to 833 dwellings, contingent on the treatment plan not being located on the property. The council, however, approved construction of the plant. PGA Tour, Inc. bought the rest of the farm and proposed a stadium golf course and a related residential community. The council approved a second Potomac Plan amendment, eliminating the sewage plant contingency and designating the property, which was zoned for two-acre cluster development, as eligible for development with TDRs at a maximum density of two units per acre.

The West Montgomery Citizens Association appealed the planning board's approval of subdivision and site plans using TDRs for Avenel. It argued the council could not increase density using TDRs merely by designating receiving areas on master plans, but must create and apply a distinct zone for each TDR-enabled density increase. To do otherwise, it contended, improperly delegated the council's zoning authority to the planning board. The Maryland Court of Appeals agreed, holding that the council had to adopt specific TDR zones and a zoning map amendment applying them to specific properties.[24] The planning board quickly drafted a set of TDR zones, which the council adopted and then applied them as recommended by master plans, including to Avenel. The board then re-approved the subdivision. As new master plans were prepared, additional receiving areas were designated and TDR zones were applied in fifteen master plan areas.

Market Issues

As the Avenel case moved through the courts the private market in TDRs began to function, making the bank unnecessary. Builders used them in the strong housing markets of Olney, Potomac-Travilah, Germantown, and Fairland where most receiving areas were located. Over 21,000 acres of farmland were protected by TDR easements in the program's first ten years. By 2013 privately acquired TDRs easements accounted for 52,000 of the 72,000 acres of farmland protected by all state and local farmland preservation programs.[25] Only 1,500 TDRs remained attached to Montgomery farms. Another 3,500 TDRs had been severed by easement, but had not been attached to projects in receiving areas.

With capacity for only 4,600 TDRs remaining in the county's receiving areas, the perennial issue remained of providing the right balance between the supply of TDRs and receiving area capacity to use them. Many builders used only 40 to 60 percent of the full TDR bonus density available, either to reduce local opposition to a project or because the market for detached homes was so strong they could make more money building fewer but larger houses. Although enough receiving area capacity probably existed to provide a competitive market for several years, the high rate of underutilization led the planning staff to estimate the county should identify additional receiving areas with capacity for 3,700–7,800 more units as new master plans were developed and old ones revised.[26]

When TDR prices fell, farmers complained that the government was breaking faith with them by not providing enough receiving areas to induce competitive builders to offer TDR prices at levels they regarded as a fair return on their equity in the land. Superficially, this complaint seemed justified. As a general rule of economics more receiving areas should increase demand, and thus, move prices upward. However, a 1988 study of the program found that:

> [I]ncreasing receiving capacity was followed by increasing utilization of TDRs but not by an increase in price. Total TDR receiving capacity appears to have a weak linkage to price indicating that the factors influencing price must lie elsewhere.[27]

The average TDR prices reported in Table 8.1 suggests that TDR prices tended to vary with the strength of the housing market. They gradually increased as the market expanded through the mid-1990s and declined with market contraction in the latter years of the decade. Average TDR prices rose with the housing bubble of the early years of the twenty-first century and as national development firms entered the new Clarksburg housing market. They peaked at $42,000 before the bubble burst and the discovery of building violations that temporarily suspended Clarksburg development. The TDR market was chilled for the remainder of the decade and had not recovered by 2015.

TABLE 8.1   TDR transactions, 1982–2006

YEAR	NUMBER	AVG. PRICE ($)	TDR EASEMENT ACREAGE	CUMULATIVE VALUE ($)
1982	101		505	
1983	396	5,000	2,485	1,980,000
1984	470	4,750	4,835	4,212,500
1985	1,100	4,050	10,335	8,667,500
1986	1,053	3,970	15,600	12,847,910
1987	397	3,750	17,585	14,336,660
1988	197	4,200	18,570	15,164,060
1989	290	5,200	20,020	16,672,060
1990	215	7,500	21,095	18,284,560
1991	32	6,000	21,255	18,476,560
1992	543	8,250	23,970	22,956,310
1993	427	8,500	26,105	26,585,810
1994	479	10,000	28,500	31,375,810
1995	492	10,500	30,960	36,541,810
1996	216	11,000	32,040	38,917,810
1997	132	10,500	32,700	40,303,810
1998	402	8,000	34,710	43,519,810
1999	167	7,500	35,545	44,772,310
2000	178	7,000	36,425	46,018,310
2001	291	6,500	37,890	47,909,810
2002	225	7,500	30,015	49,597,310
2003	452	11,500	41,275	54,795,310
2004	407	18,000	43,310	62,121,310
2005	627	35,000	46,445	84,066,310
2006	380	42,000	48,345	100,026,310

Source: TDR Program Overview. December 8, 2006. Montgomery County Department of Economic Development, Agricultural Services Division. p. 6.

Market Supplement

In 1987 as TDR transactions sharply declined in a cooling housing market, Council Member Neal Potter discovered the county had remitted $2.5 million of agricultural land transfer tax revenues to the state since 1980 under a statutory "use it or lose it" rule. He urged the council to establish a county program using those funds to purchase agricultural easements to supplement the private TDR market and the MALPF easement program in the county.[28] The council enacted the Agricultural Easement Program (AEP), which provided for county supplemental payments to farmers selling easements to MALPF and to purchase TDR easements.[29]

Unlike the private TDR market, in which prices were negotiated between buyer and seller, the AEP established an annual offering price based on a formula that gave priority to larger farms with the most productive soils. Over a twenty-year period, it acquired TDR easements on over 8,000 acres. To avoid competing with farmers, county policy did not permit resale of TDRs it purchased. A significant effect of the program was to set a benchmark price for TDRs.[30] Landowners were reluctant to sell at a price lower than the county offer, even though the odds of selling to the county were quite small, given the funds available.

AEP acquired only "excess" TDRs that could not be used for a dwelling. Like most private TDR sales, landowners retained the right to build one dwelling per twenty-five acres. A more strategic approach might have used the public funds to extinguish as many of the "buildable" development rights as possible, thus, reducing the number of rooftops in the Reserve and preserving more land for farming.

The problem was illustrated in the case of the 233-acre Hilltop Farm, with 46 TDRs. The AEP purchased the thirty-seven excess TDRs for approximately $900,000 from its owner, a limited liability partnership comprised of a family—husband and wife and their seven adult children. The easement reserved one lot for "the owner and each of its children." The LLP initially applied to subdivide the property for the existing house and seven "child lots," notwithstanding the well-established legal rule (and biological fact) that corporations and business partnerships cannot have children. The county attorney's office, which had participated in crafting the 1994 easement, ruled the provision for child lots was proper and in accord with state MALPF practice when an LLP was composed solely of family members. The assistant county attorney's letter in support of the subdivision stated that "it is probably more appropriate to consider the requested lots 'owner' lots in that each prospective lot will be owned by and titled in the name of a partner."[31]

By this reasoning, some of the partners were their own children. The planning board denied Hilltop's subdivision application based on the size and configuration of the lots, but on appeal the courts ordered its approval.[32] The county received almost no added value for its expenditure, since RDT zoning limited the property to a maximum of nine residences. It was clear from the planning board hearing of the case that few, if any, family members would occupy any of the lots, as none currently lived on the farm and negotiations for its sale were apparently in progress as the subdivision was under review.

Keeping the Reserve

Creation of the Agricultural Reserve did not guarantee its survival as a working and cultural landscape. Four major threats to its integrity soon emerged. The introduction of sand mounds as a method of waste disposal made development

FIGURE 8.2 Farming in Montgomery County's Agricultural Reserve. Photo courtesy Lee Langstaff

feasible on land that was unsuited to traditional deep trench septic systems. Large private institutions found the less expensive land of the Reserve attractive for relocation and expansion of their facilities. Some landowners exploited the child lot exception to the density requirements to create additional lots their children never occupied. Finally, the strong market for exurban mansions, especially when combined with the sand mound opportunity and abuse of the child lot exception created a need to extinguish as many of the retained buildable development rights as possible to preserve a working landscape.

The Sand Mound Problem

A core assumption of the AROS plan was that the capacity of the Reserve's soils to absorb wastewater would result in a lower density of development than one dwelling per twenty-five acres.[33] The plan recommended against extension of public water and sewerage facilities into the Reserve, and declared the county should "Deny private use of alternative individual and community systems in all areas designated for the Rural Density Transfer Zone."[34]

For the first decade following adoption of the AROS plan, the need to find "perkable" sites for septic systems limited residential development. In 1986, however, the Maryland Department of Environment classified sand mounds as "conventional" technology.[35] Developers and landowners seized this semantic reclassification and urged the county to approve their use in the Reserve. Rather a plan amendment, the vehicle for policy change was a 1994 health regulation that recognized sand mounds as a generally acceptable substitute where soils could not support trench systems. The regulation was accompanied by a "Statement of Health Department Policy" that concluded: "It is the purpose and intent of the Health Department to render friendly and helpful assistance to citizen landowners to the end that they may use their property as permitted by zoning laws provided there is no significant health risk."[36]

The council approved, adding a resolution reinforcing the policy statement, declaring it "encourages the Department of Health to exercise flexibility provided for in the regulation and explore with applicants ways in which particular site restrictions can be dealt with to allow development allowed by zoning to be constructed."[37]

This health department regulation became a de facto amendment of the AROS plan. Both the planning board and council seemed oblivious that it created the potential for as many as 500 additional homes in the Reserve on land otherwise suitable only for agriculture and forestry. The board in the following decade approved fourteen subdivisions using sand mounds for all or part of their home sites. Confronted by environmental and rural community advocates in 2005 when Winchester Homes proposed development of over 30 large estate homes served by sand mounds on a 704-acre farm adjacent to the C&O Canal National Historical Park, a State Wildlife Refuge, and an Izaak Walton League property, a divided board ultimately approved only fourteen lots, requiring preservation of a large contiguous area for continued agricultural use.[38]

In 2007 the planning board urged the council to rescind the 1994 resolution, pointing out:

> the density limitations in a zone are not an entitlement, but an upper limit, and each subdivision must conform to the Master Plan and meet any other applicable regulations. . . . the resolution should be amended to conform with, and to be consistent with, the Master Plan.[39]

The council's agricultural working group recommended continued but limited use of sand mounds.[40] In the face of strong opposition from landowners in the Reserve, no proposal could attract more than four votes, one short of a majority. The issue remains unresolved.

Private Institutional Facilities

Even at development prices, land in the Reserve was cheaper than the shrinking supply of large vacant tracts in suburban Montgomery, making it attractive to large institutions that had outgrown their original sites. In the early twenty-first century several mega-churches began searching for new sites large enough for their sanctuaries, administrative offices, schools, playing fields, recreation centers, senior housing, parking, and other facilities. Land prices in the Reserve were within the capacity of capital campaigns, or if prayers were answered, land might be received as a testamentary gift of a congregant passing through the eye of a needle. What was good for religious institutions was good also for secular ones—schools, conference centers, country clubs, and so on—that needed to expand in new locations. Down county property could be sold by the square foot; new country sites could be bought by the acre.

The zoning code permitted houses of worship in all residential districts, including the RDT zone. The Reserve contained some sixty village and country churches, most of which had existed for decades and some for well over a century, serving rural congregants. Along with other public and private institutions of modest scale, such as schools, they were integral parts of rural community life. All were served by wells and septic systems, except for those in the town of Poolesville or the Damascus sewer service area. Lack of public water and sewerage was a substantial barrier to relocation of large private institutions. Council policy was to consider applications for extension of public sewer or water service to private institutional facilities (PIFs) on a case-by-case basis.

In April 2001 Farm Development Company requested extension of public water and sewer to serve four 1,000-seat church facilities on a 119-acre property just inside the Agricultural Reserve east of Germantown. The council deferred Farm's request until completion of the mandatory triennial review of the water and sewerage plan.

In the review, both the county executive and the planning board recommended a complete ban on PIF approvals in the Reserve, citing problems of traffic congestion and parking overflow during times of peak usage, the scale of such facilities compared to surrounding residential and agricultural uses, creation of large impervious surfaces, and other environmental concerns. Reflecting the lack of cohesion in the Pure Political Regime, the ten-year plan adopted by the council in November 2004 included neither the blanket prohibition of PIFs nor a cap on the amount of impervious surface, as recommended by the board. It did include a requirement that a PIF applicant must be the actual institution seeking service and prohibited the Washington Suburban Sanitary Commission from undertaking a capital project that served only a PIF.

In March 2004 Bethel World Outreach Ministries of Silver Spring identified itself as the applicant. It proposed a sanctuary accommodating 3,000 worshipers, a school and day care center for 250 children, a social hall with a capacity of 600–800 people, administrative offices, and surface parking. The council again deferred a decision while it considered an amendment to the RDT zone to limit impervious surface coverage to 15 percent of any site.[41] In the meantime, Derwood Bible Church, located near the Shady Grove Metro station acquired a 226-acre site near Laytonsville. It proposed a 1,500-seat sanctuary, educational facilities, and playing fields. It did not request public water and sewer but proposed serving its facilities with a well and a special septic system with capacity for 19,500 gallons of wastewater a day.

These proposals, added to others in the queue for decision and still more rumored to be imminent, galvanized opposition from farmers and other residents of the Reserve, concerned not only about loss of farmland but the effect of such large-scale developments on the sole source aquifer on which their wells relied, traffic on narrow rustic roads, and the impact on rural communities. The Laytonsville Council was particularly concerned about the Derwood Bible Church proposal's effect on the town's water wells. There was also general fear among supporters of the Reserve that if these projects were approved they would be precursors of more that would be hard to deny.

The council, besieged with demands from Reserve residents to deny the applications of the churches and from church members to approve them, formed an interagency working group in January 2005 to study the impact of PIFs in rural zones. Six months later the group again recommended prohibiting PIFs in the RDT zone and an impervious surface cap of 15 percent of the total lot area. Committee and full council hearings were held during the fall of 2005 on the service category change requests and the impervious cap.

Following council hearings the Transportation and Environment Committee recommended approving the Bethel request conditioned on the church granting a ten-acre conservation easement and limiting impervious surface to 25 percent of the parcel. The latter was apparently the smallest footprint possible under the church's proposed development plan. The planning board, however, recommended denial of public water and sewer as contrary to the AROS master plan. The County Department of Environmental Protection warned the council that the state Department of the Environment might deny future amendments to the water and sewerage plan if they conflicted with the master plan.

On November 29, 2005, the council acted on the package of requests before a packed hearing room. Although Bethel agreed to the committee's recommendations, the full council denied its request on a 6–2 vote. It then approved an amendment to the ten-year plan prohibiting public water and sewerage to PIFs in the RDT zone. State courts upheld summary judgment against Bethel[42] but the U.S. Court of Appeals for the Fourth Circuit ordered trial of whether the county's actions imposed a substantial burden on the church's exercise of religion under the Religious Land Use and Institutionalized Persons Act (RLUIPA).[43] The case was settled in 2013 and the church acquired a site outside the Reserve.[44]

Because Derwood Bible Church did not request public water and sewer service it was not covered by the new PIF policy. The council took up its proposal in February 2006. It denied the church's request for a 19,500-gpd septic system. It unanimously approved an amendment to limit the capacity of any institutional septic system to the number of residences that could be built on a tract, but not to exceed 5,000gpd, the level that required review of a project by the Maryland Department of the Environment. Derwood Bible sold the property and expanded at its Shady Grove site. In 2007, the council tightened restrictions on large facilities, amending the zone to exclude churches from land under TDR easement.[45]

The mega-church cases were a significant challenge to the integrity of the Reserve. Courts generally sustain ordinary regulations, such as restrictions on water and sewer service, impervious surfaces, or bulk of buildings as reasonable means of protecting a legitimate governmental interest in preventing conversion of farmland. RLUIPA subjects regulations to strict scrutiny against a claim that they impose a substantial burden on the religious exercise of the church. Thus, the county must demonstrate that it has a compelling interest in protection of the Reserve and that it chose the least restrictive means of protecting it from such facilities, which could fragment the critical mass of farmland and adversely impact its integrity and function. If Montgomery, in light of its history of land preservation, the public and private funding that has been expended to protect the land, the extensive easements held by the county to preserve farmland, and the neutrality of its regulations with regard to types of land users, cannot meet those high standards, then local neutral land use regulations will be impotent against challenges by religious institutions.

Child Lots

The child lot "exception" in the RDT zone was designed to facilitate transition of a family farm from one generation to the next. Ambiguous language in the zone was interpreted to permit child lots in addition to the limit of one unit per twenty-five acres, so long as a development right was retained for each lot.[46] Enterprising realtors and landowners with several children quickly recognized that one who retained a TDR for each twenty-five acres, plus one for each child, could create an exurban subdivision for buyers willing to pay a premium for a country "estate."

Between 1981 and 2006, 103 child lots were approved on fifty-four properties. Only five child lots were created on farms larger than 150 acres. Abuse increased as parcel size declined. Several cases stood out. An owner of a 103-acre farm added lots for his five children to four "market" lots to create an "estate" subdivision. Three 53-acre tracts were increased from two lots each to five, six, and seven lots. Seven parcels ranging from 25 to 50 acres added child lots to produce densities ranging from one residence per 4.8 acres to one per 13 acres. In some cases children of owners never took title to the lots ostensibly created for them. The child lot exception was not sustaining family farming but contributing to the impermanence syndrome the plan sought to arrest.

The planning staff in 2005 recommended including child lots in the overall density limit of one dwelling per twenty-five acres, requiring the child to own it for five years, and ending the child lot exception entirely in 2011.[47] The county's Agricultural Preservation Advisory Board, strongly objected, asserting that such a provision would "be tantamount to a taking and a betrayal of trust to Rural landowners."[48] In the face of vigorous opposition, the board did not forward the amendments to the council but began reviewing proposed child lots more rigorously, denying especially egregious proposals.[49]

In 2007 a majority of the council's Agricultural Preservation Working Group, composed of farmers, environmentalists, and rural community leaders, proposed minor adjustments but left intact the practice allowing child lots to exceed the density limits of the RDT zone. The planning board proposed including child lots in the overall allowable density of 1:25 acres. "The practice has nothing to do with equity for farmers. . . . Its purpose was to facilitate intergenerational transfer of the farm within the family, not to provide a windfall for owners with large families,"[50] the board said. Confronted with conflicting advice, the council did not act.

Over the next two years I explored different approaches with Mike Knapp, the council member representing most of the Reserve. Callum Murray, the planner responsible for the area, vetted draft proposals with the county staff and agricultural advisory groups to gauge support. In 2010 the planning board proposed three changes. First, it clarified the purpose of the child lot exemption was to facilitate intergenerational transfer of family farms. Second, it limited the total number of child lots to three and limited their size to no more than three acres. Finally, it required the person creating the lot and the child taking title to grant a covenant to the county providing that if a child lot was sold out of the family within five years, a remaining TDR would be lost, or if none remained attached to the land, the owner would pay the county the value of one Building Lot Termination (BLT) easement, with a *pro-rata* reduction for each year of child ownership.

As finally adopted in October 2010, the amendment allowed larger lots if necessary to meet septic field requirements, required a minimum parent parcel size of 25 acres for the first child, 70 acres for the second, and 120 acres for the third. Two additional lots could be permitted if the Agricultural Preservation Advisory Board found they would promote family farming, and the tract contained an additional 50 acres for each of them. Enforcement was left to the planning board to try to recover any funds "improperly obtained" from a sale or lease of a child lot earlier than five years after final inspection of the house.[51] Council staff in 2012 concluded that the effect of the amendments would restrict future child lots to no more than 67 for the entire reserve, but a smaller number was likely to materialize.[52]

The "Fifth" TDR

When the Reserve was created in 1981, planners expected landowners to sell four of the five development rights for each 25 acres and retain one for an existing or future farmhouse. They did not anticipate emergence of a robust market in land with buildable rights to construct ostentatious exurban homes in a pastoral landscape. By the late 1990s, it was apparent that the "fifth"[53] or "buildable" development right was far more valuable than the four "excess" rights.[54] Country buildable lot prices ranged from $300,000 to $750,000, many times the agricultural value of a 25-acre parcel with no retained development right.[55] Such prices virtually precluded new farmers from buying land and proliferation of McMansions generated a serious long-term threat to the Reserve's rural character and to fragmenting the critical mass of a working landscape. A large farm could be carved into a cluster of several three to five acre lots plus a remaining outlot ostensibly for "agriculture," but more likely to become uncultivated open space.

Shortly after the turn of the century, the hot private market for TDRs in Clarksburg induced a sharp drop in AEP applications just as the county received $6.5 million in transfer taxes when a large farm was sold. Faced with the prospect of having to remit unused revenues to the state, Jeremy Criss and John Zawitoski, who managed the fund for the county, recommended using it to acquire easements terminating the "fifth" buildable development right.[56] James Clifford, an attorney and farmer in the Reserve championed this proposal for a BLT program that would offer a premium price for these "super TDRs." The idea was attractive to both landowners and other supporters of the Reserve. The council's Agricultural Policy Working Group and the planning board strongly endorsed it.[57] The council's Planning, Housing and Economic Development Committee urged the planning board and county executive to develop means of implementing a BLT program.[58]

Retained development rights in the Reserve could potentially yield about 1,600 home sites. With the agricultural land transfer tax averaging about $2,000,000 annually it could take 200 years for the county to buy them all. A private market analogous to the one created for TDRs was essential to provide a reasonable chance of making a difference in the character of the Reserve. The best opportunity to create such a market was in the redevelopment of older commercial areas, such as White Flint.[59] Developers were required to purchase BLT easements (or make equivalent contributions to a county fund set up to buy them) to justify a percentage of the increased density they proposed to build in these zones.[60]

As the planning staff and board drafted the zoning regulations, the county executive staff prepared amendments to the county's Agricultural Preservation Ordinance and accompanying regulations to establish the BLT easement purchase program and the special fund to receive contributions from developers that could not find a willing seller of buildable rights or needed only a portion of a development right to satisfy density requirements.[61] The council secured legislation transferring $5 million from the M-NCPPC's Advance Land Acquisition Fund to seed the new BLT fund. The first eight easements were acquired in 2012 at an average price of $246,000. A private market formed as developers began filing project applications that required them to purchase BLT easements.[62]

The Future of Farming

The Agricultural Reserve was the last significant accomplishment of the Progressive Regime. It affirmed the vision of the General Plan and set the development pattern of the county. Its creation and survival in one of the fastest growing metropolitan regions in the country was the result of the fortuitous conjunction of natural constraints, rational analysis, planning imagination and technique, political leadership, luck, and a strong autonomous planning institution. It fused the logic of consequentiality and the logic of appropriateness.

As *Wedges and Corridors* became a policy icon, development that threatened to fragment or diminish the wedges drew the condemnation of defenders of its sacred text. They characterized the Dickerson Advanced Wastewater Treatment plant and force main as urgent existential threats to the survival of the western wedge. The rural zone found a problem for which it seemed an appropriate solution. The professional planning, legal, and political skills developed in applying the Rural Zone were crucial to later success in gaining approval of the AROS plan and sectional map amendment. The growing national interest in agricultural preservation and the concurrent spike in commodity prices made it possible to revisit policy scarcely five years after the area had undergone comprehensive rezoning. Working closely with farm interests this time to ensure their participation in developing data and analyses that addressed issues important to them, and in particular figuring out how to use TDRs to resolve the equity issue, were keys to acceptance of the plan. An added benefit of TDR easements was they protected land in perpetuity from intense development, undercutting the impermanence syndrome.

One of the important political strokes in the success of the AROS plan was reframing the issue as one of protecting the county's agricultural economy and rural heritage rather than merely preserving a wedge of open space. Giving the area a name—The Agricultural Reserve—endowed it with cultural meaning and symbolism that was far more powerful than leaving it as merely the outer, rural reaches of "wedges" ancillary to the corridor or a low-density zoning district. It now could be defended as something of intrinsic value to the county. Indeed, in later years various officials referred to it being as inviolate as New York's Central Park.

Unlike a park in the public domain, almost all land in the Agricultural Reserve remained in private ownership. Its survival and integrity rested on the interest of its landowners in maintaining a working landscape. That in no small part depended on the determination of the planning board and its staff to make the plan work. In the first instance that required establishing enough receiving areas to create a viable market for TDRs so that land would be placed under easement. As soon as the council adopted the AROS plan, the board and its staff set about identifying receiving areas so the council could approve them before the next election, avoiding the risk of changes in council membership that might undo it. Their prompt action, ratified by the council, reinforced the plan's credibility and a TDR market flourished without financial assistance from the county. When the county's easement purchase program was established to take advantage of the available transfer tax monies, it provided further evidence of county commitment to the Reserve.

As the Pure Political Regime supplanted the Progressive Regime, interpretation and implementation of the plan became inconsistent. The board's administration of the child lot exception became lax and the provision was selectively abused. The board was slow to devise a correction. The use of sand mounds to increase opportunity to maximize residential development in the Reserve originated with landowners and the county executive's staff. It was abetted by the council's inattentive concurrence in a health regulation that circumvented a master plan amendment, thus avoiding planning board review and more intense public scrutiny. The board initially acquiesced in the decision and approved sand mound subdivisions. Although it ultimately urged restrictions on their use, councils of the Pure Political Regime, beset by conflicting interests and without a cohesive majority on land use policy, did not respond to undo the mischief fostered by the 1994 resolution.

As the Reserve proved itself it won over interests that initially opposed its creation. Tensions remained among landowners and farmers that wanted to protect the area for farming but still be able to cash out at development prices rather than at the land's agricultural value. In a sense, the success of the Reserve generated an inherent danger: it became increasingly attractive to "estate" homebuyers and institutions seeking large acreages. Selling to them was temptation hard to resist.

Executive branch employees and farmers initiated the BLT idea to address the threat of estate subdivisions posed by the "fifth" TDR. The council endorsed it with almost indiscriminate enthusiasm. The planning staff and board figured out how to make it work, crafting the changes in the zoning code that provided a way to terminate a substantial number of buildable development rights as an incident of redevelopment of obsolete commercial areas.

The Reserve husbanded passionate advocacy by many old and new residents. Individuals, such as Mike Rubin, invested heavily in land, buying farms, placing them under easement to extinguish most development rights, and attracting conservation buyers. An avid horseman, Rubin was instrumental in creating and providing seed money for two miniature republics, Montgomery Countryside Alliance (MCA) and Equestrian Partners in Conservation. The Sugarloaf Citizens Association and Sugarloaf Conservancy, a land trust, also provided critical support. MCA began a broad education campaign reaching out to groups and individuals in the urbanized parts of the county, with a focus on the Reserve's role in providing fresh food and cultural and recreational resources. The Farm

Bureau remained an advocate of traditional farming interests, and in 2014 commodity farmers organized as Montgomery Agricultural Producers to advance their particular interests.

Assessing the extent to which the Agricultural Reserve serves the public interest requires a more critical examination of its role and consequences. It has sustained a working landscape for over thirty years, substantially slowing but not fully stopping conversion of farmland to residential subdivisions. It facilitated—some might say, imposed—a more compact pattern of growth and development than Montgomery's neighbors.

In 2014 the county had 577 farms and 350 horticultural businesses. The average farm was 121 acres. The average value of a county farm's land and buildings was over $1 million. Total sales of traditional agricultural products in 2007 exceeded $33 million. The horticultural industry generated revenues of $125 million and the equine industry added another $85 million.[63] Over 72,000 of the 78,000 acres assessed as farmland were under easements restricting residential development to no more than one house per twenty-five acres.

In addition to preservation of agriculture, the Reserve provides significant environmental services. Most of its streams maintain good water quality. Its commodity farmers generally use no-till practices, which reduces run-off and sedimentation. Forest acreage increased with establishment of forest banks and replanting areas used by developers to comply with off-site forest conservation requirements. These services must be balanced against the increased densities and associated externalities that result from the transfer of development rights to receiving areas.

Clearly, TDR receiving areas were not distributed equally across the county but located where land had not yet developed. Some civic activists in the five planning areas that received three-fourths of the TDRs complained they were burdened by an unfair share of the added density, resulting in diminished amenity, congestion, and inconvenience. Since developers rarely used the full number of TDRs permitted by the zone, impacts were less than anticipated by master plans. There are no reliable data on the effect of these marginal increases in density, but they appear to be negligible. Even in Olney, where 1,704 TDRs were incorporated into projects, the increase is a small fraction of the total number of households and the homes built using TDRs are not distinguishable from their neighbors.

An argument can be (and, indeed, was) made that the same result in land conservation might have been achieved simply by downzoning, without use of TDRs. This is true to a point. Simple rezoning would not have ensured protection of land in perpetuity. It may well have been regarded as a holding action until the housing market demanded more land, followed by rezoning and extension of public water and sewerage facilities. By placing perpetual TDR easements on the land, the impermanence syndrome was arrested and owners were willing to invest in farming rather than wait for the development market to ripen. Straight downzoning would have ignored the "equity" argument made by farmers. TDRs blunted resistance to what owners understandably saw as a radical and abrupt reduction in the value of their land. Ironically, even after being shorn of its "excess" TDRs, the land retained its value for estate homes, necessitating the BLT program. Extinguishing these "fifth" rights added a marginal cost to redevelopment of older areas down county, but it appears to be low enough to have little, if any, effect.

Housing advocates occasionally argued that protection of land in the Reserve increased land values elsewhere in the county, resulting in higher housing costs than would have prevailed if all the land in the county were available for development. This does not appear to be the case. Fairfax County, Virginia, developed all its farmland and its average land and housing values are slightly higher than Montgomery's. Moreover, because a TDR typically costs less than an additional lot, it lowers the average per-unit cost of producing a TDR-enhanced subdivision. The price to a buyer in a strong market, however, may not reflect that lower cost to the builder.

A more persuasive argument is that the presence of the Reserve induced some development to "leap-frog" to Frederick and Carroll counties to build less expensive homes than were available in Montgomery County. Growth in these counties increased congestion on Montgomery roads. Causality is not clear. Land is less expensive in outlying counties and regulations are less stringent. Lack of an analog to the Reserve in Fairfax did not retard the rush toward development in Loudoun or Prince William counties. Planning is not just economics. It is infused with politics, and as Mr. Dooley reminded us, "Politics ain't bean bag." And it is rarely Pareto optimal.

A Model of Farmland Conservation

In 2010 there were 239 TDR programs in thirty-four states.[64] As one of the first and the nation's most successful program of farmland preservation at the edge of a metropolitan area, Montgomery's Agricultural Reserve is often cited as a model for other areas. Its emulators should examine its experience closely to make effective use of its strengths and avoid problems it has confronted.

Key elements in its success begin with adoption of a master plan based on consensus that a critical mass of contiguous farmland should be protected from intensive development to arrest the impermanence syndrome and sustain farming as an important component of the local economy and as way of life. Zoning was designed to prefer agricultural uses and scaled to support an economically viable farm. Permitted densities were low enough to encourage sale of transferable development rights, which were provided in sufficient number to permit a reasonable recovery of equity in the land. An essential condition that made the program work was a robust market for housing and, thus, for TDRs that builders could use to increase density without acquiring more land. This required designation of enough receiving areas to create a competitive market for TDRs.

Finally, operation of the program was kept simple to minimize transaction costs and bureaucracy. Prices were established by direct negotiations between private buyers and sellers. Public involvement was limited to serializing TDRs, accepting and recording easements on land from which TDRs were extinguished and identifying their use on record plats of subdivisions built in receiving areas. The county Agricultural Services Division was helpful in providing information about the TDR and AEP programs and supporting the farm community.

Some newer programs have established TDR banks to serve as purchasers of last resort during slow markets. A program such as Montgomery's Agricultural Easement Program to purchase strategically important development rights can be a useful complement to a market-based system. A few jurisdictions have permitted developers to build with the bonus density by paying a "density transfer charge" when no TDRs are available. The funds accumulated from these payments can then be used to acquire land or easements for public benefits. Montgomery's experience suggests such devices are unnecessary if a strong market exists.

Perhaps the most important long-term issue Montgomery's experience suggests designers of farmland conservation programs should address is how to deal with retained rights to build on land from which "excess" TDRs have been severed. If at the outset the county had substantially increased the number of units a purchaser of those rights could build it could have precluded the need to establish the BLT program after some damage had been done to the integrity of the Reserve. The failure to address large private institutions, sanitary technologies, and child lots until after they became problems also offers a cautionary lesson for others.

GROWTH PAINS AND POLICY

Of all the planning decisions made in Montgomery County, none encompassed the continuing tensions and interdependence of planning and politics as fully as the forty-year debate over managing growth. The General Plan established a pattern for growth but had little to say about its rate. The builders of the commercial republic were prepared to lead the market with a constant supply of homes. The citizens of the miniature republics, having bought homes in a suburban garden, wanted no more development that added traffic to roads, students to schools, and leveled forests next door that were not parks after all. "Staging" growth to sustain the commercial republic without excessively annoying the miniature republic became a continuing challenge for the planners' logic of consequentiality and the politicians' logic of appropriateness.

The rise of the Progressive Regime coincided with a paradigm shift in urban planning. The value of growth, long almost synonymous with American patriotism, was questioned in places low and high. Silver Spring resident Rachael Carson's 1962 book, *Silent Spring*, transformed discourse on the relationship of humans and development with the natural world. Pictures astronauts captured of earth as a "big blue marble" floating in space captured public imagination of the planet's fragility. The policy literature of the 1970s was replete with concern for the decline of central cities, the remorseless consumption of ever more land per dwelling as suburbs sprawled outward, growing congestion on streets and highways, and the frailty of the nation's waterways and air. A 1973 study by the Task Force on Land Use and Urban Growth, supported by the Rockefeller Brothers Fund, declared:

> A new mood in America has emerged that questions traditional assumptions about the desirability of urban development. The motivation is not exclusively economic. It appears to be part of a rising emphasis on human values, on the preservation of natural and cultural characteristics that make for a humanly satisfying living environment.[1]

The Costs of Sprawl, released the same year by the U.S. Council on Environmental Quality, challenged the economic benefits of the dominant pattern of growth.[2] These reports coincided with the oil embargo imposed by the Organization of Petroleum Exporting Countries, which induced sharp increases in gasoline prices and long lines at filing stations. The costs of sprawl became personal. Even the development industry acknowledged a need to do things differently. The Urban Land Institute observed:

> The ethic of growth in America is increasingly being challenged; no longer is it being accepted unquestioningly as a promise of progress. Its effects on the quality of life are widely debated, and its management and control are seen by many as essential elements of modern land use policy.[3]

Several communities across the country pushed at the limits of their land use powers as they sought ways of controlling the amount, location, and pace of growth. Ramapo, New York, adopted a new master plan and zoning map, an eighteen-year capital improvements program, and an ordinance that required coordination of development with the provision of facilities, essentially limiting the amount of growth that could occur during each phase of facility construction.[4] Challenged by developers, the New York Court of Appeals in 1972 held phasing of development was within the town's planning powers and delaying some development as long as eighteen years was not a regulatory taking.[5] The case provided planners a legal foundation for plans and regulations that required "concurrency" of development and public facilities.

Other jurisdictions experimented with growth controls. Oregon required municipalities to set urban growth boundaries.[6] Petaluma, California set a cap on the number of residential units that could be approved in a year.[7] Boulder, Colorado established growth boundaries and service districts to restrict suburban sprawl.[8] Congress enacted the Water Quality Act of 1965 and the Air Quality Act in 1967.[9] The Nixon administration seized the popular momentum of heightened environmental concern to shift the agenda from explicitly "urban" policies, with their overtones of racial and class conflicts.[10] The National Environmental Protection Act of 1969 was followed by reorganization of various federal bureaus into the Environmental Protection Agency.[11] The Clean Air Act in 1970, and the Clean Water Act of 1972 established a new regulatory system.[12] Funds became available for state programs to clean up rivers and reduce pollution while restricting emissions of pollutants and imposing penalties on underperforming facilities. Many drafters and administrators of these laws and regulations lived in Montgomery County, and together with a growing environmental constituency began urging that master plans meet or exceed federal and state standards.

Alarmed over deterioration of the Chesapeake Bay, the Maryland General Assembly enacted legislation requiring each county to prepare and regularly update a ten-year plan for water and sewerage facilities.[13] Significantly, the law shifted control over the extension of facilities from the sanitary commission to the county executive and council. It required the council to approve the plan after review and comment from the planning board, which included reports on the consistency of service extensions with the county's comprehensive plan. When combined with the requirement of the county charter for annual approval of a six-year Capital Improvements Program (CIP),[14] the Progressive Council took office with new powers to stage the provision of all county-financed public facilities. Along with power to zone, these were key elements for staging envisioned by the Blue Ribbon Committee. What remained to be fashioned was a means of coordinating provision of public facilities with private development.

The Adequate Public Facilities Ordinance

Revision of the Germantown Master Plan provided the opportunity to adopt the Adequate Public Facilities Ordinance (APFO). Less ambitious than Rampo's eighteen-year program, it was tied to the CIP and the Water and Sewerage plan. Initial experience with them showed need for substantial adjustments in construction schedules each year. Because neither the General Plan nor existing master plans had staging elements and with more than twenty planning areas, some master plans could not be revised for many years, short-term coordination seemed the best way to meet legal and political challenges of getting something adopted in the face of certain opposition from developers. The logic of consequentiality provided the rationale for concurrency. The logic of appropriateness provided the rationale for the APFO's scope. A simple subdivision regulation consisting of two sentences was proposed:

> *Adequate public facilities.* The planning board must not approve a preliminary plan of subdivision unless the board finds that public facilities will be adequate to support and service the area of the proposed subdivision. Public facilities and services to be examined for adequacy include roads and public transportation facilities, sewerage and water service, schools, police stations, firehouses, and health clinics.[15]

Though adopted in conjunction with approval of the Germantown Master Plan, the ordinance was written to enable the planning board to enforce it to prevent "premature" development anywhere, whether or not there was an up-to-date master plan with a staging element. Feedback from administration of the ordinance would also indicate where and when additional facilities should be added to the CIP.

The APFO administration was made part of the subdivision approval process because that was when the presence or absence of facilities was determined and when dedications for facilities were required. It was also the earliest point in the regulatory process at which a developer could know whether it could proceed. Therefore, a subdivision would be rejected if the board found it was not in an area designated for water and sewer service within four years, or the roads necessary to serve it were not programmed for construction in the first four years of the CIP. Sewers and roads were facilities essential for development to proceed because without them new residents could not get there and their waste could not leave. Other facilities, with the possible exception of schools, were unlikely to be determinative in an individual case, but including them was politically necessary. A developer of property where necessary facilities were neither available nor programmed could avoid denial by building them itself.

Inventing Growth Policy

The Adequate Public Facilities Ordinance was reasonably effective in restricting development where facilities were not available or programmed. In this respect it had a greater effect on the location of development than on the amount or pace of it. But regulation of subdivision activity was not management of growth at countywide scale. Comprehensive growth management would be even more controversial than the APFO.

Mindful that the first rule of Montgomery's planning politics was that everyone should get into the act, the planning board initiated a broadly inclusive process of public participation and education to determine if public support for growth policy existed. To ensure an open, transparent process free of a predetermined outcome, the board contracted with the League of Women Voters to manage a citizen advisory committee and a series of "Chautauquas." These forums offered food and entertainment as well as presentations of alternative growth scenarios. Following discussion of issues and alternatives, instant voting technology was used to record preferences of the several hundred participants. The board held concurrent public work sessions with experts on growth management, including Anthony Downs, the author of the *Costs of Sprawl*.

The advisory committee endorsed the idea of a growth policy, noting: "We now realize that our land, water and air are limited, and that in the future, progress will be based on our ability to manage these resources."[16] It recommended a countywide staging program to manage and time growth where it was desirable; take leadership in the Council of Governments to set regional standards for environmental constraints on growth; and analyze the impact of the then current population forecast of 17,000 people a year and two alternative forecasts—one lower and one higher.[17] It provided only a general sense of what growth policy should do and even fewer specifics about how to do it.

The Conceptual Model

Tustian and I agreed growth policy had to have a solid conceptual foundation and a decision-making system grounded in professionally accepted analyses and legally defensible rules. Blunt instruments, such as annual growth caps or demarcation lines, did not seem politically feasible, even if legal. Because there was no well-trod path to follow, an incremental approach was necessary to craft policies that could pass professional, political, and legal muster. Most important, everyone—staff, board, council, and key stakeholders—needed time to assimilate the ideas and assess the utility, wisdom, and political risks of becoming pioneers in uncharted policy territory. Therefore, the board started with a series of annual informational reports to the council.

In the first report, "Framework," Tustian presented a tightly constructed rationale for growth policy. It modeled how growth occurred as people moved where there were jobs, creating demand for housing, community services, and amenities. Transportation systems created opportunities for development and responded to demands it generated. Growth produced congestion, stressing natural and community systems, constraining future growth of population and jobs. Each element in the model—people, jobs, shelter, community, transport, and nature—generated land uses that affected the quality of life for residents and workers. Most jobs and shelter were produced by the private sector. The private and public sectors both produced community facilities and services, while most transportation facilities and much of the natural system were in the public domain.

Local government influenced the location, character, and timing of growth through the exercise of its three inherent, but limited powers. The police power included authority to plan and regulate land uses. The power of the purse enabled local government to tax and spend. And the power of eminent domain allowed acquisition of land for public uses. The county would need to design and coordinate the use of these powers to guide development in accord with the public interest embodied in the General Plan. To keep the system in balance, regulation had to be coordinated with public expenditures and acquisition of land. An analytical section of the report discussed trends and problems that affected the rate, location, and costs of growth.

The board made fifteen general recommendations, the most prescient of which were that the county should focus in the near term on producing the transportation and sanitary facilities that would encourage concentration of future development in the corridor cities and mixed-use centers in the urban ring; subsidize expansion of high density rental housing, especially for moderate-income households and empty nesters; and develop a set of "quality of life" indicators to evaluate the effectiveness of growth policy and master plans. Staging elements were recommended for all master plans.[18]

Tustian, Robert Winick, chief of the planning department's transportation division, and Drew Dedrick, chief of the research division, worked at the Metropolitan Washington Council of Governments with professional colleagues from other jurisdictions to improve regional population, economic, and transportation models. These tools were urgently needed to prepare the board to address recommendations of the citizens' advisory committee to evaluate the reasonableness and impacts of higher and lower growth scenarios on the county's fiscal condition and quality of life.

The Risk of Forecasting Risks

The council in early 1975 agreed the board should focus the second growth policy report on the fiscal impact of alternative growth rates. Forecasts of population and jobs drove strategic capital budget decisions. The population forecast influenced school construction and expansion of a wide range of other county services and facilities. If the resulting scale and pattern of development did not produce a commensurate revenue base, the tax burden would adversely impact residents and businesses.

The second report examined the fiscal impact of three ten-year population growth scenarios: an adjusted trend annual rate of 15,000; a high rate of 21,000; and a low rate of 5,000. It found that regardless of the growth rate, a substantial revenue increase would be necessary to maintain current service levels. It concluded that concentrating development down county where infrastructure existed would provide some cost savings for services and produce the greatest increases in assessable base. Low growth produced the greatest per capita deficit.[19]

A sequel, published a month later, illustrated the practical applications of the fiscal analysis for infrastructure decisions. The most important and controversial finding was that "the anticipated orderly growth of the County would not suffer if the [Dickerson] AWT [Advanced Wastewater Treatment] plant's capacity were cut from 60 mgd to 30 mgd."[20] A companion analysis recommended reducing the size of a proposed 160 mgd water filtration plant. The second stage of each plant could be postponed until after 1990, assuming the "trend" scenario, which looked comfortably high. Reducing their size would save $46 million in debt service over twenty years.

Rather than welcome this news, County Executive James Gleason and the Washington Suburban Sanitary Commission responded angrily that the board was undercutting the plan for the Dickerson plant, on which a substantial amount of money (and political capital) had been spent. They questioned the board's methods of population forecasting, arguing that the "trend" forecast, on which the treatment plant plan was based, should not have been modified based on the board's inter-census survey conducted to validate it. Their position seemed to be that the old forecast may have been wrong, but it was official and should be used. They could have saved their umbrage because U.S. Environmental Protection Agency vetoed the Dickerson plant and county needs were met by a much smaller plant on Rock Run in Potomac and enhancements to the regional Blue Plains plant.

Lost in the controversy was a key planning idea: population and job forecasting were inexact practices. They relied on assumptions, and therefore, alternative scenarios should be analyzed in terms of the level of fiscal and service risk the county was willing to accept. A smaller population would bear the costs of excess capacity in a facility built on high growth assumptions that failed to materialize. On the other hand, if facilities were scaled to meet a low growth assumption and resulted in less capacity than needed, congestion, rationing, and moratoria would occur while additional facilities were constructed.

Instead of conducting risk analysis, the executive and council demanded a full explanation of the methods employed by the board in forecasting population, jobs, and housing. Thus, the third growth report laid out the technical details of the forecasting process.[21] It made three significant findings: the 1976–1986 rate of population increase would be lower than in prior decades due to lower household size, fertility, and immigration rates; households would grow faster than population; and jobs would grow faster than either households or population. The report found that for the first time a majority of the county's workforce was employed within the county and recent additions to the housing stock contained a lower proportion of detached single-family homes than townhouses and multi-family buildings.

Moving from Ideas to Policy

The first three reports developed a conceptual model for growth management, demonstrated means of measuring the impact of growth on fiscal resources, and perfected an approach to using growth forecasts to assess risks of alternative levels of public investment aimed at sustaining acceptable levels of service. What remained was devising a legally defensible means of regulating the overall amount of growth to correspond to the capacity to serve it and guiding it to locations that could most efficiently assimilate it. The next two reports addressed those issues and in so doing laid the foundation of the growth management system that endured for the next thirty years.

Carrying Capacity and Staging

Borrowing a concept from ecology, the fourth growth policy report proposed using the "carrying capacity" of the county's principal existing and programmed infrastructure—transportation, sanitation, and schools—to stage residential and nonresidential development in each planning area and, in the aggregate, for the county as a whole.[22] This set no absolute ceiling for growth, recognizing it could rise or fall based on expansion or contraction of facilities and public tolerance of changing levels of service. The ultimate ceiling was the zoning envelope, which could also rise or fall as master plans were amended and zoning was changed.

Putting this system in operation required coordination of several moving parts. The CIP and the Water and Sewerage Plan had to be coordinated closely with forecasts of future growth and development projects to avoid long lags between the population of new subdivisions and the presence of facilities. The council agreed the board should take the next step and prepare a staging element for the General Plan.

The 1979 growth policy report recommended the council approve a comprehensive staging element as an amendment to the General Plan to synchronize private development activity with public investment in infrastructure. The staging element would consist of a set of future growth ceilings for each of eleven policy areas calibrated to the "carrying capacity," or "adequacy," of facilities available at each stage.

The policy areas were the key innovation of the staging element. Analogous to watersheds, they were based on "traffic sheds"—neighborhoods in which traffic flowed from a limited number of collector streets onto the arterial system. The planning department's transportation model simulated the level of congestion on the road network of each traffic shed. Traffic sheds tributary to segments of the arterial system were aggregated into eleven policy areas. Each was assigned an acceptable level of roadway congestion based on its pattern of transit service. This resulted in four tiers of service, with down-county areas served by Metro expected to tolerate higher levels of traffic congestion, while rural areas with little to no bus service were expected to experience almost none.

Once the policy areas and their levels of service were established, the transportation model set ceilings for the number of jobs and homes that could be added in each stage without reducing levels of service, based on existing and programmed facilities. When the number of homes or jobs reached the "ceiling" for a stage of growth, the planning board would deny further subdivisions until a new "lump" of infrastructure was programmed to raise the ceiling.

The board argued this approach had several advantages over the case-by-case approach used to administer the Adequate Public Facilities Ordinance, which addressed only the adequacy of facilities directly serving the subdivision under review. It could not account for "downstream" or cumulative effects on a larger area. Subdivisions rarely contained more than a few hundred homes. This did not match the much larger scale at which public infrastructure was added, making it virtually impossible to maintain an equilibrium between aggregate private land development and production of facilities needed to serve it without some limit for the larger service area of which each subdivision was a small part.

Having the council establish service levels and thresholds for each policy area would set clear legislative standards for administration of the APFO. Regular monitoring of development activity would inform the CIP's priorities and the construction schedule for facilities. Reviewing and amending the staging element of the General Plan every two years could establish a contrapuntal rhythm with the CIP and the Ten-Year Water and Sewerage Plan. The CIP would provide information needed to adjust growth policy to the county's fiscal realities. This process would ensure expansion of facilities corresponded to demand in each area and that private development would not overburden existing and programmed facilities.

Rational Planning and Political Reality

This felicitous outcome, of course, depended on the willingness of the council and executive to set up such a system and live by it. The political environment for planning shifted. The reception for growth policy was cooler than in prior councils, but not out of reach, so, the board recommended adoption of a staging element for the General Plan. Joint council-planning board work sessions were arranged to acquaint the council—especially its new members—with what was involved in creating an effective growth policy. Following a detailed briefing by Tustian, the challenge confronting the policy was captured when Council Member Rose Crenca pleaded: "Could you just give us the Sesame Street version."

As the council began its work sessions, the new county executive, Charles Gilchrist, elected with strong backing from much of the old guard and many civic leaders, was wary of the planning board. He defeated me in the 1978 Democratic primary and my Republican colleague, Max Keeney, in the general election. He took a passive-aggressive stance toward a council-adopted growth policy. An assistant county attorney, ostensibly sent to offer legal advice, objected that it conflicted with the county charter by limiting the executive's discretion in preparing the CIP. Civic activists found the proposed levels of service too relaxed.

Developers thought them too rigid. Several council members were uneasy about approving service standards. That made them responsible for stopping or allowing development in some areas. After several weeks of discussion, it was clear the council preferred to avoid a decision. Adoption of the growth policy would precipitate a confrontation with Gilchrist; rejection would be seen as repudiation of the planning board, which the council majority was unwilling to do. Since no council resolution had been introduced, I withdrew the policy for further refinement and testing. With both the miniature and commercial republics unhappy, the logic of consequentiality could not be squared with the logic of appropriateness.

With bleak prospects for council approval of a comprehensive growth policy, the planning board remained responsible for case-by-case administration of the APFO. Taking an expansive view of its authority, the board adopted the staging ceilings and levels of service calculated for the proposed growth policy as guidelines for administration of the ordinance. Ceilings were refreshed annually based on updated development, facilities, and population trends. The staff improved the transportation model, testing methods in professional conferences and peer-reviewed papers.[23] Transportation capacity ceilings were adjusted to account for the effect of upstream traffic on congestion within policy areas.[24] Developers of subdivisions containing more than fifty units were required to conduct a Local Area Traffic Review (LATR) to ensure that intersections in the immediate vicinity of their subdivisions would operate at acceptable levels of service after new trips were added. Projects were approved only if applicants passed this test or proffered improvements necessary to meet the standard.

None of the major stakeholders was satisfied. The board and its staff felt trapped in a system that emphasized only the regulatory side of growth management. The authority to enforce the development ceilings rested on the board's general power to deny a subdivision if it found facilities inadequate. The ceilings were objectively set but they exerted no serious leverage on scheduling capital projects. Developers despised the staging ceilings and the cost of traffic studies and intersection improvements they had to make to gain approval of their projects. During robust housing markets, they denounced ceilings that limited growth as products of the "black box" transportation model. In soft markets they blamed the APFO for discouraging development. Housing advocates worried the ceilings caused land values to rise in areas with excess capacity, pricing out affordable housing and compromising long-standing policy to disperse it throughout the county. Community activists in the urban ring considered the standards too lax and the ceilings too high. They tended to attribute all increases in local traffic congestion to excessive development although part of the increase resulted from trips originating in outlying areas of the region. An additional source was closer to home: the increase in the number of automobiles and trips per household as women entered the workforce and suburban children gained drivers' licenses. Civic critics and PTA leaders complained that the board had no standard for school capacity that could ever deny a subdivision. The board relied on the advice of the Superintendent of Schools to determine whether schools were "adequate." It received no adverse opinions. Trends in demography and work could not be stopped, but community leaders seemed confident that policy could curb growth.

Adversaries in the commercial and miniature republics assailed council inaction. Some members proposed moratoria or caps on growth until facilities and services caught up. Gilchrist was concerned that moratoria in certain areas impaired economic development and growth of the tax base. He complained that "bad planning" produced imbalances between growth and facilities, although the problem lay not in the master plans, which balanced future land uses and transportation, but in the failure of the CIP to provide the planned facilities in concert with growth. The advantage for elected officials was they could blame the planning board for results that displeased them and their constituents. For its part, the board was frustrated by the complaints as it tried to manage growth in the absence of a clear, comprehensive policy that coordinated regulation with capital investments and system management.

To further heat the debate, growth surged. Housing production rose from an average of about 4,400 units a year from 1980 through 1982 to over 8,000 between 1983 and 1985. Non-residential construction rose from 2.6 million square feet in 1980 to 6.0 million in 1985.[25] Most growth in the first half of the decade occurred in the corridor cities along I-270 and in the Route 29 area, causing traffic to converge on the Capital Beltway and arterial roads in the urban ring.

Council members and the executive flailed for congestion relief or at least the appearance of doing something about the connection between growth and traffic. The council resorted to a Consensus Committee on Growth Management. It recommended expansion of infrastructure financing, new taxes, tighter development regulation, impact fees, and a new procedure for listing roads that could be counted in APFO review. Since none of these recommendations were self-executing, little happened.

Growth Policy Returns—It's about Congestion

Growth was a central issue in the heated 1986 Democratic primary contest for county executive between Council Member David Scull and State Senator Sidney Kramer. Scull was supported by civic leaders and slow growth advocates, while Kramer had the backing of business and development groups as well as County Executive Gilchrist. Scull proposed a moratorium on building permits and a countywide construction excise tax. Gilchrist, with Kramer's agreement, recommended a more limited impact fee for transportation in Germantown, Eastern Montgomery County, and Clarksburg. With payment of the fee, developers would be allowed to proceed in these areas, where robust growth was expected.

In the face of massive opposition from business interests the council killed Scull's moratorium proposal but enacted the construction excise tax on a 4–3 vote. Scull could not muster a fifth vote to override Gilchrist's veto. The council, left with no alternative, approved the transportation impact fee.

An Interim Policy

As these events were unfolding, Tustian suggested to Council President Scott Fosler that at least some of the finger pointing (if not the congestion) might be alleviated if the council adopted an annual growth policy that established ceilings on the amount of new development the planning board could approve, metering it to match its decisions on capital improvements or management measures. In this way, the council and executive could set the ceilings for growth in particular areas but decide if special circumstances justified exceeding them for projects providing unique economic, amenity, housing, or other benefits.

Fosler embraced staging development based on the carrying capacity of infrastructure. He introduced legislation calling for an interim growth policy for 1986 and an annual growth policy thereafter. The executive was empowered to review and revise the planning board draft before its submission to the council for public hearing and action.[26] Gilchrist, who opposed adoption of growth policy in 1980, now supported the legislation, which tightened transportation standards for approval of subdivisions and approved a set of short-term traffic alleviation measures. The council also imposed an impact fee on development in Germantown and Eastern Montgomery County, the areas with the greatest deficits in transportation capacity.[27]

Consideration of a more comprehensive policy was postponed until after the November election. The planning board was directed to prepare an annual growth policy, which the council would adopt after receiving recommendations from the county executive.[28] The council also amended the APFO, adding standards and procedures for its administration.[29] Fourteen years after it was first proposed the council decided a comprehensive growth policy was appropriate.

Limits of Managing Growth

The planning board presented the draft 1987–1988 growth policy to County Executive Sidney Kramer and the new council, with progressives now in the minority, a week after they took office in December 1986. The draft refined the policy areas first proposed in 1979, updated the test for transportation adequacy, and added the LATR test for local intersection performance. A new test for school adequacy would deny a subdivision if the students it added would cause enrollment at any level (elementary, middle, high) of schools in a "cluster"—a high school attendance area—to exceed 110 percent of capacity by the fourth year of the school system's capital program.

Kramer rewrote the board's draft, recommending major changes. Instead of using the high school clusters to test for school capacity he recommended using the school system's three administrative districts, each containing a number of clusters, making it virtually impossible to deny a subdivision. He proposed requiring council and executive approval of assumptions used in the transportation model and joint ownership of it by the executive and planning board. He urged separating the Silver Spring Central Business District from a larger policy area, freeing capacity for the Silver Triangle.

In an effort to shift power over growth management from the board to the executive, Kramer proposed transferring administration of the APFO from subdivision approval to issuance of building permits by the County Department of Environmental Protection.[30] This proposal ostensibly aimed to assuage concerns expressed by both builders and community groups. Builders complained that road capacity was artificially reduced by counting estimated trips from approved subdivisions along with existing traffic against the growth ceiling. Dormant projects in the development "pipeline" could not hoard capacity if APFO tests were administered at building permit. An area would go into moratorium only when the number of building permits issued hit the capacity ceiling. Community groups, conversely, claimed that because an area's capacity for growth was based on the construction schedule in the CIP, subdivisions were approved and occupied before facilities were provided because the council and executive regularly delayed them. Limiting building permits to the amount of development served by roads that existed or would be in service within a year would ensure closer concurrency with private development. Subdivisions that did not win the race for building permits would be out of luck until actual improvements were made.

Ultimately, both developers and civic leaders rejected "test at permit" once they understood its practical consequences. Builders and bankers realized that delaying APFO testing until building permit made it uncertain an approved subdivision could proceed, imperiling the ability to finance projects and make the front-end investments and site work necessary before reaching the building permit stage. This was especially the case for large projects that involved extensive engineering and site preparation. Building permit applications for such projects were issued over many years as building and sales progressed. Land stripped of cover to prepare it for building could remain a vacant eyesore and become an environmental and safety hazard if permits were denied. Community leaders realized that moving the APF test would remove constraints on approval of subdivisions, gorging the pipeline and inducing pressure on the county to issue building permits even though the supporting facilities were not programmed.

The council, confronted with dissatisfaction with both existing practice and the executive's alternative, referred the proposal to a thirteen-member advisory committee. The committee quickly concluded that APFO testing at the permit stage was too late in the process. It rejected two alternatives proposed by the executive for the same reason. While most committee members thought the existing system fell short of the ideal, several concluded that the problem arose primarily from the failure of the county's CIP to maintain the construction schedule called for in master plans.[31] The committee accepted a Christeller proposal to allow the board to approve additional subdivisions if capacity to serve them was programmed in the CIP for construction six to ten years in the future.[32] This raised ceilings but required a leap of faith that the county would keep the out-year construction schedule.

The council made none of these changes in adopting the 1988 growth policy. It later created a separate policy area for the Silver Spring Central Business District (CBD). Christeller's revised test for transportation adequacy was accepted the following year and the council added an exception to ceilings for up to 750 affordable housing units. The number of policy areas grew to twenty-two by carving out central business districts and dividing one other large area. Six areas were placed in moratorium for housing and five for jobs. None was placed in moratoria for inadequate school capacity.

These first three years of experience with a council-adopted growth policy revealed it was easier to propose than achieve concurrency of growth and facilities. The market was segmented and diffused across the metropolitan area. It was difficult enough to forecast when approved development projects would reach completion, let alone estimate the rate of growth for housing and jobs in subareas of the county six to ten years ahead. The reliability of the CIP's construction schedule deteriorated beyond the current year as the council reduced, delayed, or eliminated projects in the next CIP cycle. State transportation funding was even less predictable. The fact that some approved subdivisions would not be completed, or even started within four years led to a "paper" scarcity of available capacity in the near-term, but if "ready" projects were approved and dormant projects suddenly sprung to life, the system would become congested and levels of service would decline.

There was one hard way to accommodate additional growth: fund increases in infrastructure capacity. There were four easy ways to allow it on paper: raise the ceilings by counting capacity programmed for the "out" (fifth and sixth) years; discount dormant pipeline projects to provide more room below the ceilings; divide policy areas to separate more constrained sectors from those less congested; or assign lower levels of service. The last two approaches were used for the Silver Spring CBD. Separating it from the larger policy area produced a better level of service for the surrounding suburban area by taking out the most congested roads. Simultaneously lowering the level of service for the CBD allowed the Silver Triangle to be approved. Setting a high level of service for traffic in Fairland, as demanded by Council Member Isiah Leggett in 1987, kept it in moratorium for almost twenty years.

The council invented a fifth method. "Ceiling flexibility" allowed the board to approve subdivisions recommended by the county executive and for which the developer proffered additional facility capacity. This was initially designed to facilitate development of the life sciences complex between Rockville and Gaithersburg. It was used later to accommodate the proposed Marriott headquarters and a shopping center in East Germantown.

Separate allocations of capacity for jobs and housing was problematic. The ratio for a given year was based on the long-range goals of master plans for a policy area. But factors beyond county control, such as changes in depreciation schedules in the 1986 federal tax reforms, were more influential in determining what was built. After overbuilding during the first half of the decade, commercial construction in the county fell 25.5 percent from 1986 to 1987.[33] Unreached commercial ceilings effectively restricted capacity available for residential development. The ratios for a policy area might be adjusted to avoid placing it in moratorium. This involved art more than science.

Starting Over in the Same Place

Seeking consensus on how best to deal with the vicissitudes of growth and the unsettling conundrums of growth policy, the council appointed a Commission on the Future. It was charged with recommending how best to cope with the cascading changes in demography, economics, environment, and energy that were placing communities under stress. After eighteen months of deliberation, the commission recommended returning to a moderate growth rate of about 10,000 jobs a year (in contrast with the recent 20,000 rate) while increasing housing production by 50 percent. It had no advice on how to achieve this. It proposed a comprehensive reassessment of the General Plan, retaining the Agricultural Reserve, and planning for more compact living patterns at selected Metrorail stops.[34]

The council exercised its appetite for expert analysis and directed the planning board to produce a comprehensive growth policy study to answer four questions: Can we grow without excessive congestion? Can we afford the cost of growth? How should we approach these problems? Are present management tools adequate?

Tustian and the planning staff produced a four-volume report that proposed shifting growth management toward "Centers and Trails" within the General Plan's corridors and activity centers. It found growth could occur without excessive congestion only if the average share of auto trips were reduced from 75 to 50 percent. This would require doubling the percentage of non-auto trips; creating new travel networks for light rail and buses, vans, bikes, and pedestrian systems; concentrating future development in pedestrian-friendly urban centers; and adopting pricing policies and subsidies to discourage auto use and encourage travel by transit. The county could afford growth if it increased taxes and fees and secured more state and federal funding for infrastructure and services. To contain urban sprawl and its environmental and social costs, growth management tools would need to be enhanced by new revenue sources for infrastructure and services, revision of master plans to concentrate growth, and expansion of efforts to increase housing affordability.[35]

The staff draft of the 1991 growth policy pointed out the pattern of growth was more important than its pace in determining the level of traffic congestion and policy that directed development to uncongested areas was generating more congestion.[36] The Planning, Housing and Economic Development (PHED) Committee dismissed the report. Council members complained of its cost, size, and (if they read it) declared it was impractical. The planning board, seeking to repair relationships with the council and executive, ignored it. The board's final draft of the 1991 Growth Policy deleted the section of the staff draft that recommended creating small "allocation areas" within policy areas, thus, enabling the growth policy to be "more sensitive to and supportive of pattern considerations as well as pace and proportion."[37] The board fudged the issue, recommending only that the council consider adjusting residential staging ceilings in areas close to transit stations but defer making any significant changes to the basic structure of policy areas.[38]

County Executive Kramer agreed and proposed removing some roads from the CIP, including improvements in Germantown that would have served the soon to be cancelled Marriott headquarters.[39] The council resolution adopting the 1991 growth policy made no mention of the development pattern. Instead it set the course of growth policy for the next decade: it would not become the vehicle for coordinating the police and purse powers of the county to produce a salubrious pattern of development. Instead, it would be narrowly focused on setting standards for administration of the Adequate Public Facilities Ordinance.[40]

Meanwhile, two developers appealed the denials of their subdivision plans for lack of transportation capacity. The courts upheld the denials, holding that the establishment of jobs and housing ceilings was a reasonable exercise of the county's police power. The courts also rejected the claim that the delay constituted a taking of their property since they were not deprived of reasonable uses pending the availability of facilities sufficient to support their projects.[41] In a separate case the Maryland Court of Appeals held the impact fee lacked the necessary nexus to the project it was charged against because the improvements did not benefit it and its primary purpose was not to regulate development, but to raise revenue.[42] The council quickly re-enacted the assessment as an excise tax on development, substituting "tax" for "fee" wherever it appeared, and made the amendments retroactive.[43]

By the end of 1991, three things had occurred that profoundly affected growth policy for the next decade. The General Assembly restored the council's power to appoint all planning board members and repealed executive power to rewrite or veto plans. Repeal ended opportunity for the county executive to build a governing regime in coalition with the development sector. Christeller and Tustian retired and the board no longer viewed growth policy as a vehicle for making major course corrections in the county's development pattern. With departure of the two main characters on whom the council had relied for planning advice, Glenn Orlin, who joined the council staff in the late 1980s, became the council's principal adviser on growth policy.

Exceptions Consume the Rules

When recession slowed growth officials sought ways of encouraging development. Even County Executive Neal Potter, long associated with the planned growth movement, urged the council to consider relaxing staging ceilings in selected areas to permit more housing.[44]

Between 1992 and 2002 the number of policy areas increased from twenty-two to twenty-nine. The council unsuccessfully sought ways to discount the pipeline and to create an effective test for adequate school capacity. It adjusted levels of service for areas where a majority wanted to encourage or discourage development, and lowered ceilings when fiscal constraints forced delays in programmed facilities. More exceptions to moratoria were made for projects of "special merit," such as low and moderate-income housing or projects deemed important to county economic development goals. Such projects occasionally emphasized *special* more than *merit*. An example was Council Member Leggett's sponsorship of the "6–12" exemption to the moratorium, which allowed a construction of a convenience store at a heavily congested intersection in East Germantown on the questionable assertion that such enterprises generated little or no traffic in addition to that already on the road. Planning and council staff uniformly opposed such "red-eyed Eskimos" but the council continued to approve them as aid and comfort to distressed constituents.

In 1994 the council adopted a new test of policy area transportation capacity, labeled PATR (Policy Area Transportation Review). It included a measure of transit accessibility, a new equation-based method of calculating auto congestion standards, and separated treatment of freeways from local roads in determining capacity ceilings. Applying it removed three areas from moratoria for jobs, but added one area with no room for housing. Growth policy was separated into two biennial elements: a "ceiling element" that set limits on the amount of residential and non-residential development that could be approved under the APFO; and a "policy element" that reported research and analysis of specific issues of concern to the council and planning board.[45]

Growth policy became an exercise in tweaking administration of the APFO but not an instrument for comprehensively and strategically coordinating development and facilities or steering growth to sustain the county's economy and the quality of life for residents.[46] By 2002, of twenty-four policy areas, two had been in housing moratoria for sixteen years, another two for nine years, and an additional five for five or more years. Half had been in moratoria for jobs for five years or more; six of those for eight years or more, all but one served by Metro stations.

From Moratoria to Pay & Go

David Levinson, a former M-NCPPC staff member who helped develop the transportation tests and ceilings, ruefully concluded that the effect of the county's growth policy, "is imposing the highest costs on new housing and employment in places with the highest congestion, precisely the locations where the government should encourage development to take advantage of the correlated access to jobs and housing."[47] He pointed out the system worked against itself; when roads were improved to reduce congestion it discouraged transit usage. Higher densities supported transit usage but could also increase road congestion. He concluded that the "top down" rational planning model used to set ceilings for growth had neither kept congestion in check nor matched provision of facilities with development. Nonetheless, travel times for county commuters had not increased for thirty years and it was not possible to know if moratoria resulted in more or less congestion.

Levinson recommended a "reactive" approach to growth management. Instead of relying on setting area ceilings and imposing moratoria until facilities caught up with demand or created excess capacity, he proposed assessing impact fees or taxes on development to recover the economic costs it imposed on the county. Such charges could be calibrated to encourage development where it would provide the greatest benefits and discourage it where it was less supportive of county goals.

Encouraged by the experiment with the Alternative Review Procedure for Metro station areas, the development industry and some council members embraced impact fees as a way around moratoria. Interest in the idea grew as the recession ended but development in the county did not recover as fast as in Fairfax County. Council president Gail Ewing proposed a "pay-and-go" system. Developers could bypass the tests if they made a transportation facilities payment. The tax would be higher in moratorium areas. County executive Douglas Duncan endorsed the proposal as a way to make the county more competitive in the regional development market.[48] The planning board opposed it, arguing that allowing any project paying to proceed effectively eliminated all moratoria, without which there was no way to identify areas where projects should pay the higher tax. The board proposed that if the council accepted the idea it should be restricted to areas where growth was encouraged and negative impacts on the transportation system could be minimized.[49]

With eight policy areas in moratoria for housing and seven for jobs when the 1998 Annual Growth Policy was adopted, a divided council finally agreed with Duncan and approved a pay-and-go amendment.[50] It limited "expedited review" for both residential and non-residential development to a five-year period and established different tax rates for moratorium and non-moratorium areas. But in May 1998 Marilyn Praisner, whose district included the eastern county, persuaded the council to limit pay-and-go to nonresidential projects.[51]

Weaving in Traffic

As the twentieth century ended, the economy recovered, Planning Board Chair William Hussmann tried to steer growth policy back toward its broader purpose. Transmitting the 1999 policy element report to the council, he suggested restoration of healthy residential and commercial markets provided an opportunity to consider changes to growth policy and infrastructure financing "that support true Smart Growth."[52] The board proposed broadly restructuring growth policy, noting it had "identified areas where the AGP [annual growth policy] does not appear to produce the desired results, procedures which restrict development unnecessarily or permit development where it should not, and procedures which create an unequal [allocation] of costs of infrastructure."[53]

To increase funding for transportation facilities while allowing more development in areas best suited for growth the board recommended converting the pay-and-go system into a countywide development impact tax designed to encourage development where transit service was available. Revenues would be earmarked for transportation management programs and master-planned facilities in the areas where the taxes were collected. To allow more growth at transit centers, the board proposed letting APFO approvals expire if building permits had not been obtained in twelve years, making unused capacity available for projects that were ready to proceed.[54] The council accepted only a recommendation to count five instead of four years of the CIP in estimating the capacity of roads to accommodate new growth. The following year it approved a countywide transportation impact tax but rejected earmarking the revenues to help finance area-specific projects. A revised APF test for schools temporarily placed the Damascus cluster in moratorium until the Clarksburg High School was programmed for construction. Policy areas in moratoria were reduced to four for housing and five for jobs in 2001.

The council's resistance to major changes reflected a deep division over the utility of policy area staging ceilings. Members advocating slower growth and opposing construction of the Inter-County Connector (ICC) favored maintenance of moratoria in their districts and strongly defended the system. Those favoring more development were skeptical of ceilings, arguing the critical issue was the increased congestion new subdivisions generated at nearby intersections. Revalidation of the transportation model resulted in significant changes to staging ceilings for several policy areas but the council declined to accept them. Instead it ordered the planning board to conduct a "top to bottom" review of growth policy during the next two years.

The Pause in Policy Area Review

The 2002 council election changed the growth policy landscape as profoundly as the 1990 election had done. Douglas Duncan was re-elected county executive for an unprecedented third term. The victory of his "End Gridlock" slate shifted the council's center of gravity toward acceptance of more and faster growth along with support for key highway projects—especially the ICC.

While the next round of growth policy was expected to deal with impact taxes and adequacy of schools, the survival of policy area review was the most critical matter addressed in the "top to bottom" review. Presenting the 2003–2005 policy element, the planning board declared: "The existing formulas for Policy Area Review simply do not reflect reality, and the Planning Board believes they should be abandoned."[55] Instead, it recommended a countywide biennial growth cap of 1 percent of the existing base for jobs and housing. Within that growth rate, a ratio of 1.6 jobs per housing unit would be permitted. Instead of retaining the twenty-nine policy areas, the county would be divided into eight areas reflecting different levels of transit usage and growth pressure. Slightly more than half of the growth in jobs and housing would be allocated to Metro station areas, and another quarter of it to other locations on the eastern and western branches of Metro's Red Line. The board proposed increases in the transportation impact tax and establishment of a school impact tax, with the revenues from both dedicated to funding capacity improvements.[56]

With the End Gridlock majority in firm control, the council eliminated policy area review and rejected the proposed annual growth rate. It directed the board to report annually on subdivision approvals accompanied by a list of high priority road and intersection improvements, based on existing and projected conditions. The council tightened standards for adequacy of local intersections everywhere but in Metro station areas and authorized the board to require large subdivisions to test intersections located farther from the site. If it found them inadequate, the developer would be required to make improvements or take other trip mitigation measures. The school test was tightened, but no areas were placed in moratorium. Impact taxes were raised, but the effective date was delayed for six months. This precipitated a rush by developers with approved projects to secure building permits before the higher rates took effect. Developers were allowed to receive a credit against the impact tax for road improvements they made.[57]

The changes had little effect. Of the 9,902 housing units in subdivisions approved the following year, only 813 would not have been approved under the prior policy. None of the approvals for commercial and office space could be attributed to the new policy. The council in 2005 made some minor changes in time limits for APFO approval, but approved no policy for the 2005–2007 period.

The 2006 council elections returned a narrow majority committed to restoration of policy area review and the planning board was directed to submit a new growth policy.[58] The board tried once more to pivot from obsession with congestion to a focus on managing growth in ways that contributed to the sustainability of communities and resources. The draft policy proposed:

> a conceptual adjustment from thinking of growth policy as primarily an instrument governing administration of the Adequate Public Facilities Ordinance (APFO) through the denial or delay of subdivisions until facilities—primarily roads—meet certain standards for levels of service. While growth policy continues to perform its traditional function, our recommendations are designed to perform a broader set of functions.[59]

The Council Deconstructs Growth Policy

To paraphrase an old hymn, the council didn't want to get adjusted. Its members were far from united in their expectations. The board structured the proposed policy as a single, comprehensive system with mutually reinforcing elements. Council procedure for considering the policy, however, was disjointed and narrowly focused. The PHED Committee considered most components but the Management and Fiscal Policy (MFP) Committee separately reviewed the impact tax. Only Council President Marilyn Praisner was a member of both committees.[60] Council members that took an interest in the deliberations were primarily concerned with outcomes and the effects on constituencies that mattered to them. They remained uncomfortable with key elements of the policy.

PHED Committee work sessions focused on reviving policy area review for transportation.[61] The board recommended a new approach, labeled Policy Area Mobility Review (PAMR).[62] A significant departure from past practice, PAMR measured *mobility* instead of congestion or *capacity*. This was done by estimating the speed at which peak hour auto trips for commuters from each policy area moved relative to free flow speed (Relative Arterial Mobility [RAM]) and the speed by which the journey to work could be made by transit, compared to driving (Relative Transit Mobility [RTM]). These measures were assigned Levels of Service (LOS) "grades" of A to F. Relative arterial and transit mobility were inversely related, as shown in Table 9.1, reflecting the principle that areas with better transit service could tolerate slower road travel. The levels of service for each policy area were plotted on a chart, shown in Figure 9.1. Each "step" in the chart indicated a change in arterial and transit service levels a traveler would experience, at the extreme upper left of the chart, LOS "A"—uncongested travel by car—but LOS "F" for travel by transit, to the far lower right, where auto travelers would experience LOS "D" but transit riders would enjoy LOS "B."

TABLE 9.1 Relationship of relative arterial mobility and relative transit mobility

IF AUTO TRAVEL SPEED AS PERCENT OF FREE-FLOW SPEED IS:	RAM LOS IS:	RTM LOS IS:	IF EFFECTIVE TRANSIT SPEED AS PERCENT OF ROADWAY SPEED IS:
At least 85%	A	F	Less than 42.5%
At least 70%	B	E	At least 42.5%
At least 55%	C	D	At least 50%
At least 40%	D	C	At least 60%
At least 25%	E	B	At least 75%
Below 25%	F	A	100% or more

Source: Montgomery County Planning Board. May 21, 2007. *Toward Sustainable Growth for Montgomery County: A Growth Policy for the 21st Century.* Final Draft 2007–2009 Growth Policy. MNCPPC. pp. 143–145. Arterial speed ranges based on Transportation Research Board. 2000. *Highway Capacity Manual;* Transit speed ranges based on Transportation Research Board. 2003. *Transit Capacity and Quality of Service Manual.*

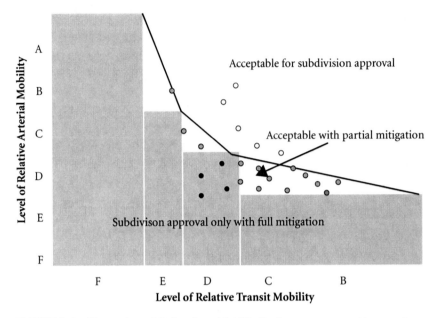

FIGURE 9.1   Illustration of Policy Area Mobility Review as approved by county council

Source: Montgomery County Planning Board. May 21, 2007. Toward Sustainable Growth for Montgomery County: A Growth Policy for the 21st Century.

PAMR replaced staging ceilings for each policy with a binary system. Projects would be approved in policy areas "above the PAMR steps" where mobility was "acceptable." Projects proposed for areas below the steps would be approved only if developers mitigated 100 percent of the transportation deficiency. The advantages of this approach were that it was simple, did not require developers to commission expensive studies of the impact of their projects on policy area transportation capacity, and avoided placing large numbers of policy areas in moratoria. To avoid overbuilding an area and inducing a moratorium the board proposed impact taxes on development set at levels sufficient to recover the marginal cost of improvements in transportation and school facilities needed to serve it at acceptable levels of service. The LATR test was required of all projects to mitigate local intersection congestion.

The board found past practice often frustrated smart growth objectives by channeling development into low-density areas with excess road capacity instead of encouraging mixed-use, pedestrian, and transit-oriented redevelopment where existing infrastructure investments could be leveraged, the tax base enhanced, and environmental conditions could be improved. No separate allocations of transportation capacity to jobs and housing were proposed. Staging ceilings had achieved neither concurrency of development and infrastructure nor a balance of housing and jobs in policy areas or countywide. Since master plans and zoning determined the maximum amount of each use that could be built, trying to decide in advance how much should be allowed to go forward in a two-year growth policy cycle was an unrealistic guessing game at which the board and council had an unimpressive record.

Council members were less interested in whether PAMR accurately measured mobility or capacity than that its results squared with their judgments about where relief from congestion was required. If few areas were placed into moratoria, more mitigation of congestion should be exacted. Council Member Marc Elrich attacked the idea that the county should accept a decline in arterial mobility if an area had a high level of transit service. Council Member Roger Berliner argued no one would consider a grade of D or E acceptable at school and should not be done for commuters. Elrich challenged PAMR methodology on several grounds. He argued that the standards used for transit service were too imprecise; that transit was not a full substitute for driving for most commuters; and that area-wide mobility averages were artificially favorable because they included traffic moving in both directions during peak periods, and that the wrong peak period had been used for some of the traffic modeling.

The council made two modifications to PAMR. It set "D" as the lowest level of service allowed for arterial roads even if transit in a policy area operated at level "A." The immediate effect was purely symbolic since no area was forecast to experience a level of arterial service lower than D, even by 2030. As a statement of policy, however, it was counterproductive of smart growth goals by requiring expensive road widening to improve driver experience in the county's most heavily developed areas, discouraging use of transit.

The second modification inserted a diagonal line connecting the tips of each step on the PAMR chart to create a "partial mitigation" category, turning a binary system into a complex one. Projects in the twelve affected policy areas shown in Figure 9.1 would be required to make payments costing from 5 to 45 percent of full mitigation. Four areas required full mitigation. This change provided a palliative for council members favoring restoration of staging ceilings and moratoria. It arguably prevented an area from falling into an unacceptable range of transportation mobility, and prevented early developers from being free riders on available capacity, forcing those coming later to mitigate fully all trips their projects generated. The fairness of this measure was debatable in light of the tax covering the marginal cost of transportation improvements required to offset each project's impact.

Glenn Orlin's staff report to the full council recommended against policy area review on grounds that it was too complex and its methods and results were not transparent to the general public. Since most arterial roads and fixed-route transit were in place, he argued the focus should be on trip reduction measures and curing congested intersections where most travel delay occurred.[63] Therefore, he recommended tighter LATR standards and requiring all development to undertake mandatory trip reduction.

The council adopted tighter LATR standards and required the planning board to consider only those facilities in the first four years of county and state capital programs in administering the APFO.[64] The alternative review procedure was retained for Metro station areas. PAMR and LATR tests in those areas would be waived (a LATR study was still required), but projects had to take measures to reduce trips by 50 percent, participate in a transportation management organization, and pay 75 percent of the applicable development tax.

A viable test for the adequacy of schools had eluded the planning board and council since the earliest days of growth policy. Like a single student graded on a curve, schools always passed. In devising recommendations for 2007–2009, the board, with concurrence from the school system, recommended that when schools at any level in a cluster reached 110 percent of program capacity, a developer would make a facilities improvement payment, based on the per-student cost of facilities at that level. When any level reached 135 percent of programmed capacity, the board would deny housing subdivisions until sufficient facilities were programmed for construction. Under this test, six clusters required facilities payments at the elementary level, one at the middle school level, and one at the high school level. No cluster required a housing moratorium.

Except in newly developing areas, growth affected enrollment less than neighborhood demographic changes. The board, therefore, recommended that in addition to the school impact tax on housing developments, the portion of the recordation tax dedicated to school improvements should be increased. This would provide relief for down-county schools where there was little growth but large increases in enrollment.

The council, eager at last to have a school test with bite, responded to constituents clamoring to rid their schools of portable classrooms and eager for renovation of older buildings. It lowered the threshold for impact fees to 105 percent of capacity and imposed a moratorium at 120 percent. Two years later, to avoid imposing moratoria resulting from this policy, the council amended the CIP to add funding for affected schools. In this sense, the growth policy did what it was supposed to do: link private development with a concurrent expansion of public facilities, and provide a means of financing the expansion.[65]

The council's enthusiasm for impact taxes was moderated by concerns that Montgomery would be perceived as less hospitable to economic development than its Northern Virginia neighbors. The council accepted the board's approach to recovery of marginal costs of transportation and school facilities required to serve new development but trimmed the rates to 90 percent of marginal cost.[66] The recordation tax was increased on home sales over $500,000 and earmarked for capital improvements and rental assistance.[67]

As a complete policy package, the adopted 2007–2009 Growth Policy was slightly more sustainable from a fiscal perspective than the initial proposal by the board because the partial mitigation amendment to PAMR more than offset any losses occasioned by reducing impact taxes.

One Step Forward, One Step Back

In its 2009–2011 Growth Policy Report, the planning board made another effort to shift the focus from congestion to sustainability. It pointed out past growth policy had almost no effect on the amount or pace of growth. However, concern for congestion directed growth to areas with excess road capacity but poor transit service, contributing to low-density sprawl, more and longer auto trips, increased downstream congestion and higher levels of energy use and greenhouse gas emissions. With little vacant land left to develop, the board urged reorientation of policy toward mixed-use, higher-density, transit-oriented redevelopment of older commercial centers and strips. This would achieve smart growth objectives and meet needs of a changing and more diverse population. When transportation was included, household costs could be competitive with those in outlying areas.

To fund necessary facilities in transit-oriented areas, the board proposed special taxing districts to replace the transportation tests. It recommended setting the standard for arterial mobility in these areas at LOS "E" rather than "D" if transit operated at LOS "B." Residential parking requirements should be reduced to conform to recent experience with such development. Mitigation of local intersection deficiencies would be monetized at a cost of $11,000 per trip to pay for a wide range of non-auto facilities. The threshold for payment of a school impact fee would be raised to 110 percent of programmed capacity. The board recommended reducing dormant projects in the "pipeline" by allowing holders of APFO entitlements to sell them to others ready to build in the redevelopment centers.[68]

By the time the report was published, the economy was in recession and development stagnated. The partial mitigation rule increased transaction costs and raised, in hard times, the level of discontent among developers. Having increased its complexity, council members now complained PAMR was difficult to understand, first, because its transit mobility calculation was a ratio of a ratio; but mainly because it measured mobility rather than congestion. Civic leaders paying attention to growth policy remained fixated on congestion and echoed the contention that PAMR was not transparent and insufficiently accounted for congestion.

Elrich continued his assault, asserting PAMR allowed intolerable levels of congestion and delay on roads, insisting urban arterial mobility should not be allowed to decline even where a high level of transit service existed. County Department of Transportation operatives opposed PAMR, contending that it allowed too much congestion and did not provide clear guidance on which roads or transit projects to move forward. County Executive Leggett expressed concern "that the proposed 2009 Growth Policy includes assumptions and directions that could significantly impair the quality of life in Montgomery County." He recommended replacing PAMR with some other approach. While he agreed that focus should be on mass transit, he argued: "it is untenable to intentionally impose congestion upon the residents and businesses of Montgomery County with the hope that it will force them out of their vehicles as congestion becomes intolerable."[69] He directed the county Department of Transportation to retain a consultant (the same one that devised PAMR) to invent a new transportation test to replace PAMR for the next growth policy cycle.[70]

Because it had not yet acted on the draft plans for White Flint and the Life Sciences area, the council declined to create separate policy areas for them or for Germantown Town Center. It refused to lower the adequacy standards for schools or roads, even for transit-oriented areas, or allow transfer dormant of APFO entitlements to ready projects in transit areas. The $11,000 per trip payment was accepted as an alternative to construction of facilities of equal value.

As the debate over growth policy extended into 2010, both the board and council concluded that, given the amount of time and resources consumed its production and consideration, and the lack of change that occurred between reports, it should be placed on a four-year instead of a two-year cycle. The council approved Orlin's recommendation to reduce its scope and change the name of the exercise to "Subdivision Staging Policy."[71]

Congestion Trumps Sustainability

The decision to restrict policy to establishment of rules for approval of subdivisions under the APFO was an official surrender to a Gresham's Law of politics in which the trivial drove out the important. The council was relieved of the unpleasant chore of contemplating the consequences and strategic implications of its land use and transportation policies. It had generally eluded this task under earlier incarnations of growth policy but was at least confronted with the issues by planning board reports on conditions and trends.

The substitution of the executive's proposed Transportation Policy Area Review (TPAR) for PAMR provided a better specification of road and transit deficiencies, thus making a better connection to the capital program. TPAR also identified more precisely deficiencies in transit service, but in contrast with its roadway analysis, it was less able to specify improvements to cure them. The cumulative effect of these changes in the technical approach was to revert to a more comfortable focus on amelioration of congestion rather than on the sustainability of growth. A suburban mind-set prevailed.

Planning Politics and Growth Policy

Montgomery's primary contributions to the national discussion of growth management were its conceptual model of growth and, though never adopted, a strong rule structure for synchronizing the regulatory and capital improvement systems to manage the timing of development and influence its location and character. Invention of techniques for measuring levels of service at small geographic scale was an important technical achievement. The use of risk analysis in making capital improvement decisions was another contribution to the design of growth policy, although it was first condemned, then ignored in practice.

Montgomery's growth policy experience demonstrates that people pay attention to things they measure. The early planning board proposed maintaining a series of indicators of changes in conditions affecting the quality of life in the county. The 2009 report reprised that recommendation, proposing a set of economic, social, and environmental sustainability indicators. This advice was rhetorically admired and studiously neglected. Congestion was the only thing regularly measured, sharply limiting the policy imagination.

Obsession with congestion had one arguably salutary effect. In 1986 it resuscitated growth policy when development surged ahead of the expansion of facilities. But in the face of fiscal constraints and local opposition it was easier to place an area into moratorium than fund facility improvements to relieve its congestion. The consequence was more congestion.

Planning politics in the Pure Political Regime produced exceptions to the carrying capacity rule by permitting some projects—for example, Marriott corporate headquarters or Silver Triangle—that caressed the political erogenous zones of an executive or council. The rule was tightened to prevent development where slow-growth constituencies opposed both new subdivisions and transportation improvements that might have relieved congestion but enabled more growth. Growth policy was converted from a rule-based system into a policy bazaar at which council members, executives, developers, and civic leaders bargained over the distribution of capacity and growth for the next policy cycle. Surely, some exceptions to general policy were justified. The erosion of the system, however, and the repeated search for a method that would produce more satisfying outcomes led to failure to deal with the contradictions in a policy designed to reduce congestion and promote concurrency of development and facilities, which in practice did neither very well.

As the system devolved it came to resemble practice in many other jurisdictions, whether they used a system similar to Montgomery's, growth boundaries, or population caps. It essentially delayed development in areas where smart growth policies would have been advanced and shifted it to lower density areas with excess road and school capacity.[72] Shedding the strategic vision of the original 1979 proposal and the 1989 Comprehensive Growth Policy Study, it became a short-range tactical policy tool, focused on administration of the Adequate Public Facilities Ordinance. Practical people with electoral constituencies, as the executive and council members became familiar with its moving parts they realized that "carrying capacity" was elastic. Interest grew in manipulating it to achieve politically acceptable results. One could stand on principle to keep an area in moratorium or take it out, to oppose pay-and-go fees and taxes or support them. Micromanagement of the rules for APFO administration imbedded in public consciousness the idea that the sum and substance of growth policy was fine-tuning it to prevent congested roads and overcrowded schools. It became an exercise in the logic of appropriateness.

Growth policy was invented to manage the rate of growth but had more impact on its location than on its amount, type, or timing. The annual fluctuation in the number of households corresponded to economic cycles, and except for the sewer moratorium in the 1970s, the amount of growth had little relationship to the stringency of policy.

Growth was not the sole cause of growing congestion, but growth policy was a solution that found its problem. Proposals aimed at inducing behavioral changes, such as congestion pricing or a carbon tax, were regularly elided and growth policy was truncated to deal only with rules for denying approval of subdivisions where facilities were inadequate to prevent congestion. Although the council could have used the findings of the growth policy reports to direct the executive to include in the CIP the projects necessary for development to proceed in response to forecasted demand that was politically inappropriate—and expensive.

With all its imperfections, trimming, and asymmetries, growth policy stimulated a continuing public dialogue about growth and its consequences. The analytical studies conducted by the planning staff that accompanied growth policy reports gradually changed official and public perceptions of the kind of development that should occur. The widespread support for the wedges and corridors concept slowly fused with growing support for more compact pedestrian and transit-oriented forms of development that were reflected in master plans and modernization of the zoning code. The need to refine and explain the methods used to measure the adequacy or acceptability of service strengthened staff capabilities and official and public knowledge of the problems of growth and the limitations of its management. The result was development of better and more effective policy tools. And in a place where development was at the center of its political economy, decisions about growth were kept high on the public agenda and made in transparent deliberation about the public interest.

THE PUBLIC INTEREST

Montgomery County has enough flaws to make it an interesting place to live and work. Looking back at how planning politics affected its development, some policies were followed and worked; some, very well. Others fell short of promise or expectations or failed because they deserved to do so, or because circumstances or opposition denied them secure footing. A perfect place would be quite dull.

A century of growth transformed Montgomery County. The first half was shaped by two regimes anchored in interests of the commercial republic. Its development in the past fifty years was guided by two regimes reflecting greater influence by suburban miniature republics. The worth of the policies of the four regimes is not measured by how thoroughly their plans stirred one's blood or how elegant or messy was their logic, but whether, in the fullness of time, the results on the ground reasonably can be said to have advanced the common good and public welfare of the community. Otherwise, they were at best empty gestures; at worst serious mistakes. Judgments about the extent to which planning decisions serve the public interest should be made not upon publication of a plan but after a substantial amount of development pursuant to it has occurred on the ground.

Defining *Public Interest* is an exercise of Miles's Law: "Where you stand depends on where you sit."[1] Each school of thought and generation imposes its own standards for the public interest. In this sense public interest is a continuing reasoned argument. In any political system, however, that argument is bounded by basic, widely shared—public—values about what constitutes the common good and how it should be obtained. Values, as noted in the discussion of the miniature and commercial republics, involve traditions and reasons for supporting particular interests. Thus, one test of whether the outcomes of decisions served the public interest involves an assessment of the extent to which they embodied broadly accepted understandings that span generations. It is of course possible that such understandings may fail other, more empirical tests.

Utilitarianism is the most common framework for assessing policy outcomes for public interest. It is the philosophic foundation of the logic of consequentiality. Its cost-benefit calculus awards equal weight to each person's utility and derives the net of pleasures and pains to find the public interest in those measures that produce the greatest happiness for the greatest number. To pass utilitarian muster, the development pattern should produce net benefits to both the county as an entity and to a substantial majority of its residents.

A mutation of utilitarianism, Public Choice Theory assumes individuals, including public officials and bureaucrats, are rational actors that advance their own interests. All are utility maximizers. Thus, government is not an organic entity or artificial "person," but a bunch of officials, each of whom is acting in his or her own interest, such as retaining office or influence. Public interest is an oxymoron if considered as no more than the utility maximization of the greatest number of officials. Public Choice also assumes that people rationally shop for homes and "packages" of taxes and services that give them the best deal and greatest net happiness. Public Choice theorists further argue that small, homogeneous groups are more effective in gaining benefits from government because they can maintain cohesion, have higher stakes in the outcome of decisions, and do not have to deal with the distractions of free riders with weak attachment to their goals. For adherents to this school of thought, public interest is served when individuals have wide choices, enabling them to vote with their pocketbooks and feet.[2]

Pluralism is less demanding of evidence of aggregate benefit. It finds the public interest in the legitimacy of decisions achieved through inter-group bargaining and accommodation of interests. Where utilitarianism is focused on the allocation of resources among individuals, pluralism is more concerned with the distribution of power and resources among groups and its exercise in ways that prevent its consolidation by a single group or coalition that excludes others. Deliberation, negotiation, and experimentation through open processes are more important than specific outcomes because pluralists tend to doubt that perfection will or can be achieved in a world of imperfect knowledge and self-interested actors. Public interest is, therefore, to be found in the continuous seeking of it.[3]

John Rawls's *A Theory of Justice* is one of the most influential and hotly debated philosophical treatises of the twentieth century.[4] Its implication for this discussion is its insistence on fairness in the distribution of primary goods and liberties. In the context of planning politics, the public interest would require an equitable distribution of facilities, services, and amenities among the citizenry and communities of the county. It would also insist upon open and equal access to the processes of government.

A different standard for the public interest can be found in Regime Theory. It is concerned with whether a stable governing coalition exists and is able to sustain itself by facilitating social production—"The capacity to assemble and use needed resources for a policy initiative."[5] That capacity depends upon the ability of those participating in and engaging the regime to develop civic capital—to learn how to govern, expand participation and adapt to new actors and circumstances, and build knowledge and bonds of trust that facilitate alliances and solve problems.[6]

This quick survey of the theoretical maze offers no sure pathway to discovering the public interest. Rather than holding a county map before the light of each theory to see how well their respective contours match, I offer a reduction of these various schools of thought to six questions about whether the results of Montgomery's planning politics served the public interest:

1. Has the General Plan and the pattern of development fostered by it embodied widely accepted public values?
2. Has the overall pattern of development been more beneficial than costly to the county as a whole?
3. Have the benefits and costs of development consistent with the plan been equitably distributed among groups and geographic areas?
4. Have the consequences of development in accordance with the General Plan provided current and future generations a reasonable range of choices?
5. Have decisions been made in ways that honor core principles of fairness and democratic governance?
6. Has the politics of planning fostered the development of civic capital and problem solving?

Ground Proofing Outcomes

Montgomery County is generally regarded as one of the nation's planning successes. But it is a qualified success. In a 2002 study, Harrigan and von Hoffman concluded:

> Montgomery County has had some extraordinary successes in fostering "smart growth" and yet has failed to attain many of the goals of its 1964 Plan. Those failures, however, are the product of its own ambivalence on the matter of growth and development. There has been constant political tension between those whose focus is jobs, growth and tax base and those whose paramount values are preservation of neighborhoods and environmental protection.[7]

A 2004 report prepared for the Cooperative Highway Research Program comparing Montgomery with five other jurisdictions with strong growth programs reached a similar conclusion:

Although strong growth management policies have successfully preserved the rural character of northwestern Montgomery County, the policies may have served to divert development to other areas in Metropolitan Washington, such as Loudon County, Virginia. In addition, since I-270 extends north from Montgomery into Frederick County it provides access to employment in Montgomery County and Washington, D.C., contributing to Frederick County's 30 percent population growth between 1990 and 2000. Most of Frederick County's growth has been concentrated on the southern edge of the county adjacent to Montgomery County's rural preserve.[8]

That the General Plan's vision of wedges and corridors achieved greater success in protecting the "wedges" than in designing and building the corridors merely demonstrates that it is easier to use the police power, upon which the authority to plan and regulate land use rests, to prevent things than to create them. In the former case the instrument can be rather sharp; in the latter, blunt. Even with that caveat, and the ambivalence Harrigan and von Hoffman noted, the extent to which the goals of the General Plan were achieved over almost fifty years of rapid growth is remarkable. Montgomery is the only jurisdiction in the Washington Metropolitan Area that even tried to follow the basic structure of the Year 2000 Plan.[9] Except for Arlington County, it has also been more successful in retrofitting key centers in its suburban ring than other jurisdictions of metropolitan Washington.

Plans and Public Values

Two basic features of the General Plan must be emphasized: it has not been static and it has enjoyed broad public support. From council approval of the updated version in 1969, it has been a work in progress, amended by each master, sector, and functional plan for over forty years. These amendments have refined, adjusted, added, reinforced, and in some cases, rescinded original features of the plan. Notwithstanding these changes, the basic contours of the General Plan survived and were followed into a third generation.

There are good reasons, if not indisputable evidence, to think the plan reflects a widely accepted set of common values and embodies the county's corporate understanding of the public interest. By the time of its approval by the county council in 1969, after almost a decade of robust public discussion, debate, and two election cycles, a consensus evolved in support of the wedges and corridors model for county development. This consensus included the civic and political classes, and, with more reluctance and some truculence, the development sector.

Within a decade of its approval by the council, the basic structure of wedges and corridors had become politically sacrosanct.

Although it did not suppress the conflict between them over specific policies, the General Plan's broad framework provided room for both the commercial and miniature republics to flourish. No candidate for council or executive has seriously questioned it, although disagreements persisted about various elements—some of them critical, such as the Inter-County Connector. There was always a risk that the plan would lose salience, more through neglect than malice, or gradually be rendered irrelevant by incremental decisions, none singly grave, but cumulatively fatal. Temptations always existed to accept proposals that were inconsistent with the plan but appealed to the edifice complexes or revenue-generation aspirations of elected officials. Desire occasionally overwhelmed reason. Some departures from plans could be politically risky; others were popular.

The Progressive Regime's planning and development decisions cemented the General Plan's basic pattern to the land, leaving successors little alternative to continuing the same path. Although specific policies, such as the Adequate Public Facilities Ordinance, the Central Business District sector plans and zones, the Germantown master plan, and the creation of the Agricultural Reserve, excited controversy as they were produced; once adopted, they were largely accepted. Following the decline of the Progressive Regime, the 1988 report of the Commission on the Future of Montgomery County and the 1993 update reaffirmed the basic architecture of the General Plan.

Acceptance of the plan was a triumph of experience more than ideology. In particular, the successful redevelopment of Bethesda while preserving the quality (and raising property values) of adjacent residential neighborhoods overcame resistance from civic and development interests to transit-oriented development in the urban ring. Success in Bethesda nurtured envy, then support for redevelopment in Silver Spring. Just as the initial wave of suburban growth in the pre- and postwar eras shifted the county's center of political gravity and attitudes toward development, the changes in development patterns and demography in the final decades of the twentieth century reinforced support for the redevelopment of older commercial centers and strips. Consensus on the principles of the General Plan did not dampen the intensity of disputes over specific plans or projects, but rechanneled the debate to one of interpretation, with adversaries invoking the General Plan and its principles to justify their opposing positions. *Wedges and Corridors* became the constitution for county land use, a sacred text subject to interpretation by a priesthood of all believers, each earnestly operating under Miles's Law.

Finally, the Montgomery County Planning Board became the institutional guardian of the General Plan. As its authors, the planning board and its key staff were deeply invested in it by the time council approval elevated it to a new level of legitimacy. It became a policy mandate that converted the board's role from advocate to steward. Achieving its goals became the overriding mission of the planning board during the Progressive Regime and continued to inform its decisions and initiatives. It is the architectural skeleton to which all area and functional master plans, sector plans, growth policies, and regulatory measures have been fastened. In performing its advisory and regulatory functions the board is often required by state or county law to make findings of consistency with approved plans, making it the authoritative interpreter of the General Plan.

Development Pattern and the Public Interest

The local popularity and institutionalized perseverance of the General Plan begs the question whether adhering to it has been in the public interest. That requires subjecting the resulting development pattern to empirical evidence rather than abstract argument. The first step in conducting such an analysis involves providing a more precise characterization of the development pattern. A common way of characterizing suburban development patterns is by the extent of urban *sprawl*. The term tends to connote unmanaged, random, low-density, leapfrog growth, with unfortunate consequences for the local economy, society, and environment. The first goal of Maryland's Smart Growth policy is "Reduce Urban Sprawl."

Defining and measuring sprawl and its consequences is something of a cottage industry among urbanists. In a series of papers published over the last decade, my colleagues and I defined sprawl as consisting of several dimensions of urban development that can be measured empirically and compared across any number of jurisdictions, using a common geographic unit of analysis.[10] Adapting and applying the techniques developed in these papers to Maryland's five urban counties, Jason Freihage and I measured residential and non-residential density, the continuity of development, the extent to which development is dense, concentrated, centralized, and diverse.[11] The results are shown in Table 10.1.

Overall, Montgomery's development pattern exhibited less sprawl than the other urban counties. It achieved higher density of businesses in transit centers and the I-270 corridor, and a tighter concentration of development due to the constraining effect of the Agricultural Reserve. Even though Montgomery's density scored best among the state's urban counties, slightly more than a fourth of its residential communities had densities lower than the state's Smart Growth goal of more than 3.5 units per acre, reflecting the extensive amount of land made available for large-lot homes in the "low-density residential wedges" of Potomac-Darnestown, Goshen, Fairland, and around satellite communities of

TABLE 10.1   Ranking of Maryland urban counties on dimensions of sprawl
(higher rank = less sprawl)

COUNTY	RESIDENTIAL DENSITY	BUSINESS DENSITY	CONTINUITY	CONCEN-TRATION	DIVERSITY	SUM OF RANKINGS	OVERALL RANK
Montgomery	3	5	3	5	4	20	5
Prince George's	5	3	4	3	3	18	4
Baltimore	5	4	2	4	1	16	3
Howard	1	1	5	2	5	14	2
Anne Arundel	2	2	1	1	2	8	1

Source: Adapted from Royce Hanson & Jason Freihage. 2001. Is Maryland Growing Smart? Maryland Institute for Policy Analysis & Research.

Damascus and Olney. Montgomery's middle ranking on continuity is largely a function of its protection of stream valley parkland, which produced a distinctive pattern of development. It was edged from the top rank on the measure of diversity of land uses by Howard County, the development of which was dominated by a single project—Columbia—and by the fact that almost half of Montgomery's land area is protected for agriculture and parks.

That the General Plan retained its popularity as the icon of planning policy or that Montgomery is Maryland's best example of central goals of state Smart Growth policy only establishes a rebuttable presumption that development consistent with it served the public interest in practice as well as it captured it as an aspiration. Addressing that proposition first requires defining which public's interest is of concern. There are several.

Benefits and Costs

A place to start is to think of the county as a single entity with interests distinct from those of its individual citizens, communities, or interest groups. Public Choice theory would hold that its officials each have utilities they wish to maximize, but would probably concede that utility coincides with their roles as fiduciaries to advance the county's fiscal well-being. As politicians they understand realizing this objective could place unwelcome burdens on taxpayers and inconvenience residents. Therefore, there is a compelling interest in minimizing constituent unhappiness, which entails finding the sweet spot that balances taxes and services, growth and inconvenience. Thus, planning politics ought to find the public interest in "a core consensus in the dynamics of the market: tax base maximization . . . at the direct intersection of the interests of the diverse sets of individual actors."[12]

Politicians and bureaucrats needed enough growth to provide revenues that could be used to expand programs. Developers needed growth to expand their businesses and profits by building homes that attracted upscale buyers, who, in turn, would demand better services. While new arrivals would doubtless join earlier settlers in opposing more nearby subdivisions, they had an interest in allowing enough growth elsewhere to sustain a robust market in home sales that would foster rising property values. Underlying the disagreements over how much and where to build was an unspoken consensus that growth should be managed to ensure that the county could provide an acceptable level of services at a reasonable cost in taxes levied on continuously rising property values.

From that perspective, the public interest of the county was served if the assessable base of property grew at a rate that allowed an acceptable tax burden to maintain a constant or improving level of services. The tax/services "package" represented the county's competitive niche in the metropolitan market for residents and businesses. If the taxes are perceived as too high, or the services as inadequate, the county would lose market share of population as people and firms voted with their feet and relocated to a jurisdiction that better suited their preferences.

The real world, of course, is not that simple. Many other factors affect the location decisions of households and firms and their mobility among jurisdictions within a region. Attachments to place, neighbors, friends and familiar surroundings may override costs and inconveniences. Home equity and other sunk investments, both financial and psychic, make citizens more than mere consumers. To be sure, some services, such as schools, parks, or safety, may be valued more than others. Property taxes appear to be a relatively minor consideration in location choices, as they tend to be invisible to most mortgagees.

Nonetheless, it is reasonable to consider whether growth of the tax base kept pace with population and the demand for services, but in doing so, it is worth remembering that neither the demand for services nor tolerance for taxes is fixed or constant. As a general proposition people prefer low taxes and better services over high taxes and poor services. It is also important to consider other indices of community well-being that are directly related to the pattern of physical development and land use. These include transportation conditions and costs; environmental quality; housing costs and affordability; income inequality; and access to employment and amenities. Thus, I have included them in assessing the how Montgomery's development pattern affected the public interest of the county as a whole.

The county's assessable base of real property grew 611 percent in 2012 constant dollars from 1970 to 2010, while population increased only 88 percent. Median home values increased 164 percent, making the rise in value of property and an expanding private business sector the principal sources of growth in the assessable base. Although over 20,000 employees were added to government

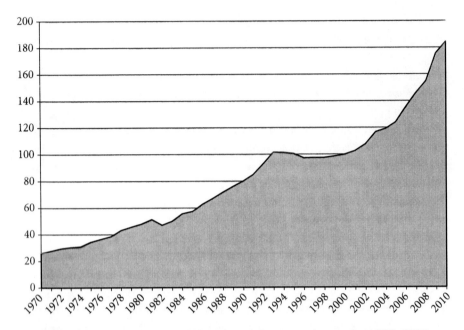

FIGURE 10.1   Market value of Montgomery County real property, 1970–2010 in 2012 constant dollars (billions)

Source: Montgomery County Annual Financial Reports 1970–2010.

payrolls during these forty years, the public sector's proportion of county jobs dropped from 27 to 15 percent. Personal income grew by 410 percent in constant dollars, from $14 billion to $71 billion, keeping ahead of county expenditures, which increased 355 percent over the same period. The per person cost of county government expenditures rose 243 percent. In 1970 county taxes were 3.7 percent of county personal income and had increased to slightly above 4 percent in 2010. The property tax rate declined, from $3.245 per $100 in 1970 to $0.904 in 2010, a function of the substantial increases in property values and the introduction of an income tax in the 1960s, which became the second principal source of county revenue.[13] The tax burden does not fall equally across the population, of course, depending on sources of income, and the ratio of property to income taxes paid by different individuals. It should be pointed out that the tax base changed relatively little compared to the change in the economic base of the county.

As a gross measure of the effect of the county's development on the overall tax burden for the services it provides, the results on the ground produced rising property values and attracted a population with incomes that grew faster than the county budget. It is not possible to say that a different pattern of development would have produced a greater or lower tax burden. We can only say that however weak the path of causation from the development pattern, the overall tax burden, as a percentage of income, did not increase substantially even as some services were improved while others appear to have declined.

Traffic has been a constant source of public dissatisfaction. The transportation system provided the basic structural element of the General Plan, and was central to its implementation and administration through area master plans, growth policy, and the subdivision process. By far, the most important transportation project contemplated by the General Plan was Metro. It not only spurred development in Friendship Heights and Bethesda, and finally in Silver Spring and White Flint, it provided the opportunity for the planning board to establish a clear linkage between transportation capacity and land use. Plans that led to the development of high-density mixed uses at key Metro stations and expansion of feeder bus service resulted in 15 percent of Montgomery commuters using public transportation by 2010, compared with only 9 percent in Fairfax County.

If the county was relatively aggressive in capitalizing on the development and mobility opportunity provided by Metro, it was far less enthusiastic about the original highway recommendations of the General Plan. In collaboration with the District of Columbia, plans for the northwestern and north central freeways were abandoned shortly after the General Plan was approved. The western leg of the Outer Beltway was first moved, then eliminated. Ultimately its remnant, the euphemistically designated Rockville Facility faded away to a segment, Montrose Parkway, running from I-270 to Rockville Pike. An eastern segment became a state park in which the once proposed freeway was reduced to a hiker-biker trail.

The Inter-County Connector remained on the plan. The planning board used its Advanced Land Acquisition Fund to acquire its right-of-way. This made construction possible once county and state political support was in accord, thirty years after the alignment was established. Although various arterial roads were improved and a few new ones were constructed, a substantial backlog of roadway improvements languished because of absence of support as often as shortage of funds. Lack of capacity for roads to function at acceptable levels of service placed many areas of the county in building moratoria for much of the two decades following adoption of the first growth policy in 1986.

By and large, the major highways removed from the General Plan were in response to local objections, although the decisions were supported by more broadly based interest groups. Their elimination benefited the affected local communities in some respects and burdened them in others. It remains debatable whether not building them was contrary to the interests of the county as a whole. It seems reasonable to conclude that eliminating the western leg of the Outer Beltway helped reduce pressure to develop the Agricultural Reserve. Successive generations of county and state officials resisted sporadic efforts to resurrect the project. That seems to ratify the judgment that the original decision to remove the freeway and river crossing was in the county's long-term public interest. It is harder to judge whether it was in the public interest of the region. Its absence probably contributed to tighter concentrations of high technology and defense firms near Dulles Airport in Virginia and of bio-medical institutions in Montgomery County.

Although complaints of congestion were persistent and loud, the overall mobility of county commuters changed little. The average travel time during the morning peak period rose from twenty-eight to thirty-three minutes, but was still twenty-nine minutes for auto commuters in 2010. The higher all-modes average was due to the high percentage of transit commuters. In 2010 there were approximately 7.5 billion vehicle miles travelled (VMT) on Montgomery roads—21,000 miles per household. This compares with 10.5 billion VMT in Fairfax, or 28,000 miles per household.[14] The county's congestion index and minutes of delay per person were also lower than Fairfax's and the average for the region.[15] Some amount of Montgomery's congestion is attributable to a development pattern that is a combination of its legacy of arterial ridge roads, which reinforce the corridor plan, exacerbated by cul-de-sac neighborhoods that foreclosed creation of a grid street system in the urban ring.

There are reasons to ascribe at least some of these attributes of the development pattern to following the General Plan. High concentrations of employment and housing at Metro stations and in the I-270 corridor increased use of public transportation and facilitated employment of 60 percent of Montgomery's workforce in the county (compared with just over half the Fairfax workforce). The deep reach of both branches of Metro's Red Line into heavily populated areas served a large portion of the 25 percent of commuters working in the District of Columbia. Protection of the Agricultural Reserve limited residential sprawl and contributed to lower VMT for county residents, although some argued that it may have increased VMT for the region by encouraging leap-frog residential development into Frederick County, thus, producing longer trips for those commuters.

Two features of Montgomery's development strategy shaped its pattern and provided its chief environmental benefits. The 57,000 acres of parkland and the 106,000 acres of the Agricultural Reserve occupy 47 percent of the county's land area. The Maryland-National Capital Park and Planning Commission's (M-NCPPC) 35,000-acre park system includes all major stream valleys. Augmented by state parks, Sanitary Commission land adjacent to water supply lakes, and the C&O Canal National Historical Park, this extensive network protects flood plains from development, preserves woodlands and wildlife corridors, and reinforces the "corridor" structure of the General Plan. The stream valley park system provides natural areas and an extensive trail system close to neighborhoods throughout the county. Over 400 local parks and playgrounds, five regional parks, 56 recreation, conservation and special-purpose parks, and Revenue Authority golf courses offer a wide variety of outdoor and indoor recreation facilities. County residents consistently rank the park system the most used county service (other than mandatory recycling) and over 86 percent of those surveyed in 2007 reported visiting a park at least once in the prior year. M-NCPPC's is the only park system in the country to have won the National Parks and Recreation Association's Gold Medal for excellence in park management six times.

The Agricultural Reserve made "wedges" permanent features of the county's development pattern by placing most of the Reserve's land under easements in perpetuity. The Reserve fostered a resilient agricultural sector that produces about a quarter billion dollars annually to the county economy and supplies a growing local fresh food movement. Together, the Reserve and the park system contain most of the county's significant historic and cultural resources.

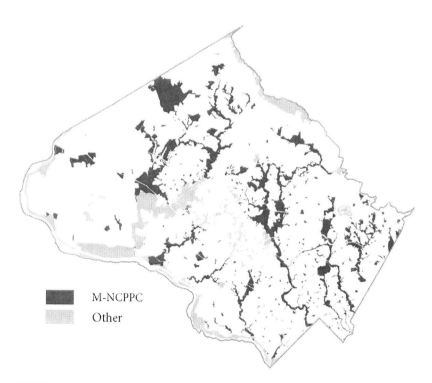

M-NCPPC
Other

FIGURE 10.2   Public parklands in Montgomery County. Courtesy Montgomery County Planning Department M-NCPPC

Stream valley parks contain a significant proportion of the county's tree cover and almost all riparian forest buffers, especially in the urbanized parts of the county. After better technology became available, park taking lines were drawn to include the 100-year flood plain, based on assumptions of full development of watersheds in accordance with approved master plans. The result has been a virtual absence of flood damage to homes and businesses in the county. Public ownership of stream valleys reduced costs for trunk sewer construction and made possible the development of over 200 miles of paved and natural surface trails for recreation and travel.

The trees, forests, protected floodplains, wetlands, and working farms in the Reserve contribute environmental services such as carbon sequestration and reduction of pollution loads into tributaries of the Chesapeake Bay. The Reserve contains most of the land in the county with less than 10 percent impervious cover and watersheds with good or excellent stream health. Even in the highly developed areas, stream health is better where there is less impervious surface and more riparian buffer.

The Reserve's taxpayers produce more revenue for the county than the cost of services delivered to them.[16] Its presence marginally reduces overall county infrastructure capital and operating costs. Because there is no need in the Reserve for a dense road network to serve sprawling suburbs, Montgomery has 126 fewer miles of public roads than Fairfax County even though is about 100 square miles larger.

Development Pattern and Equity

The most substantial criticism of the wedges and corridor development pattern concerns its effect on social and geographic equity. The broadest form of this argument is a generic criticism of the constraints on land availability imposed by protection of the Agricultural Reserve.[17] By restricting the supply of land available for development, land values increase in areas zoned and serviced for development, which increases the price of housing, excluding lower-income households from the developable area and forcing the market for more affordable homes to leapfrog the restricted area to vacant land farther from the center.

The real market is not as elegant as the theory. Because land values are related to zoning and the availability of infrastructure, it is probably rash to assume that the Reserve would be zoned and provisioned for the suburban and urban densities available in the rest of the county. Even before the imposition of five-acre zoning, it was zoned for densities ranging from two units per acre to one unit per two acres. Even half-acre zoning would not support moderately priced housing. There is little evidence that the limitation on land available for development resulting from establishment of the Reserve affected housing prices. The 2009

American Community Survey found median home values for the previous three years $34,000 higher in Fairfax County than in Montgomery.[18] In a suburban housing market with median household incomes more than twice the national level there is an almost inexhaustible demand for upscale housing. Even the low end of that market carries prices above the national median.

The transferable development rights (TDR) program arguably helped lower some housing costs while providing greater equity for land owners in the Reserve. In some cases TDR purchases allowed builders to double or triple the unit yield permitted by the underlying zone. Clarksburg's unimproved land zoned half-acre was being offered at approximately $100,000 per lot. It was less expensive for developers to purchase TDRs than additional land to increase their yield. This process also resulted in higher densities, fewer miles of roads and sewers, and lower new home prices than if development had proceeded on large lots.

Montgomery's Moderately Priced Dwelling Unit (MPDU) program further mitigates the equity issue inherent in high land and housing prices. One of the most successful inclusive zoning programs in the country, it produced over 14,000 units, approximately half of all affordable units built in the county over a forty-year period. Unlike the voluntary TDR program, MPDUs are mandatory. All projects containing twenty or more units must make a minimum of 12.5 percent of them available for moderate-income buyers or renters. In return, developers receive a density bonus to offset the lower value of the MPDUs. Unfortunately, MPDUs built during the early decades were allowed to migrate to the general market after a certain number of years of controlled prices. The result was a reduction of MPDU stock by 4,672 sale units and 1,400 rental units in 2015. The law was recently amended to extend the control period to ninety-nine years, ensuring maintenance of the stock. There is no evidence that the MPDU program had a material effect on land values or the price for market housing in Montgomery County.[19] Its principal effect since the mid-1970s has been to distribute moderately priced housing across the county.

The county's Housing Opportunities Commission (HOC) manages 1,603 units of public housing and 6,384 Housing Choice Vouchers.[20] HOC has followed a policy from its inception to scatter assisted housing rather than concentrate it in one or two locations. It has right of first refusal for a third of all MPDU units produced.

The principal impediment to low and moderate income housing is the robust demand for upscale homes from affluent buyers, combined with a diminishing supply of land and rising construction costs, which kept prices high. While the MPDU, HOC, and TDR programs modestly ameliorated the problem of providing affordable housing they have far from solved it. In 2008, the planning department estimated a net shortage of 43,000 housing units available for households earning less than $90,000 a year. When household size was taken into account, the deficit in affordable units reached 50,000 and was forecast to reach 62,000 by 2030.[21] In 2015, the county Department of Housing and Community Affairs' waiting list for public housing stood at 34,107 and 15,550 for vouchers.[22] Montgomery, however, provided a larger share (15%) of homes valued less than $300,000 than Fairfax County (11%). While median rents are lower in Montgomery than Fairfax,[23] 50 percent of Montgomery's renters pay more than 30 percent of their monthly income for housing.[24]

Because Montgomery concentrated employment in its transit corridors, access to it is better than in other suburban jurisdictions. Except for Washington and Arlington—both within the ten-mile square of the original federal district— fewer Montgomery commuters than those of other suburbs spend 45 percent or more of their household incomes on transportation and housing.[25] It seems fair to conclude that Montgomery's development pattern has not induced greater inequity in housing costs than those with fewer restrictions on the location of growth.

Income inequality increased over the life of the General Plan. The GINI coefficient, which measures inequality among households, rose from 0.38 in the mid-1970s to 0.45 in the 2006–2009 period, placing Montgomery in the second quintile of inequality among U.S. counties.[26] This is largely a function of displacement in recent decades of older residents of the stock of affordable older garden apartments, townhouses, smaller single-family detached houses with younger minorities, immigrants, and single-person households, all of which have increased. At the same time, incomes have risen for the most affluent residents.

By any measure, Montgomery is relatively affluent, consistently ranked among the counties with the highest median household incomes, ranking second only to Fairfax in affluence among Washington Metropolitan counties, and second in Maryland behind Howard County. While there are variations in household incomes across census tracts in Montgomery there are no areas of extreme poverty or minority ghettos.[27] In only ten of its 550 census-defined neighborhoods are more than 20 percent of households living in poverty. To some degree, this is a result of policies deliberately designed to distribute moderate and low-income housing throughout the county.

This pattern of inclusionary zoning has had a significant indirect benefit. A Century Foundation study found that children from highly disadvantaged families attending elementary schools serving their low-poverty neighborhoods benefitted academically. The achievement gap narrowed significantly between them and classmates from higher income families. Children attending schools serving communities with moderate levels of poverty, however, did not significantly close the learning gap even though the school system devoted substantial additional resources to them.[28] To the extent the development pattern at the neighborhood scale mirrored the general pattern, the county benefitted in lower costs for schools. Even more important, by increasing opportunity for social and economic mobility of its students, the economy and stability of the county was enhanced. As the author of the study concluded:

> Since education is an investment with both individual and societal benefits, improving low-income students' school achievement via integrative housing is a tool that not only can reduce the income achievement gap but also can help stem future poverty. Furthermore, the experience of Montgomery County shows that it can be in the self interest of both localities and low-income families to create economically integrated neighborhoods and schools.[29]

Planning politics involves tradeoffs among interests over the location and character of land uses. A use that provides net benefits to the county, considered as a single entity, might inflict burdens on the places where they alight. These locally unwanted land uses, such as landfills, prisons, freeways, sewage treatment facilities, high voltage transmission lines, cell towers, and public housing, are uses that are both necessary and beneficial to the "public," of the whole county, but may be regarded as an abomination by the neighborhoods on which they are bestowed.

Averages inherently obscure the extremes and mask disparities among communities. Countywide there were 1.41 jobs per household in 2009, but there was a wide variation in the ratio among different areas of the county. Urban areas of the county contained 4.64 jobs per household, while in the rest of the county it was 1.11.[30] Unequal distribution of employment is inevitable, since agglomeration is essential for business success, and results in shorter travel times for residents in denser mixed-use areas with transit access than for those living in low-density residential communities and commuters that depend on the limited east-west routes. Some willingly traded those costs for the privacy and amenity of their sylvan suburbs. Cost-benefit analysis can take us only as far as our ability goes to convert preferences and sensibilities into a common currency.

Montgomery's development pattern has contributed to disparities in the quality of life among local communities in the county to the extent that it produced a mosaic of economically homogeneous subdivisions. Almost all homes in subdivisions built before the approval of the General Plan and the MPDU ordinance were exclusively of a single type and spanned a narrow price range. The saltbox homes of Veirs Mill Village, three-bedroom bungalows of Wheaton, and garden apartments in Takoma-Langley Park and Glenmont housed households of returning veterans and employees of a burgeoning federal government.

These homes became the bottom of the county housing market as the original residents leveraged their windfall equity from a hot market to meet down payment requirements of new single-family homes with a family room, three baths and a two-car garage. The older less-expensive housing stock filtered to the next generation of less affluent strivers, many of them minorities or immigrants. As their incomes rose they followed the upward mobility pattern of earlier residents but at a slower pace than in earlier decades.[31]

Before 1970, the minority population was small; primarily African Americans with deep roots in the county. A number of African-American communities traced their communities to early emancipation by Quakers or settlements of Freedmen established after the Civil War. The county enacted the first fair housing legislation in the state, ahead of the 1966 federal Fair Housing Act but did not see a substantial increase in the proportion of minorities until the 1980s. Since that time, the minority population of the county has increased from 14 to 53 percent and it has diversified. Almost one-third of the current population is foreign-born, chiefly from Asia and Latin America. Although minorities are well dispersed throughout the county, housing patterns affected their settlement. Older, wealthier single-family areas such as Bethesda, Potomac and the rural up-county areas generally remain heavily Anglo. Minorities constitute high percentages of the population in eastern down county areas of Takoma-Langley, Fairland, and Wheaton, as well as mid-county Gaithersburg, Montgomery Village, and Germantown. None of the county's 215 census tracts has no minority residents and only one tract has fewer than 10 percent. Minorities make up 90 percent of the population in five tracts and another twenty-nine tracts are 75 percent or more minority. The median tract in 2010 was 47.8 percent minority.[32] Asians, Hispanics, and blacks are geographically dispersed, respectively comprising 10 percent or more of the population in 137, 122, and 125 census tracts. Of the tracts with minority populations greater than 75 percent, blacks are the dominant group in sixteen and Hispanics in thirteen. The U.S. Agency for Healthcare Research Quality calculated the racial dissimilarity index for all minorities in Montgomery at 0.277, indicating a relatively high level of integration, which compares favorably with an index of 0.452 for the metropolitan area. The county's economic dissimilarity index was 0.223 compared to 0.345 for the entire area.[33]

The combination of demographic changes, land values, and inflation produced simultaneous and contradictory market responses. Single-family homes grew larger and occupied larger lots even as households became smaller. Townhouses and multi-family high-rise apartments accounted for a larger share of new construction, catering to newly forming households, singles, and some empty nesters. Concentrations of townhouses arose in Fairland and Germantown, producing high-density, modest income communities with a large percentage of renters, as Potomac, Darnestown, and Goshen-Woodfield were populated with estates that pushed at the edges of the Agricultural Reserve. As is almost invariably the case, homeowners, especially affluent ones, were more engaged in the politics of land use (as well as other policy arenas) than less affluent owners and renters. Since squeaky wheels tend to be greased there is a good prospect that differences in the level and quality of service among sectors of the county will widen rather than converge. This may be ameliorated by the redevelopment of the old commercial centers of the county, such as White Flint and Wheaton, producing an "urban inversion,"[34] that brings the affluent back toward the centers rather than the periphery and in the process generates a cross-subsidized housing stock that provides greater income integration. Friends of White Flint offers a model of a new form of political coalition that embraces both the miniature and commercial republics.

The carrying capacity concept embedded in master plans and growth policy tended to narrow variations in local transportation and school services. Few places experienced unacceptable levels. Provision of facilities lagged development in less affluent sections of the county and in areas undergoing rapid development. In 2007, for example, Clarksburg, which was undergoing rapid development, lacked adequate classroom capacity in all levels of its schools. Of the other five areas with over-capacity elementary schools, all served areas where household incomes were below the county median.[35] None of these areas experienced much new development, but the affordability of their housing resulted in substantial turnover to younger and immigrant households. The school system, as indicated above, enhanced resources for these and other schools with increasing numbers of disadvantaged and ESL students, so there were efforts to ameliorate inequities.

Planning Politics and the Public Interest

Facts on the ground constrain future choices; some for the near term, others for far longer. The historic pattern of ridge and mill roads became the arterial transportation system and established the nodes and strips for commercial and high-density residential development. Metro furthered that process. The stream valley park system reinforced a development pattern established along these routes. Sewers affected the pattern and intensity of development. These bits of engineered environment were not impossible to change, but it was difficult and expensive to do so. The first half-century of the county's development was purposive, but followed no overarching plan. The master plans of the Lee and Builders and Bar regimes were not regarded as much more than advice and did not seriously constrain development decisions, which were privately made and publically ratified.

Land Use Policies and Future Choices

As the planning reforms of the Progressive Regime took hold, public decisions played a larger role in constraining future private choices. The linkage of master plans with zoning and the use of sectional map amendments to implement plans shifted the vital center of planning politics from ad hoc rezoning cases to making and revising comprehensive area master plans. Future private choices and public options were inhibited by public decisions. Easements on land in the Agricultural Reserve, for example, have made about a third of the county forever unavailable for urban uses, even if a future generation should fervently desire it.

All plans involve explicit and implicit promises and obligations to future as well as current residents. Both are part of the "public" whose interests a plan addresses, although only the current public can act on them. Because any plan, if followed, reduces choices, planners have a duty to envision as best they can the effect of the plan on the welfare and opportunities of future publics. In this sense, the establishment of the park system and the Agricultural Reserve conserve resources for the enjoyment of future generations by not consuming them. It also means designing the built environment in ways that make it economically sustainable by keeping the debt service for infrastructure within manageable bounds and fostering an economic system that can produce a revenue stream sufficient for gradual improvement in services and amenities.

For Montgomery's planners, the General Plan provided the moral framework of a 50-year dialogue with the public and its officials about how to balance the political imperatives of the moment with the needs of the future. The path has not been straight or always easy. Occasionally, people wandered from it and did not always return, or could not because of changed conditions on the ground. It is difficult for officials to admit error, even those made by predecessors. The challenge in a system in which planning plays such a prominent role is to institutionalize practices of organizational learning that allow decision makers to get smarter. That occurred, albeit slowly, in the case of Silver Spring and most recently in Clarksburg.

Plans are unique forms of public policy. Both art and science, they embody a vision of a future for which there is no proof. If well done, they include strategy for reaching their goals and make convincing arguments about the ends and means of serving the public interest. We plan because our collective experience suggests that things work out better than if we leave them alone. This judgment is not undisputed and there are poorly drawn, overly ambitious, excessively restrictive, and inadequately implemented plans. A more measured view of its value would claim only that when effective, planning makes a marginal but important correction of market failures, provides greater coherence and harmony for the public realm, and improves the efficiency of public investments, without which private development could neither occur nor succeed.

Fairness

In an open, democratic, and pluralistic political economy, planning is one of many elements influencing the uses of land and the shape of the built environment. Our constitutional system places a high value on protection of private property rights but recognizes that there are public interests in the use of property. In this constitutional order, planning politics involves public deliberation to find an equitable balance among those interests; to imagine and create places for current and future inhabitants that produce a greater common good than would be probable if each property owner were left alone. The Constitution demands deliberation and fair procedures.

The way decisions are reached affects their content, legitimacy, and acceptance. It is hard for an outcome to be regarded as fair if reached through procedures seen as unfair. Land use controversies are freighted with moral arguments about rights, opportunities, liberties, and fairness. The economic stakes are often high, as they are for the quality of community life. Adversaries from the commercial and miniature republics pursue their interests, which can be nefarious or noble, but are certain to be extolled as embodiments of the public interest. Fairness in resolving such conflicts requires application of principles of transparency, reciprocity, and accountability.[36]

Transparency

Transparency requires an open process where interested parties present and debate their views. Opportunity must exist for timely review and comment on staff and consultant studies and reports. Officials must be open to persuasion and reach decisions after weighing evidence and argument in the course of public discussion. Montgomery planning politics is reasonably transparent. The open processes for preparing and approving plans has produced an informal rule that everyone should get into the act. Advisory committees, forums, work sessions and hearings by board and council may be inefficient from an administrative perspective, but they are efficient from the perspective of producing legitimate outcomes.

Planning and regulatory actions are process-intensive. They require referrals and on-the-record comments from county and state agencies and reconciliation with more comprehensive planning policies in an open review process culminating in public hearings in which anyone with a pulse can be heard. Planning board and council decisions are made in open session and memorialized in published plans and resolutions. Transparency forces public deliberation and debate when agencies and parties disagree. Staff reports are published in advance of board meetings. Staff regulatory review procedures were designed to prevent a single person from making decisions without consultation with others. Deviation from this practice in the Clarksburg case illustrated its importance.

Deliberation, Reciprocity, and Civic Capital

Transparency is easy. For a plural body such as the planning board, with a bipartisan membership and overlapping terms, it is both necessary and expedient, since it is hard for more than one person to keep a secret. Information inherently leaks. Reciprocity is harder. It cannot be mandated or enforced but must become part of an organization's culture. It involves participants making claims grounded in reasons others are morally obliged to honor.[37] Advisory committees that include adherents of the commercial and miniature republics are venues that implicitly convey the idea that each participant's perspective has a reasoned moral basis worthy of mutual respect. The process encourages antagonists to listen to and understand each other's interests, even if they cannot accept them. This lays a basis for bargaining, accommodation, and in the best of circumstances, cooperation, and consent.

Reciprocity, as a principle of fairness requires the planning board to treat with dignity and respect the views of those that appear before it, including staff and advisory committees. Honoring the views of others does not demand agreement, but does require engaging them and giving reasons for decisions that are reached. Finally, reciprocity expects officials and other participants to accept empirical evidence produced by reliable methods of inquiry.[38] The logic of consequentiality is most persuasive when participants accept the factual underpinnings and analytical approaches of a plan or policy.

Deliberation of land use matters often requires time for participants to acquire a level of mutual trust and confidence that the staff and board are seeking fair and workable solutions that balance private property rights with the liberties and convenience of others. A common complaint is that plan gestation takes too long, but like Lincoln's legs—which, he told a critic who criticized their length, were just long enough to reach the ground—planning takes just enough time to reach acceptable decisions. As the contrast between acceptance of the plans for White Flint and the Great Seneca Science Corridor illustrates, a plan is more likely to be considered fair if it not only does the right thing, but does it the right way. When reciprocity was achieved in White Flint, disagreements narrowed, fostering bargaining among parties to reach accommodations so the board or council had to make only modest adjustments to reach an appropriate and acceptable result. Plans for Bethesda (1975) the Agricultural Reserve (1980), and Silver Spring (2000), achieved high levels of reciprocity. Planning board drafts enjoyed wide support and were approved with little substantive change. In contrast, opposing interests failed to achieve either moral or empirical reciprocity in Friendship Heights (1974), Great Seneca Science Corridor (2010), and the Ten Mile Creek Amendment (2014). Resolution of major issues moved to the board or council. In Friendship Heights they fostered careers in litigation.

As some of the cases suggest, reciprocity among participants was not invariably achieved. Those unwilling to honor different viewpoints or to accept facts contrary to a frozen position learned different lessons from their experience. Some became disenchanted and withdrew. Others turned resentment into fuel for careers as civic gadflies, issuing sporadic jeremiads and filing lawsuits against officials and sundry other imagined conspirators against honor, justice, and the common good. Their zeal and litigiousness sometimes made their targets envy Job, who only had to endure boils and dead camels, before remembering they deserved the dignity of being heard, and that even obnoxious people could sometimes be on to something that needed to be attended.

When reciprocity worked it produced a corollary benefit to the public interest. Engagement of a cross section of civic, business, legal, and environmental interests in planning politics provided a platform for development of civic capital. Participants brought knowledge of their communities and skills from their professions, trades, and experience. They educated each other, the board and staff, and helped all those involved understand better the nature and intensity of concerns of those affected by land use decisions. Most participants absorbed the ideas, technical information and methods of planning, developed negotiation and problem solving skills, and had an impact on the issues being addressed. They formed associations, friendships and built trust with other stakeholders. Development of "the power to" solve problems often resulted in continuing involvement with land use issues and carried over into other civic endeavors. Some leveraged the experience and knowledge gained to launch civic or political careers, including service on the planning board, council, and legislature.

Accountability and Autonomy

Accountability requires public justification of official performance for consistency with norms of democratic governance, law, and public interest. For planning organizations in general, and the planning board in particular, accountability is complicated by the function planners perform in a democratic system. Public administration theory regards a government bureau as an *agent* of elected officials who represent *the public*. It is accountable for following the instructions and serving the interests of its principal. This arrangement embodies a positivist notion of the public interest as an expression of the preferences of those endowed with the power to proclaim it here and now. It tends to work best in a centralized executive branch, where formulation of policy is not fully visible to the public and the finished position is enforced by budgetary and executive discipline so the administration speaks with one voice.

Montgomery County planning does not operate in such a hierarchical system of accountability and its pure form is rare elsewhere because government organizations are more than simple agents of elected officials. In a constitutional government, they have a higher obligation to the law.[39] Some government organizations, like M-NCPPC, provide special services in an environment relatively free from political or ideological direction but subject to statutory standards for the exercise of authority delegated by law. The autonomy of M-NCPPC's planning function departs from orthodox administrative theory in that it is specifically charged with initiation of land use policy rather than merely administering it. Since the planning board is not elected, the exercise of this responsibility elevates the need for accountability and requires strong justification for its autonomy in the framework of democratic governance.

The Montgomery County Council appoints all five planning commissioners, establishes the budget and work program for the board, approves all plans, and enacts the ordinances under which the board exercises its regulatory functions. But the board-council relationship is not and cannot be one in which the board is simply accountable for faithfully carrying out the wishes and commands of the council. There are several reasons for a more relaxed arrangement. First of all, the council is a plural body. Its guidance to the board must be given in open session, may involve nuance in the form of differences in emphasis or opinion among members, and rarely is made in specific detail. Sometimes council direction is quite Delphic.

The board is half of a bi-county commission governed by state law. Direct management of its professional staff makes it less an *agent* of a current council or regime, than a quasi-*trustee* of the future of the county. Its historic mission, illustrated by the General Plan and the Functional Master Plan for Preservation of Agriculture and Rural Open Space, has been to act in the best interest of an intergenerational public. The idea that each generation has a duty to ensure that certain natural resources are available for the continuing benefit of the people is deeply rooted in the Public Trust Doctrine of Roman and Common Law and in modern planning and public administration theory.[40] Planners in a democracy are only quasi-trustees because their advice is contingent upon modification and final approval by elected officials. The board and staff, therefore, must persuade the council that their recommendations are not adverse to the latter's current understanding of the public interest, or if they are, their merit outweighs concern for immediate political pain.

The board remains accountable to the council but its autonomy allows it a greater degree of freedom to speak truth to power than if its staff were controlled by the council or executive and if commissioners served "at the pleasure" of the council rather than for fixed, overlapping terms. This arrangement fostered an organizational culture that placed high value on the integrity of professional staff and on devising creative solutions to land use problems—even when they were not requested and regardless of preconceptions of their likely popularity.

At the same time autonomy provides room for innovation, it adds intensity to the scrutiny the council gives the explanations offered for plans and policy recommendations. The mechanisms for accountability have kept the board anchored to the reality that its good ideas must be framed and presented in ways that can secure a council majority. Autonomy at the front and accountability at the end of the process has worked well. It often induced a broader deliberation about what should be done even if some ideas were initially outside the comfort zones of stakeholders and officials.

Institutional autonomy and accountability to the council undoubtedly exacerbated tension over turf and policy with executive agencies. County executives chafed at the board's autonomy and its occasional challenge of policies or practices of operating agencies, such as those dealing with transportation, environment, housing, and economic development. Exercise of the board's mandatory review powers to comment on public projects and to enforce forest conservation and water quality regulations against other agencies occasionally raised uncomfortable issues and required revision or delay of projects. A common complaint of developers was that disagreements between staff from the planning department and executive agencies delayed project approvals, a condition that led to periodic interagency and ad hoc committee efforts to "streamline" the development review process. Executives have opposed granting the planning board final authority to overrule agencies under their control, so various ordinances and agreements have assigned the "final" word on elements of a proposed development to the agency with primary jurisdiction. This does not work well in practice. If two agencies with overlapping responsibilities, such as transportation and storm water management make conflicting decisions someone must reconcile them with each other and with other elements of the project plan, or the board must deny the proposal. These are usually minor and resolvable issues. The most significant aspect of the board's autonomy from executive control is that it prevented forming a regime centered on a strong executive in partnership with the development industry—a modern echo of the Lee Regime. This resulted in a more equal balance of political power between the development industry, as the driving force in Montgomery's commercial republic and the watchful guardians of its miniature republics.

Council attitudes toward the planning function varied with experience, connection to constituencies, and further political ambitions. Some valued, or at least tolerated an autonomous voice that blended professional analysis and lay judgment on development policy. Other members resented the board's autonomy, and would have preferred that it either be refashioned as a direct agent of the council with no autonomous will, or made part of the executive branch where its position and that of operating agencies would be confirmed. And some members—perhaps all at some point in their council careers—vacillated between the extremes.

Although the board was sometimes an irritant for council members or the executive when it disagreed with their positions or that of a favored constituency, there were advantages for elected officials in the arrangement. It served as a lightning rod for land use controversies and through its advisory committees, hearings, and work sessions with stakeholders the board resolved some issues before they reached the council and narrowed others for council decision. It could raise issues, serve as a sounding board and build a base for acceptance of ideas and policy innovations, preparing them for public acceptance, leaving council members free to embrace or disown them.

In a governmental system on a four-year electoral calendar, long-term thinking was institutionalized in the planning board. Because of the council's factionalism and the press of other county business, the planning board set the long-term and immediate agendas for public consideration of land use policy through preparing master plans, growth policy, semi-annual and special reports. It produced data and analysis, framed issues, and proposed responses to them. Debate and deliberations were conducted largely on terms laid out by the board. Ultimate council decisions usually found the board's recommendations appropriate when it followed the logic of consequentiality.

The sporadic efforts since the 1940s to dismantle the M-NCPPC, transfer all or part of the planning or parks functions to the county manager or county executive, bend the planning board and/or its staff to agents of the council or executive have all failed. There have been both formal and informal erosions of its autonomy but most of its authority and influence have survived for two basic reasons. It is difficult to unscramble the egg. By virtue of being a component of a state bi-county commission a majority of both Montgomery's and Prince George's delegates and senators must agree on the precise nature of any organic surgery. The nuances of legislative comity have allowed minor adjustments that accommodate each county, but the advantages of retaining the commission have repeatedly frustrated efforts to abolish it emanating from one county or the other. Secondly, there generally has been strong support for retaining the autonomy of the board and for its accountability exclusively to the council among the leaders of the miniature republics. Even development interests that regularly complain of its regulatory oversight of their activities value its staff's professionalism and the board's freedom from political influence in its decision-making.

The system is valuable, not because it is invariably right, but because (with the unfortunate exception of Clarksburg) it maintained a high standard of integrity in a policy arena fraught with conflict, political influence, and opportunity for corruption. It nurtured policy innovation within a consensus General Plan and sustained a development pattern that arguably served the public interest. The institutional autonomy of the planning board provided continuity of policy, stability for planning, and the expectation that it should serve as trustee for the future.

THE IMPORTANCE OF PLANNING AND POLITICS

It is hazardous to overgeneralize from the experience of Montgomery County. This examination of how well the planning politics of one place served the public interest is useful mainly for insights, examples, models, analogies, and cautionary tales it offers others confronting the challenges of rapid growth and transitions from rural to suburban to urban forms and functions. Montgomery's story emphasizes that the roles and reasoning processes of planners and politicians were complementary as they sought to act in the public interest. Treating suburban politics as an exercise in competing values and interests of virtual commercial and miniature republics that are reflected in the composition and decisions of governing regimes suggests a way toward broader and more nuanced understanding of why decisions get made as they do and of the mixture of interests they serve.

If there is an American public philosophy it is, to paraphrase Oliver Wendell Holmes, that the life of policy making is experience, not logic. This pragmatic view sees case studies as virtual experience; next best to the real thing. Their lessons are disseminated as best practices by professional societies, government agencies, and advocacy organizations. Others can adapt them to their distinctive circumstances to help fashion policy for their places and times.

Perhaps the most valuable lesson planners and political leaders can take from these cases is the importance of persistence in land use policy. It took a decade to achieve approval of the General Plan. Conservationists struggled from 1950 to 1980 before establishing the Agricultural Reserve and another thirty-five years to secure it. Reviving Silver Spring involved forty years of trial and error before succeeding. Germantown is not complete after a half-century of development. Each effort spanned two or more governing regimes. The constant was the institutional presence of the planning board and its staff serving as stewards of the General Plan.

Persistence distinguishes *planning* from *plans*. The former involves the continuous process of administering, adjusting, adapting, and revising policies and actions. Indeed, a corollary to persistence is willingness to adapt to new circumstances and abandon things that did not work well or failed to gain public support. The aphorism that planning is improvisation on a general sense of direction captures the conjunction of strategy and tactics that should be as natural to

THE IMPORTANCE OF PLANNING AND POLITICS

planners as speaking prose. A plan is but the first move in a three-dimensional game that requires linking plans to strategic use of public powers and feedback from markets and publics.

Montgomery's policy successes usually involved some form of improvisation or innovation, whether it was the hybrid Central Business District and Commercial-Residential zones, different ways of using existing public facility and regulatory tools in concert to enforce staged development in Germantown, new methods of measuring congestion and mobility, or expanding the transferrable development rights concept to protect the Agricultural Reserve. When planners failed to question conventional wisdom and standard procedures in proceeding with Clarksburg as a corridor town mainly because the General Plan suggested it, or applied the same techniques that worked in Friendship Heights and Bethesda to Silver Spring without recognizing its economic and social distinctions, things did not go smoothly. Taken together, the Montgomery cases illustrate the importance of designing the planning and decision making system and fostering organizational cultures to allow those working in it to get smarter; to learn from mistakes rather than repeat them because it is easier than admitting error or abandoning outmoded methods that worked in the past.

Above all, Montgomery shows planning matters even if planning politics is hard. In a democracy it should not be otherwise because liberty and property, certainly happiness and sometimes, even life, are at risk. But when planning is taken seriously it can make a material difference in influencing development patterns and their consequences for public well being. Montgomery teaches taking seriously the way the roles of planners and politicians are configured. It is highly unlikely any other place will replicate the autonomy of the Maryland-National Capital Park and Planning Commission, but that is unnecessary. Even statutory insulation is no firewall against politicizing planning. The essential lesson is not about formal structure but the value of giving citizen and professional planners, wherever they reside in a government, the latitude to practice the logic of consequentiality before their governing regimes temper it with the logic of appropriateness. Institutionalizing that behavior so that it is habitual rather than an eccentric happenstance has to be constantly refreshed.

However helpful Montgomery's experience may be for others struggling with similar challenges, this tale of how it got this way should be most instructive at home. Much of what the county accomplished can be attributed to a General Plan that presented a persuasive vision that looked forward half a century rather than fixate on immediate challenges. By 1969 *On Wedges and Corridors* had been adjusted and compromised but retained its basic integrity. Its approval by the council was a defining moment in the county's development. The general direction it mapped is fast receding behind the inexorable pace of change and the improvisations made to adapt to them.

As it was fifty years ago, Montgomery County is at a moment when it will need to define its future anew. The suburban era is complete. The Agricultural Reserve, for the most part, is protected in perpetuity. The corridor is mostly built. The county has entered a period of redevelopment and urbanization. The interests of the miniature and commercial republics that defined planning politics over the past century are becoming more entwined and their relationship more nuanced as demography, property tenure, social cohesion, the nature of work, and economic structure are undergoing tectonic shifts.

In face of these transformative events Montgomery County is still improvising, sometimes brilliantly, sometimes with limited imagination, and sometimes in desperation. But it has not rethought its general direction. Development of a new general plan to guide a more diverse and economically interesting place is more important even than in 1964. All tactics and no strategy is less than half the game in planning politics.

Planning for the next half-century will require a fusion of traditional land use planning with a broader capacity for rethinking the county's role in the metropolitan, state, national, and world political economies. Understanding its role as the host of several specialized activity centers in a polycentric regional economy and building on their comparative advantages is critical to its future. Unlike the relatively homogeneous population of the twentieth century, the county now shares with much of America the need to house and assimilate a far more diverse population. Changing technologies in information, transportation, and energy will need to be understood and employed in the service of the public lest they induce greater economic stratification and social discord. A fiscal system based on exponential growth in the value of homes must be redesigned to take account of slower growth in residential property values and the strength of emerging economic sectors of a knowledge-based economy. The county will need an articulated philosophy of development as evocative as *Wedges and Corridors* to guide the development of centers that offer high quality housing, services, economic opportunity, mobility, and amenity.

The framework for the institutional capacity to plan for the county's future is available. It will require a determination to populate the planning board and its staff with talent to offer intellectual leadership and some forbearance as it generates ideas and proposals that invade protected turf and rattle the cages of the comfortable.

Analytical Table of Contents

Considerations of space, page size, legible reproduction of complex plans, and cost limited the number of illustrations it was feasible to include in this book. Links to most of the referenced documents and others that may be of interest to professionals, students, and others are available at MontgomeryPlanning.org/community, the web site of the Montgomery County Planning Department. Click on the county map for the appropriate area for a list of master plans and related documents.

Growth policy reports and other publications may be found at: MontgomeryPlanning.org/research/.

Archived documents, including staff reports, may be found at: http://www.montgomeryplanningboard.org/meetings_archive/. Click on the date, then search for the document in the agenda.

The 2014 Montgomery County Zoning Ordinance is at: http://permitting-services.montgomerycountymd.gov/DPS/pdf/FULLCh59APPROVEDclean3.5.14.pdf

For the Rockville comprehensive plan: http://www.rockvillemd.gov/index.aspx?NID=200.

For the Gaithersburg comprehensive plan: http://www.gaithersburgmd.gov/~/media/city/documents/government/master_plan/2011/Land_Use.pdf

Notes

INTRODUCTION

1. Stilgoe, John R. 1990. *Borderland Origins of the American Suburb, 1820–1939.* Yale University Press; Gans, Herbert, J. 1967. *The Levittowners: Ways of Life and Politics in a New Suburban Community.* Pantheon Books; Keats, John.1957. *The Crack in the Picture Window.* Riverside Press; Garreau, Joel. 1991. *Edge City: Life on the New Frontier.* Random House. Panetta, Roger, ed. *Westchester: The American Suburb.* Fordham University Press; Hanlon, Bernadette. 2012. *Once the American Dream: Inner-Ring Suburbs of the Metropolitan United States.* Temple University Press; Ehrenhalt, Alan. 2012. *The Great Inversion and the Future of the American City.* Alfred A. Knopf.

2. Ihlanfeldt, Keith R. June 1995. The Importance of the Central City to the Regional and National Economy: A Review of Arguments and Empirical Evidence. 1(2) *Citiscape: A Journal of Policy Development and Review* 125–150.

3. Elizabeth Kneebone, Job Sprawl Revisited: The Changing Geography of Metropolitan Employment. Brookings Institution, April 2009, http://www. brookings.edu/~/media/Files/rc/reports/2009/0406_job_sprawl_kneebone/20090406_jobsprawl_kneebone.pdf. See also Brennan, John, and Edward W Hill. November 1999. Where Are The Jobs? Cities, Suburbs, and the Competition for Employment. Brookings Center on Metropolitan and Urban Policy; Garreau, *Edge City*; Lewis, Paul G. 1996. *Shaping Suburbia: How Political Institutions Organize Urban Development.* Pittsburgh University Press.

4. Metropolitan Washington Council of Governments. July 14, 2010. Economic Trends 2005–2009.

5. See, for example, The Urban Institute. 2012. *Expanding Housing Opportunities through Inclusionary Zoning: Lessons from Two Counties*; Rusk, David. 1999. *Inside Game Outside Game: Winning Strategies for Saving Urban America.* Brookings Institution Press; Schwartz, Heather, Liisa Ecola, Kirstin J. Leuschner, and Aaron Kafner. 2012. *Is Inclusionary Zoning Inclusionary? A Guide for Practitioners.* Rand Corporation; Burchell, Robert W., David Listokin, and Arlene Pashman. 1994. *Regional Housing Opportunities for Lower Income Households: Resource Guide to Affordable Housing and Regional Mobility Strategies.* Google eBook; Jakabovics, Andrew. 2004. *Building Equity: The Evolution and Efficacy of Montgomery County.* MA thesis, Columbia University.

6. Meyerson, Martin, and Edward C. Banfield. 1955. *Politics Planning and the Public Interest: The Case of Public Housing in Chicago.* Free Press.

CHAPTER 1. PLANNING POLITICS

1. March, James G. and Johan P Olsen. 1989. *Rediscovering Institutions: The Organizational Basis of Politics.* Free Press; March, James G. and Johan P. Olsen. 1995. *Democratic Governance.* Free Press.

2. Cohen, Michael D., James G. March, and Johan P. Olsen. 1972. A Garbage Can Model of Organizational Choice. 17(1) *Administrative Science Quarterly* 1–25; March and

Olsen *Rediscovering Institutions*; Kingdon, John W. 1984. *Agendas, Alternatives, and Public Policies*. Little, Brown.

3. Simon, Herbert. 1945. *Administrative Behavior*. Free Press; Lindblom, Charles E. 1959. The Science of Muddling Through. 19(2) *Public Administration Review* 79–88.

4. March and Olsen, *Rediscovering Institutions*.

5. Jones, Bryan D., and Lynn W. Bachelor. 1993. 2d ed. *The Sustaining Hand: Community Leadership and Corporate Power*. Kansas University Press.

6. Simon, *Administrative Behavior*.

7. Lindblom, The Science of Muddling Through.

8. For an extended discussion of the commercial republic, see ch. 7 in Elkin, Stephen L. 1987. *City and Regime in the American Republic*. University of Chicago Press.

9. Petersen, Paul. 1981. *City Limits*. University of Chicago Press.

10. Perin, Constance. 1977. *Everything in Its Place: Social Order and Land Use in America*. Princeton University Press. p. 45.

11. Wood, Robert C. 1959. *Suburbia: Its People and Their Politics*. Houghton-Mifflin.

12. Stone, Clarence N. 1989. *Regime Politics: Governing Atlanta, 1946–1988*. p. 6; Stone, Clarence N. 1993. Urban Regimes and the Power to Govern: A Political Economy Approach. 15 *Journal of Urban Affairs* 1–28. See also Elkin, *City and Regime in the American Republic*; Stone, Clarence N., and Heywood Sanders. 1987. *The Politics of Urban Development*. Kansas University Press; Hanson, Royce. 2003. *Civic Culture and Urban Change: Governing Dallas*. Wayne State University Press.

13. *Md. Laws 1918*, ch. 122; *Md. Laws 1916*, ch.313.

14. *Md. Laws 1927*, ch. 448. M-NCPPC was modeled on the National Capital Park and Planning Commission, which Congress had established a year earlier.

15. P.L. 284, 71st Congress, 2d Session (May 29, 1930), chap. 354, 46 *Stat.* 482.

16. The average cost for an acre of stream valley land during depression years was $923. Calculated by the author from data in the M-NCPPC, Montgomery County Parks Department. March 22, 2011. Park Inventory System, Land Transaction by Year.

17. DeLeon, Richard. 1992. *Left Coast City: Progressive Politics in San Francisco, 1975–1991*. Kansas University Press; DeLeon, Richard. 1999. San Francisco and Domestic Partners: New Fields of Battle in the Culture War. pp. 117–136 in Sharp, Elaine. B., ed. 1999. *Culture Wars and Local Politics*. Kansas University Press; Mossberger, Karen, and Gerry Stoker. 2001. The Evolution of Urban Regime Theory: The Challenge of Conceptualization. 36 *Urban Affairs Review* 810–835.

18. A Survey Staff of the Brookings Institution. 1941. *The Government of Montgomery County, Maryland*. Brookings Institution Press.

19. A more detailed history of the struggle over commission control can be found in Garber, Marie M. 1964. *E. Brooke Lee vs. Charter: The Fight to Modernize Montgomery County Government, 1938–1950*. MA thesis, George Washington University; Baker, Madeline. 1966. *The Politics of Planning in Montgomery County Maryland*. MA thesis, George Washington University; Puffenberger, Charles W. 1963. Montgomery County Planning: A Study in Politics. Unpublished paper.

20. Garber, *E. Brooke Lee vs. Charter*.

21. *Montgomery County Code*, § 59-H.5 Hearing Examiner. In *Hyson v. Montgomery County*, 242 Md. 55 (1966) the Maryland Court of Appeals held that while the final action on rezoning an individual property was legislative in character, when the council was considering and determining these adjudicative facts concerning particular parties, it necessarily was performing a quasi-judicial function, even though its final action, in granting or denying the reclassification, which was required to be based on its findings of adjudicative facts, was quasi-legislative in character.

22. Mann, Jim. March 12, 1971. Bills Underscore Planning Split. *The Washington Post and Times Herald.* p. C-2.

23. Mann, Jim. March 20, 1971. Compact Benefits Gleason. *The Washington Post and Times Herald.* p. B-1.

24. Hardy, David W. March 24, 1971. Feud Flares Again Over Plans Post. *The Washington Post and Times Herald.* p. A-23; Johnson, Ruth. March 24, 1971. Council Fails to Approve Its Own Planning Nominee. *The Frederick Post.* p. 1; Council Approves Plans Appointment. April 7, 1971. *The Washington Post.* p. C-2. Montgomery Bureau. April 7, 1971. Council Confirms Hanson Commission Appointment. *The Frederick Post.* p. 1.

25. Montgomery County Code, §50-35 (k): *Adequate Public Facilities.*

26. *Montgomery County Code,* § 25-A Housing, Moderately Priced; 1974 L.M.C., ch. 17, §1. The MPDU program became a highly regarded inclusionary zoning program. Rusk, David. 1999. *Inside Game/Outside Game: Winning Strategies for Saving Urban America.* Brookings Institution Press.

27. See chapter 8.

28. *Montgomery County Code,* Chapter 24A. Historic Resources Preservation.

29. *Maryland Code* (1957, 1987 Repl. Vol.) Art. 28, § 2-101; § 7-108 (d) (2).

30. Developers contributed 61 percent of his campaign funds. Developers fueled Kramer campaign. *Montgomery Journal* (July 7, 1989). pp. A-1, 9.

31. Laws of the Maryland-National Capital Park and Planning Commission: *Md. Ann. Code,* Article 28 (2006 edition) § 7-108 (2) (ii).

32. The Advance Land Acquisition Fund allows the planning board, with council approval, to acquire land for public facilities shown on master plans but not contained in current county or state construction programs. Commission bonds support the fund. Upon transfer of the land to the state or county the commission is reimbursed the purchase price plus interest. *Md. Ann. Code, Art. 28, § 7-106.*

33. In this respect it did not fit comfortably into the usual regime typology. See Stone, Clarence N. 1987. Summing Up: Urban Regimes, Development Policy, and Political Arrangements. Ch. 14 in Stone and Sanders, *The Politics of Urban Development.*

34. For a full discussion of these factors and their implications, see Hanson, Royce, Harold Wolman, David Connolly, Katherine Pearson, and Robert McManmon. 2010. Corporate Citizenship and Urban Problem Solving: The Changing Civic Role of Business Leaders in American Cities. 32(1) *Journal of Urban Affairs* 1–23.

35. *Transportation Policy Task Force Report.* February 28, 2002. Final Report to Montgomery County Planning Board; Montgomery County Council. p. 1.

36. Montgomery County Planning Board. January 15, 2002. *Montgomery County Planning Board's Transportation Policy Report.* p. 6.

37. Hofstadter, Richard. 1952. *The Paranoid Style in American Politics.* Vintage Books.

38. One observer of county politics estimated that the Federation had fewer than two dozen paid-up members in 2009. Pagnucco, Adam. January 28, 2010. Change or Die. Maryland Politics Watch. http://maryland-politics.blogspot.com/2010/01/change-or-die.html,

39. In 2010 the average age of board members was sixty-five.

CHAPTER 2. ON WEDGES AND CORRIDORS

1. The Joint Committee issued eighteen reports summarized in Joint Committee on Washington Metropolitan Problems.1960. *A Discussion Guide to Washington Area Metropolitan Problems.* Staff Report. 86th Congress, 2d Session. United States Printing Office.

2. *National Capital Transportation Act of 1960.* P.L.86-669.

3. Hanson, Royce. 1964. *The Politics of Metropolitan Cooperation: Metropolitan Washington Council of Governments*. Washington Center for Metropolitan Studies.

4. National Capital Regional Planning Council. 1961. *A Plan for the Year 2000 for the National Capital Region*. p. v.

5. Ibid., p. 26.

6. The specific alternatives were: (1) Restricted Growth, (2) New Independent Cities, (3) Planned Sprawl, (4) Dispersed Cities, (5) Ring of Cities, (6) Peripheral Communities, and (7) The Radial Corridor Plan. Ibid., pp. 34–60.

7. Baker, Madeline. 1966. *The Politics of Planning in Montgomery County*, Maryland. MA thesis, George Washington University. pp. 80–88.

8. To rezone a parcel of land to a different Euclidean zone the council must find a change in the character of the neighborhood since the last comprehensive rezoning, or that the existing zone was the result of a mistake. The rule does not apply to floating zones. Barlow Burke, Jr. 1976. The Change-Mistake Rule and Zoning in Maryland, 25 *American University Law Review* 631–657.

9. The goals were: (1) Promote economical use of land; (2) Open land sequentially for development; (3) Expand public and private outdoor recreation opportunities; (4) Efficient provision of public facilities with staged, compact development; (5) An efficient transportation system, including mass transit; (6) Encourage greater variety of living environments; (7) Special attention to amenities: (8) Invite imaginative urban design; and (9) Assure implementation of the Plan. M-NCPPC. 1964. *On Wedges and Corridors. A General Plan for the Maryland-Washington Regional District in Montgomery and Prince George's Counties*. pp. 16–20.

10. Ibid., p. 36.

11. National Capital Transportation Agency, 1962. *Recommendations for Transportation in the National Capital Region: A Report to the President for Transmittal to Congress;* Schrag, Zachary M. 2006. *The Great Society Subway: A History of the Washington Metro*. Johns Hopkins University Press.

12. Report of the Committee to Evaluate the General Plan. 1967. M-NCPPC Archives. pp. 5–6.

13. Schrag, *The Great Society Subway*.

14. Takoma Park and Silver Spring on the eastern branch; Twinbrook, Rockville, and Shady Grove on the western branch.

15. Montgomery County Planning Board. December 1969. *Updated General Plan for Montgomery County*. M-NCPPC.

CHAPTER 3. RETROFITTING SUBURBIA

1. Hagman, Donald G., and Dean J. Misczynski. 1978. *Windfalls for Wipeouts: Land Value Capture and Compensation*. American Society of Planning Officials.

2. M-NCPPC. 1964. *On Wedges and Corridors: A General Plan for the Maryland-Washington Regional District*. p. 39

3. The Rockville Station was not under M-NCPPC jurisdiction, but under that of the city of Rockville.

4. *Beall v. Montgomery County Council*, 240 Md. 77 (1965). 212 A.2d 751, held a floating zone was analogous to a special exception and could alight any place that met the requirements of its purpose clause without having to prove that a change had occurred in the character of the neighborhood.

5. FAR is the amount of floor space relative to the size of a parcel. For example, FAR 2.0 on a 22,000 square foot parcel would yield 44,000 square feet of floor space. A building

covering the entire lot would have two stories. If half of the lot were covered, it would have four stories.

6. *M-NCPPC*. 1972. *Planning, Zoning, and Development of Central Business Districts and Transit Station Areas.*

7. M-NCPPC. 1964. *Master Plan for West Chevy Chase and Vicinity.*

8. *Funger v. Mayor and Council of Somerset*, 249 Md. 314, at 314–315, 239 A.2d 748 (1968).

9. *Funger v. Mayor of Somerset*, 244 Md. 141, 223 A.2d 168 (1966); *Chevy Chase Village and Town of Somerset, Maryland v. Montgomery County Board of Appeals*, 249 Md. 334, 239 A.2d 740 (1968).

10. Maryland is a "late vesting" state and requires evidence of "substantial construction" to prevent a change in regulations, such as rezoning of the property, from overriding any prior entitlements, such as zoning, subdivision, or construction permits. *Prince George's County v. Sunrise Ltd. Partnership*, 623 A.2d 1296, 1304 (Md. 1993); Delaney, John J. and William Kominers. 1979. He Who Rests Less Vests Best: Acquisition of Vested Rights in Land Development. 23 *St. Louis University Law Journal* 219.

11. Quoted in *Washington Suburban Sanitary Commission v. TKU*, 281 Md. 1, at 12, 376 A2d 505 (1977). The opinion contains a succinct summary of the Woodies decision.

12. 281 Md. 1, 376 A2d 505 (1977).

13. *Montgomery County v. Woodward & Lothrop*, 280 Md. 686, 378 A.2d 483 (1977); cert. den. 434 U.S. 1067 (1978).

14. Knopf, Norman. February 7, 1974. Statement of Chairman, Citizens Coordinating Committee on Friendship Heights at Public Hearing on the Friendship Heights Sector Plan. M-NCPPC Archives.

15. Barron, H.C., Jr. Extension of Remarks on the Proposed Zoning of the Bergdoll Tract Submitted on behalf of the Citizens Coordinating Committee on Friendship Heights. Undated. M-NCPPC Archives.

16. *Friendship Heights v. Funger*, 265 Md. 339, 289 A.2d 329 (1972).

17. Donahoe sued, claiming denial of his applications for permits constituted a taking of his property. The U.S. Court of Appeals for the Fourth Circuit held it was not. *Donohoe Construction Company, Inc., v. Montgomery County Council*, 567 F.2d 603 (1977).

18. Mitric, Joan McQueeney. April 2, 1988. Somerset Casts Off Condo Complex: Residents Snub Extra Tax Revenue to Maintain Small-Town Feeling. *The Washington Post.*

19. Simon, Herbert A. 1976, 3d ed. *Administrative Behavior. A Study of Decision-Making Processes in Administrative Organization.* Free Press; Lindblom, Charles E. 1959. The Science of Muddling Through. 19 *Public Administration Review* 79–88.

20. *Montgomery County Code*, Sec. 59-C-4.30. C-T Zone-Purpose and Development Standards.

21. M-NCPPC. 1982. *Amendment to the Sector Plan for the Bethesda CBD.* pp. 19–20.

22. Montgomery County Planning Board. July 13, 1983. In the Matter of: MCPB Public Hearing on rankings of projects, final comments, decisions, and approvals on optional method of development in Bethesda CBD. Transcript. M-NCPPC Archives.

23. Montgomery County Planning Board. June 22, 1983. In the Matter of: MCPB Public Hearing on the Bethesda Optional Method Applications Staff Report. Transcript, M-NCPPC Archives; Montgomery County Planning Board. July 13, 1983.

24. Meyers, Allen. September 8, 1988. Testimony of, Chairman of the Bethesda Coalition. Montgomery County Planning Board. Public Hearing: Project Plan Review No. 9–8806 (Lorenz building) Project Plan Review No. CBD-81-5 (Bethesda Metro Center) Site Plan Review No. 8-88045 (Bethesda Metro Center). Transcript, M-NCPPC Archives.

25. Pearson, Bradford. June 18, 2008. Planners reject Bethesda Metro tower. *Gazette. Net.* http://ww2.gazette.net/stories/061808/chevnew203128_32355.shtml

26. Bethesda Row has received awards from the Congress for the New Urbanism, the Washington Smart Growth Alliance, the Urban Land Institute, the National Association of Home Builders, and U.S. EPA. For a description, visit http://www.epa.gov/dced/case/bethesda.htm.

27. M-NCPPC. July 1994. Approved and Adopted *Bethesda CBD Master Plan.*

CHAPTER 4. THE DEATH AND LIFE OF SILVER SPRING

1. M-NCPPC. May 22, 1957. *Report and Recommendations on Proposed Revisions to the Street and Zoning Plan for Silver Spring and Vicinity.*

2. *Evening Star.* February 2 1971. Dream of an Instant City.

3. Brinkley, David. February 1975. Facing the Future. *Preservation News.*

4. M-NCPPC. 1975. *Approved and Adopted Silver Spring CBD Plan.*

5. Mitric, Joan McQueeney. July 7, 1988. Silver Spring Tract Is again in Spotlight. *The Washington Post.*

6. Montgomery County Planning Department. June 1988. Silver Spring Central Business District: Issues Report. p. 29.

7. For a chronology of the struggle to redevelop Silver Spring, see Bauman, Gus. 2011. The Silver Spring War and Rebirth: The Rise and Fall of an American Downtown. Unpublished paper.

8. Johansen, Bruce Richard. 2005. Imagined Pasts, Imagined Futures: Race, Politics, Memory, and the Revitalization of Downtown Silver Spring, Maryland. PhD diss., University of Maryland College Park.

9. Leclair, Vincent. January 15, 1988. Nordstrom Not Seeking Silver Spring Location. *The Record.*

10. Montgomery County Council. September 12, 1989. Resolution No. 11-1612. *Disapproval of Silver Spring Central Business District Final Draft Sector Plan, Dated June 1989.*

11. *Montgomery County v. Singer*, 321 Md. 504 (1991).

12. HSG/Gould Associates. October 1991. Retail Market Analysis: Downtown Silver Spring, MD. Technical Appendix, The Silver Spring CBD Approved and Adopted Plan for the Revival of Downtown Silver Spring. M-NCPPC, 1993. pp. 30–67.

13. Urban Land Institute. February 9–12, 1992. Downtown Silver Spring, Maryland: An Evaluation of the Development Potential and Revitalization Strategy for the Silver Triangle Site. An Advisory Services Panel Report.

14. For a summary of the American Dream's failure and analysis of problems of Urban Entertainment Districts (UED), see Hannigan, John. 1998. Chapter 7: Calling the Shots: Public-Private Partnerships in Fantasy City, in *Fantasy City: Pleasure and Profit in the Postmodern Metropolis.* Routledge.

15. Silver Spring Redevelopment Advisory Board. February 1996. *Final Report and Recommendations on Triple-Five's Redevelopment Proposal.*

16. Duncan, Douglas M. November 11, 1996. Letter to Triple Five Development Eastern, Ltd.

17. The transportation center's construction was plagued with problems and cost overruns. Bill Turque. November 19, 2013. Silver Spring Transit Center will require additional repairs, county says. *The Washington Post.*

18. The final agreement with Live Nation is summarized in Montgomery County News Release. January 18, 2008. Montgomery County & Live Nation Sign Lease to Bring Live Music, Entertainment & Community Use Venue to Downtown Silver Spring; Substantial Annual Cash Profit to Public Estimated.

19. Sernovitz, Daniel J. April 8, 2013. The JBG Cos. To Redevelop Falkland Chase, but Not Now. *The Washington Business Journal*. http://www.bizjournals.com/washington/breaking_ground/2013/04/the-jbg-cos-to-redevelop-falkland.html

20. For a fuller explanation of the psychology of this behavior, see Hirschman, Albert O. 1970. *Exit, Voice, Loyalty: Responses to Decline in Firms, Organizations, and States*. Harvard University Press.

21. Charles E. Lindblom. November–December 1979. Still Muddling, Not Yet Through. 39(6) *Public Administration Review* 517–526.

22. For robust discussions of the formation of social and civic capital, see Putnam, Robert D. 1992. Chapter 6: Social Capital and Institutional Success, in *Making Democracy Work: Civic Traditions in Modern Italy*. Princeton University Press; Stone, Clarence N. 1989. Chapter 11: Rethinking Community Power: Social Production versus Social Control, in *Regime Politics: Governing Atlanta, 1946–1988*. University of Kansas Press.

CHAPTER 5. THE END OF SUBURBIA?

1. Testimony on the preliminary draft sector plans for the North Bethesda Area. September 19, 1977. M-NCPPC Archives.

2. Mike Knapp, March 8, 2008. Letter from President, Montgomery County Council to Royce Hanson, Chairman, Montgomery County Planning Board.

3. Judy Daniel, Team Leader, Bethesda-Chevy Chase/North Bethesda, Community Planning Division and Pamela Dunn, Planning Coordinator, Research and Technology Division. June 3, 2008. Memorandum to Montgomery County Planning Board: Twinbrook Sector Plan, TOMX ZONES and New TMX ZONES with Building Lot Termination (BLT) Program Provisions.

4. M-NCPPC. May 1978. *Approved and Adopted North Bethesda Sector Plans.* p. 80.

5. Montgomery County Planning Board. September 19, 1977. In the Matter of: North Bethesda preliminary draft sector plan public hearing; Grosvenor, Nicholson Lane, and Twinbrook. Hearing Transcript. M-NCPPC Archives, p. 56.

6. M-NCPPC. 1992. *Approved and Adopted North Bethesda Garrett Park Master Plan.*

7. Members included Federal Realty, JBG, Lerner Enterprises, The Tower Companies, Combined Properties, Gables Residential, and the Holladay Corporation.

8. *Montgomery County Code*, § 59-C-15 COMMERCIAL/RESIDENTIAL (CR) ZONES. Subsequently, the board and council approved two additional CR zones: CRN, with a lower base density designed for neighborhood-scale development, and CRT, designed for transition areas between high density centers and residential communities.

9. *Montgomery County Code*, § 59-C-15.87.

10. Montgomery County Planning Department. December 2008. *White Flint C^3: Midtown on the Pike*. Public Hearing Draft. M-NCPPC. p. 80.

11. They are not. See 2013 MD Land Use Code § 21-104 (b) (1) (viii) and (ix).

12. Isiah Leggett. January 12, 2009. Testimony of the County Executive on the Public Hearing Draft White Flint Sector Plan.

13. Montgomery County Council. November 30, 2010. *Bill 50-10*: Special Taxing District—White Flint Development Tax District; Ch. 52: *Laws of Montgomery County 2010*; Montgomery County Council. November 30, 2010. *Resolution 16–1570: White Flint Sector Plan Implementation Strategy and Infrastructure Improvement List*.

14. Christensen, Clayton. 2000. *The Innovator's Dilemma*. HarperBusiness.

CHAPTER 6. TRIALS IN CORRIDOR CITY PLANNING

1. Stein, C.S. 1967. *Toward New Towns for America*. MIT Press; American Institute of Planners. 1968. *New Communities: Challenge for Today*. A.I.P.; Von Eckardt, Wolf. The

Case for Building 350 New Towns. December 1965. *Harper's Magazine*; Mayer, Albert. January 1951. A New-Town Program. 15 *Journal of the American Institute of Architects* 5. See also U.S. Department of Housing and Redevelopment Office of Policy Development and Research. 1984. *An Evaluation of the Federal New Communities Program.*

2. City of Rockville. 2002. *Comprehensive Master Plan.* p. 1.6.

3. M-NCPPC. January 1971. *Approved and Adopted Master Plan Gaithersburg Vicinity.*

4. The city did not adopt its first comprehensive plan until 1997; three decades after its expansion began. The plan contained no allusions to being a corridor city, although it referenced state smart growth requirements. City of Gaithersburg. 2009. *Master Plan.* Chapter 1: Land Use.

5. Forty percent of the Gaithersburg's 2010 population was foreign born, versus 31 percent for the county. Its home ownership rate was 56 percent, compared with 69 percent countywide.

6. For a full account of the history of the project, see Hurley, William N., Jr. 2006. *Montgomery Village: A New Town.* Fortieth Anniversary Edition. Montgomery Village Foundation.

7. *Montgomery County Code*, §59-C-7.21.

8. Each single-family-detached house represented 3.7 people, a townhouse 3, and a unit in a multiple-family building 2.

9. M-NCPPC. 1977. *Approved and Adopted Shady Grove Sector Plan.*

10. M-NCPPC. 1990. *Approved and Adopted Shady Grove Study Area Master Plan.*

11. M-NCPPC. 2006. *Approved and Adopted Shady Grove Sector Plan.*

12. M-NCPPC. 1985. *Approved and Adopted Gaithersburg and Vicinity Master Plan.*

13. M-NCPPC. 1996. *Approved and Adopted Amendment to the Gaithersburg and Vicinity Master Plan.*

14. Donna Baron, Coordinator. Undated letter from The Gaithersburg-North Potomac-Rockville Coalition to each Council Member.

15. Leggett, Isiah. September 10, 2009. Memorandum to Phil Andrews, Council President.

16. Montgomery County Council. July 20, 2010. Resolution 16-1447.

17. *Newell v. The Johns Hopkins University*, No. 1861. Md. App. (Nov. 21, 2013); cert. den. *Newell v. Johns Hopkins University*, Pet. Docket No. 612, Md. (March 24, 2014).

18. M-NCPPC. 1966. *Master Plan for Germantown.*

19. Germantown Inventory. November 12, 1971. M-NCPPC Archives.

20. Vosbeck Vosbeck Kendrick Redlinger. July 1972. Review and Proposed Amendments to the 1967 Germantown Master Plan. M-NCPPC Archives.

21. M-NCPPC. 1974. *Comprehensive Amendment to the Master Plan for Germantown Montgomery County, Maryland.* p. 61.

22. *Montgomery County Code*, § 59-C-7.1 P-D Zone-Planned Development Zone. The zones ranged in density from 2 units per acre to 100 units per acre.

23. O'Donnell, James J., Acting State Highway Administrator. March 2, 1973. Letter to Royce Hanson, Chairman, Montgomery County Planning Board

24. *Montgomery County Code*, § 50-35(k). See chapter 9 for a more extensive discussion of the adoption of the ordinance and its evolution in administration of county growth policy.

25. Hillard, Arthur J. March 12, 1973. Statement at Public Hearing on the Comprehensive Amendment on the Germantown Master Plan. M-NCPPC Archives.

26. Hoffberger, Stanley, and Robert Mitchell. March 12, 1973. Testimony for Germantown Investment Co., Inc. and Croyder Irvin & Co., a division of Ervin Atlantic Company. Public Hearing on Comprehensive Amendment to the Germantown Master Plan; Mitch-

ell, Robert L., Vice President & Manager, Croyder, Irvin & Co. April 11, 1973. M-NCPPC Archives.

27. D. Wright Associates. September 27, 1976. Germantown: Its Social/Institutional Development. M-NCPPC Archives.

28. Ibid. p. 2.

29. Christeller, Norman L. March 24, 1988. Memorandum to Planning Board Members. Subject: Germantown Housing Mix. M-NCPPC Archives.

30. Montgomery County Planning Board. October 8, 1987. Informal Transcript of Item 28, Work Session on Germantown Master Plan. p. 10. M-NCPPC Archives.

31. Montgomery County Planning Board. December 21, 1987. Transcript of staff briefing on Comprehensive Amendment to Germantown Master Plan. M-NCPPC Archives.

32. Blackburn, Carol. August 8, 1988. Germantown Development Brings on "Growing Pains." *Gaithersburg Gazette.*

33. Ellis, Ruth W. August 3, 1988. Marriott Gets Go-Ahead to Build in Germantown. *Frederick Post;* Hamblin, Matt. August 3, 1988. Development Rule Eased: Builders Would Help Pay for Road Improvements. *Montgomery Journal.*

34. Planning Board Slaps Kramer Planning Staff. September 15, 1988. *Montgomery Journal.*

35. Master Plan Mystery. September 28, 1988. *The Germantown Gazette.* p.10.

36. Wheeler, Timothy B. April 8, 1999. Assembly Approves Deal with Marriott: $44 Million Incentives Pass Despite Questions. *Baltimore Sun.*

37. Urban Land Institute. June 25–30, 2006 *Germantown Maryland Strategies for Development of the Germantown Business Distric*t. An Advisory Services Panel Report.

38. Ibid. p. 14.

39. Montgomery County Planning Department. October 2009. *Germantown Forward: Approved and Adopted Germantown Employment Area Sector Plan.* M-NCPPC.

CHAPTER 7. ERRORS IN CORRIDOR CITY PLANNING

1. M-NCPPC. 1968. *Master Plan Clarksburg and Vicinity.*

2. M-NCPPC. June 1, 1967. Public Hearing on a Preliminary Plan for Clarksburg and Vicinity Area, Montgomery County, Maryland. Transcript. M-NCPPC Archives.

3. Montgomery County Council. July 24, 1968. Resolution No. 6-1433 Re: Proposed Clarksburg and Vicinity Master Plan—Approved with Modifications and Revisions. This was the first plan requiring council approval before commission adoption.

4. *2013 MD Code, Natural Resources* § 5-1601-1613. : Forest Conservation; *Montgomery County Code*, Chapter 22A. Forest Conservation Law.

5. *Ann. Code Md*, Art. 66B, Zoning and Planning. The Economic Growth, Resource Protection, and Planning Act Amendments of 1992.

6. Montgomery County Planning Department. October 1991. Staff Draft Clarksburg Master Plan and Hyattstown Special Study Area.

7. Montgomery County Planning Department. February 1992. Preliminary Draft Plan. Clarksburg Master Plan & Hyattstown Special Study Area: A Transit-Serviceable & Pedestrian-Oriented Town that Preserves the Environment.

8. M-NCPPC. 1994. *Approved and Adopted Clarksburg Master Plan & Hyattstown Special Study Area.*

9. Ibid.

10. M-NCPPC. June 1994. Fiscal Impact Analysis Summary. *Clarksburg Master Plan & Hyattstown Special Study Area: Technical Appendix.* pp. 191–194.

11. Hanna, William. November 16. 1993. Memorandum to Robert Marriott.

12. The General Assembly enacted legislation in 1994 authorizing local governments to create development districts. 2010 *Md. Code* § 12–203.

13. Hussmann, William. April 19, 1994. Letter to William Hanna, Chairman PHED Committee.

14. Klebanoff, Steven M., President, Sumner Development Company. May 16, 1994. Letter to William Hanna, County Council President.

15. M-NCPPC. June 1994. Fiscal Impact Analysis Summary. p. 204

16. Agular, Louis. May 26, 1994. Clarksburg's Days as a Peaceful Village Are Numbered. *The Washington Post.*

17. *Montgomery County Code.* Chapter 14; 20-A.

18. Montgomery County Planning Board. March 26. 1996. Revised Opinion: Preliminary Plan No. 1-95042. Clarksburg Town Center. pp. 2–3.

19. White, Suzanne. November 17, 2003. Small town now sees where it fits into a large plan. *Washington Business Journal.*

20. Shiley, Kimberly A. and Carol L. Smith, August 16, 2004. Letter to Derick Berlage, Chairman, Montgomery County Planning Board.

21. Maskal, Nellie Shields. April 7, 2005. Memorandum to Wynn Withans, Development Review.

22. Krasnow, Rose, Chief, Development Review Division. July 7, 2005. Memorandum to Montgomery County Planning Board: Clarksburg and Vicinity Master Plan. pp. 2–3; Craig, Tim. July 1, 2005. Montgomery to Probe Alteration of Site Plan. *The Washington Post.*

23. Krasnow, Rose, Chief, Development Review Division. July 7, 2005. Memorandum to Montgomery County Planning Board: Reconsideration of Alleged Height Violations; Consideration of Alleged Setback Violations.

24. Montgomery County Council. July 26, 2005. Resolution 15-1125: Short Term measures to Assure Compliance with Site Plans.

25. Krasnow, Rose, Chief, Development Review Division. November 25, 2005. Controlling Development Plan Approval Documents for the Clarksburg Town Center Project. Memorandum to the Montgomery County Planning Board; Mooney, Bill, Deputy Director of Park and Planning. November 25, 2005. Controlling Development Plan Approval Documents for the Clarksburg Town Center Project. Memorandum to Montgomery County Planning Board.

26. Carter, John, and Rose Krasnow. June 1, 2006. Plan of Compliance: Clarksburg Town Center. Memorandum to Montgomery County Planning Board.

27. Montgomery County Planning Board. June 15, 2005. Compliance Program: Clarksburg Town Center.

28. Hanson, Royce May 17, 2007. Letter to Council President Marilyn Praisner; Spivak, Miranda. May 20, 2007. Planners Question Repaying Clarksburg Developers. *The Washington Post.*

29. Montgomery County Council, Bill No. 36-07: Development Districts-Amendments. Introduced December 4, 2007; Enacted October 14, 2008; Effective January 26, 2009.

30. Montgomery County Council. November 30, 2010. Resolution No. 16-1551: Appointment of. Clarksburg Infrastructure Working Group.

31. Report of the Montgomery County Council's Clarksburg Infrastructure Working Group. April 1, 2011.

32. Kronenberg, Robert, Supervisor, Development Review Division and Catherine Conlon, Supervisor, Development Review Division. October 22, 2008. Staff Report: Project Plan Amendment 91994004B, Preliminary Plan 11995042A, Final Water Quality Plan and Site Plan 820070220 Clarksburg Town Center.

33. Ibid. p. 21.

34. Commissioner Amy Presley recused herself. She had been president of CTCAC before her appointment to the Board in 2008.

35. The Planning Board's action is contained in the following resolutions: Clarksburg Town Center Preliminary Plan 11995042A, ADOPTION OF MCPB RESOLUTION No. 08-163 (04/30/2009); Clarksburg Town Center Preliminary Plan 11995042A, ADOPTION OF MCPB RESOLUTION No. 08-163 (11/06/2008); Clarksburg Town Center Preliminary Plan Amendment #11995042A (correction) (11/06/2008); Clarksburg Town Center Preliminary Plan Amendment #11995042A (correction 07/16/2009) (12/11/2008); Clarksburg Town Center Site Plan #820070220, ADOPTION OF MCPB RESOLUTION No. 09-15 (11/06/2008); Clarksburg Town Center Site Plan #820070220 (correction) (11/06/2008); Clarksburg Town Center, Site Plan #820070220, ADOPTION OF MCPB RESOLUTION No. 09-15 (correction) (11/06/2008); Clarksburg Town Center, Site Plan #820070220, ADOPTION OF MCPB RESOLUTION No. 09-15 (correction) (12/11/2008); Clarksburg Town Center Project Plan Amendment #91994004B (correction) (11/06/2008); Clarksburg Town Center Project Plan Amendment #91994004B (correction) (11/06/2008); Clarksburg Town Center Project Plan Amendment #91994004B (correction) (12/11/2008); Clarksburg Town Center Project Plan Amendment #91994004B (correction) (12/11/2008).

36. Singer-Bart, Susan. June 16, 2010, Mediation resolves dispute over Town Center: Clarksburg community hopeful decision will spur construction of retail district. *Gazette. Net.*

37. Montgomery County Council. June 28, 2011. Resolution No. 17-188: Approval of Planning Board Draft Limited Amendment to the Clarksburg Master Plan & Hyattstown Special Study Area.

38. Singer-Bart, Susan. December 7, 2011. Clarksburg Town Center prepares for new owner. *Gazette.Net.*

39. Montgomery County Planning Board. September 14, 2015. MCPB Resolution No. 15-85. Project No. 91994004D. Clarksburg Town Center; Montgomery County Planning Department. July 23, 2015. Clarksburg Town Center. Project Plan No. 91994994D; Preliminary Plan No. 11995042B; and Site Plan No. 82007022D.

40. Neibauer, Michael. July 18, 2013. Planning Board backs one Clarksburg outlet mall plan, another to come. *Washington Business Journal.* http://www.bizjournals.com/washington/breaking_ground/2013/07/planning-board-backs-one-clarksburg.html?page=all; Montgomery County Planning Board. July 18, 2013. Development Plan Amendment 13-02: Cabin Branch Community.

41. Dolan, Mary, and Ronald Cashion. July 7, 2009. Memorandum to Montgomery County Planning Board: Next Steps for Clarksburg Development Stage 4—Recommendation to County Council. Some areas could reach 50 percent imperviousness if developed at the maximum level permitted by the proposed zoning. See appendix to the staff memorandum. p. 14.

42. Montgomery County Council. October 13, 2009. Resolution No. 16-1149.

43. Ad Hoc Water Quality Working Group. July 16, 2010. Report to the Montgomery County Council. p. 47.

44. Montgomery County Planning Board. October 2013. *10 Mile Creek Limited Amendment.* Planning Board Draft.

45. Montgomery County Planning Department. July 2014. *Approved and Adopted 10 Mile Creek Area Limited Amendment Clarksburg Master Plan and Hyattstown Special Study Area.* M-NCPPC.

46. Montgomery County Council. October 26, 2010. Resolution No. 16-1544: Termination of Clarksburg Town Center Development District.

47. Rittel, Horst W. J., and Melvin M. Webber. 1973. Dilemmas in a General Theory of Planning. 4 *Policy Sciences* 155–189.

CHAPTER 8. THE AGRICULTURAL RESERVE

1. 2005 *Md. Code* § 8-209.

2. Nielsen, Craig A. 1978–1979. Preservation of Maryland Farmland: A Current Assessment. 8 *University of Baltimore Law Review* 429. For analyses of the effects of preferential assessment and taxation programs, see Kashian, Russell. 2004. State Farmland Preferential Assessment: A Comparative Study. 34 *Journal of Regional Policy & Analysis* 1–12; Kashian, Russ, and Mark Skidmore. 2002. Preserving Agricultural Land via Property Assessment Policy and the Willingness to Pay for Land Preservation. 16 *Economic Development Quarterly* 75–87; Blewett, Robert A., and Julia I. Lane. 1988. Development Rights and the Differential Assessment of Agricultural Land: Fractional Valuation of Farmland Is Ineffective for Preserving Open Space and Subsidizes Speculation. 47 *American Journal of Economics and Sociology* 195–203; Lynch, Lori, and Wesley N. Musser. 2001. A Relative Efficiency Analysis of Farmland Preservation Programs. 77 *Land Economics* 577–594.

3. Mandel, Marvin, Governor. October 25, 1973. Letter to Dr. Royce Hanson, Chairman, Montgomery County Planning Board.

4. Montgomery County Planning Board. November 1973. Rural Zone Sectional Map Amendment.

5. Hewins, John. Summary of testimony prepared by M-NCPPC staff. M-NCPPC Archives.

6. Montgomery County Planning Board. December 13, 1972. Resolution MCPB 72-54; M-NCPPC Resolution 72–72.

7. Montgomery County Council. June 19, 1973. Resolution CR 7-1272.

8. See Dawson, Grace. 1977. *No Little Plans: Fairfax County's PLUS Program for Managing Growth.* The Urban Institute. For the story of Fairfax's development from the viewpoint of its pro-growth champions, see Banham, Russ. 2009. *The Fight for Fairfax: A Struggle for a Great American County.* George Mason University Press.

9. M-NCPPC. May 1979. Draft Master Plan for the Potomac Subregion. p. 70.

10. Dennis, Steven T. and Catherine Dolinski. May 14, 2004. Study inspires little support for Techway bridge. *Gazette.Net*; Ginsberg, Steven. May 11, 2004. Traffic Study Renews "Techway" Debate: Most Md. Drivers Who Cross Legion Bridge Turn West. Researchers Find. *Washington Post.* p. B1.

11. American Land Forum. 1970. Land and Food: The Preservation of U.S. Farmland. Report No. 2; U.S. Department of Agriculture and Council on Environmental Quality. 1981. *The National Agricultural Lands Study.* U.S. Government Printing Office.

12. *Md. Ann. Code* §§ 2-501-519, et. seq.

13. *Md. Ann. Code* §§ 3-201-211.

14. Johnson, Rene. 1981. APPENDIX B: SMALL FARM ECONOMICS. *Approved and Adopted Functional Master Plan for Preservation of Agriculture and Rural Open Space.* M-NCPPC. p. 95.

15. Montgomery County Planning Department. 1979. Issues and Alternatives for the Protection of the Rural Wedge.

16. The TDR concept was initially proposed some years earlier by Costonis, John J. 1973–1974. Development Rights Transfer: An Exploratory Essay 83 *Yale Law Journal* 75. The use of TDRs in New York City to preserve Grand Central Station was upheld in *Penn Central Transportation Co. v. New York City*, 438 U.S. 104 (1978) and a few other jurisdictions had used them in limited ways.

17. Montgomery County Planning Department. 1978. Staff draft, Olney Area Master Plan. The RDT zone was renamed the Agricultural Reserve zone when the Zoning Code was revised in 2013.

18. M-NCPPC. October 1980. *Functional Master Plan for the Preservation of Agriculture and Rural Open Space in Montgomery County.* p. 43.

19. Research Division, Montgomery County Planning Department. January 26, 1981. Proposal for a Montgomery County Development Bank to Assist in Agricultural Preservation. M-NCPPC.

20. *Montgomery County Code*, §§ 50-23 (c); (d). Also see *Gruver-Cooley Jade Corp. v. Perliss*, 252 Md. 684, 251 A2d 589 (1969).

21. Montgomery County Council. September 30, 1980. Resolution No. 9-979.

22. *Dufour v. Montgomery County Council*, Law No. 56964 (Circuit Court for Montgomery County, Md. Jan. 20, 1983).

23. Price, Robert S. November 25, 1980. Testimony at Public Hearing before the Montgomery County Planning Board.

24. *West Montgomery County Citizens Assn. v. Maryland-National Capital Park and Planning Comm.*, 309 Md. 183, 522 A.2d 1328 (1987).

25. Agricultural Services Division. 2012. The Montgomery County Farmland Preservation Program Certification Report 2011–2012. Montgomery County Department of Economic Development. The other programs were: MALPF—4,433 acres; Montgomery County AEP—8,176 acres; Maryland Rural Legacy—4,875 acres; MET—2,086 acres; and CREP—1,909 acres.

26. Research & Technology Center, Montgomery County Planning Department. January 14, 2008. Tracking Transferable Development Rights. p. 4.

27. Timothy W. Warman. October 30, 1987. Agricultural Preservation in Montgomery County. Appendix C in Report of the Working Group to Evaluate the Agricultural and Rural Open Space Preservation Programs (February 2, 1988). p. 113.

28. Potter, Neal. December 3, 1987. Memorandum to Council Members: Bill 56–87, Agricultural Land Preservation.

29. *Montgomery County Code*, Chapter 2-B.

30. American Farmland Trust. May 4, 2001. Purchases of Development Rights and Transfer of Development Rights Case Studies. Prepared for Boone County Planning Commission. Confirmed by Jeremy Criss. Director, Division of Agricultural Services, Montgomery County Department of Economic Development. Email response to questions, July 14, 2011. Author's files.

31. Gault, Vicki L., Associate County Attorney. Letter to Tariq A. El-Baba, Esq., Associate General Counsel, M-NCPPC, p. 4, n. 3.

32. *Hilltop Farm, LLP v. Montgomery County Planning Board*, Circuit Court for Montgomery County No. 294120 (December 5, 2008); aff'd. in part, rev. in part, Md. App. No. 02511 (August 12, 2010); remanded to Cir. Ct. October 28, 2010; cert. den. Md. Pet. No. 458 (January 24, 2011); Order of Remand entered, Cir. Ct. for Montgomery County No. 294120-V (March 30, 2011). The appellate opinion was not reported.

33. AROS, p.17.

34. Ibid. p. 62.

35. Sand mounds, as the name implies, filter septic tank effluent delivered by pump into a large above-ground sand mound typically about five feet high and occupying a ground area thirty-five feet wide by ninety-eight feet long. State of Maryland Department of the Environment, Water Management Administration, On-Site Systems Division. June 2003. *Design and Construction Manual for Sand Mound Systems*, 4th ed.

36. Office of the County Executive. March 24, 1994. *Executive Regulation 28-93AM*. Montgomery County, Maryland.

37. Montgomery County Council. February 22, 1994. Resolution 12-1503: On-Site Water and On-Site Sewage Disposal Systems.

38. Montgomery County Planning Board Opinion. December 20,2005. Preliminary Plan 1-05029 Stoney Springs (Casey Property).

39. Hanson, Royce. March 12, 2007. Letter to Marilyn J. Praisner, President, Montgomery County Council.

40. The working group proposed that three sand mounds be allowed for the first seventy-five acres and one for each additional fifty acres. A minority of the group proposed limiting them to one for each fifty acres. Final Report of the Ad Hoc Agricultural Policy Working Group. January 2007.

41. The history of the case is summarized in *Bethel World Outreach Church v. Montgomery County*, 184 Md. App. 572, 967 A.2d 232 (2009).

42. 184 Md. at 607–608.

43. *Bethel World Outreach Ministries v. Montgomery County Council*, USCA (4th Cir.) No. 11-2176 (January 31, 2013).

44. Marshall, Ryan. September 16, 2013. Montgomery County pays $1.25 million to settle with church. *Gazette.Net*. www.gazette.net/article/20130916/NEWS/130919403/-1/montgomery-county-pays-125-million-to-settle-with-church&template=gazette.

45. Montgomery County Council. October 2, 2007. ZTA 07-07.

46. See: Montgomery County Planning Board. 2001. *Plowing New Ground*. The original child lot provision is at: Montgomery *County Code* § 59-C-9.74. Exempted Lots and Parcels-Rural Density Transfer Zone.

47. Daniel, Judy, Rural Area Team Leader, Community Planning Division. December 19, 2005. Memorandum to Montgomery County Planning Board from Zoning Text Amendment—Proposed Modifications to Child Lot Provisions in the Rural Density Transfer Zone. p. 11.

48. Ibid. p. 7

49. In one case, five heirs to a vacant forty-two-acre tract filed a plan to subdivide it to provide a house for each of them although the deceased owner had expressed no desire to create child lots. In another, owners of an eighty plus acre farm proposed to create the three market lots plus five additional lots for each of their children.

50. Hanson, Royce. March 12, 2007. Letter to Marilyn J. Praisner. p. 3.

51. Montgomery County Council. July 26. 2010. Zoning Text Amendment No. 10-12 Child Lot Standards.

52. Michaelson, Marlene. July 26, 2012. Memorandum to Planning, Housing and Economic Development Committee: Economic Trends and Land Use Issues in the Agricultural Reserve.

53. So-called because a twenty-five-acre tract had five development rights. If four "excess" TDRs were sold, the fifth right, if retained, could be used to construct a dwelling.

54. Thompson, Edward Jr. 1999. "Hybrid" Farmland Protection Programs: A New Paradigm for Growth Management. 23 *William & Mary Environmental Law and Policy Review* 831 at p. 841 n. 54.

55. For a more extensive discussion of the market for TDRs and the buildable lot issue, see McConnell, Virginia, Margaret Walls, and Francis Kelly. 2007. Markets for Preserving Farmland in Maryland: Making TDR Programs Work Better. Harry R. Hughes Center for Agro-Ecology (HRHCAU Pub. 2007-03).

56. Criss, Jeremy. and John Zawitoski. Undated. Enhanced Farmland Preservation Program Initiatives for Montgomery County. Unpublished paper.

57. Final Report of the Ad Hoc Agricultural Policy Working Group. January 2007. Montgomery County, MD.

58. Michaelson, Marlene L., et al. September 13, 2007. Memorandum to Planning, Housing, and Economic Development Committee: Overview of Short-Term Measures to Implement Recommendations of the Ad Hoc Agricultural Policy Working Group.

59. See chapter 5 for a description of the mechanics, economics, and politics of setting up the BLT easement program in the new Commercial-Residential zones.

60. *Montgomery County Code* §59-C-15.856 (a) Building *Lot Termination*.

61. *Montgomery County Code*, Chapter 2B; *Executive Regulation No. 3-09AM*.

62. Michaelson, Marlene. July 26, 2012. Memorandum to Planning, Housing and Economic Development Committee.

63. Montgomery County Department of Economic Development, Agricultural Services Division. 2011. Farm Characteristics, Montgomery County 1949–2007. https://www.montgomerycountymd.gov/agservices/resources/files/agdata1949-2007.pdf.

64. Nelson, Arthur C., Rick Pruetz, and Doug Woodruff, et al. 2012.*The TDR Handbook: Designing and Implementing Transfer of Development Rights Programs*. Island Press.

CHAPTER 9. GROWTH PAINS AND POLICY

1. Reilly, William K., ed. 1973. *The Use of Land: A Citizens' Policy Guide to Urban Growth. A Task Force Report by the Rockefeller Brothers Fund*. Crowell. p. 17.

2. Real Estate Research Corp. 1974. *The Costs of Sprawl*. U.S. Government Printing Office.

3. Urban Land Institute. 1975. *Management and Control of Growth: Issues, Techniques, Problems, Trends*. p. 2.

4. Development proposals were evaluated on a point system, based on the availability of various facilities, and design quality. Emanuel, Manuel S. 1974. Ramapo's Managed Growth Program. 4(5) *Planner's Notebook*. Reprinted in Urban Land Institute, *Management and Control of Growth*, vol. 2. pp. 301–313; Freilich, Robert H., Robert J. Sitkowski, and Seth D. Mennilo. 2010. *From Sprawl to Sustainability: Smart Growth, New Urbanism, Green Development, and Renewable Energy*. American Bar Association.

5. *Golden v. Ramapo Planning Bd.*, 285 N.E.2d 291; *appeal dismissed*, 409 U.S. 1003 (1972). The legal literature on *Ramapo* is exhaustive. See, for example, Nolan, John R. 2003. *Golden* and Its Emanations: The Surprising Origins of Smart Growth. 35 *The Urban Lawyer* 15.

6. Nelson, Arthur C. and Moore, Terry. 1993. Assessing Urban Growth Management: The Case of Portland, Oregon, the USA's Largest Urban Growth Boundary. 10(4) *Land Use Policy* 293. Gerrit J. Knapp. 1985. The Price Effects of Urban Growth Boundaries in Metropolitan Portland, Oregon. 61 *Land Economics* 26–35.

7. Petaluma's growth cap was ultimately upheld by the courts. *Construction Industry Association, Sonoma County, v. City of Petaluma*, 522 F.2d 897 (9th Cir. 1975).

8. de Raismes, Joseph N., II, et al. Undated. Growth Management in Boulder, Colorado: A Case Study. http://www.bouldercolorado.gov/files/City%20Attorney/Documents/Miscellaneous%20Docs%20of%20Interest/x-bgmcs1.jbn.pdf

9. P.L. 89-234 (1965), 81 *Stat.* 485, P.L. 90-148 (1967).

10. Hanson, Royce. 1982. *The Evolution of National Urban Policy 1970–1980*. National Academy Press.

11. 83 *Stat.* 852; P.L. 91-190 (1969).

12. 84 *Stat.* 1676; P.L. 91-604 (1970); 86 *Stat.* 816; P.L. 92-500 (1972).

13. *Md. Ann. Code* Art. 9-505; *Code of Maryland Regulations (COMAR)* § 26.03.01.04.

14. *Montgomery County Charter*, § 302. The Charter was amended in 1996 to provide for biennial submission of the CIP in odd-numbered fiscal years.

15. Montgomery County Code § 50-35(k).

16. Advisory Committee on County Growth Policy. February 1974. *Interim Report of the Advisory Committee on County Growth Policy*. Montgomery County Planning Board. Quoted in Montgomery County Planning Board. October 1974. *Framework for Action: First Annual Growth Policy Report for Montgomery County*. M-NCPPC. p. 6.

17. Advisory Committee on County Growth Policy. August 1974. *Directions for Growth Policy*. Montgomery County Planning Board.

18. Montgomery County Planning Board. October 1974. *Framework for Action: First Annual Growth Policy Report for Montgomery County*. M-NCPPC.

19. Montgomery County Planning Board. September 1975. *Fiscal Impact Analysis: Second Annual Growth Policy Report.* M-NCPPC.

20. Montgomery County Planning Board. October 1975. *Sequel No. 1 Environment & Transportation: Second Annual Growth Policy Report—Fiscal Impact Analysis.* M-NCPPC. p. 15.

21. Montgomery County Planning Board. October 1976. *Forecast of People, Jobs & Housing in Montgomery County: Third Annual Growth Policy Report.* M-NCPPC.

22. Montgomery County Planning Board. October 1977. *Carrying Capacity and Adequate Public Facilities: Fourth Annual Growth Policy Report.* M-NCPPC.

23. Owolabi, Babtunde O., and Robert M. Winick. 1987. Performing Traffic Impact Reviews at Different Stages of the Development Review Process. Presented at the ITE Annual Meeting, August 1987; Winick, Robert M. 1985. Balancing Future Development and Transportation in a High Growth Area. *Compendium of Technical Papers,* Institute of Transportation Engineers, 55th Annual Meeting, August 1985. pp. 55–59; Winick, Robert M. et al. 1986. Appropriate Development Limitations to Reduce Transportation Impacts. Presentation to the National Conference on Site Development and Transportation Impacts, Orlando FL, March 23–26, 1986.

24. By 1984, standard Transportation Analysis Zones prepared by the Bureau of the Census, replaced the "traffic sheds" that had originally been developed in-house.

25. Montgomery County Planning Department. November 12, 1986. *Trends & Forecasts: Jobs, Housing, Population & Births.* M-NCPPC.

26. Montgomery County Council. April 29, 1986. Bill No. 7-86. Growth Policy.

27. *Montgomery County Code,* §§ 49A-1 et seq.

28. Montgomery County Council. April 15, 1986. Bill No. 11-86; *Montgomery County Code,* Ch. 33-A. Planning Procedures.

29. Montgomery County Council. April 22, 1986. Subdivision Regulation Amendment No. 86-4; *Montgomery County Code,* § 50-35 (k) Adequate Public Facilities.

30. Montgomery County Executive. January 1, 1987. *County Executive Recommended FY 88 Annual Growth Policy. Montgomery County, Maryland.*

31. Titus, Roger W. August 1987. Separate Statement of Roger W. Titus, in Test at Permit Advisory Committee. Placement of the Adequate Public Facilities Test in Montgomery County's Development Process: Report to Montgomery County Executive; Montgomery County Council.

32. Test at Permit Advisory Committee, Placement of the Adequate Public Facilities, p. 25; Appendix: Christeller, Norman L. July 22, 1987. Memorandum to: TAP Committee. Amendments to APF Ordinance.

33. Montgomery County Planning Board. December 1988. *Trends & Forecasts: Jobs, Housing, and Population.* M-NCPPC.

34. Commission on the Future of Montgomery County. December 1988. *Envisioning Our Future.* Google Books.

35. Montgomery County Planning Department. August 1989. *Comprehensive Growth Policy Study. Vol. 1. A Policy Vision: Centers and Trails.* M-NCPPC. p. 64.

36. Montgomery County Planning Board. October 1989. *FY 91 Annual Growth Policy Montgomery County, Maryland.* Staff Draft. M-NCPPC. pp. 23–24.

37. Ibid. p. 24.

38. Montgomery County Planning Board. December 1989. *FY 91 Annual Growth Policy Montgomery County.* Final Draft. M-NCPPC.

39. Montgomery County Government. January 1, 1990. *County Executive's Recommended FY 91 Annual Growth Policy.*

40. Montgomery County Council. June 26, 1990. Resolution No. 11-2104: Approval of FY 91 Annual Growth Policy.

41. *In the Matter of John E. Schneider; Kettler Brothers v. Montgomery County*, Civil No. 39760, Circuit Court for Montgomery County. Unreported opinion. March 11, 1991; aff'd, *Schneider v. Montgomery County*, No. 683, Md. App. Unreported opinion June 5, 1992.

42. *Eastern Diversified Properties, Inc. v. Montgomery County*, 319 Md. 45, 570 A2d 850 (1990).

43. Montgomery County Council. 1990. Emergency Bill No. 33-90; 1990 *Montg. Co. Laws*, Ch. 40. The tax was later upheld. *Waters Landing Ltd. Partnership v. Montgomery County*, 337 Md. 15, 650 A2d 712 (1994).

44. Potter, Neal. January 11, 1993. Memorandum to Marilyn Praisner, President, Montgomery County Council: County Executive comments on the FY 94 Annual Growth Policy.

45. Montgomery County Council. June 29, 1993. Resolution 12-1187: Approval of FY 94 Annual Growth Policy.

46. See: Montgomery County Planning Board. May 26, 1995. Final Draft 1995–1997 Annual Growth Policy Element. Montgomery County Government Office of Planning Implementation. August 1, 1995. The County Executive's Recommendations on the 1995–1997 Policy Element of the Annual Growth Policy.

47. Levinson, David 1997. The Limits to Growth Management: Development Regulation in Montgomery County, Maryland. 24 *Environment and Planning B: Planning and Design* 689–707.

48. Douglas M. Duncan. July 31, 1977. Memorandum to Marilyn Praisner, President, Montgomery County Council: County Executive recommendations on the 1997–1998 Annual Growth Policy Element.

49. Montgomery County Planning Board. July 1, 1997. Addendum to Final Draft 1997–1998 Annual Growth Policy-Policy Element.

50. Montgomery County Council. June 8, 1996. Resolution No. 13-977: Approval of FY 98 Annual Growth Policy; Montgomery County Council. October 28, 1997. Resolution No. 13-1087: Amendment of FY 98 Annual Growth Policy.

51. Montgomery County Council. May 13, 1998. Resolution No. 1271.

52. William H. Hussmann. June 15, 1999. Letter to Isiah Leggett, President, Montgomery County Council, transmitting the Final Draft 1999–2001 *Annual Growth Policy: Policy Element.*

53. Montgomery County Planning Board. June 15, 1999. *1999–2001 Annual Growth— Policy Element.* M-NCPPC. p. 35

54. Ibid.

55. Derick Berlage. August 6, 2003. Letter to Hon. Mike Subin, President, Montgomery County Council and Douglas Duncan, County Executive.

56. Ibid.

57. Montgomery County Council. October 28, 2004. Resolution No. 15-375: 2003–05 *Annual Growth Policy—Policy Element.*

58. Montgomery County Council. December 12, 2006. Resolution No. 16-7: Planning Board Study of Growth Policy Issues.

59. Montgomery County Planning Board. May 21, 2007. *Toward Sustainable Growth for Montgomery County: A Growth Policy for the 21st Century: Final Draft 2007–2009 Growth Policy.* M-NCPPC. p. ii.

60. Nancy Floreen and Marc Elrich were the other PHED Committee members. The other two MFP Committee members were Duchy Tractenberg and Roger Berliner.

61. Montgomery County Planning Department, Growth Policy Team. September 24, 2007. Memorandum to Montgomery County Planning Board. Further *"Toward Sustainable Growth for Montgomery County: A Growth Policy for the 21st Century."* Addressing Issues Raised in Response to the Planning Board's Final Draft 2007–2009 Growth Policy.

62. Hardy, Dan, Eric Graye, and Royce Hanson. 2011. Are We There Yet? Smart Growth, Travel Forecasting, and Transportation Adequacy in Montgomery County, Maryland. 7(2) *Sustainability: Science, Practice & Policy.*

63. Orlin, Glenn, deputy council staff director, and Michael Faden, senior legislative attorney. October 12, 2007. Memorandum To: Planning, Housing, and Economic Development Committee: 2007–2009 Growth Policy.

64. Montgomery County Council. November 11, 2007. Resolution No. 16-376: *2007–2009 Growth Policy.*

65. Ibid.

66. Montgomery County Council. November 23, 2007. Expedited Bill No. 10-07: Impact Taxes Amendments; Ch. 16, Laws of Mont. Co. 2007.

67. Montgomery County Council. November 23, 2007. Bill No. 11-07: Recordation Tax-Rate; Ch. 17, Laws of Mont. Co. 2007.

68. Montgomery County Planning Board. 2009. *Reducing Our Footprint: Growing Smarter.* M-NCPPC.

69. Isiah Leggett. September 22, 2009. Testimony before the Montgomery County Council on the Planning Board Draft 2009 Growth Policy.

70. Known as TPAR, the new approach required separate tests for the adequacy road congestion and transit service. Motion Maps, LLC. July 2012. Final Report: 2012 Transportation Policy Area Review.

71. Montgomery County Council. July 20, 2010. Resolution No. 38-09: Growth Policy Amendments; Chapter 35, *Laws of Mont. Co.* 2010.

72. Ott, Stephen H. Mayer, and Dustin C. Read. 2006. The Effect of Growth Management Strategies: Adequate Public Facilities Ordinances and Impact Fees: A Review of Existing Research. Center for Real Estate at UNC Charlotte; National Center for Smart Growth. 2006. Adequate Public Facilities Ordinances in Maryland: Inappropriate Use, Inconsistent Standards, Unintended Consequences. The National Center for Smart Growth Research and Education, University of Maryland; Christopher J., and C. Tsuriel Somerville. 2000. Land Use Regulation and New Construction. 30(6) *Regional Science and Urban Economics* 639–662; Pelham, Thomas G. 1992. Adequate Public Facilities Requirements: Reflections on Florida's Concurrency System for Managing Growth. 19 *Florida State University Law Review* 974, 980; White, S. Mark, and Elisa L. Paster. 2003. Creating Effective Land Use Regulations through Concurrency. 43 *Natural Resources Journal* 753, 756.

CHAPTER 10. THE PUBLIC INTEREST

1. Miles, Rufus E. 1978. The Origin and Meaning of Miles' Law. 38(5) *Public Administration Review* 399.

2. Downs, Anthony. 1957. *An Economic Theory of Democracy.* Cambridge University Press; Olson, Mancur. 1965. *The Logic of Collective Action: Public Goods and the Theory of Groups.* Harvard University Press. Peterson, Paul E. 1981. *City Limits.* University of Chicago Press; Tiebout, Charles. 1956. A Pure Theory of Local Expenditures. 64 *Journal of Political Economy* 416–424; Schneider, Mark. 1989. *The Competitive City: The Political Economy of Suburbia.* University of Pittsburg Press.

3. Pluralist works of particular relevance to local planning include various works by Dahl, Robert A. 1960. *Who Governs?* Yale University Press; Dahl, Robert A., and Bruce Stinebrickner. 2002. *Modern Political Analysis.* 6th ed. Prentice Hall; Dahl, Robert A. 2006. *A Preface to Democratic Theory.* Expanded ed. Chicago University Press. Dahl, Robert A. 1989. *Democracy and Its Critics.* Yale University press. See also Long, Norton E. 1958. The Local Community as an Ecology of Games. 44 *American Journal of Sociology* 251–261.

4. Rawls, John. 1971. *A Theory of Justice.* Harvard University Press.

5. Stone, Clarence N. 1989. *Regime Politics: Governing Atlanta: 1946–1988.* p. 227.

6. See Putnam, Robert D. 1993. *Making Democracy Work: Civic Traditions in Modern Italy*. Princeton University Press.

7. Harrigan, Lucille, and Alexander von Hoffman. October 2002. Forty Years of Fighting Sprawl: Montgomery County, Maryland, and Growth Control Planning in the Metropolitan Region of Washington, D.C. Joint Center for Housing Studies, Harvard University.

8. Cambridge Systematics, Inc., with Elizabeth Deakin. May 2004. *Transportation Impacts of Smart Growth and Comprehensive Planning Initiatives*. Final Report NCHRP 25-25 Task 02. National Cooperative Highway Research Program. p. E-10.

9. Harrigan, Lucille, and Alexander von Hoffman. 2004. *Happy to Grow: Development and Planning in Fairfax County, Virginia*. Joint Center for Housing Studies, Harvard University.

10. Galster, George, Royce Hanson, Harold Wolman, Jason Freihage, and Stephen Coleman. 2001. Wrestling Sprawl to the Ground: Defining and Measuring an Elusive Concept. 12(4) *Housing Policy Debate* 681–709; George Galster, Hal Wolman, Royce Hanson, and J. Cutsinger. 2003. *Patterns and Processes of Sprawl: Phase II*. Final Report to U.S. Geological Survey; Hal Wolman, George Galster, Royce Hanson, Michael Ratcliffe, R. K. Furdell, and Andrea Sarzinski. 2005. The Fundamental Challenge in Measuring Sprawl: Which Land Should Be Considered? 57(1) *Professional Geographer* 94–105; Andrea Sarzynski, Hal Wolman, George Galster, and Royce Hanson. 2006. Testing the Conventional Wisdom about Land Use and Traffic Congestion: The More We Sprawl, the Less We Move? 43(3) *Urban Studies* 601–626.

11. See Hanson, Royce, and Jason Freihage. 2001. *Is Maryland Growing Smart: A Growth Indicators and Reporting System for Measuring Achievement of the Goals of Maryland's Smart Growth Policy*. Maryland Institute of Policy Analysis & Research.

12. Peterson, *City Limits*. p. 148.

13. Source data for these calculations are from Montgomery County, Maryland. *Comprehensive Annual Financial Report* for Fiscal Years 1971–1972 through 2009–2010. Expenditure figures for 1970 and 1971, and population, personal income, and per capita income for 1971 are estimates. Financial reports before 1972 do not include expenditures for schools, which were not part of consolidated financial reporting until 1972. The raw data reported in current dollars was converted to 2012 constant dollars using the BLS CPI-U-R-S conversion factor.

14. VMT per household calculated from data in Office of Legislative Oversight. January 26, 2010. Comparative Data on Montgomery County and Fairfax County. Report Number 2010-5. Montgomery County Council.

15. Transportation Planning Staff. February 14, 2003. Memorandum to Montgomery County Planning Board: Impact of AGP on Montgomery County Traffic Congestion. The memorandum reported that Texas Transportation Institute Congestion Index (average volume to capacity ratio based on LOS-C) for Montgomery was 1.32; for Fairfax, 1.41; for the Washington region, 1.35. Annual delay per capita for Montgomery was forty-three minutes, compared to fifty-two for Fairfax and forty-five for the region.

16. See Lynch, Lori, and Joshua M. Duke. 2007. Economic Benefits of Farmland Preservation: Evidence from the United States. WORKING PAPER 07-04 Department of Agricultural and Resource Economics, the University of Maryland, College Park.

17. Bruegmann, Robert. 2005. *Sprawl: A Compact History*. University of Chicago Press; Cohen, James R., and Ilana Preuss. September 3, 2002. An Analysis of Social Equity Issues in the Montgomery County (MD) Transfer of Development Rights Program. Unpublished paper.

18. U.S. Bureau of Census. 2008. *American Community Survey*.

19. For a comparative study of affordable housing programs in eleven jurisdictions, see: Schwartz, Heather, Liisa Ecola, Kirstin J. Leuschner, and Aaron Kafner. 2012. *Is Inclu-*

sionary Zoning Inclusionary? A Guide for Practitioners. Rand Corporation. See also Rusk. David. 1999. *Inside Game Outside Game: Winning Strategies for Saving Urban America.* Brookings Institution Press.

20. Montgomery County, Maryland. 2015. Analysis of Impediments to Fair Housing Choice. http://montgomerycountymd.gov/DHCA/Resources/Files/community/fair_housing/2015_Analys is_of_Impediments_to_Fair_Housing_Choice.pdf.

21. Tate, Lisa Madigan, and Megan Taylor. June 26, 2008. Analysis of the Supply and Demand for Housing. Montgomery County, Maryland. M-NCPPC Research & Technology Center, Montgomery County Planning Department.

22. Montgomery County, Maryland. Analysis of Impediments to Fair Housing Choice.

23. Office of Legislative Oversight. Comparative Data. p. 40.

24. Montgomery County, Maryland. Analysis of Impediments to Fair Housing Choice

25. Center for Neighborhood Technology. July 2011. Housing + Transportation Affordability in Washington, DC.

26. The GINI Coefficient is a summary statistic widely used to measure inequality in a population, where a GINI of 0.0 represents complete equality; 1.0 represents extreme inequality.

27. Only 1.2 percent of Montgomery households received public assistance income in 2012, and the most households receiving public assistance in any census tract was 6.7 percent. Healthy Communities Institute. http://www.healthymontgomery.org/modules. php?op=modload&name=NS-Indicator&file=index.

28. Schwartz, Heather. 2010. *Housing Policy Is School Policy: Economically Integrative Housing Promotes Academic Success in Montgomery County, Maryland.* The Century Foundation.

29. Ibid. p. 35.

30. Montgomery County Planning Board. 2009. *Reducing Our Footprint: Planning Board Draft 2009–2011 Growth Policy.* M-NCPPC.

31. Montgomery County Planning Department. 1997. Census Update Survey Report. http://www.montgomeryplanning.org/research/data_library/census1997update/census_res_mobil.pdf.

32. Calculated from the 2010 U.S. Census.

33. Billings, John, and Robin M. Weinick. 2003. Community Context—Indices of Racial and Economic Separation. U.S. Department of Health and Human Services Agency for Healthcare Research Quality. http://archive.ahrq.gov/data/safetynet/databooks/v1_sec09_02.htm.

34. Ehrenhalt, Alan. 2012. *The Great Inversion and the Future of the American City.* Alfred A. Knopf.

35. All were down-county school clusters. Montgomery County Planning Board. May 21, *Toward Sustainable Growth for Montgomery County: A Growth Policy for the 21st Century.* 2007. Final Draft 2007–2009 Growth Policy. M-NCPPC.

36. Gutmann, Amy, and Dennis Thompson. 1996. *Democracy and Disagreement.* Belknap Press of Harvard University.

37. Stoker, Laura. 1992. Interests and Ethics in Politics. 86(2) *American Political Science Review* 369–380.

38. Gutmann and Thompson. *Democracy and Disagreement.* pp. 55–57.

39. Rohr, John A. 1998. *Public Service, Ethics, & Constitutional Practice.* University Press of Kansas.

40. Bento, Lucas 2009. Search for Intergenerational Green Solutions: The Relevance of the Public Trust Doctrine to Environmental Protection. 11 (Autumn) *Common Law Review* 7–13; Frederickson, George. 1994. Can Public Officials Correctly Be Said to Have

Obligations to Future Generations. 54(5) *Public Administration Review* 457–464; National Academy of Public Administration. 1997. *Deciding for the Future; Balancing Risks, Costs, and Benefits Fairly across Generations.* Report for the U.S. Department of Energy; Lewis, Carol W. 2006. In Pursuit of the Public Interest. 66(5) *Public Administration Review* 694–701.

Index

Adams, Bruce, 177
Agricultural Reserve. *See* Montgomery County, Agricultural Reserve
Alfandre, Jay, 147, 149, 151
Allied Civic Group, 33, 92
American Community Survey (2009), 257
American Film Institute, 93, 97
Anderson, Thomas, 23
Andrews, Phil, 175
Antonelli group, 89
APFO (Adequate Public Facilities Ordinance), 24, 144, 147, 152–153, 159, 216–217, 223; administration of, 231, 234, 238, 242; proposal to shift administration County Department of Environment, 226–227
Archawsky, Harriet, 107
Arms, Richard, 85–86
Aron, Ruthann, 27
AROS (Agriculture and Rural Open Space). *See* master plans: Functional Master Plan for Preservation of Agriculture and Rural Open Space (AROS)

Bagg, Lester, 67
Banach, Melissa, 189, 194
Banfield, Edward, 6
Banks, Elizabeth, 138
Baron, Donna, 138
Bartholomew, Harland, 36, 37, 49
Bauman, Gus, 26–27, 63, 93, 95
Beall v. Montgomery County Council, 282n4
Bergdoll Tract litigation, 60–62
Berlage, Derick, 28, 162–163, 165, 167, 181
Berliner, Roger, 175, 237
Berman, Perry, 115, 185, 189, 192, 194
Bethel World Outreach Ministries, 204–205
Bethesda, 74–75, 125; Bethesda Row, 79–80, 284n26; CBD sector plan, 76–77, 80, 81; CBD sector plan amendment "beauty contest," 78–80; Commercial Transition Zone proposal, 75; Elm Street Park, 76; Metro access and surrounding area, 77–78; opposition to additional high rise tower, 80; parks as buffers between residential and commercial, 75–76; successful redevelopment, 248

Bethesda Coalition, 78
Bethesda Naval Hospital, 17
Bible, Alan, 35, 49
Bienenfeld, Paula, 115
Blair, Montgomery, 84
Blair estate, 83, 84, 89
Blocher, Joseph, 19
"Blue Ribbon" committee: Blair Lee III chair, 43, 50; General Plan review, 43–44; staging of county-financed public facilities, 216
Braddock, Edward, 154
Bradshaw, Douglas, 18
Brewer, Newton, 61
Brinkley, David, 87
Broderick, Thomas, 112
Brookings Institution: county government study (1941), 17; metropolitan area and jobs study (2009), 1
Brooks, Gene, 146
Builders and Bar Regime, 19–20; CAP Council and transportation policy debate, 38; commercial republic and, 49; interest in development, 30, 32–33, 261; Silver Spring policy and, 102

C&O towpath, 42
Cabrini-Green public housing site, 6
CAP (County Above Party) Council, 20; builders' prodevelopment slate, 20; Friendship Heights commercial zoning approved, 60; lame duck zoning actions, 20–21; Somerset and Bergdoll Tract dispute, 61; "Town Sector" (TS) floating zone approved for Montgomery Village, 134; zoning rulings and General Plan, 30, 42
Carson, Rachael, 214
CBD (central business district). *See* zoning
Christeller, Norman, 25–26, 69, 72, 146, 227, 230
Christensen, Clayton, 128
CIP (Capital Improvements Program), 42, 144, 216, 229
Citizens Coordinating Committee for Friendship Heights, 62, 64, 65; Bergdoll Tract small lots or parkland proposed, 68; objections to sector plan, 66–68

"Koubek Plan." *See* Friendship Heights and the Hills
Kramer, Rose, 44
Kramer, Sidney, 26, 91, 93, 104, 107, 147, 224–226

Lamb, Gordon, 23
land use planning and policy, 6, 10, 262; battles at boundaries of districts, 81; evolutionary process, 34, 125–126, 155, 218; innovation in, 128–129; local government powers, 218; methods of planners and politicians, 10–11; new town planning, effect of time on, 182–183; planning and plans, difference of, 270. *See also* logic of appropriateness; logic of consequentiality
Lawrence, Rod, 115
League of Women Voters, 17, 32, 37, 217
Lee, Blair III, 18, 43, 49–50, 186
Lee, E. Brooke (the Colonel), 15–18, 85, 88
Lee Regime, 14; political battle with reformers, 17–18; politics of land use, 15–16, 30; Silver Spring policy and, 102. *See also* Maryland-National Capital Park and Planning Commission (M-NCPPC); Washington Suburban Sanitary Commission (WSSC)
Leggett, Isiah, 29, 100, 124–125, 136–138, 147, 173, 228, 230, 240
legislation, federal: Air Quality Act (1967), 215; Capper-Cramton Act, 16; Clean Air Act (1970), 215; Clean Water Act (1972), 215; National Environmental Protection Act of 1969, 215; Religious Land Use and Institutionalized Persons Act (RLUIPA), 205; Water Quality Act of 1965, 215
legislation, local: 1980 Master Plan for Historic Preservation, 89; development districts process ordinance, 160; Moderate-Priced Dwelling Unit Ordinance, 5, 24, 149. *See also* APFO (Adequate Public Facilities Ordinance)
legislation, state: Council power to appoint planning board, 230; Maryland Agricultural Land Preservation Foundation, 188–189; Maryland Environmental Trust, 189; M-NCPPC law amendments, 26; Regional District Act (1957 and 1960 amendments), 37, 43; water and sewerage ten year plan statute, 215–216
Lerch, Harry, 21, 43
Leventhal, George, 175
Levinson, David, 231
Lieb, David, 117

Linowes, Robert, 19, 84–85, 87, 95, 102
Livable Clarksburg, 175
Loehr, Charles, 27
logic of appropriateness, 11, 24, 50, 134, 138, 152; CBD zones and, 72; failure in Silver Spring, 103; Gaithersburg "Town Sector" (TS) floating zone, 134; Lee Regime, in the, 30–32; Metro access and, 77; Progressive Regime, in the, 81; Silver Spring failures, 103
logic of consequentiality, 24, 181; farmland preservation and, 191; Friendship Heights plan, 72; General Plan and, 49–50; Radial Corridor alternative, 36; Silver Spring misdiagnosis, 103; Ten Mile Creek Amendment, 174–175; utilitarianism and, 244–245; White Flint Sector Plan, 116

Mandel, Marvin, 186
Marriott, Robert, 159
Maryland Board of Public Works, park acquisition funding ended, 76
Maryland Department of Environment, sand mound septic systems, 202
Marylanders for a Second Crossing, 187
Maryland-National Capital Park and Planning Commission (M-NCPPC), 3, 20, 30; 1957 General Plan, 35; Advance Land Acquisition Fund, 27, 208, 281n32; Bartholomew to prepare plan for two counties, 37–38, 46; bills for abolition then expansion of, 18–19; Council and executive power dispute, 22–23; critical to Progressive Regime, 23; Gold Medal for excellence, 255; Little Bennett Regional Park, 155; members appointed by County executive, 22; pressure to move to Rockville, 90; Regional District Act (1957 and 1960 amendments), 37, 43; rural zone in wedges, 185; Silver Spring report on zoning, 83; Somerset and Bergdoll Tract dispute, 61. *See also* master plans; Montgomery County Planning Board
Maryland's Change/Mistake Doctrine, 40, 282n8
mass transit, 9; Bethesda-New Carrollton light rail, 29; Bethesda-Silver Spring light rail transit route, 27; comparable plans to Planning Commission, 58; park & ride facilities in General Plan, 42; redevelopment of White Flint, Great Seneca Sciences Corridor and Germantown, 29; urban ring transformation, 128. *See also* Metro; Washington Metropolitan Area Transportation Authority (WMATA)

CPSIA information can be obtained
at www.ICGtesting.com
Printed in the USA
LVOW12*1349140317

527174LV00001B/2/P